THE 1st BATTALION
THE FAUGH-A-BALLAGHS IN THE GREAT WAR

Photo by]   [*H. Allison & Son, Armagh*

THE LATE PRIVATE ROBERT MORROW, V.C.

THE 1st BATTALION
THE FAUGH-A-BALLAGHS IN THE GREAT WAR

BY
BRIGADIER-GENERAL A. R. BURROWES, C.M.G., D.S.O.
(LATE ROYAL IRISH FUSILIERS)

Printed and Published for the Regimental Committee by
GALE & POLDEN, LTD.,
WELLINGTON WORKS, ALDERSHOT
ALSO AT LONDON AND PORTSMOUTH

"THERE is a promptness to obey, a hilarity, a cheerful obedience and willingness to act, which I have rarely met with in any other body of men, but whether, in this particular case, those qualifications had been instilled into them by the rigid discipline of their corps, I know not, or whether these are characteristics of the Irish nation; but I have also observed in that corps (I mean the 87th Regiment, or Prince's Own Irish) a degree of liberality amongst the men I have never seen in any other corps—a willingness to share their crust and drop on service with their comrades, an indescribable cheerfulness in obliging and accommodating each other, and an anxiety to serve each other, and to hide each other's faults. In that corps there was a unity I have not seen in any other; and as for fighting, they were very devils."

Memoirs of Lieutenant John Shipp, 87th Regiment.
2nd Edition, page 179.

PREFACE

THERE are only two points connected, with the following war diary, which the writer wishes to bring to notice. First, that it is entirely unworthy of the men whose deeds it commemorates. Not only has the writer no claim to literary ability, but the difficulty in obtaining details of authentic incidents, partly due to the inherent modesty of the persons concerned, has made it very difficult to produce a really interesting narrative. The second point is that the account, so far as it goes, is accurate. It would have been easy to produce a thrilling tale of adventure had the writer relied on reports which appeared in the Press at the time. But these reports, on investigation, proved to be so inaccurate that it has been thought best to ignore them.

On the other hand, the practice of collecting all messages and orders, etc., daily, and forwarding them weekly to the Regimental Depot for safe custody, has proved a mine from which the best evidence of facts has been drawn. This practice was first started at the commencement of the war by Captain and Adjutant W. H. C. Wortham, and was carried on by his successors up to the beginning of 1918, when it was unfortunately abandoned, and this has made the narrative of 1918 a difficult one to verify.

The amalgamation of the 1st and 2nd Battalions, in 1922, suggested the advisability of continuing the narrative up to the date of amalgamation.

The best thanks of the writer are due to Brigadier-General J. E. Edmonds, C.B., C.M.G., and the staff of the Historical Section (Military Branch) of the Imperial General Staff, for most kindly help and advice; to Sergeant-Major P. J. Clancy for his roll of officers, and to all those who have so kindly lent diaries and notes.

The authorities of the Imperial War Museum kindly gave authority to reproduce the war photographs. Thanks are also due to Sir William Orpen, A.R.A., for kindly permitting a reproduction of his sketch of a Royal Irish Fusilier after coming out of the trenches at the Chemical Works, Roeux.

A. R. B.

CONTENTS

CHAPTER		PAGE
I.	1914	1
II.	1915	27
III.	1916	59
IV.	1917	87
V.	1918	107
VI.	THE ARMISTICE AND AFTER	129

APPENDICES

NUMBER		
I.	ROLL OF HONOUR, AND NOMINAL ROLL OF OFFICERS WHO SERVED BETWEEN AUGUST 23RD, 1914 AND NOVEMBER 11TH, 1918	147
II.	ROLL OF HONOUR, OTHER RANKS	150
III.	DECORATIONS AND HONOURS AWARDED TO COMMISSIONED OFFICERS	164
IV.	DECORATIONS EARNED BY WARRANT OFFICERS, NON-COMMISSIONED OFFICERS AND MEN	170
V.	REINFORCEMENTS AND STRENGTH IN OTHER RANKS FROM AUGUST, 1914, TO OCTOBER, 1918	177
VI.	A LIST OF SOME OF THE STORES BROUGHT INTO USE FOR TRENCH WARFARE	178
VII.	THE "BARROSA" SONG	180
VIII.	BATTLE HONOURS IN THE GREAT WAR	182

LIST OF ILLUSTRATIONS

The Late Private Robert Morrow, V.C.	*Frontispiece*
	FACING PAGE
Cemetery at Ferme Phillipeaux, "Sydney Street"	16
Shells Bursting on Messines Ridge, 8-6-17	30
Ypres, The Cloth Hall and Cathedral, Oct. 1917	36
A Night Scene on The Western Front	56
The Redan and Quadrilateral from Air Photographs	61
The Village of Monchy-au-Bois, 1917	64
Sketch of Royal Irish Fusilier by Sir William Orpen	94
Canal-du-Nord near Moeuvres, 28-11-17	102
Scene in Ypres Salient, 15-2-18	118
General View of Bailleul, 1-9-18	120
Memorial to Officers	144

LIST OF SKETCHES AND MAP

SKETCH		FACING PAGE
I.	Battle of Le Cateau	4
II.	Action at Meteren	12
III.	Houplines and Frelinghien	14
IV.	The Douve Sector	22
V.	The Salient South of St. Julien	34
VI.	The Quadrilateral and Redan	60
VII.	Trenches near Monchy-au-Bois	66
VIII.	The Chemical Works and Rœux	92
IX.	The Battle of Cambrai	104
X.	Twig Farm	124
Map: Western Front		128

CHAPTER I—1914.

AUGUST, 1914.

IN August, 1914, the 1st Battalion Royal Irish Fusiliers—the 87th, or, as the Regiment is known throughout the British Army—the "Faugh-a-Ballaghs," were quartered in Moore Barracks, Shorncliffe.

It was under this last and best-known name that the Regiment gained many of its battle honours; it corresponds to other and celebrated titles in use in the British Army, like "The Buffs," "The Black Watch," and "The Die Hards." Those who in action have once heard it as a battle-cry (and understand its meaning, "Clear the way") will appreciate how it expresses the soul of the Regiment. For this reason it will be frequently used in the following pages instead of the formal and official description.

It was at 6.40 p.m. on August 4th that the telegram ordering mobilization was received with a calm satisfaction commensurate with what all felt to be an event unprecedented in history.

After the telegram had been read out to the officers assembled in the ante-room of the mess there was a short silence, which was broken by the question "Will company commanders wear spurs?"—an incident which, perhaps, well illustrates the attitude of the junior British officer towards the most formidable army in the world.

The high ideals which permeated the Army as a whole are best expressed in the two following letters addressed to the troops by His Majesty the King and Lord Kitchener:—

"*Buckingham Palace.*

"*You are leaving home to fight for the safety and honour of My Empire.*

"*Belgium, whose country we are pledged to defend, has been attacked, and France is about to be invaded by the same powerful foe.*

"*I have implicit confidence in you, My soldiers. Duty is your watchword, and I know your duty will be nobly done.*

"*I shall follow your every movement with deepest interest, and mark with eager satisfaction your daily progress; indeed, your welfare will never be absent from my thoughts.*

"*I pray God to bless you and guard you, and bring you back victorious.*

"*GEORGE, R.I.*"

"You are ordered abroad as a soldier of the King to help our French comrades against the invasion of a common enemy. You have to perform a task which will need your courage, your energy, your patience. Remember that the honour of the British Army depends on your individual conduct. It will be your duty not only to set an example of discipline and perfect steadiness under fire, but also to maintain the most friendly relations with those whom you are helping in this struggle. The operations in which you are engaged will, for the most part, take place in a friendly country, and you can do your country no better service than in showing yourself in France and Belgium in the true character of a British soldier.

"Be invariably courteous, considerate and kind. Never do anything likely to injure or destroy property, and always look upon looting as a disgraceful act. You are sure to meet with a welcome and to be trusted; your conduct must justify that welcome and that trust. Your duty cannot be done unless your health is sound. So keep constantly on your guard against any excesses. In this new experience you may find temptation both in wine and women. You must entirely resist both temptations, and, while treating all women with proper courtesy, you should avoid all intimacy.

"Do your duty bravely.

"Fear God.

"Honour the King.

"KITCHENER."

The Faughs formed part of the 10th Infantry Brigade, the other infantry units being the 1st Battalion Royal Warwickshire Regiment, 2nd Battalion Seaforth Highlanders, and 2nd Battalion Royal Dublin Fusiliers. Brigadier-General J. A. L. Haldane, C.B., D.S.O., commanded the Brigade, which formed part of the 4th Division under Major-General T. D'O. Snow, C.B. The Battalion had good reason for believing, as it did, that it belonged to the best brigade of the best division in the Army.

In such circumstances the work of mobilization worked smoothly, in spite of difficulties which are inherent in every military problem.

On July 29th, during the precautionary period, a composite battalion, to which the Faughs contributed their allotted quota, left, according to a long pre-arranged plan, for the defence of the Isle of Thanet, for, until the Territorial troops were mobilized, Regular troops had to be employed to garrison the local defences.

On August 6th the Colours of the Battalion were deposited at the Regimental Depôt, Armagh, by Captain Bull and Lieutenant Tuely.

On August 8th the Battalion moved to Exhibition Hall, York.

On August 9th the Faughs and 2nd Battalion Seaforth Highlanders moved to Darlington, the former being quartered in the Drill Hall. The above moves were part of the move of the whole of the 4th Division to the East Coast as a precautionary measure against invasion.

THE LANDING IN FRANCE

On being relieved half the 10th Brigade moved to Strensall Camp, where some useful training and route marching, of which the Reservists stood in need, were carried out. The Battalion was comfortably billeted in Rowntree's factory, at York, during this period.

On August 18th the Brigade moved to Harrow Weald and joined the rest of the 4th Division under canvas, the 4th Division being at this time the sole division in the III Army Corps, under command of Major-General W. P. Pulteney, C.B., D.S.O.

On August 21st the welcome orders to entrain the next day were received, and very early in the morning of the 22nd the Battalion entrained in two trains at Kenton station. Daylight found the Battalion at Southampton Docks, and little time was lost in transferring to the s.s. *Lake Michigan*. It was a beautiful morning as the vessel steamed down Southampton Water to the examination anchorage, all the ships in harbour bidding us good-bye, the men in the highest spirits, singing and cheering. And thus the soldiers set forth on the great adventure from which, alas, so few of them were to return.

The 87th did not disembark at Boulogne till the morning of the 23rd, when they marched through the town, amidst the acclamations of the inhabitants, to St. Martin's Camp, about one-and-a-half miles south-east of the Colonne de la Grand Armée, a monument erected to commemorate Napoleon's concentration on the north-east coast for the projected invasion of England.

When the 87th landed in France the situation was this: Germany, after forty years of preparation, had violated the neutrality of Belgium and was sweeping through that country in accordance with a plan for the execution of which she considered she had ample means. It is true that the gallant little Army of Belgium, by sustaining the first shock, had given breathing time to the armies of the Allies who were rallying to her support, and it is also true that the British Commander had no thought of retirement until the night of August 23rd, when, in conformity with the French Fifth Army on his right, he commenced what is known as the retreat from Mons. But there is no doubt that on this date the Germans were pressing forward in what they believed would be a rapid and decisive march on Paris.

The British Army was northwards of Maubeuge, covered by its cavalry holding the line of the Condé Canal, at about Mons.

After a short rest at St. Martin's Camp, orders were received for the Battalion to entrain, and, early on the morning of the 24th, the Battalion left Boulogne, via Amiens and St. Quentin, detrained at Le Cateau in the afternoon, and marched to a bivouac south of Inchy, passing on the way large numbers of civilians, who were busy digging long, straight lines of trenches to the south of the Le Cateau—Cambrai road. The inhabitants, who had, of course, never seen British soldiers, were a nuisance in this bivouac, especially in their eagerness to collect "souvenirs." The Battalion transport wagons came up just before dark, and advantage was taken of this opportunity to distribute maps—as it turned out, a very fortunate coincidence.

At 2 a.m. on August 25th the 10th Brigade broke up from its bivouacs about Inchy and marched north to the neighbourhood of St. Python, the task of the 4th Division this day being to cover the withdrawal of the 3rd and 5th Divisions, which had fought at Mons and were now retiring. The Brigade eventually took up an entrenched position about Fontaine-au-Tertre Farm, the 87th being detailed to guard the left flank, Major Phibbs's company entrenching to the south-west of Quievy. There was desultory firing all the afternoon, chiefly by cavalry and machine guns mounted on lorries. The 87th were the extreme left of the British Expeditionary Force, and in this, their first contact with the enemy, had no reason to doubt their superiority to the soldiers of the Kaiser.

After dark orders were received to withdraw to a position about the village of Haucourt, the 10th Brigade being rear-guard and the 87th flank guard. The Battalion marched via Herpigny Farm, west of Bethencourt and Beauvois. The first part of the road was extremely bad, so bad that the bicycles had eventually to be abandoned, and the night was very dark, but lit up to the north by the lurid glare of burning farmsteads and stacks. About 6 a.m. on August 26th the 87th and Seaforth Highlanders halted close to the cemetery at Haucourt, the 10th Brigade having been detailed Divisional Reserve, and the weary soldiers threw themselves on the ground and immediately slept.

August 26th.—Battle of Le Cateau.

The rest was short, for about 6.15 a.m. heavy machine-gun fire was heard from the north. The Germans' II Corps cavalry, who were following with its five Jäger battalions in motor lorries, was attacking the outposts of the 4th Division.

The 87th moved south of Haucourt, and then deployed as follows:

"A" Company east of the village, "D" Company west of the village, and "C" Company on their left, "B" Company in support.

After the preliminary skirmishes the battle commenced with artillery fire about 8 a.m., and as the German infantry divisions which came up—III Corps, IV Corps and IV Reserve Corps—did not dare to close, was in the main an artillery duel, in which the British artillery were outnumbered and outranged, and the gallantry with which they fought earned the keen admiration of their comrades of the infantry.

A feature of the day was the lull which occurred in the early part of the afternoon, variously estimated at from one to two hours. During this lull on a typical August day the stillness was remarkable; even the birds were silent, as if overawed by the recent thunder of the guns. The Faughs were under the impression that the enemy had had enough, especially as his infantry were seen retiring from the northern ridges, but he was, in fact, only concentrating still

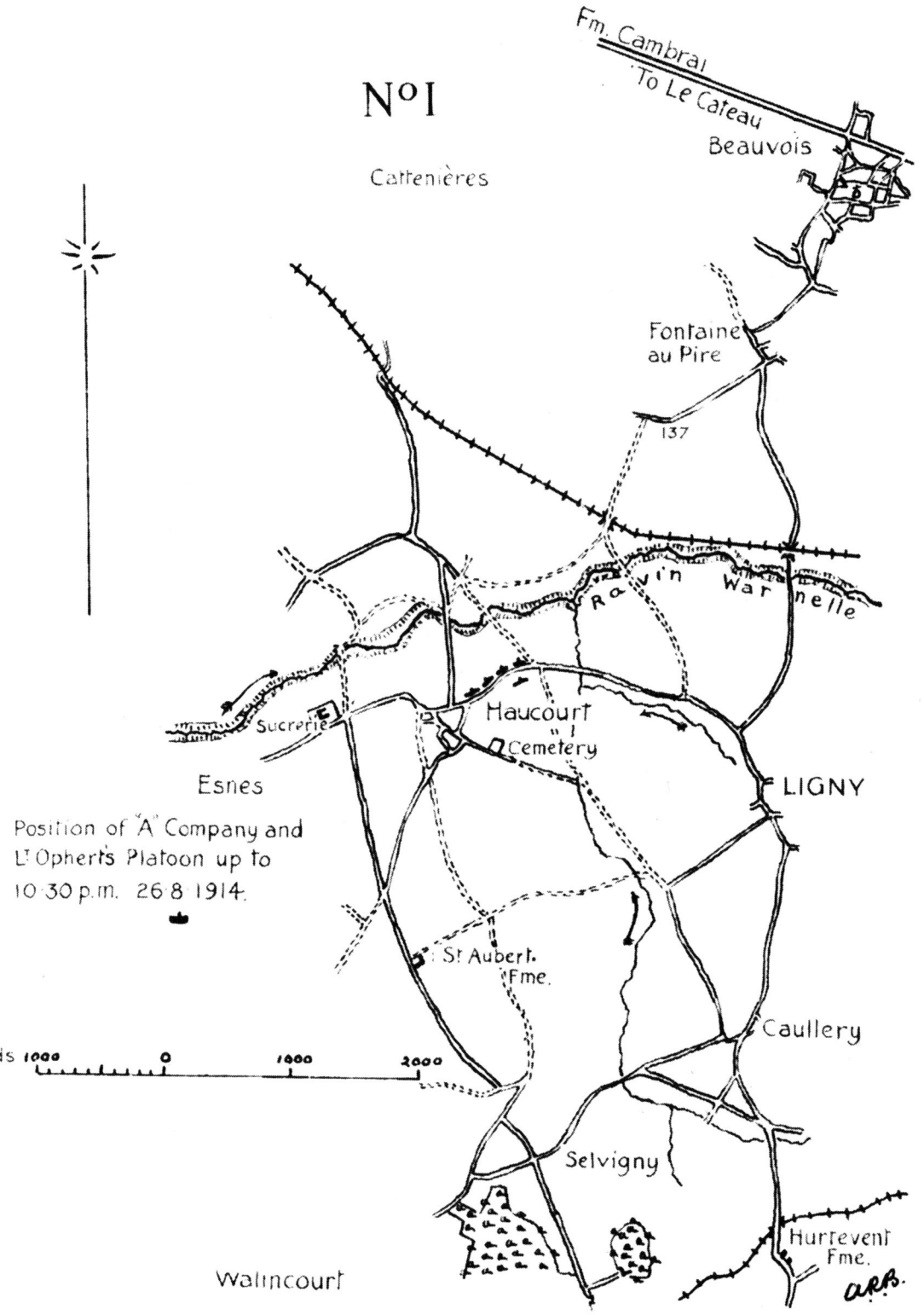

BATTLE OF LE CATEAU

more batteries of artillery, and about 4 p.m. his fire had increased to a bombardment comparable with those so frequently developed later in the war.

There were several tactical moves during the day, *e.g.*, "A" Company was reinforced by Lieutenant Olphert's platoon of "B" Company, and support was given both to the Seaforths and Dublin Fusiliers, but in the main the companies maintained their original positions.

Battalion headquarters, "B," "D" and part of "C" Company eventually bivouacked in the vicinity of Hurlevent Farm, south-east of Selvigny.

Owing to the difficulty of communication, the Signal Company was not present in this action, and the Brigadier had small means for sending instructions, orders were not received to withdraw, and "A" Company, with Lieutenant Olphert's platoon attached, who had received orders from a staff officer to "hold the position till all was blue," remained on the Haucourt—Ligny road, where they dug in and prepared to spend the night. Whilst thus occupied, German words of command and a bugle-call were heard in the village of Haucourt. All platoon commanders appear to have instinctively formed their men to meet the German attack. Lieutenant Olphert, whilst leading a charge, was hit in the foot and then in the head, and his platoon-sergeant, Godwin, a very promising non-commissioned officer, was killed at his side. The enemy fled. About midnight a conference of the senior officers was held, and at about 2 a.m. on August 27th "A" Company was ordered to concentrate at the crossroads north-east of Haucourt, where they met Major Poole, of the Warwickshire Regiment, with a number of his men.

Under command of Major Poole the column started south through Selvigny, and it was chiefly due to the skill with which this officer led his men, often within sight of the enemy, that they eventually regained their units. Major Gray, who was very ill, and had been carried, first on a horse and then on a country cart, had to be left at a Red Cross dressing station.

On August 28th the little column marched for some time parallel to, and only about 1,000 yards from, a German battalion.

During these days there were, of course, no rations forthcoming, and the men existed for the most part on apples. Tired and hungry as they were, the men gave what help they could to the French refugees who crowded the roads.

The little force crossed the Somme at Ham just before the bridge was blown up, and it was here that they got in touch with the British rear-guard.

From Ham the men were taken in wagons and lorries to Compiègne. During this journey Lieutenant O'Donovan and No. 4 Platoon became separated from the rest of the company, and, with other troops, proceeded to Rouen and then to Le Mans, where the British troops were put into a French cavalry barracks, and after a few days the men were drafted back in train-loads of 1,200, Lieutenant O'Donovan and his men rejoining the Battalion at Maisoncelles on September 7th.

Whilst the regimental transport was at the village of Caudry, where it had assembled with the transport of other units, a staff officer collected the greater part of the personnel, including the cooks, for the defence of the village. It was here that Lieutenant R. O. B. Wakefield, the transport officer, was mortally wounded. He was carried to a place of safety by Sergeant Stevenson, who had considerable difficulty in getting through the enemy lines and rejoining. Lieutenant Wakefield was not seen again, but it was ascertained that he died of his wounds on August 28th. A very promising young officer and a general favourite in the Regiment. The transport marched south through St. Quentin, under Lieutenant T. E. Bunting, D.C.M.

At daylight on August 27th the writer, who had been temporarily incapacitated the day before and had been carried from the field on a gun-limber, found himself at the northern entrance to the village of Le Catelet, on which troops of the 4th and 5th Divisions were converging, and the relative positions of these divisions being known, it was possible to sort them out and send those of the 4th Division on the Vendhuille road and those of the 5th Division due south. Here the greater part of "A" and "C" Companies were collected, and proceeded via Lempire and Templeux-le-Guerrard to Roisel, where touch with the main column was regained, some food was obtained, and where French engineers were busy breaking up the railway line just south of the village. The main portion of the Battalion, under Lieutenant-Colonel Churcher, from near Selvigny, followed the same route from Le Catelet, but the two portions did not meet.

The day was oppressively hot and steamy, as there had been heavy rain during the night, and the men were very weary. The 4th Division was concentrated in the neighbourhood of Haucourt, the 10th Infantry Brigade being rearguard in the neighbourhood of Nobescourt Farm, and as an attack was expected, this farm was put in a state of defence by the Royal Irish Fusiliers and Seaforths. This work temporarily incapacitated the men for further effort, and, as a number were physically unable to march farther without rest, the services of artillery drivers were used in making up teams from the farm horses to draw country wagons, in which the worst cases were placed. Whilst near Nobescourt Farm a few aeroplanes manœuvred over us, and French cavalry, who showed signs of having seen some hard times, passed us on their way south; but no attack developed, and as night fell the march was resumed. The route lay through Tertry—Monchy—Lagache—Croix and Matigny. At daylight the Somme was crossed, and the whole Battalion once more reunited at Voyennes.

Here it may be remarked that the regimental spirit and the stern march discipline of the 4th Division stood them in good stead during the retreat from Mons. The writer has seen fusiliers obliged to abandon their equipment from weakness, with only the remains of boots, but still retaining their arms and ammunition, and with every intention of using them to the last. As the French interpreter remarked: "I do not understand you Irish; we Frenchmen are glad when we go forward but sad when we come back; you Irish are always the same, you laugh always and all you want is bully beef."

There was little rest at Voyennes, for by 7 a.m. on August 28th the 10th Brigade was again on the move, first to Canizy, where for some time it took up a position south of and parallel to the Somme Canal, presumably to cover the withdrawal of the 3rd Division farther eastward; then, again becoming rear-guard, proceeded by Esmery—Hallon—Flavy-le-Moldeux—Tirlancourt and Muirancourt to Bussy, which was not reached till about midnight.

During August 29th some rest was obtained, and what was still more welcome, ablutions were possible to a limited extent. In the evening the Faughs had their first sight of an aerial combat, an Allied plane driving a German back to his lines; it had the appearance of a small bird mobbing a much larger one. A few of the enemy cavalry were seen this day by the outposts, but there was no fighting. The Battalion held the section of the outpost line immediately north of Bussy.

At about 11 p.m. the outposts were withdrawn, and, acting as rear-guard, the Battalion moved to Beaurains and halted for some time in what appeared to be the grounds of a château. The night was cold and dark; the stillness was suddenly broken by a few men bursting open the door of an outhouse, uttering uncouth yells. They turned out to be French civilians, mad with terror, who had mistaken us for Prussians.

At about 6.45 a.m. on August 30th the Battalion arrived at the bridge over the Oise at Pont l'Evèque, which it held for some time for two reasons. First, because the bridges were to be blown up, and secondly because "D" Company, under Major Phibbs, was absent. It did not receive orders to withdraw from Bussy till 8 a.m., and did not reach the bridge till after 10 a.m., having been ably helped in their withdrawal by the Divisional Cyclist Company, which had had a brush with the Uhlans in doing it. About 1 p.m. the march was continued and the welcome shade of the Bois de Carlepont was now reached, and the sound of explosions in the rear told us that the bridges had been destroyed—as it turned out, only just in time, as the enemy were working round the demolition party, who acted with the usual gallantry of the British sapper.

The route lay through Carlepont, Tracey-le-Mont, Berneuil-sur-Aisne to Genancourt. The bivouac in a field south of the latter place was reached about 10 p.m., where the supply wagons afforded a welcome meal to the tired soldiers.

On August 31st the 4th Division moved through the Foret de Compiègne in two columns; the 10th Brigade marched with the right, *i.e.*, the most northern column, and nearest the enemy. The pleasant shade and absence of dust formed a pleasant change, but a sharp look-out had to be kept, as Uhlans were reported to be in the forest. The Faughs were diverted to form a rear-guard to the left column, and after dark bivouacked in the streets of St. Sauveur. This day the troops heard the welcome news of the French success at Guise, when the French Fifth Army, under General Lanrezac, drove the Germans back.

SEPTEMBER, 1914.

Before dawn on September 1st the Battalion moved to Verberie. It was a foggy morning, and about 5 a.m. troops of the 1st Cavalry Brigade were attacked in the village of Nery. This was a surprise, but the Germans were driven off with the loss of two complete batteries.

The Faughs were ordered to support the 19th Infantry Brigade, and were directed against the northern portion of Nery, but the fight was practically over when they arrived. About 3 p.m. the retreat was continued due south to Rully, crossing the line of a Roman road. The day was hot, and marching over cultivated land was trying. The Brigade was again rear-guard, and did not reach bivouac at Baron till after dark, where, on account of the proximity of enemy mounted troops, a perimeter bivouac was formed. It was here that the first letters from home reached the Battalion. At 3 a.m. on September 2nd the Division was again on the move, and after a hot but uneventful march, the Battalion settled down in a pleasant bivouac, an orchard near the little town of Dammartin-en-Goële.

Before daylight on September 3rd the march was resumed, the 10th Brigade again rear-guard. A hot day and the troops weary. The march lay through Juilly—Claye—Souilly—Annet to Lagny, due east of Paris, where the Marne was crossed, and at which place the bridges were being prepared for demolition and heavy guns being placed in position. Thence to bivouacs in a stubble field south-east of the Bois de Chigny.

After a most welcome night's rest and the receipt of a commendatory order from the British Field-Marshal Commanding-in-Chief, dated August 25th, 1914, September 4th was spent in beginning to replace deficiencies due to fighting and the prolonged retreat. In the evening the Battalion moved to a pleasant bivouac in an orchard east of Magny-de-Hongres. Very early on the morning of September 5th, Lieutenant-Colonel Churcher, whose period of command expired on September 10th, left the Battalion and proceeded home, where he took up staff employment. Major A. R. Burrowes assumed command, as, at 3 a.m., the Faughs took up their position in the line of march, still moving south, through Serris-Ferrières and the Foret d'Armainvillers to the village of Chevry, where Lieutenant Penn, with the first reinforcements, joined the Battalion.

It was at Chevry that the great retreat from Mons ended, so far as the Battalion was concerned, for long before dawn on September 6th, when the 10th Brigade took up their formation as advanced guard, the delighted soldiers found that their faces were set northwards, and they longed to come to grips with the enemy. The situation was this: The British Expeditionary Force had on its right the Fifth French Army, while on the left was the Sixth French Army which, unknown to the Germans, had assembled under the cover of Paris and was now attacking them on their right flank. This strategic move was an important feature in the Battle of the Marne, now commencing.

The moon shone brightly as the troops retraced their steps through the forest, and, following the route of the previous day, halted at Serris. Towards evening the Battalion took up a position west of Crecy, with picquets at that place and Serbonne. It was a calm night, and the rumble of wagons as the enemy retreated was distinctly heard.

An hour before dawn on September 7th the troops stood to arms, a time-honoured custom in the British Army. It was hoped to come to grips with the enemy on this day, but the sound of the battle to the northward was all the 10th Brigade knew of it. The Royal Irish Fusiliers and the Royal Warwickshire Regiment were sent across the Grand Morin River to Ferrolles, to cover the crossing of the troops at Crecy; thence a slow advance was made during the day, via Maisoncelles to Giremoutiers, where bivouac was formed. During the day the Battalion witnessed for the first time the wanton destruction carried on by the enemy in the shape of ransacked houses, and the inhabitants had pitiful stories to relate of outrages on women. The first prisoners, three German cyclists taken this day, were an object of interest to the men. On September 8th the 10th Brigade were in reserve, and about noon, with other troops, reached Petit Courraïs. The enemy was retreating across the Marne at La Ferté, covered by rear-guards. The Battalion halted for the night on the main road not far from l'Hotel des Bois, at which place Brigade headquarters was established. Amongst the debris of fighting it was strange to see the cuirasses of the French heavy cavalry, but the French, as also the Germans, took the field in their peace-time uniforms, and it was not for some months that the blue of the poilu and the field grey of the enemy became universal. On this day Lieutenant O'Donovan and 99 other ranks, who had become detached during the Battle of Le Cateau, rejoined the Battalion. The following words of the Field-Marshal, spoken to the General Officer Commanding 4th Division, were conveyed to the troops as a special order of the day:—

"*I have been wanting to meet you, your brigadiers and commanding officers, to enable me to tell them how much I appreciate the splendid work of all ranks of the 4th Division during the retirement of the past ten days. I consider you saved the situation, and I look upon it as ranking as one of the finest bits of work ever done by the British Army.*"

Recommendations for decorations awarded by the French Government for gallantry at Le Cateau were submitted this day. They were written in a ditch by the road-side and handed to Brigade headquarters under a cart in the farm-yard. All those recommended received awards.

On September 9th the 10th Brigade was still in reserve, and did not move till 4.30 p.m. to Les Poupelains; during this march the Divisional Commander met with a serious accident owing to his horse falling with him, and Brigadier-General H. F. M. Wilson, C.B., commanding 12th Infantry Brigade, as senior officer, took over command.

Lieutenant G. M. H. Wright rejoined from the staff. About this time the service post card was taken into use, and proved a great boon. The privilege was seldom abused, though the non-commissioned officer who sent one to all his friends with all sentences crossed out except " I have not received your parcel " was not considered to be quite playing the game. There was considerable disappointment that we had not caught up the enemy. On the morning of September 10th the 10th Brigade crossed the Marne, without opposition, by the railway bridge at Le Saussoy. The work of dragging the laden wagons along the permanent way and over the bridge was heavy. The route lay by Dhuisy and Coulombs to Hervillers. There was ample proof of the temper of the enemy in ransacked houses, and of their haste in half-consumed carcasses found in their bivouacs.

On September 11th the 10th Infantry Brigade was advanced guard; the route ordered lay through the Bois de Gandelu, but the track became a forest path, and the remainder of the troops were diverted to the west of the forest. A few prisoners, some wounded, were picked up, and on emerging at St. Quentin the vanguard found themselves on the same road as the 5th Division. French troops, Turcos, were now on the left, and their quaint dress was a novelty to Irishmen. There were now frequent signs of the enemy's retreat, in the form of abandoned wagons and equipment. The march was continued, via Passy-en-Valois, across the River Ourcq to Chouy, where fighting had taken place and the first dead civilians, presumably shot by the Germans, were seen. There is something peculiarly shocking in the sight of dead habited in ordinary clothes, which conveys a feeling entirely different to that of a battlefield, however numerous the dead soldiers may be. Heavy rain had fallen during the march, and it was therefore a great comfort to billet in the large farm of La Loge, the first time the Battalion had been under cover since landing in the country. The men were well housed in the ample lofts and barns, and the officers slept well on the stone floor of the kitchen. The platoons on picquet at the farms of Bellevue and La Couture did not fare so well.

On September 12th the 10th Brigade was again on advanced guard, and, to the booming of guns, advanced by Louatre and Villemontoire to Septmonts. The British and French Armies were in touch, the nearest troops being the Chasseurs d'Afrique, in sky blue uniforms and mounted on grey horses, either Arabs or Barbs. About 4.30 p.m. the advanced guard was drawn up on the ridge north of Septmonts, overlooking the Aisne valley, when the 60-pdr. battery of the Division came into action against the retreating Germans, cheered by the whole Brigade. The scene was not unlike that from the top of Talana Hill, in South Africa, on the evening of October 20th, 1899. On being relieved, the 10th Brigade was ordered into billets in Septmonts, where it arrived in pitch darkness and pouring rain, and never was shelter more welcome.

On the night of September 12th/13th the 4th Division forced the passage of the Aisne, being the first of the Allied troops to cross the river, and seized Bucy-le-Long and the heights to the north of it, but the 10th Brigade was in in reserve and advanced slowly, by Billy-sur-Aisne, to a covered position in woods adjacent to La Tuilerie, where it lay for some time, the only excitement being the shells from German heavy guns passing overhead. After nightfall on September 13th the Battalion crossed the Aisne by the damaged bridge at Venizel, and bivouacked in the open during a cold and wet night.

On September 14th the Battle of the Aisne was continued, and the Battalion lay on the southern side of Bucy-le-Long.

The situation was now this: The British Army, having forced the Aisne, had seized the high ground to the north and was clinging on to the southern edges of these heights, whilst a big turning movement was being carried out by the French Sixth Army on their left. This was the commencement of the prolonged struggle in trench warfare, for the British found the enemy strongly entrenched, whilst they naturally entrenched the positions gained. The position was precarious because, owing to the wide level plain which lay behind the British lines and the river, artillery support was inadequate, and all movement of reinforcement by day was in full view of the enemy.

During the battle the troops had become intermingled, and from September 14th to September 30th the 87th was in support to various parts of the line. For this reason they suffered more from shell fire than the troops actually in the line, who were in trenches and natural caves, whereas troops in support, being on the slopes of the hills, were exposed to the searching fire of the enemy, who employed heavy 8-in. howitzer batteries, hereafter known as "Crumps," "Black Marias," "Woolly Bears," etc. On the 17th the Battalion suffered considerably from these heavy shells, losing a number of excellent non-commissioned officers and men and a number of horses. Lieutenant and Quartermaster Bunting and Company Sergeant-Major Fynne were amongst the wounded. The Battalion behaved splendidly under a very trying ordeal. The streets of Bucy-le-Long presented some horrible sights after this bombardment. On the 16th one of those little incidents occurred which cemented the good feeling between the French and British. A French battery in action had to be supplied with ammunition across the open plain mentioned above; as the artillery wagons galloped through the zone of bursting shells they were loudly cheered by the men of the 87th.

During the last days of September the Battalion was employed in various duties, such as guarding bridges over the Aisne, clearing the battlefield of dead horses, and working on trenches, but there were welcome opportunities of washing, as lice, the unavoidable result of long periods in the open without means of ablution, had begun to be troublesome.

On the 28th Major Phibbs was sent by motor car to Paris to purchase necessaries for the officers of the Brigade. At the time this was looked upon as a great privilege. It was on September 17th that the famous order of the Kaiser, issued at Aix-la-Chapelle on August 19th, was published to the troops.

"It is my Royal and Imperial command that you concentrate your energies for the immediate present upon one single purpose, and that is that you address all your skill and all the valour of my soldiers to exterminate first the treacherous English; walk over General French's *Contemptible little Army* . . . ."

It was also about this time that the Intelligence Department commenced the issue of daily summaries, which were eagerly looked for by the troops. Also measures against hostile aircraft were first undertaken, the first being a light gun (pom-pom) mounted on a cart-wheel.

The Battalion was very fit—only seven men were admitted to hospital during the last week of September. It must be borne in mind that during the retreat and advance the troops had marched 260 miles in twenty-two days without a rest.

OCTOBER, 1914.

On October 1st a readjustment of the line took place, and the 87th took over the right of the 10th Brigade from the King's Own Regiment and the Essex Regiment, the trenches of the latter being particularly good. The line, which lay to the north of St. Marguerite, was held as follows: "B" Company on the right, "D" Company on the left, "A" Company in support, Machine Gun Section on right of "A" Company; "C" Company was detached, guarding bridges.

The enemy trenches were plainly visible about three quarters of a mile in front. The shelling was fairly continuous, but owing to good trenches and the configuration of the ground, casualties were slight. Battalion headquarters were in a ruined house under the brow of the hill. It was in this house that our senior French interpreter, Sergeant Henri B. de la Rancheraye, 24th Regiment Territorials, cooked one of the best meals the headquarters had had for a long time. These interpreters were most useful, and the Battalion was fortunate in those detailed for the duty.

Life in the trenches was a pleasant change, and much work was put in in improving them. We were warned against spies and authentic cases of the Germans wearing British and French uniforms.

On October 4th the Battalion were very pleased at the announcement of Regimental Sergeant-Major W. Murphy being promoted to a commission in the Regiment; his was the first of these promotions, and, like all subsequent promotions from the ranks, he was heartily welcomed by his brother officers. At this time the non-commissioned ranks of the 87th were filled with men second to none in the British Army, and they amply repaid the care taken in selecting and training them.

However, the first tour in the trenches was not to be a long one, for on October 6th the 10th Brigade was withdrawn, the 87th being relieved by the 63rd Regiment of Chasseurs-Alpins, and as the column crossed the bridge at Venizel hopes were high, for a staff officer informed the Commanding Officer that a big surprise was being arranged for the enemy.

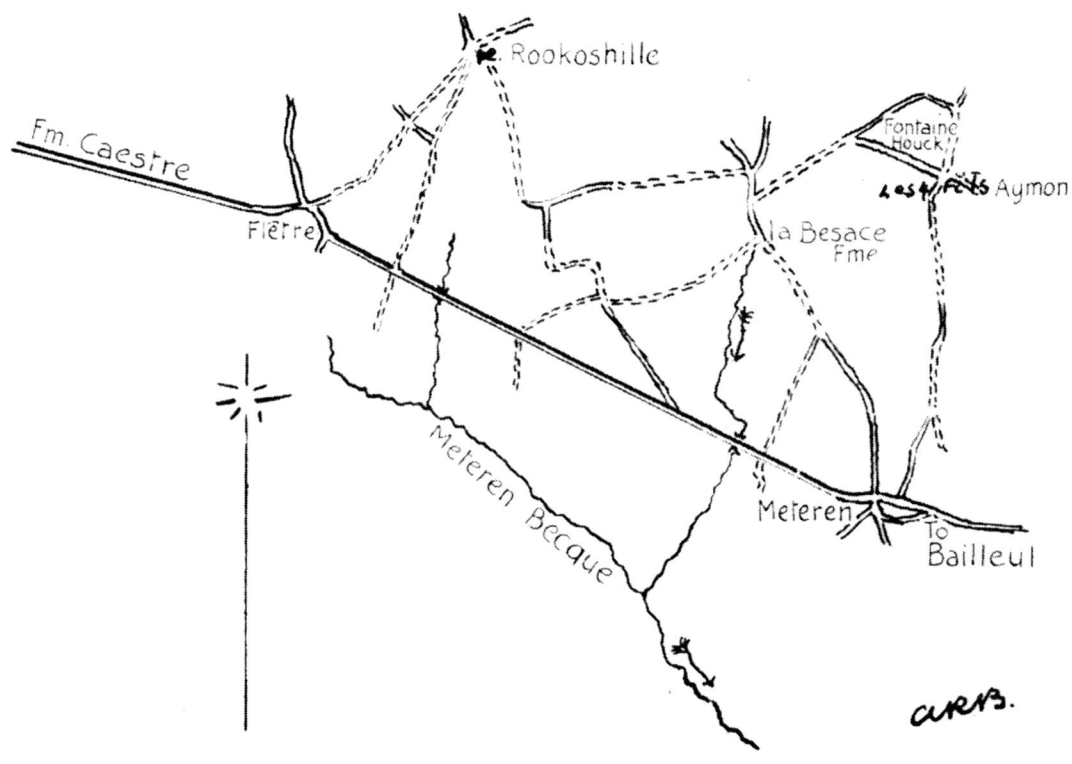

MOVE TO THE NORTH

Marching by Septmonts and Rozières, where some of the fallen Fusiliers lie buried, the Battalion reached good billets about 7 a.m. on October 7th at Hartennes, where blankets were issued to the men, with two country carts to carry them. At 8 p.m. the Brigade was again on the move, marches being carried out at night to avoid the enemy's observation by aeroplanes, and reached Rozet St. Albin, via Oulchy-la-Ville, at 2 a.m. on October 8th. Battalion headquarters were at an inn, from which the Germans had looted a number of prehistoric stone implements found in the neighbourhood. At 4.30 p.m. the march was resumed via Chouy, where the line of advance last month was crossed, Ancienville (halt for two hours for a meal), Dampleux Pisseleux, Vauciennes, to a large sugar factory, which was reached at 3 a.m. on October 9th. Marched again at 4.15 p.m. via Crepy-en-Valois to Rully, arriving at 10 p.m., where the line of retreat from Mons was crossed. The Battalion was comfortably housed in two large farms, the proprietor making the officers welcome in his dining-room, the panelling of which had been broken by Germans seeking for hidden treasure.

At 3 p.m. on October 10th the Battalion marched via Raray to Verberie, its resting place before entraining.

On October 11th the Battalion entrained at Longueil St. Marie, and proceeded by Creil, Amiens, Abbeville, Etaples, Boulogne, and Calais to St. Omer, where they arrived early on the morning of October 12th. It was bitterly cold, and, owing to inexperienced officers in charge, the detraining arrangements were not good. The whole Battalion billeted in the College de St. Joseph, but about noon took its place in the Grande Place to wait for French motor buses to proceed to Hazebrouck. The buses did not arrive, but a German airman did, and dropped bombs, with what effect was not known, but it was fortunate he did not hit the 10th Brigade, which was in mass.

October 13th.—Action at Meteren.

At daybreak, after a night spent in the French buses, the Faughs found themselves in the neighbourhood of Hazebrouck, and, leaving the French buses, concentrated at l'Hazeminde, where food and a little rest were obtained. But they were soon again on the move, and, passing through Caestre, Flêtre was reached at 1 p.m. At 2.25 p.m. orders were received to attack, and the Battalion moved to its rendezvous on the first by-road leading north, east of Flêtre. The situation was this: The enemy were holding an entrenched position running north and south through Meteren, the 4th Division attacking with the 6th Division on its right and General Allenby's Cavalry Division on its left. The objective allotted to the Battalion was Fontaine—Houck inclusive and 660 yards south of that farm. The Seaforths were on the right, and eventually the Dublin Fusiliers on the left. The Battalion dispositions were as follows: "C" Company (Captain Carberry) on the right, with orders to direct; "D" Company (Captain Incledon-Webber) on the left, "A" Company (Captain

Kavanagh) in support, and " B " Company (Captain Bull) echeloned on the left rear. The attack was launched at 3.15 p.m.; there was mist, which prevented effective artillery support; rain also commenced, which rapidly reduced the cultivated ground to soft mud, and, to prevent the rifles jamming, the soldiers carried their ground sheets loose and lay on them after each advance. The country was difficult, being cut up with hedges and other obstacles, which made adherence to the direction difficult. The advance was carried out in a spirited and workmanlike manner, and, as night closed in, Irish cheers coming from the heights north of Meteren proclaimed that the enemy position was in our hands. This was not a big affair, in the light of after events, but it was an eminently satisfactory one to the Regiment, because everything was done on the principles laid down in the training manuals as practised in peace, with most satisfactory results. There was no disorganization after the fight, and the enemy position was held and entrenched in fighting formation; moreover, thanks to the good leading, the losses were small. Lieutenant A. M. Samuels, who was hit early in the fight, died of wounds during the night.

October 14th, which was dull, was spent in entrenching the position and replenishing ammunition, etc. The Brigadier expressed himself as well pleased with the manner in which his Brigade had fought on the previous day. A prisoner of the 1st Bavarian Regiment was captured this morning under peculiar circumstances. Some soldiers were frying bacon on the roadside, the smell of which was too much for this hungry individual, who emerged from a culvert. He stated he was a non-commissioned officer, but he had a complete kit for reconnaissance work, and was probably hiding with a purpose. Later in the evening the Battalion moved into billets in Meteren, which had not suffered much from our shelling. The men were accommodated in the church, which they cleaned out after the Germans, and headquarters at the house of the Curé, l'Abbé a'Gryson, a most charming old gentleman; he had had German officers billeted on him, and the signs of their visit were too disgusting to mention here.

On the evening of October 15th the 10th Brigade moved into billets in Bailleul, the 87th being accommodated in the church. It was a weird sight to see the dimly-lit church crowded with soldiers, some in prayer and the remainder carrying on their usual occupations, but all showing reverence for the sacred building. There were many enemy wounded left in the town, and a house-to-house search was made for enemy soldiers in hiding. On this day the first honours awarded to the Regiment appeared in 4th Division Orders. They were:—

Legion of Honour Croix de Chevalier.—Second-Lieutenant W. H. Liesching.

Medailles Militaires.—Company Sergeant-Major Scrafield, Sergeant H. A. Wilson, Drummer Corrigan, and Company Sergeant-Major R. Neville.

October 16th, a short march to billets in farms east of La Crèche.

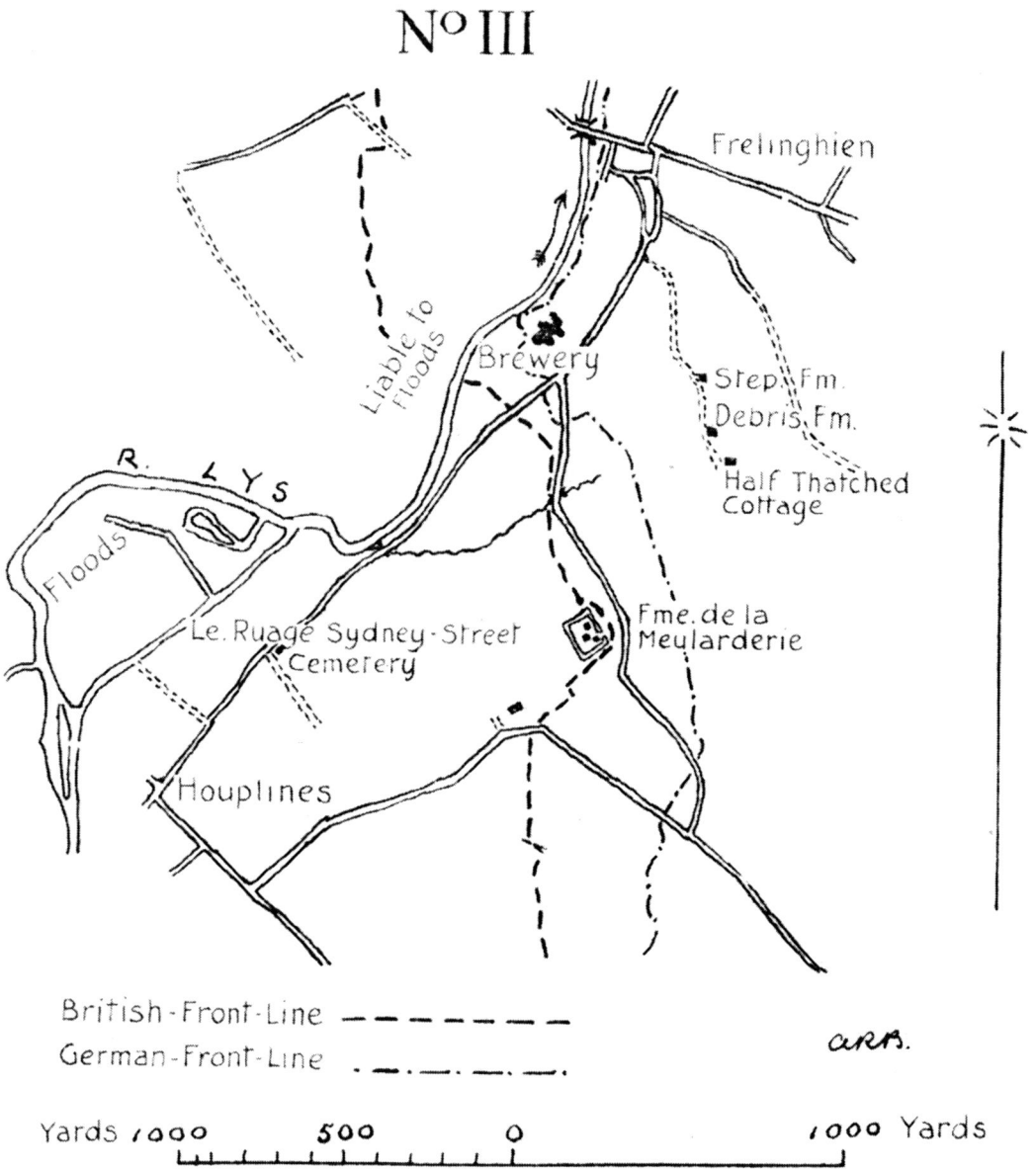

THE TAKING OF ARMENTIÈRES

The Taking of Armentières.

At 6.45 a.m. on October 17th the Battalion formed the advanced guard of the 10th Brigade, "B" Company, under Captain Bull, being the vanguard. The River Lys was crossed at Erquinghem, the troops being accompanied by a crowd of refugees. At 8.30 a.m. "C" Company, under Captain Carberry, reinforced Captain Bull, and by 9.30 a.m. the whole Battalion was acting as advanced guard, with the Royal Dublin Fusiliers in support, the whole under command of the Officer Commanding Royal Irish Fusiliers.

The welcome given to the troops was extraordinary; the poorest inhabitants literally overwhelmed the soldiers with bread, fruit, flowers, chocolates, etc., and would take no denial. But street fighting began soon after entering the town, which made progress slow. However, about noon Lieutenant Penrose, with his platoon of "C" Company, rushed the Farm Phillipeaux at Le Ruage. Captain Carberry, coming up in support, was mortally wounded—a most gallant officer, and a great loss to the Regiment. He had been severely wounded in the South African campaign. When Captain Carberry fell, Captain Elkan took command of "C" Company and continued the attack on the farm, which he set on fire. This farm was held by a few Saxons, who refused to surrender, and from after events was known in the Regiment as Sydney Street, so called after a desperate fight which took place in London about this time. For the present a guard was left over the farm.

By noon Armentières was in our hands but not clear of the enemy, as stragglers remained concealed for days, and lost no opportunity of firing on the soldiers in the streets. At 12.45 p.m. Captain Hill, "D" Company, was at Pont Ballot Ferme, having skilfully led his men to this position. "B" Company was on his left, linked up with "C" Company about Le Ruage, and this was, roughly, the position as night fell, the orders being to hold on to the ground won.

In this action Captain Wright, of "B" Company, who, with his platoon, had fought his way well in advance of the general line, was severely wounded, and certainly owes his life to the action of No. 6484 Private John Copeland, a Reservist of the Regiment, who carried him to safety under enemy fire. Private Copeland was one of the first private soldiers of the Battalion to be mentioned in despatches during the war.

To return to Le Ruage. At 2.10 p.m. authority had been received to blow up the farm, but as no guns were available there was delay in doing so. Several valuable lives had been lost in endeavouring to rescue the wounded from the tiles which were falling on them from the burning roofs. No. 7074 Lance-Corporal E. McCarthy and Private J. Murrogh both fell in a gallant attempt. Had the former lived he would have been recommended for the Victoria Cross.

Captain Kentish behaved with great gallantry in this affair, and it was chiefly through his initiative that a party of engineers were obtained to blow in the side of the farm next the road. He was assisted by Lieutenant Corblet, of the French Navy, who was awarded the Military Cross for his share in this fight.

Late at night, all being in readiness, the farm was blown in, and the gallant defenders met the death they had courted throughout the day. On November 6th the remains of Private Kavanagh were found in the debris of this wall. For this affair Captain Kentish was awarded a well-earned D.S.O., and the following were awarded the D.C.M.:—

Private A. Barton, Private B. Leddy, Private F. McKenna, and Sergeant C. Jones, since killed in action.

From midnight to 1.30 a.m. on October 18th the enemy attacked the line held by the Irish Fusiliers, using star shells and machine guns. The firing line was in trenches dug with the light entrenching tools in the root-fields to the north and east of Houplines, and nowhere did the enemy make any impression, though some of his men were killed close to the firing line. Before the attack the enemy endeavoured to find our exact positions by calling out for various companies in English, but as, amongst others, they called for " E " Company, no longer in existence under the four-company system, the ruse did not succeed.

During October 18th the Battalion was in support of the Seaforth Highlanders, and a little progress was made.

On October 19th " C " and " D " Companies were in action about Le Ruage, but at night, owing to the losses suffered by the 10th Brigade, it was relieved by a battalion of the Rifle Brigade, from the 11th Brigade, and went back into billets, except the Machine Gun Section, under Lieutenant Herrick, which remained in the line.

October 20th.—Attempt on Frelinghien.

The attack on Frelinghien, which had begun on the 19th, was continued this day, and at 5.15 a.m. the Irish Fusiliers were in a position of readiness about Le Ruage. The enemy were in trenches to the south of Frelinghien, and north of a horse-shoe shaped depression, the heels of the shoe being joined by the River Lys. The Seaforths were between the Fusiliers and the river. The right being the uncertain flank, the attack was made in echelon from the left. At 9.10 a.m. Captain Elkan, " C " Company, on the left, reported that he was in possession of the German trenches. This company attacked with considerable skill, using a muddy ditch as an approach. The German trenches were covered by a low wire entanglement, painted green, amongst a crop of roots. The trenches were taken by a combined charge of the Seaforths and Fusiliers. For skilful leading of his company before Frelinghien, and for gallantry at Le Ruage, Captain Elkan was awarded the D.S.O.

By 1.30 p.m. the following line had been established: Captain Webber,

Cemetery at Ferme Phillipeaux, "Sydney Street," taken in 1924, looking west. Debris of old farm in background.

"D" Company, held Ferme de la Meularderie on the right, and "A" Company linked up this company with "C" Company on the left.

Frelinghien was not taken, for the simple reason that the Germans had been driven back into a fully-prepared entrenched position, and it is an interesting fact that the trench-line now established by the Faughs was held by the British up to the closing months of the war.

The First Battle of Ypres—called by Lord French, in his first despatch, the Battle of Ypres—Armentières—was now being fought to the north of the Lys. The British attempt to turn the German left flank had been changed into a determined attempt on the part of the enemy to reach the Channel ports, and the rôle of the 10th Infantry Brigade, much weakened by losses in action, was to hold an extended line and thus free troops required farther north.

About 7 p.m. on October 21st the enemy attacked the right of the line with field guns, machine guns, rifle-fire and star shells. They had no success, and their discomfiture was announced by three cheers from the Faughs. The Brigadier congratulated the Battalion on this occasion.

On the night of October 23rd Frelinghien Church was burnt down; this was, apparently, a deliberate act on the part of the Germans. On October 26th the enemy brought trench mortars into action for the first time against the 10th Brigade. They were employed to dislodge the Seaforths from the Brewery in Frelinghien, and the adjacent houses. The huge projectiles could be seen rising and falling almost perpendicularly. They were most effective, and the buildings were literally blown to pieces.

The loss of these buildings, unfortunately, exposed the Fusiliers to enfilade fire from their left. It should be explained that the German trenches had been dug on the edge of a steep bank, and when these trenches were taken and reversed there was no parados. To obviate this a huge traverse of sandbags was made, the work being partly done under fire, and this did give protection, but only whilst the men stood close to the parapet. Casualties were suffered from this galling fire, amongst them Lieutenant Penrose, wounded. These trenches could not be approached by daylight, but on one occasion the Germans suffered four stretcher-bearers to carry a wounded man to the rear in daylight, an act of German chivalry so uncommon as to be worthy of record.

During these days the Battalion had the support of one howitzer, under Second-Lieutenant A. G. Hess, Royal Field Artillery. This young officer spent his whole time in working out targets and angles, and never failed when called upon. He and his gun detachment earned not only the gratitude, but the affection of the Faughs, and any comforts available were always shared, first share to the gunners. This gallant young officer was given his Horse Artillery jacket as a reward, but was killed shortly afterwards near Ypres, on February 24th, 1915.

At this time the Battalion headquarters was in Nos. 87 and 89, Rue Lutin, Houplines, and an adjacent dug-out, as the enemy shelled pretty frequently;

and on October 28th the Chateau at Houplines, just across the road, was destroyed. It was on this day that a welcome present of matches from their Majesties the King and Queen was received. The following message from the Secretary of State for War was also issued to the troops:—

"*To Sir J. French, General:*

"*The splendid courage and endurance of our troops in the battle in which you have been engaged during the last few days, and the boldness and capacity with which they have been led, have undoubtedly given the enemy a very severe blow, successfully frustrating all their efforts. Let the troops know how much we all appreciate their services, which worthily maintain the best traditions of the Army.*"

"KITCHENER."

The Intelligence summaries were eagerly scanned by all ranks. Although only taking a secondary part, the heavy and continuous fighting to the north was within sight and hearing, and the anxiety as to how the British fared was great. The authorities seemed to have formed an opinion as to the general state of the enemy which was not shared by those in touch with them—that is to say, the enemy on our front showed no signs of weakness or loss of *moral*.

On October 29th the enemy sent up a captive balloon east of Frelinghien, and continued to do so. It was very annoying, as we felt we were being overlooked.

On October 30th five loophole plates were issued for sentries. It must be remembered that in these early days trench stores were unknown, and though by this time the trenches were strong, all materials had to be looked for and gathered together under cover of darkness. This day the Battalion suffered a great loss in Major W. G. B. Phibbs, a splendid officer. He had been ailing for some time, and at last had to give in. His last words on leaving were to express regret that he could not see the thing through. Shortly after reaching England he died of disease contracted in the trenches.

On October 31st five Very pistols, or flare pistols as they were called, were issued to the Battalion, with a few cartridges—a small beginning, when it is considered that the Ypres Salient was for years illuminated nightly. The Germans always used these lights more freely than the British.

Authority was also given for an issue of rum to troops in the trenches. Whatever doctors may say, it is certain that when a hot drink such as cocoa is not available, the issue of a tot of rum to men in the early morning, after a night of exposure, is not only a great comfort, but also a most effective preventative of disease.

NOVEMBER, 1914.

Very heavy fighting was now taking place to the north, under the personal supervision of the Kaiser, and at 2.5 p.m. on November 2nd the reserve companies of the Seaforths and Irish Fusiliers were ordered to proceed at once

HELP FOR THE 11TH INFANTRY BRIGADE

to the assistance of the 11th Infantry Brigade, in the neighbourhood of Ploegsteert, since known throughout the British Army as "Plugstreet." Accordingly, "A" Company, under Major Shuter, left at 2.55 p.m.

This was an anxious time; every man, from the Commanding Officer downwards, was in the trenches. An attack was expected, and it was recognized that we must hold on without much chance of support. Reassuring messages were received in the Commander-in-Chief's Orders of the Day. On November 6th the following telegram was received by Sir John French from Lord Roberts:—

"Please accept yourself, and convey to your splendid troops, the expression of my highest appreciation of the magnificent gallantry displayed by all ranks, British and Indian."

This was the last message from the veteran Field-Marshal, who died at General Headquarters on November 14th.

At 7.30 p.m. on November 11th our lines were attacked, the enemy using field guns, but the attack, which met with a warm reception, was not pushed home.

At 10.30 a.m. on November 14th, "A" Company, under Major Shuter, rejoined headquarters. We had been in communication with them daily, but beyond the fact that they were engaged in heavy fighting, and had suffered severely and done very good work, we had no details.

The history of their expedition is as follows:—

On the night of November 2nd the company was in billets, in reserve to the 11th Infantry Brigade. On November 3rd took over trenches, near the crossroads at Le Gheer, from a company of the East Lancashire Regiment, and remained there till November 6th. They were within one hundred yards of the enemy, and worked hard at the defences, Captain Fitzgerald doing specially good work wiring at night under fire. On November 6th the company relieved the company of the Seaforths in trenches at the north-east corner of Bois de Ploegsteert. At 7 a.m. on November 7th the enemy made a strong attack, under cover of thick fog, and overwhelmed a company of the Worcestershire Regiment. In response to a call for help, Major Shuter, Captains Kavanagh and Fitzgerald, and Lieutenant Forde, with twenty men, went to their assistance and established a secondary position. Lieutenant Cooke and six men did good service by advancing into the open and enfilading the German advance. November 8th was a day of heavy shelling, the company being now in a very exposed position. They also suffered from our own shrapnel fire; this is bound to occur when the fighting lines are in close proximity. Major Shuter was wounded this day, but remained at duty. The company held these trenches until relieved by a company of the Rifle Brigade on November 13th, during which time they were subjected to heavy shell and rifle fire. The proximity of the enemy, and constant attacks, necessitated half the company being on watch day and night. All the officers were hit, the total killed and wounded being 41, or about one half the strength of the company. The company well maintained the credit of the Regiment, and their services were appreciated. Captain Kavanagh was severely wounded, and the Battalion permanently lost the services of a most gallant and brave officer. There were several recommendations made for awards, amongst them No. 11158 Private W. Hanvey, who died of wounds in a gallant attempt to save a wounded comrade. At this time the Germans were shooting our wounded who lay in the open. One section specially asked that their commander, 8667 Lance-Corporal W. Dunne (wounded) might be brought to notice for the way he had led them; he received a card of commendation from the Divisional General.

Major Shuter's wound would have been very serious had not the bullet been diverted by a cigarette case which contained a four-leaved shamrock and a lucky bean.

Whilst attached to the 11th Infantry Brigade, "A" Company received great kindness from Lieutenant-Colonel Prowse, of the Somerset Light Infantry, and the medical officer attached to that battalion.

On November 16th the Battalion were warned for relief the next day, and the opportunity for a few hours' rest was very welcome. The weather had for some time been wet and cold, with occasional frost, and the men, although cheery enough, had become numbed in mind and body; so much was this the case that at night, sentries standing in the trenches with their eyes fixed on the enemy lines, had to be spoken to more than once before they could divert their minds from the actual duty of looking out. At this time there were still fourteen of the original twenty-seven officers serving with the Battalion. On the night of November 17th the Battalion was relieved by the Royal Welch Fusiliers and Scottish Rifles, and marched to billets in farms south of Ploegsteert. On the night of November 18th the Fusiliers relieved a battalion of the Royal Scots in what was known as the Douve Sector. The Battalion marched by companies from their billets. It was a short but trying march, as rations, ammunition and trench stores had to be carried by hand. The route lay to the road fork south of Hill 63, well known as Hyde Park Corner, thence to Red Lodge, and from there in single file through the château grounds, by White Gates to La Plus Douve Farm, and from thence due east across country to the trenches. The ground was a sheet of ice and very trying to the heavily-laden men. The reason for this wide detour was that the main Messines road was swept by enemy fire.

As the Battalion held this sector alternately with their friends the Seaforths until April 12th, 1915, a description of the ground will not be out of place. The right rested on the road at Anton's Farm, where it linked up with the sector held by the Royal Dublin Fusiliers and Royal Warwickshire Regiment, and ran north-west across ploughed fields to the moated farm subsequently known as Seaforth Farm, then turned west across the Messines road, and taking in Donnington Hall and Red Cottage, ran north to the River Douve, which was the dividing line between divisions—a trench line of 1,200 yards. The names are taken from the trench map.

The soil was the usual deep Flanders loam, easy to work, but in wet weather forming a tenacious mud. The Douve is a military obstacle, but fordable; in wet weather it rises rapidly, and on many occasions the northern end of the line was under water. The mud in this part of the line was so bad that the Battalion invented what were afterwards known as "duck-boards." They were made from wood cut in the copses behind the line, and their primary use was to enable the men to lie down, which was otherwise impossible. At the close of the war there were thousands of miles of trenches and tracks constructed with "duck-boards." The position was dominated by the Messines Ridge, and from the church and buildings of that place the enemy had a bird's-eye view of our trenches and could observe the effect of his artillery fire. Our own artillery position was on and south of Hill 63. On November 18th there were no trenches in the southern part of the sector, and indifferent ones in the northern portion. Severe fighting had taken place on this ground, and hasty defences had been made by the French. Battalion headquarters were at first in a dug-out west of Irish Farm, but were frequently moved to different points in the support trenches, and at one time were at Red Lodge, and finally at Barrosa. But the spot which will be best remembered was a small cellar under the ruins of Seaforth Farm. It was about 12 feet by 6 feet, below the level of the moat, and unapproachable by day; but at night, behind the blanket which concealed the entrance, lay what was known as the "little bit of comfort." By bailing, the place could be kept moderately dry, and a brazier in one corner made it warm. It was to this underground shelter that visitors and new arrivals were conducted and made welcome.

On November 19th, Major-General Haldane, having been promoted to that rank for good service in the field and ordered to assume command of the 3rd Division, was succeeded in command of the 10th Infantry Brigade by Brigadier-General C. P. A. Hull, Middlesex Regiment. On this date also the first leave was granted to officers, and Captain Bull was selected, one officer per battalion being allowed to go. Winter clothing was also authorized, and was most welcome, especially the goat-skin coats and mackintosh capes. The regulation coat was unsuitable for the trenches. The Divisional Commander had a soldier's great-coat weighed just as he came out of the trenches, and the wet and mud were found to increase its weight by at least fifty pounds.

The remainder of the month was spent in settling down to trench life. The Seaforths and Fusiliers, relieving each other every four days, officers and men came to know their position so well that on the darkest night these periodical reliefs were carried out rapidly and without a hitch. Billets behind the lines were not yet organized, and battalions were billeted in Armentières and Nieppe. At the latter place the billet was in the Brasserie Esperance, a most difficult place to get a large body of men in and out of, but it had the great advantage that, by cutting beer barrels in two, the men got a much-needed bath. The farms south of Hill 63 were also used as billets, the best being "The Piggeries." The pig sties, all under cover in large buildings, were thoroughly cleaned out, and formed really comfortable quarters for sections of men.

Much work was put in improving the defences; the weather was hard, and this favoured work in the otherwise soft and sticky soil, but as revetting material was scarce, the occasional thaws played havoc with the earthworks.

The enemy also did his best to destroy the works. At this time the British artillery were short of ammunition, and retaliation was not forthcoming. So bold did the enemy become that he formed a habit of bringing field guns up to what was practically point-blank range and having daily shoots, every shot being accurately observed from Messines. For protection from this fire deep, narrow trenches were dug, which, although probably seen, were exceedingly hard to hit.

Gradually small comforts were provided, amongst them braziers, with a supply of coke and charcoal. Small hand-carts, with old motor tyres on the wheels, one per company, were found very useful for bringing up stores, etc. The officers purchased a country cart, which enabled the mess sergeant to do some catering; these mess carts afterwards became part of the Regimental transport, and were issued by the Ordnance Department. A small proportion of gum-boots were a welcome addition to trench stores.

But the greatest boon to all ranks was the supply of comforts sent out by an organization of which Mrs. Douglas Churcher, wife of the late Commanding Officer, was the head. The Battalion owes a very deep debt of gratitude to Mrs. Churcher, who continued throughout the war to supply all sorts of articles, which for the men in the trenches supplied the little comforts which, in trench warfare, are great comforts. In this connection it may here be stated that Mr. Delmege-Trimble, editor of the *Armagh Guardian,* devoted himself to the same work, and he was instrumental in sending a continuous supply of parcels to the prisoners of war. The Battalion lost few men as prisoners of war, and these chiefly the wounded and worn-out during the retreat from Mons. There is little doubt that some of these men owe their lives to the food sent through Mr. Trimble's agency. In 1920 the Battalion, then serving in Persia, sent Mr. Trimble three handsome Persian carpets; but the real reward for Mrs. Churcher, Mr. Trimble, and all those who worked with them, lies in the heartfelt gratitude of thousands of Irish Fusiliers, and especially of those who served in the trenches during the winter of 1914-15.

In 1915, Lady Dartrey was instrumental in collecting no less than £1,314 from all denominations in the counties of Armagh, Monaghan, and Cavan, and sent out three motor ambulances to France for the Royal Irish Fusiliers, and also endowed a bed in the U.V.F. Hospital in Belfast. Two of the brass plates, with inscriptions, from the ambulances are now in Lady Dartrey's possession. The third ambulance is believed to have been destroyed by shell fire.

Nº IV

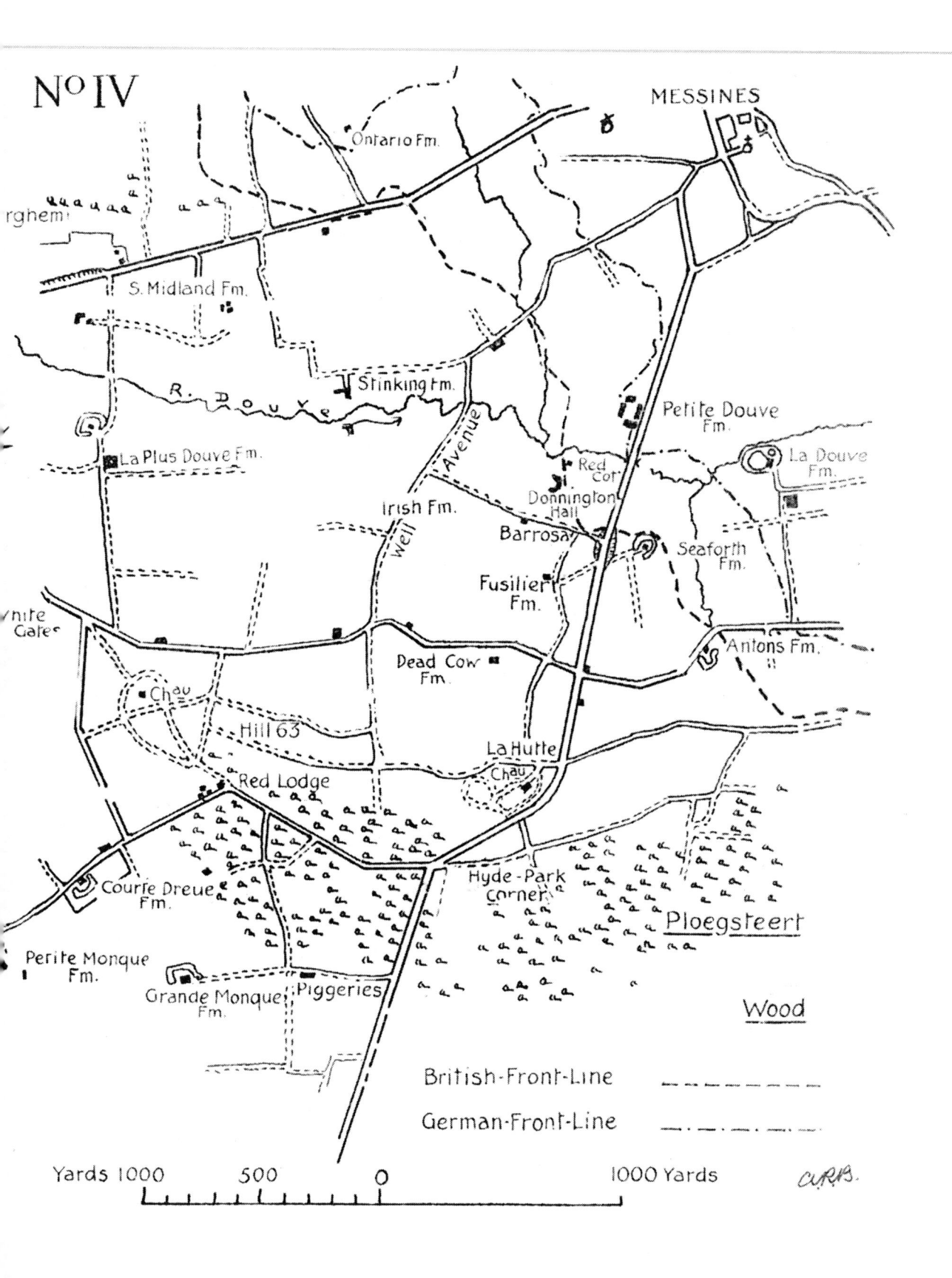

On November 23rd, Father Ryan joined as chaplain to the Faughs; he had a good influence over the men. Captain R. W. R. Jeudwine also joined, with a draft of 103, on this date, and was excessively annoyed at having a particularly smart new hat blown to pieces on his arrival in the trenches. During the last few days of the month the Battalion was subjected to a fairly heavy bombardment, the 29th being one of the worst days, on which Second-Lieutenant C. E. Cooke, a very gallant young officer, was wounded.

On November 25th the first warrant officers and non-commissioned officers were allowed to go on ten days' furlough; the first to go were Regimental Sergeant-Major Scrafield and Regimental Quartermaster-Sergeant Robinson.

December, 1914.

On December 2nd, His Majesty the King visited Nieppe and presented decorations and medals, the fortunate recipients in the Battalion being Captain R. J. Kentish, D.S.O., and Privates Barton and Leddy the D.C.M. The Battalion was in billets just behind the lines, and, as a representative platoon was to parade for the occasion, there was great furbishing up of buttons and equipment in honour of the Colonel-in-Chief. Lieutenant J. C. O'Brien was selected to command the platoon.

Conditions in the trenches were bad at this period, but all ranks were always cheery and made the best of things. In addition to our own, we occasionally had what we regarded as official jests. For example, late at night on December 3rd, a particularly uncomfortable night, the Commanding Officer and company commanders were gathered in the small cellar already mentioned, trying to work out how to maintain the defences on the Douve River, when a telephone message of ninety words was received over the slender wire which constituted our link with civilization, the subject being "Paying compliments on the march." Another message, demanding immediate information as to the number of caps, winter and summer pattern, with and without chin-straps, in our possession, was mercifully intercepted by the Brigadier. Some of the trenches could only be maintained by constant bailing, supplemented by improvised pumps made by the Royal Engineers out of corrugated iron.

On December 5th, Captain and Adjutant W. H. C. Wortham went to hospital; he had been unwell for some time, but remained at duty until he was physically unable to perform it. He was a great loss to the Battalion. Captain P. Penn took over the duties of adjutant.

In addition to the constant bombardment of the enemy, there was always a good deal of sniping in this sector, and this was a kind of fighting in which we could hold our own; there was no shortage of rifle ammunition. Both sides used "rifle batteries," *i.e.*, rifles laid on an object and fixed, a soldier being detailed to fire a round at stated intervals. This nature of fire was useful at night. Our casualties were not severe, but many good men were lost in this

this way. Company Sergeant-Major Sproule, an exceptionally fine type of Irish soldier, was shot dead on a pitch dark night by one of these snipers.

On December 7th we had on trial an "optical appliance," made of cardboard and looking-glass, to protect sentries from snipers. This was the origin of the "trench periscope."

A very good system of reliefs was adopted at this time, which consisted of four days in the trenches, four days in billets just below the lines, when the Battalion was employed at night working on the support lines, and four days at the village of La Crèche, well to the rear, where the men could rest in peace, and much necessary refitting, etc., be carried out. The first day at La Crèche was always spent in cleaning and the second in ceremonial drill, etc., which was not only necessary to maintain smartness, but was liked by the men. There was also periodical washing in Nieppe, and, above all, "The Follies."

The staff of the 4th Division were pioneers in many arrangements conducive to the happiness and well-being of the men, and not the least of these was "The Follies," a troupe of amateur entertainers who began in a small way. The first theatre was a low, ill-lighted room in Nieppe. The foot-lights were candles, and the orchestra three French instrumentalists in uniform. At this stage not the least attraction were "Vaseline" and "Lanoline," two French girls, neither of whom could speak a word of English, but who set off the troupe, seated at either end, dressed up in costumes obtained from Paris. "The Follies" held their own as a divisional troupe throughout the war. It is said that a bargain was once struck between the 4th Division and the Highland Division, the latter exchanging a female impersonator for a machine gun.

Divisional headquarters was a sort of home for weary officers, and many an officer must look back in gratitude to the welcome received in the headquarters mess, where the genial commander, Major-General Henry Wilson, did much to endear himself to all ranks.

On December 10th the news of the naval victory at the Falkland Islands was received. On December 11th, Lieutenant-Colonel Burrowes proceeded on ten days' leave, and command of the Battalion devolved upon Major Shuter.

On December 14th our artillery shelled enemy trenches about the Messines road, and a good many casualties were inflicted by our machine-gun and rifle fire.

About this time divisional machine-gun batteries were formed, the Battalion furnishing its share of the personnel. The officers were issued with Web equipment identical with that of the men. The habit of wearing badges of rank on the shoulders, instead of on the cuffs of the service jacket, also became common, the reason being that the regulation cuffs were very conspicuous. The officers' swords were withdrawn and sent home.

Mineral jelly, and afterwards whale oil, were issued as a preventive against frostbite. The Battalion were singularly free from this ailment, which can only be attributed to the proper use of these preventives, as the conditions were very bad, in many cases mud and water up to the knees.

On December 20th the Battalion assisted an attack made by the 11th Brigade on their right by fire action only.

On December 21st, Lieutenant-Colonel Burrowes resumed command of the Battalion.

The trenches were subjected to heavy shelling on this and the two following days, probably as retaliation for our action on December 20th. The enemy brought not less than twelve guns to bear on our front, both heavy and light; their practice was accurate, and they did a great deal of damage. This is not surprising, since, in the words of the official report, "Our artillery did not engage the enemy guns." These bombardments, when we were unable to hit back, were trying. That the casualties were not more than they were was due to the deep cover trenches, where officers and men stood and joked while the missiles flew over their heads. The enemy's field guns being fired, as stated above, at point blank range, the most that could be done was to repair by night the damage done during the day.

Orders were received on December 22nd to increase the number of machine guns with the Battalion from two to four.

Conditions in the trenches were now so bad that a new scheme of defence was devised. Instead of a continuous fire trench, it was suggested that the line should be held by a chain of posts, buildings or breastworks, so as to keep above the water; these posts to be connected by obstacles and supported by a second line of posts in rear. Full use was to be made of machine guns. The Douve sector was consequently modified on these lines, but, owing to the nature of the terrain, there was not much improvement as regards comfort.

Two other matters of far-reaching importance were also under consideration at this time. First, the use of hand grenades; and second, the introduction of trench mortars. In view of after events, it is interesting to note that only 300 trench mortars were available for issue to the whole Army, and it was suggested that battalion machine-gun officers should be responsible for the training of the detachments and fighting the weapons.

On December 24th, Lieutenant and Quartermaster T. E. Bunting was recommended for a step in honorary rank. He had already received two wounds during the campaign. The Battalion owes much to this fine old soldier, who never spared himself in his endeavours to minister to their well-being. Later in the war he lost a son who fought as an officer of the Faughs, and except when wounded, or on short periods of leave, he never left the Battalion during the entire war. He was, however, beaten in this respect by his storeman, Private Dougan, who never left the Regiment at all throughout the entire campaign.

December 25th, Christmas Day. After a somewhat trying tour in the trenches, the Battalion was fortunate in being in billets at La Crèche. It was a fine, frosty morning, and services were held for the Roman Catholics in the village church, and for Protestants in the school-house. The Christmas cards sent by their Majesties the King and Queen were distributed, as well as Princess Mary's chocolate-boxes. Thanks to many gifts sent by kind friends at home, the men had a really good Christmas dinner. The officers dined together in the evening, and carol-singers, led by the regimental sergeant-major, went round the village; altogether, a very pleasant day.

The usual routine was carried on up to the end of the month. On December 28th an artillery observing officer was on duty in the trenches for the first time, and proved of great service; it was not until he made his report that the impunity with which the enemy shelled us was realized behind the lines. On December 29th we had a visit of officers from the 27th Division to learn trench warfare; they turned out to be officers and non-commissioned officers of our own 2nd Battalion, and received a hearty welcome. On this day the River Douve rose considerably and flooded the trenches in its vicinity. The alternate frost and rain made the trenches very bad.

At Christmas there had been rumours that the enemy were attempting to fraternize with the British. On the morning of December 31st the enemy opposed to the Battalion got up on their parapets and made friendly signals. The Battalion stood to arms, and Captain G. V. W. Hill, having first divested himself of all identity marks, was sent out into No Man's Land to warn them that we would shoot if they did not desist. He allowed two men to approach him, from whom he learnt that there was a dead British soldier in front of their trenches. He asked them to bury him and to bring his identity disc. They returned shortly, bringing papers and letters from the body of an Inniskilling Fusilier. The identity disc was recovered shortly afterwards by Captain Bull, on night patrol—No. 9162 Private R. Boyd. From this incident we identified two units on our front, and that the River Douve was the boundary between units.

At this time a new series of maps was issued. Trench maps were not yet in existence, but the new maps, by a simple system of lettering and squares, made map references on maps of different scales identical.

In spite of the bad weather and hard life in the trenches, the end of 1914 found the 87th remarkably healthy and in good spirits. Seventeen officers and 768 other ranks had been required to replace losses, but it is noteworthy that only three of the officers who came out with the Battalion had been lost through sickness.

CHAPTER II—1915.

January, 1915.

The opening weeks of the New Year were comparatively uneventful. Both sides had settled down to the routine of trench warfare, and, in addition to the daily fighting, were fully occupied in the maintenance of defences, which suffered more from the vagaries of the climate than the actual shelling.

During January the situation improved, for the British ammunition supplies were being gradually replenished and the enemy did not have it all his own way in bombardments, and the feeling that we could, and did, hit back was a great satisfaction to those in the front line trenches.

The chief hardship was still the appalling state of the trenches during the frequent thaws and heavy rain. But the whole situation was improving; a strong second line of defence had been constructed astride of the Messines road, huts had been constructed for the supporting troops on the southern slopes of Hill 63, where they were practically immune from shell fire; and the routine of reliefs had been slightly modified, four days being spent in the front line, two days in support and two days at La Crèche. The men bathed at reasonable intervals, and football and other amusements were organized.

Great attention was paid to sanitation and inoculation, with excellent results. Up to the end of January, 1915, there had only been 212 cases of enteric in the British Army, confined almost entirely to soldiers who had not been inoculated; and whale oil proved an efficient preventive against frostbite.

During the month the 7th Argyll and Sutherland Highlanders were initiated into trench warfare, at first by platoons and then complete companies. A very fine Territorial unit, they became part of the 10th Infantry Brigade, and acquitted themselves well, both in trench warfare and later in the Second Battle of Ypres.

So smooth was the working of reliefs, and so well did officers and men know their trenches, that the Seaforths and Fusiliers could, and often did, relieve each other on pitch dark nights without the slightest hitch. The work was done by programme and was progressive, and each company kept an inventory of trench stores, which by this time were becoming important.

On January 12th, Lieutenant C. W. Sparks assumed medical charge of the Battalion; this excellent officer, with his no less efficient Sergeant H. W. Stoner, will long be remembered in the Regiment for the way in which they laid themselves out to alleviate the sufferings of the wounded and sick. Many officers and men were saved to the Battalion by sending them for a few days' rest to the transport lines. This temporary relaxation was a great boon to men who, if continued at duty in the trenches, would undoubtedly have taken months to regain their strength in hospital.

About this time a cadet school for officers promoted from the ranks was started at Bailleul, under the auspices of the Artists Rifles, a Territorial battalion with which the Faughs were on very friendly terms both before and during the war.

On January 27th instructions were received for the formation of a grenadier platoon, Second-Lieutenant Cooke to command 1 non-commissioned officer and 25 men from each company.

During the winter there were constant reports of German spies behind the lines. Some of the reports were doubtless true, but many were not. On January 31st a French woman told a circumstantial tale of meeting a party of mounted Germans on Hill 63. She described their dress and said she had been threatened with a rifle. On investigation it turned out to be an artillery party reconnoitring for observation posts.

The ordinary routine of trench life was continued throughout the month of February. In spite of the adverse weather conditions much work was done, and the trenches were brought to a state of efficiency which not only ensured that an infantry attack on the part of the enemy would be exceedingly costly, but also afforded protection to the garrisons, with the result that, in spite of the continued shelling, the casualties were light. The enemy attempted several attacks on other parts of the line, but in the Douve sector the ground was practically impassable, except during hard frost, and he contented himself with using the sector as a practice ground for his artillery, his observation from Messines making the locality an ideal one for this purpose.

Nearly all the work was carried on at night, and the Battalion were fortunate in having the assistance of Lieutenant Martell, of the 9th Field Company, Royal Engineers, an officer as brave as he was clever in designing field works; he became a great friend of the Regiment. A good deal of patrolling was done at night, which gave a zest to the work.

When out of the line there was plenty of routine work to occupy the time, and this was varied with football matches, and visits to "The Follies" helped to pass the time. The Battalion also played matches with their friends the Artists Rifles, who also had a very fine concert troupe.

On February 20th the Commanding Officer was placed on the sick list, and during his absence the Battalion was commanded by Major Shuter and Captain Kentish.

Barrosa Day, March 5th, was spent in billets south of Hill 63. The Drums played, and were now augmented with Bandsman Fincham's ragtime band. The men had a good dinner, chiefly due to the generosity of the Hon. Mrs. Gough; and the customary greetings were exchanged between the 1st and

2nd Battalions of the Regiment. The officers off duty dined at La Courte Dreve Farm, the Battalion headquarters.

The usual bombardment went on, the enemy's field gun shells being known at this time as "Little Willies" and his howitzers as "White Hopes."

The work of carrying up stores to the lines was heavy, and at this time the numerous dead cattle, the victims of shell fire, were buried. The half of a dead pig, which for a long time had been a land-mark on the Messines road on dark nights, also disappeared.

The British were making attacks farther south, and for some days reports on enemy movements had to be submitted every two hours. Nothing unusual occurred in the Douve sector, except that the enemy appeared nervous and spent much time and labour in wiring his front.

In the evolution of trench maps English names were gradually substituted for the local ones, and farms came to be known as Irish, Fusilier, Barrosa and Seaforth, the latter containing the famous cellar.

On March 16th the Battalion moved from La Crèche to Armentières, the 10th Brigade having been relieved by the 84th Brigade with a view to taking over their old lines north of that town. The Artists Rifles had kindly arranged a dinner and concert for the Fusiliers at Bailleul; at short notice they transferred the whole thing to Armentières, and a most enjoyable afternoon was spent. On March 17th the Battalion moved back and relieved the 1st Battalion Suffolk Regiment in their old sector on the Douve. On March 25th, on relieving the Seaforths, the Battalion took over 200 yards of trench north of the River Douve, communication being established by a temporary bridge. On March 27th, General Blore, Chief Engineer, inspected the trenches, expressing himself as very pleased with the work and describing them as "show trenches."

The Battalion had established a cemetery at Seaforth Farm; it is to be regretted that during the severe fighting which afterwards took place over this area, the cemetery was entirely obliterated.

April, 1915.

On April 6th, Lieutenant-Colonel Burrowes resumed command of the Battalion. At this time the newspapers kindly supplied free by the proprietors at home were much appreciated by the troops.

On April 8th the grenadiers practised with a catapult for throwing bombs; it was a crude affair, capable of throwing a jam-tin full of explosive to a maximum range of forty yards.

On this day the Battalion received a copy of a captured order, from which it appeared that the Germans in Messines found our fire distinctly unpleasant.

On April 11th orders were received for the relief of the Brigade on the following day, and for this purpose advance parties of the 5th Battalion Royal Warwickshire Regiment came into the trenches. The enemy were very active this day, both in the air and shelling the Château of La Hutte on Hill 63.

April 12th.

The last day in the Douve sector was destined to be an eventful one. In addition to other bombardments, about 5 p.m. the enemy opened with heavier guns than he had hitherto employed. The first shells burst north-west of Dead Cow Farm, and aided by his excellent observation from Messines, he systematically shortened range till he found the trench immediately south of the River Douve, and this he proceeded to demolish.

It was on this occasion that Private Robert Morrow, of "D" Company, won the Victoria Cross for conspicuous bravery and devotion to duty. The award was notified in the *London Gazette* of May 22nd, 1915, in the following words:—

"*For most conspicuous bravery near Messines on April 12th, 1915, when he rescued and carried successively to places of comparative safety, several men who had been buried in the debris of trenches wrecked by shell fire. Private Morrow carried out this gallant work on his own initiative, and under very heavy fire from the enemy.*"

Private Morrow died of wounds received on April 25th, 1915, during the Second Battle of Ypres, before his honour was known to himself or his Regiment. The late Tsar of Russia awarded him the Medal of St. George, 3rd Class.

Many Victoria Crosses have been won for isolated acts of gallantry, but Private Morrow's was much more than that.

A simple, unassuming lad from New Mills, in the County Tyrone, where his widowed mother lived on a small farm, in peace time he was not conspicuous as a soldier, but, from the first time the Battalion was under fire, Private Morrow proved that he had the heart of a lion, and many are the stories of his fearlessness still current amongst his comrades.

On one occasion water was badly wanted in a trench. Morrow volunteered to get it, and, carrying a rum-jar, he proceeded to a neighbouring farm, being under a heavy rifle-fire all the way there and back. Just as he was jumping into the trench on his return, an enemy bullet smashed the jar to pieces. Nothing daunted, Morrow got some water-bottles and again went to the farm, this time returning safely, but still fired at all the time.

The writer once met Morrow with a large rent in his trousers. On being asked the cause he replied, in his quiet way, "Only a bit of shell, sir."

The Victoria Cross was sent to Mrs. Morrow, who also received the following much-prized letter from His Majesty the King:—

"*Buckingham Palace,*
"*October 15th, 1915.*

"*It is a matter of sincere regret to me that the death of Private Robert Morrow deprived me of the pride of personally conferring upon him the Victoria Cross, the greatest of all distinctions.*

"*GEORGE R.I.*"

SHELLS BURSTING ON MESSINES RIDGE, 8-6-17.

Photo by [Imperial War Museum

Although in poor circumstances, Mrs. Morrow refused a tempting offer for her son's decoration, saying that only his Regiment should have it. A subscription was started amongst past and present officers, and in August, 1919, at a ceremonial parade held at the Depôt, Armagh, Mrs. Morrow formally handed the Victoria Cross to the Regiment, who, in return, handed her the title deeds of a piece of land she was anxious to add to her farm.

The following were also recommended for gallantry during this action:—Lieutenant C. W. Sparks, R.A.M.C., Second-Lieutenant W. E. Henry (attached), Sergeant J. Donaldson (severely wounded), Sergeant F. Thomas, and Bandsman (Lance-Corporal) F. Fincham.

During the night the Battalion was relieved by the 5th Royal Warwickshire Regiment, and marched via Ploegsteert, Romerin, and Robat to billets in Bailleul, reaching the latter place at 2.30 a.m. on April 13th. Earlier in the night a Zeppelin had dropped bombs on Bailleul, and it is interesting to note that at this time the airship flew so low that it was engaged with rifle fire.

During the next three days all ranks thoroughly enjoyed the luxury of billets after such a long spell in trenches. The mornings were taken up with training, the grenadiers practising with rifle grenades; the afternoons were devoted to sports. The inhabitants were most hospitable. Poor people, they little knew that before the end of the war their town would be reduced to a heap of rubble.

On April 16th the Battalion moved about four miles to billets in the village of Merris, where officers and men were again on the best of terms with the inhabitants. The church had been injured by shell fire, and the regimental transport assisted the Curé by bringing materials for its repair. The village was destroyed in 1918, and was one of those which marked the limit of the German advance.

On April 19th the Battalion was inspected by Major-General W. P. Pulteney, commanding the III Corps, who expressed himself as follows on the work done during the winter, and on the appearance and turn-out of the unit on parade.

"*Lieutenant-Colonel Burrowes and officers: Sir John French would like to have seen your battalion on parade, but his numerous duties have prevented him. It is a great pleasure for me to meet you. The cleanliness of the men shows great self-respect on their part, and this reflects much credit on the officers who have looked after them so well. I know full well the arduous time you have all had in the trenches, and how cheerily you have met the uncongenial conditions. I also know that the filling of sand-bags is not very interesting work; but you have made your trenches strong, and you who have been behind them know the value of this. It has been a great pleasure to me to hear from time to time that whatever duty your Battalion has been called upon to perform, you have at once undertaken that duty and carried it through well and cheerily, and that is the true high spirit which I know so well. The summer is now approaching and you have all got your backs well up, and I know that you will acquit yourselves well. Colonel Burrowes, I congratulate you on the turn-out of the men of your Battalion. They are very clean and well turned out."*

It now transpired that the Faughs were undergoing what was known as the "fattening process," that is, being got ready for a big attack. This attack was to be the taking of Frelinghien. The commanding officers and company commanders of the Brigade were sent in buses to reconnoitre their old lines in front of Houplines for this purpose. On April 20th companies visited the battlefield of Meteren, each company inspecting the ground it fought over on October 13th, 1914. There were few traces of the fight, but the grave of Second-Lieutenant A. M. Samuels was put in good order.

On April 22nd, "B" Company were defeated by a company of the 7th Argyll and Sutherland Highlanders in the final for the 10th Brigade Football Cup. It was presented by the Brigadier for competition, the silver cup being mounted on a plinth of Ploegsteert oak.

On April 23rd, at 11.15 a.m., orders were received for the Brigade to be ready to move at short notice. From the nature of the orders it was evident that the troops were going into action somewhere to the north.

The situation was this: The enemy had made their first great attack with asphyxiating gas to the north-east of Ypres. The French troops had been overwhelmed, and not only they, but the whole of the civil population, had been driven to the western bank of the Yser Canal, thus leaving the British troops who held the line on their right, with their left flank in the air. It was to restore this situation that troops were being rushed to the Ypres Salient.

At 8.20 p.m. the Battalion left Merris and marched via Bailleul to Dranoutre, reaching that place at 11.30 p.m., and billeted.

At 7.15 a.m. on April 24th the column was again on the move, and marched to Locre and rested till 2.30 p.m., when they took the road by Zevecoten to Ouderdom. Some huts 1,500 yards north-east of that place were reached at 4.30 p.m., and here extra hand-grenades and carriers were distributed. Each soldier was also given an extra 100 rounds of ammunition and two sand-bags. From this point only the fighting portion of the transport accompanied the Battalion. Marching via Vlamertinghe the Battalion reached its rendezvous, the cross-roads about 3,000 yards east of Vlamertinghe, at 7.15 p.m. The men rested by the roadside; the officers found shelter in the loft of a building at the cross-roads which was being used as a dressing-station, and all traces of which have long since disappeared.

As night fell, the scene was typical of the back area during a great battle. The Ypres—Poperinghe chaussée is one of the finest roads in Belgium, easily capable of taking four streams of traffic, and it was now crowded with ammunition and supply wagons going forward, which met the opposite stream of ambulances and wounded men, each man having his own ideas as to what was going on in the fighting line. The sides of the roads were crowded with the sleeping soldiers, oblivious to the clatter around them and the more distant sounds of artillery and rifle fire. But the whole scene was illuminated by the burning town of Ypres, the grandeur of the spectacle increasing with the darkness. The crackling of the flames could be heard, and at intervals the whole sky was lit up with a lurid glare as the fire spread to some new building. The general roar was punctuated at intervals by a dull explosion which dwarfed all other sounds, the heavy shells of the enemy bursting in the devoted city. The Commanding Officer had gone to Brigade headquarters to receive instructions for the next day, and on his return, shortly before midnight, the whole Battalion was still sleeping. By the light of a guttering candle the officers could be seen in all attitudes amongst the heterogeneous contents of the loft. It was impossible to suppress the sad thought that this must necessarily be the last sleep for many of these gallant gentlemen and their brave men.

Second Battle of Ypres.

The night was dark and rain fell heavily as the Battalion marched at midnight from its rendezvous. They were the last unit in the column, and, to avoid the burning town of Ypres, the route taken led north of that place by what was afterwards named "Salvation Corner." This road was being shelled, but no casualties occurred. A halt was made in the village of Saint Jean, and in a small cottage on the south side of the road the Brigadier issued his instructions for attack. A shell had penetrated the roof, and the water was dripping on to the little household treasures which form the typical adornment of a Flanders cottage. A canary was dying in its cage hung in the window.

The situation was obscure, but it was believed that some of the Canadians, who had made such a gallant stand against the onslaught of the enemy, still held the village of St. Julien. The following orders were issued to the Battalion at 3.15 a.m., April 25th: First objective, to make good an east and west line just north of Fortuin, the left resting on the Hanebeek in touch with the Royal Dublin Fusiliers. Second objective, to occupy a gap of about 500 yards said to exist between St. Julien and the Suffolk Regiment east of that village, care being taken not to fire on the village, which might still be occupied by our troops. Units were detailed as follows: "C" Company (Captain Elkan), firing line and supports on the left and unit of direction. "D" Company (Captain Jeudwine) prolong to the right and get in touch with the Suffolks. "A" Company (Major Kentish) and Machine Gun Section (Lieutenant Herrick) in rear of "C" Company. "B" Company (Captain Bull) Battalion reserve under the Commanding Officer, to follow "D" Company and protect the right, that being the exposed flank.

There was considerable delay in moving forward, the road being blocked with transport and Canadian troops, and dawn was breaking as the Battalion debouched from the village of Wieltje. The morning mist had not yet risen, but from rifle and machine-gun fire it at once became evident that the enemy held the farms between Wieltje and St. Julien.

On arriving at a small cottage north of the road, the Commanding Officer mistook a small stream for the Hanebeek; the column was suffering casualties from rifle fire, and the Dublin Fusiliers had already deployed and were moving east. For these reasons he ordered the Battalion to deploy at about 5.30 a.m. This was done by moving sections along the shallow roadside ditches. The mistake turned out to be a fortunate one, and as the mist rose the direction of the attack was soon corrected and the deployment was carried out as ordered, with the exception that three machine guns were sent with " C " Company and " A " Company took the place of " B " Company as Battalion reserve.

The Battalion advanced to the attack, which at this time was unsupported by artillery, with their usual dash and made good progress, in spite of a hot fire, especially of machine guns. At 6.30 a.m. the situation was as follows: Captain Elkan (" C " Company) had ascertained from an officers' patrol led by Lieutenant MacMullen, that St. Julien was held by the enemy, and had advanced to about 70 yards from the village, the whole of his company being on the right of the Hanebeek except No. 9 Platoon, under Captain Penrose, which was on the left bank. Captain Jeudwine (" D " Company) was on the right of " C " Company, and also about 70 yards from the village. Captain Bull (" B " Company), was in rear of " D " Company, with one section detached to protect the right flank. Major Kentish (" A " Company) was near the road and just west of the Hanebeek.

The losses had been heavy and the advance, made over open ground and subjected to the concentrated fire of machine guns with which the enemy had reinforced St. Julien, was brought to a standstill. " C " Company was in the act of repulsing a counter-attack which endeavoured to advance along both banks of the Hanebeek, and " B " Company was advancing by sectional rushes in an endeavour to help their comrades of " D " Company in front. Battalion headquarters were at a small farm in the angle made by the right bank of the Hanebeek and the north side of the Wieltje road, from which a good view of the battlefield could be obtained. An endeavour of the enemy to push a machine gun along the ditch of the Fortuin road had been frustrated by the fire of the headquarters orderlies.

It was at this time, 6.30 a.m., that the writer saw the troops, who were attacking what was afterwards known as Kitchener's Wood, on the left under very heavy fire of all descriptions, begin to withdraw. The apparent reason was that some British heavy guns, which now came into action, were dropping their shells short amongst the troops and creating an impossible situation. This retirement spread to the right and eventually reached the Irish Fusiliers, on the extreme right of the attack. The forward lines of the Fusiliers did not retire; they lay on the glacis-like slope in front of St. Julien, dead.

" A " Company of the Fusiliers formed a rallying point for men of all corps.

Nº V

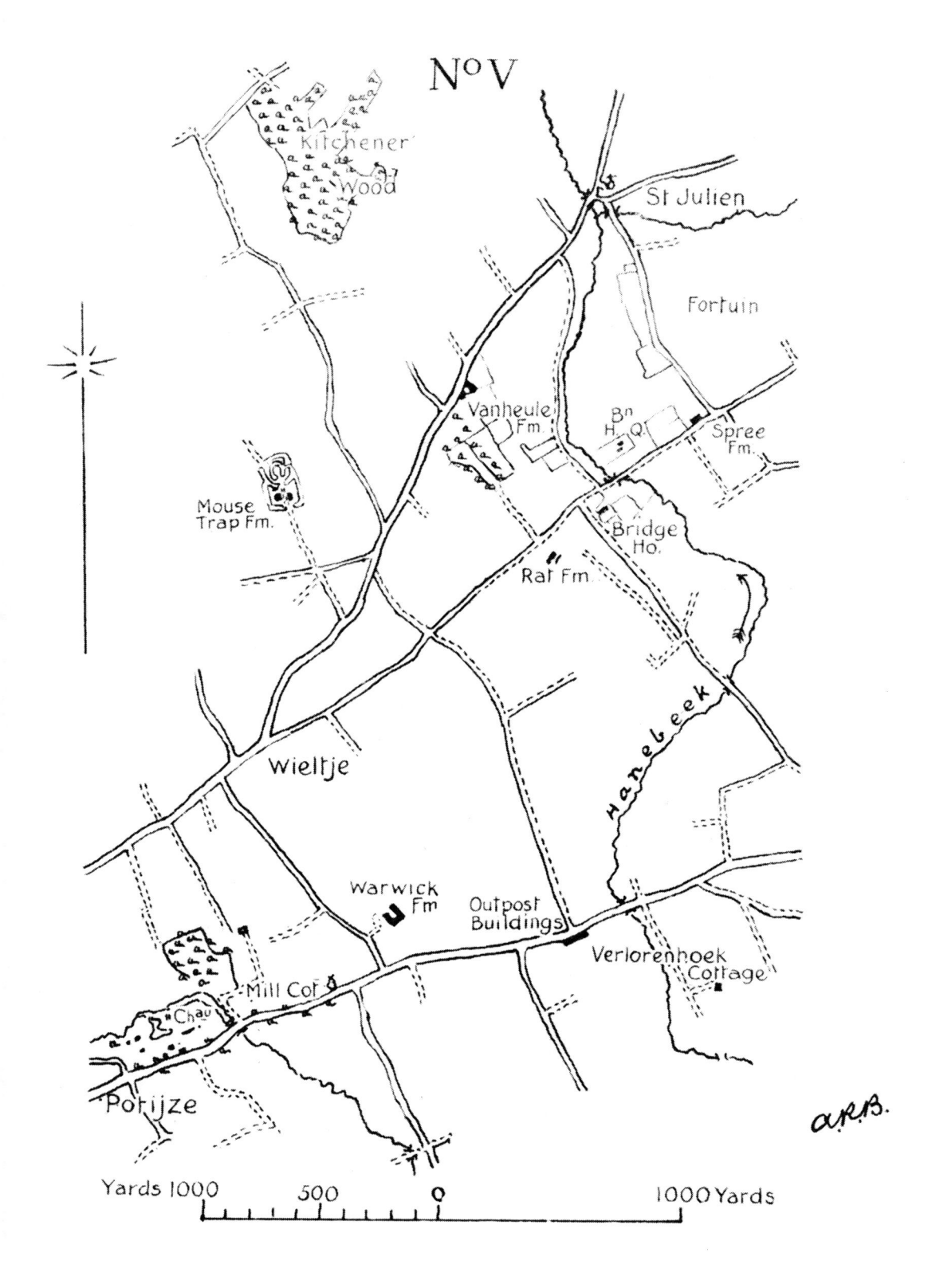

LOSSES NEAR ST. JULIEN

The withdrawal was covered by parties of the regiment holding the bed of the Hanebeek; a few men who sacrificed themselves were taken prisoners.

About 8.30 a.m. the Battalion had established a line running from the headquarters farm to near Vanheule Farm, held by the Royal Dublin Fusiliers, and were digging in under shell fire.

There is no doubt that before the retirement commenced the attack of the Royal Irish Fusiliers had reached its limit. For an infantry battalion, unsupported by artillery and with only four machine guns, to carry by assault a fortified village bristling with machine guns is not humanly possible. Yet the attack had served its purpose, and the bitterness of disappointment was alleviated when, a few months later, the objects of the attack were explained to the 10th Infantry Brigade.

The chief source of anxiety was now the right flank. An officers' patrol had succeeded in getting in touch with the Suffolk Regiment, which was, however, a considerable distance to the right rear, and it was not known if they had maintained their position.

That the enemy, who were evidently the stronger, did not make an effective counter-attack, may be partly explained by the extraordinary gallantry of troops of the Northumbrian Division. These Territorial troops, in this, their first engagement, displayed a heroism which not only called forth the admiration of their comrades of the Regular Army, but apparently intimidated the enemy. Unfortunately, their efforts were ill-directed. They knew neither their objective or direction, and the best efforts of the Irish Fusiliers to help them were of little avail.

The losses on this day were severe and increased by the fact that a number of men, who would otherwise have been in rear, knowing that a battle was imminent, joined the companies on their own initiative.

The casualties were:—Officers killed: Captain E. J. McN. Penrose, Lieutenant A. J. Millar, and Lieutenant D. P. Lynden-Bell. Officers wounded: Captains D. A. Davison and J. C. P. O'Brien, Lieutenants H. E. Herrick (machine-gun officer), J. F. R. Massy-Westropp, H. Turner and H. S. Shine, and Second-Lieutenant W. P. Oulton. Other ranks: Killed, 45; wounded, 160; missing, 150 (most of whom were dead).

The fate of Captain Penrose, a most gallant officer who had distinguished himself in every action he had taken part in, and had been recommended for reward, was for a long time a mystery. It was not till December, 1919, that his father, the Rev. John T. Penrose, received from a German professor at Aachen some papers belonging to his son, and which he, the professor, said he had found in a dug-out on the Hanebeek on April 25th, 1915.

The conduct of all ranks of the Royal Irish Fusiliers on this day was in accordance with the best traditions of the Regiment. The services of the following were brought to special notice:—

Captain G. Bull, Captain G. V. W. Hill, Lieutenant C. E. Cooke, Lieutenant A. Low, Second-Lieutenant G. Wadden, Second-Lieutenant J. C. Henry, Lieutenant G. Gough, Lieutenant W. Liesching, Captain C. J. Elkan, Second-Lieutenant H. P. Shine, Lance-Corporal R. Keenan, Private T. Steenson, Private E. Cheeny, Private S. McDowell, Company Sergeant-Major J. Cathcart, Sergeant P. Radmilovic (killed), Private A. Branagan, Lance-Corporal P. Gilbert, Lance-Corporal J. King, Corporal R. Fraser, Private J. Copeland, Sergeant F. Hodd, Private W. Douglas, Lance-Corporal M. Kirkland, Private E. Pearson, Drummer T. Woods, Private H. Lunn, Corporal A. Harden, Sergeant C. Nicholson, and Private B. McParland.

No. 6484 Private John Copeland, killed in this action, has been mentioned above as saving Captain Wright's life at Houplines. He met his death when performing the same service for Captain Davison, to whom he was acting as orderly. Captain Davison had been wounded in the foot, and Private Copeland was helping him to a place of comparative safety, when a bullet passed through both of them. Captain Davison was rendered unconscious, but he believed this bullet killed Private Copeland, a fine soldier, and one who was much respected by his officers and comrades.

In his official report, Lieutenant-General E. A. H. Alderson, commanding 1st Canadian Division, wrote as follows:—

"*It is difficult to write too highly of the gallantry of the 10th Brigade and the work done by it. It arrived on the night of the 24th April, when the situation was critical. The necessity for a counter-attack without delay was imperative. Therefore the Brigade had to go forward early the next morning over, to them, unknown and unreconnoitred ground. It advanced, in spite of heavy losses, with the utmost gallantry, and though it did not reach its objective, its attacks undoubtedly checked the German advance and relieved the situation in this part of the field. Subsequently the Brigade held its ground, and repulsed all of the numerous German counter-attacks.*"

Night brought no rest for the weary troops, and it was spent in consolidating the position, which was held by "A," "C" and "B" Companies from right to left, with "D" Company in support.

The next few days have been described by an officer as "a continuous nightmare." Day and night work was carried on consolidating the line, during daylight under bombardment, but at night the enemy devoted all his energy to shelling the roads.

During the night of April 25th-26th, a weak battalion of the Royal Irish Regiment, under Colonel G. M. Gloster, entrenched in front of our right; this mistake was rectified the next night, when they prolonged the line on our right, and the gap between the 10th and 11th Brigades was filled up. On the 26th two attacks were made, one by the Lahore Division and another by a brigade of Northumberland Fusiliers, but neither achieved much.

Photo by] [Imperial War Museum

YPRES—THE CLOTH HALL AND CATHEDRAL, OCTOBER, 1917.

FIRST EXPERIENCE OF POISON GAS

On April 27th, about 9 a.m., the Germans were seen massing in the direction of St. Julien, but they did not attack. A French attack, delivered farther north in the afternoon, met with success. On the evening of April 28th a German aeroplane was brought down near the Brigade headquarters. The small farm had been set on fire and destroyed by shell fire, and headquarters were established in a French "elephant" shelter, which somehow escaped the attentions of the enemy artillery. Near this shelter a number of soldiers of various units, including Lieutenant Lynden-Bell, were buried in a common grave and a rough cross erected. In 1917 the writer revisited the spot, then only recognizable by a plank road and muddy ditch, and by good luck found a rotten piece of wood with the letters "Bell" on it. A substantial cross was placed on the spot, and after the Armistice the bodies were removed.

On April 29th, after receiving a draft of 50, the ration strength of the Battalion rose to 453 all ranks. On the evening of April 30th a German aeroplane, accompanied by a captured Belgian aeroplane, flew over our lines—a typical instance of German ill-manners. The Germans also fired on an ambulance which ventured too far up the road.

Up to this time the country was in its full spring beauty, trees abounded, and the substantial farmsteads were surrounded with waving corn and other crops. As stated before, the civil population had fled, leaving everything, and one kind action was to let the wretched cattle free, which had been left tied up in the byres. Years of frightfulness were to convert this smiling landscape into a vast sea of mud and filth which no pen could describe and only sight could convey to the senses.

May, 1915—Battle continued.

May 1st was a fairly quiet day, but on May 2nd in the afternoon, after a heavy bombardment, the enemy made a formidable gas attack. The gas, which rolled slowly from the enemy lines, was in dense clouds of a yellowish colour, and so high that it enveloped the highest trees. It was a truly terrifying sight. The gas cloud struck the left of the Battalion, where "B" Company was posted, and officers and men suffered considerably. Some relief was got by standing up on the parapets as the heavy gas filled the trenches. The Faughs stuck to the trenches in spite of the agony caused by the gas, and as the cloud gradually rolled back and the grey-coated Germans appeared following it up, they were received with such an effective fire that they were speedily repulsed.

The only protection known at this time was to hold cloth in front of the mouth, the cloth soaked in a solution of sodium bicarbonate; some cholera belts had been issued for this purpose, but the solution was lacking.

After this attack "B" Company were no longer in a physical condition to repulse a second attack, but as no reinforcements were available they were compelled to hold their position.

About midnight a message was received from Brigade headquarters which ended with the words: "*Well done the Faughs.*"

At 8.35 p.m. on May 3rd orders were received to withdraw in conjunction with troops on the right and left. This was done to shorten the line, a new trench line having been prepared in rear of the advanced position held by the troops who had attacked on April 25th.

The trenches on which the Battalion had worked so hard were cleaned up as for general's inspection, all ammunition, tools, etc., being removed, and at 2 a.m. on May 4th the Battalion silently withdrew by companies, leaving a few snipers, under an officer, to cover the movement. When all was clear this party followed their comrades. The route lay by Potijze and La Brique to a spot on the east side of the Yser Canal and about 2,500 yards north of Ypres. This was in the French area and under artillery and long-range rifle fire, the accommodation being holes dug in the clay—not an ideal spot, but a haven of rest after the last few days.

On the road a unit which had suffered more severely from the gas attack was met, and it was pitiful to see the soldiers using their rifles to support themselves along the road, and to hear their groans. This gas had the effect of turning everything, even grass and foliage, an ashen grey.

May 5th was uneventful, except that at 8.40 p.m. the Battalion moved to La Brique, in temporary reserve to the 12th Brigade.

On the night of May 7th the Battalion moved to the canal bank nearer to Ypres, and came under orders of the 12th Brigade.

On the morning of May 8th a heavy bombardment in the direction of Wieltje announced a German attack in that direction, and at 9 a.m., having left packs in the bivouacs, all companies were at or approaching La Brique, where they came under shell fire; Lieutenant Sparks, the medical officer, who behaved most gallantly, being one of the severely wounded. At 1.20 p.m. orders were received to send two companies to occupy Wieltje and vicinity, and get in touch with any troops to the south of Wieltje and report the situation. The line was reported broken. "C" Company (Captain Elkan) was immediately ordered forward, with "A" Company (Major Kentish) in support.

At 3.10 p.m. Major Kentish reported that, finding no trenches in Wieltje as reported, and as that place was being very heavily shelled, he was advancing to what was known as G.H.Q. line east of that place. At 3.45 p.m. Captain Elkan also reported his company in position presumably on the left of "A" Company. The enemy had apparently broken the line, but had not pushed through.

At 7.30 p.m. orders were received from the 10th Infantry Brigade to concentrate at La Brique and come under the orders of the 11th Brigade. Some time after this, in consequence of a verbal report made by an officer of the Royal Irish Regiment to 12th Brigade headquarters, the remaining two companies were ordered to go forward to restore the situation. These companies were near the road fork north of La Brique. The night was very dark, and the Commanding Officer used the road to form the two companies in line. Bayonets were then fixed, and, led by Captain Jeudwine, they advanced under the following orders: "Go forward steadily. Get in touch with 'C' Company on your right. Don't fire. If you meet any Germans, charge them at once." The Regimental Headquarters, consisting of a few men and two machine guns, were then posted in the road ditch as a support in case of need.

At 9.50 p.m. a further report from Major Kentish was received. He was holding his position, but had suffered considerable losses. The troops who had sustained the original attack were in confusion, but the enemy had not followed up his initial success.

A message was also received from Captain Jeudwine saying he was in position with his right on the Wieltje road and in touch with the South Lancashire Regiment on his left.

Major Shuter had made a personal reconnaissance through Wieltje, and reported the enemy to be east of the village.

The situation was satisfactory.

At 12.15 a.m. on May 9th the 12th Brigade ordered the Battalion to concentrate at La Brique. This was not an easy task, but thanks to the excellent communication which the company commanders had maintained with Battalion headquarters, the concentration was complete by daylight, and the hungry and weary soldiers had some food.

This fight was a most unpleasant one; the Battalion did good work, but, owing to being so widely scattered, there was not that mutual co-operation to which they had been accustomed. At 9.20 a.m. the Battalion was ordered back to the canal bank, moving there under shell fire.

In the evening the Battalion was moved to bivouac west of the Château des Trois Tours—a very welcome rest, where, during the next three days, companies were reorganized with the help of a large draft. Respirators, in the form of gauze pads to be tied on with tapes, were issued.

On May 13th an increase in artillery fire was the warning for action, and at 9 a.m. the Battalion moved forward to their old position on the canal bank. Later in the day, when moving back again, they were stopped by the Brigadier of the 11th Brigade, and late at night occupied an obliterated trench line east of Wieltje which had been held by the cavalry. The night was dark and wet, and although the ground was nothing like what it eventually became, the roads and trenches were difficult to distinguish. The left was to rest on the Wieltje road, and the Commanding Officer, accompanied by Regimental Sergeant-Major Scrafield, creeping along the road by the aid of German Very lights, succeeded in getting in touch with the Royal Lancaster Regiment on the left.

During May 14th, 15th and 16th very hard work was put in reconstructing the trenches, and when relieved by the Royal Warwickshire Regiment on the night of the 16th, they were fairly defensible. There was also a good deal of work burying the dead. Battalion headquarters were in a cellar in Wieltje. The shelling on these days was not heavy. The cavalry on our right had the 2nd Battalion Royal Irish Fusiliers on their right, and were kind enough to say they approved of the sandwich. General Joffre, Commander-in-Chief of the French Army, sent his congratulations on the way the British had stood up to the German attack. On relief, the Battalion moved to La Brique. A company of the 5th Battalion Border Regiment was attached to the Battalion and one platoon allotted to each company.

After dark on May 17th the Battalion moved back to their old bivouac on he canal bank just north of Ypres, and found working parties, the mud being very bad. All movements east of Ypres were made in small bodies on account of shell fire. The Germans, being on the outer circle, had the advantage that they could, and did, concentrate their fire. The British had to endure this fire without adequate retaliation, on account of the shortage of artillery ammunition. To quote the words from a captured German letter: " In between times, the English sent a small shrapnel over."

On May 19th, Major Kentish was sent to take temporary command of a battalion of the East Lancashire Regiment, and early in the night the Fusiliers returned once more to La Brique. May 20th was spent in clearing La Brique, as far as possible, of arms and stores of all kinds which had accumulated during the battle, the countryside being strewn with the debris of protracted fighting. In the evening the Commanding Officer and company commanders went to dug-outs in the grounds of Potijze Château, preparatory to taking over a portion of the line from the 4th Cavalry Brigade.

On the night of May 21st the Battalion took over the line from the road near Verlorenhoek northward to the end of the switch trench, and thus were on the immediate right of the sector last held by them. The trenches were taken over from the 3rd Hussars and Oxfordshire Hussars. There was a good deal of sniping and shelling in this sector.

About this time apparatus for spraying the trenches during a gas attack was issued; the troops were also warned against using running water, as it was proved that the enemy had poisoned the Diependallbeek stream with arsenic.

On May 23rd the enemy artillery were very active, especially against the area immediately behind our front line. In the evening the British aeroplanes were heavily engaged from the ground, and as the wind was favourable for a gas attack, all ranks were warned to be especially watchful.

On May 24th the Battalion was distributed as follows:—" B " Company (Captain Bull) on the right; then " D " Company (Captain Hill) and " C " Company (Captain Elkan) on the left. One platoon was in a redoubt on the mound on the north side of the road, afterwards known as Mill Cot. " A " Company (Captain Fforde) was Battalion reserve in the G.H.Q. line east of the château. The machine guns, under Lieutenant Brinckman, were distributed in the fire trenches; Battalion headquarters in the château grounds.

At 2.15 a.m. the troops stood to arms, and at 2.45 a.m. gas clouds were seen issuing from the enemy trenches, the hissing noise as the gas escaped from the cylinders being distinctly audible. Almost at the same time the enemy opened a heavy artillery and rifle fire. Respirators were immediately adjusted, and, as previously arranged, a heavy machine gun and rifle fire was poured into the advancing gas clouds. As the clouds gradually rolled back behind the fire trenches, the grey-coated Germans were seen within a short distance of the wire entanglements; they were met with such an effective fire that they fell back, and, in fact, did not succeed in developing their attack on the front of the Battalion during the day.

A row of cottages on the north side of the road, and immediately in front of Captain Bull's right, were held by the battalion on our right. Captain Bull, noticing that no fire was coming from these cottages, sent a small party, under Lieutenant Liesching, to investigate; they found that the garrison had been gassed, and arrived just in time to drive off the enemy, who had worked up to the farthest cottage.

At 3.40 a.m. and 4.51 a.m. the Battalion reported "all well" to Brigade headquarters and the fire apparently dying down, but at 7.45 a.m. a further report stated that the shelling was continuous. At 11.45 a.m. the redoubt mentioned above had been blown to pieces, and the platoon forming the garrison moved to a position east of the château.

The Battalion, and especially "B" Company, did good work in helping the troops on our right, i.e., south of the road. Captain Bull manned a communication trench in rear of his right. Fire from this trench and from the above-mentioned cottages, and also from machine guns, enfiladed the enemy troops attacking farther south, and eventually drove them back. At 4.33 p.m. the Battalion reported the situation unchanged and the enemy digging in to their front.

In addition to poison gas, the enemy this day used lachrymatory shells, chiefly against the vicinity of the château. The troops had no protection against this gas, which was painful to the eyes and made it difficult to carry on the ordinary duties of a fight, but it had no lasting effect. The sprayers were found very effective in dispersing the poison gas where it accumulated in the trenches. In addition to respirators the Battalion had sixteen of the first pattern gas helmets, made of cloth soaked in the anti-gas mixture, with talc eye-pieces; these were issued to the machine gunners.

The Battalion behaved with great gallantry during this trying day. Their success was due to the excellent leading of the officers and non-commissioned officers, and to the discipline and excellent spirit of the men. The sick report of May 25th shows that only 21 men were admitted to hospital suffering from gas-poisoning, and in this connection a word of praise is due to the attached company of the Border Regiment. These men were nearly all miners, accustomed to the dangers of fire-damp, and on this, their first experience of the use of poison gas in war, they showed an unconcern which was most helpful to their comrades.

The Battalion were fortunate in having few killed that day, but amongst them were Second-Lieutenant H. P. Shine, a promising young officer, and Sergeants A. Seagrott and R. Tetherington, both excellent non-commissioned officers; the latter, who was machine-gun sergeant, behaved in a very gallant manner up to the time of his death.

Of those mentioned for good work No. 10012 Private G. Wilson, a machine gunner, deserves special mention. When the rest of the gun team were knocked out he continued to fight his gun single-handed, and when the gun was blown out of its emplacement he moved to a fresh position and again brought his gun into action.

The next few days were comparatively uneventful. The enemy confined himself to bombardment and sniping, and, subject to these annoyances, the Battalion worked hard at strengthening their position.

On the night of May 25th the Faughs had to mourn the loss of a particularly fine young officer, Second-Lieutenant C. E. Cooke, who was shot dead whilst out with a covering party. He had already been wounded once, and many times mentioned for gallant conduct in action. He was a quiet, unassuming young officer, who devoted himself unsparingly to the performance of his duties, and was known to his men as "The sand-bag king." As was necessarily the case during these prolonged battles, he was buried in the mud near where he fell, and before covering him up every man in his platoon knelt down and shook him by the hand. On the night of May 27th the Battalion was relieved by a battalion of the Hampshire Regiment, and marched to bivouac in the grounds of Vlamertinghe Château—a very welcome rest. Owing to the attentions of enemy aircraft, and in order not to disclose the position of 4th Division headquarters in the château, the troops were ordered to remain under cover of the trees during daylight.

On May 28th, Father Ryan, the popular chaplain of the Battalion, was relieved by Father Hessenauer; and the company of the 5th Border Regiment left.

The Battalion was now becoming short of senior company officers, and on May 29th Captain Elkan left to take up a staff appointment; he was much missed.

At 4 p.m. on May 30th the General Officer Commanding Second Army visited the Battalion, and subsequently the following communication was received:—

"*To the Royal Irish Fusiliers:*

"*Lieutenant-General Sir Herbert Plumer, commanding Second Army, after inspecting some of the units of the Brigade on May 30th, requested me to inform all battalions that he fully appreciated the good work done by the 10th Infantry Brigade since April 24th, and that this had been brought to the notice of the Commander-in-Chief.*

"*I wish to take this opportunity of thanking all ranks for their loyal support during the very trying time through which the Brigade has passed, and to assure them that the part played by them in no small measure helped to save the situation at a critical time, and led to a severe check of the enemy's offensive movement against Ypres. There is little doubt that the check thus delivered had considerable influence on Italy's decision to declare war."*

On May 31st, Major Shuter, who had been lent for a few days to help in reorganizing a composite battalion of the 7th and 9th Argyll and Sutherland Highlanders, rejoined.

June, 1915.

The enemy had by this time failed in his second great effort against Ypres, and a further period of trench warfare was beginning in the Salient. Trench warfare at all times called for a patient endurance on the part of the troops. In addition to unending work at the defences, there were constant bombardments and small incidents which daily added to the casualty lists.

Although the British Army was increasing in numbers, the enemy still had the advantage numerically and in armaments, and it was a matter of wonder to the troops that he did not take full advantage of his position. There were many times when only a thin line of British soldiers, worn out by continuous fighting and toil as well as the awful effects of the deadly gas, lay between him and his objective, and it was common belief that, had the positions been reversed, Ypres would have fallen to the attacker. In spite of what may be mildly termed a strenuous life, nothing could exceed the cheeriness and good-fellowship of the Faughs of all ranks; the reason for this it would be difficult to explain—certainly the men themselves would not have been able to put their feelings into words. Perhaps the nearest approach to the truth would be in the fact that each one felt he was "doing his bit," and that he meant to carry on to the end.

At 6 p.m. on June 1st the Battalion was paraded by Major-General Wilson, C.B., commanding the 4th Division, when he addressed them as follows:—

"Lieutenant-Colonel Burrowes and all ranks of the 87th:

"Before you go up into the trenches again I wish to thank you for the way in which you have fought and worked during the last month. I know you have had a very strenuous time, the whole Division has, but the 10th Brigade I think had the severest fighting perhaps we shall ever have. . . . Since I came up and resumed command of the Division you have had more fighting to do, you have stood some of the heaviest shelling of the whole campaign, and not only that, you have had poisonous gas to contend with, and I wish you to realize that the way you have fought and worked is very well appreciated."

Soldiers deeply appreciate such words as the above, especially when they come from a commander whom they respect and trust. Major-General Wilson was not only trusted, but beloved, by all those who had the honour to serve under him.

At 7.15 the Battalion left their bivouac to take over a portion of the Divisional Reserve line astride of the road leading almost due north from La Brique, since known as Boundary Road. Battalion headquarters south of Irish Farm. The Battalion relieved two companies of the Royal Lancaster Regiment and two companies of the Northumberland Fusiliers.

On the night of June 2nd "A" and "B" Companies moved to La Brique, from whence they were employed as working parties on the front line trenches. On the evening of June 3rd, Major Shuter was again wounded at Battalion headquarters, and the Battalion lost the services of this excellent officer as Senior Major.

On the night of June 5th the Battalion were relieved by a battalion of the Leinster Regiment (commanded by an officer who had lost an arm during the war), and returned to their bivouacs at Vlamertinghe Château.

The weather at this time was perfect, but, on account of gas attacks, periodical reports on the strength and direction of the wind were furnished to Brigade headquarters.

On this day the following letter, received by the British Field-Marshal from General Foch, was published to the troops:—

"*At the moment when the 45th French Division is once again about to find itself in contact with the British forces to the north of Ypres, I have to thank you for the very efficient aid rendered to this division by your troops after the incidents of the 22nd April.*

"*The 45th Division will recall how, in order to give it time to recover from the effect of the asphyxiating gasses and to return to the offensive, the V Corps, in a generous spirit of self-sacrifice, and despite severe losses, came into action on the 22nd April with heroic bravery, drawing on itself a portion of the enemy's attacks.*

"*I should be much obliged if you would be good enough to transmit to the General Officer Commanding V Corps the grateful thanks of the French troops and my warm congratulations on the superb conduct of his corps.*"

At 6.30 p.m. on June 7th the Battalion left its bivouacs to take over a sector of the line from the 3rd Battalion Second Zouaves, commanded by Captain Aymes. This battalion belonged to the 45th French Division.

The Battalion had to carry a day's rations, extra ammunition and all trench stores in the way of small arm ammunition, entrenching tools, barbed wire, grenades and sand-bags, and were heavily laden when they arrived on the canal bank at South Zwaanhof Farm about 9.30 p.m., where they were saluted by harassing fire from the enemy.

The French officers were very helpful, but the relief was not complete till 2 o'clock on the morning of June 8th.

The sector lay to the north-east of Zwaanhof Farm, in the most northern portion of the Ypres Salient, only one British battalion being on the left. The enemy had the advantage of higher ground, and in one place the opposing trenches were only a few yards apart. The trenches were not complete, there had been severe fighting in the locality, and the ground was strewn with dead bodies, mostly German, and the usual litter of a battlefield. There was no water, but by digging holes in the bottom of the trenches sufficient water percolated through to keep the gas respirators moist. The French ideas of sanitation were different to those of the British, and, as the weather was very hot, swarms of flies made their appearance. In spite of these conditions, an outbreak of enteric was avoided by scrupulous attention to sanitary measures. After a few days water in petrol tins was brought up daily with the rations.

On June 9th, Lieutenant MacMullen reported that he believed the enemy were mining at the point mentioned above where the lines were within a few yards of each other. A sentry reported that he heard a noise like an explosion which did not go off.

In reply to a request to Brigade headquarters, our friend Lieutenant Martell, of the Royal Engineers, came up to investigate. He reported that the only way the enemy could mine was by boring—that is, boring through under our parapet and inserting a small charge to make a chamber and then filling this chamber with more explosive; he did not think it probable. The enemy artillery and trench mortars were very active this day.

Soon after 4 a.m. on June 10th the enemy exploded a mine in the spot where suspicious noises had been heard the day before. He had done exactly what Lieutenant Martell had described. Fortunately he did not damage the parapet, and therefore could not see the slight damage he had done behind it. The company commander had withdrawn as many men as he could with safety, but five soldiers, including Sergeant Hodd, were killed, three missing and six wounded. Lieutenant Brinckman, whilst suffering from shock, unfortunately showed himself over the parapet and was killed by a bullet wound in the head. In a very short time the damage was repaired.

The German trench mortars were very annoying at this time; they fired bombs which the men called "sausages" from their appearance as they turned over in the air. They were very deadly when exploded close, but as they lay on the ground a few seconds before doing so, they could be avoided. The chief annoyance lay in the fact that they arrived about every fifteen minutes and prevented the men, who had to work all night, from obtaining any rest during the day. To counteract this fire the Battalion had only the very ineffective catapults and jam-tins which have been already mentioned, but on this day a trench mortar was sent up by the brigade and did good work.

This day the Battalion heard that the Commander-in-Chief had awarded the Distinguished Conduct Medal to Company Sergeant-Major F. Borley and Private J. McKenna.

Company Sergeant-Major Borley will long be remembered in the Regiment, not only for his sterling qualities as a soldier, but as a God-fearing man and as a true comrade to his officers and the men of his company. One of the proudest moments of his life was when he lay wounded in a London hospital in January, 1915, and His Majesty the King said to him: "Your Regiment has done well at the front; in fact, always do."

On the night of June 11th the Battalion was relieved by the Hampshire Regiment and moved to bivouacs at the Château des Trois Tours, where they remained until the night of June 15th, when they moved to new billets on the Poperinghe—Woesten road west of Coppernolle Cabaret, and became Divisional Reserve.

On June 16th Lieutenant-Colonel Burrowes rejoined, having been absent since June 11th in temporary command of the Brigade.

The centenary of Waterloo passed without incident. These were very pleasant quarters; the time was spent in route marching and training. The weather was perfect, and games and a visit from "The Follies" kept the men amused.

Captain and Adjutant Penn started a brigade canteen in the shelter of the woods, where the soldiers could purchase bread, butter, beer, etc., and it was much appreciated.

On the night of June 22nd the Battalion took over the trenches they last held from the Seaforths. The front held by the Division was now divided into three brigade sectors, the 10th Brigade being in the centre; the Fusiliers and their friends the Seaforths relieving each other under the same arrangements as the previous winter.

At this time coloured screens were issued to be erected in rear of the trenches, to help artillery observation officers and obviate the difficulty found in distinguishing our own from the enemy lines. An endeavour was also made to conceal new work from enemy aeroplanes by covering it with grass and corn.

During this time there was a good deal of shelling on both sides. On June 28th the Battalion systematically bombed the German sap-head opposite to where the mine was sprung on June 10th. The Seaforths took over, and the Battalion went into support on the canal bank, where it was employed in fatigues of various sorts, the principal one being the digging of what was called the "Alley Way," a very deep and wide trench on the east bank of the canal and parallel to it. This trench was roofed over and used as dressing stations.

About this time a most useful order, forbidding the use of the word "retire," was issued. Before the war this obnoxious word had been deleted from the training manuals. A peculiarity of the British Army is that it keeps on discovering the same thing over and over again. Another principle discovered several times during the war was that whatever the duty, it is better to detail troops by units than by numbers.

JULY, 1915.

On July 4th the Battalion relieved the Seaforths in the trenches. By dint of continuous fire at the German sap-head so often mentioned, the parapet had been lowered sufficiently to disclose a few cogs of a wheel which evidently formed part of their mining apparatus. A small bombardment was arranged, after which the Highlanders raided the sap-head and destroyed the machinery, one German officer flying in his pyjamas. Unfortunately the excited Highlanders did not think of consolidating their gains, and, by the time the Fusiliers relieved them, the enemy were back in their old position.

At 6 a.m. on July 6th a company of the Rifle Brigade, on our left, made a successful attack, taking an enemy trench, which they held. The Fusiliers were ordered not to leave their trenches, but to co-operate with fire and show fixed bayonets in the communication trenches, to divert the enemy's attention. Plans were made accordingly. The morning broke too misty for any ruses to be seen, but the machine-gun and rifle fire were so effective that the Battalion received a message, " Well done, Irish Fusiliers!"

The enemy naturally retaliated, and the trenches were much knocked about on this and the following day by heavy bombardments. There is something peculiarly trying in having to sit down under a prolonged bombardment of heavy guns, and the strain is plainly marked on the faces of those who undergo it. It wears off as the fire again becomes normal. On this day the Battalion lost 9 killed and 1 officer and 32 other ranks wounded.

Of those brought to notice for good work on this day the case of No. 7937 Sergeant P. Collier, of " A " Company, was peculiar. This non-commissioned officer, who had only rejoined, recovered from wounds, a few hours before, displayed great gallantry; he was posted opposite the sap-head, and kept up a continuous fire until, towards the close of the bombardment, he was shot through the head. Although it was not believed that he could live, he was brought down to the dressing-station, and on July 9th Father Hessenauer reported that he had seen Sergeant Collier that morning at the casualty clearing station, that he was smoking a pipe and had forgotten all about the war, and that the doctor thought there was a chance of his recovery.

Sergeant Patrick Collier had been severely wounded in the abdomen at St. Eloi on February 12th, 1915, when serving with the 2nd Battalion of the Regiment, and, though not really fit, he insisted on rejoining. When on this occasion Captain Bull found him lying at his post desperately wounded, he was trying to raise himself, and, on being spoken to, replied " It's all right, sor, I'm only waiting for the ninth second." He had been a boxer, and evidently thought he was in the ring. He died on July 10th, 1915, and is incorrectly shown in the Roll of Honour as belonging to the 2nd Battalion. Sergeant Collier has been described as " the straightest and most respected non-commissioned officer of his Battalion." This account of his death is given not only as a tribute to a very gallant soldier, but as typical of the rank and file of the Irish Fusiliers.

It took a lot of hard work on the night of the 6th to reconstruct the trenches, and, as the enemy continued his bombardment on the 7th, the work was continuous.

On the night of July 8th the Battalion was relieved by the 7th Battalion of the West Riding Regiment, and left the Salient.

Trench life in the Salient was always strenuous. An anomaly was that the nearer the combatants were to each other the less they saw of each other. Firing was carried on by snipers from prepared places of concealment, and observation was carried on by periscope. To show one's head above the parapet was to court death. It should be borne in mind that artillery and rifle fire never ceased day or night—it was only a matter of degree. At night the whole semi-circle of the Salient was brilliantly lighted up with flares, mostly sent up by the Germans, who were much more subject to " wind up," as it was called, than the British troops. Sometimes, on calm nights, the opposing lines hurled abuse at each other in between the bursts of fire. The winter was, of course, the worse time on account of the mud, cold and wet.

The losses in trench warfare were not as a rule heavy, but, being continuous, made a considerable total each month. As an example, between July 1st and July 6th, exclusive of casualties on the latter date, the Irish Fusiliers lost 2 killed and 1 officer and 13 other ranks wounded—that is, in six days, only two of which were spent in front-line trenches.

The Battalion halted for a few hours' rest about 1,000 yards west of Peselhoek, and on the morning of July 29th marched to Houtkerque, in France, where the officers were billeted and the men bivouacked.

The rest at Houtkerque was very welcome; the Battalion had now been fighting and marching continuously since August, 1914, and the mere fact of being out of gunshot, and not being liable to be called upon to fight at any moment, was a welcome relief. The time was spent in all sorts of training and sports, and a thorough overhaul was made of equipment.

On July 14th the 10th Infantry Brigade was visited by General Sir Herbert Plumer, commanding Second Army, who addressed them as follows:—

"*Colonel Poole, officers, non-commissioned officers and men of the 10th Infantry Brigade:*

"*I much regret that your Brigadier, General Hull, is not present to-day, and if I could have deferred my visit I should have done so. This is a visit and not an inspection, though I feel bound to say that, had it been an inspection, the appearance of the men and their general turn-out could not have been better. After your two-and-a-half months of hardship, and in spite of your severe fighting, you are able to turn out as soldiers, march as soldiers, and handle your arms as soldiers.*

"*I should like you to know the part you have been playing in this campaign since you came to the Ypres Salient.*

"*When our line was broken, through no fault of the British troops, two tasks devolved upon us. One was to repel the enemy's attacks, and the other to* make frequent counter-attacks, which, to troops already engaged, seemed meaningless, and which were necessarily very costly. The result was that we were able to maintain our front, and withdraw to a fresh position at a time when it suited us to do so.

"When the history of this war comes to be written, the part which you have taken in holding that salient will be an episode not the least creditable among the many heroic deeds of the British Army.

"You are now leaving the VI Corps, and I, its commander, bid you farewell. I am sorry to lose you. You are going to form the nucleus of a new corps in a new army. Your task will be to give the new units the benefit of your experience. If you succeed, as I am sure you will, in bringing them up to your high standard, you will form a highly-efficient division, and the general who commands you will be a fortunate man. I wish you all the best of luck."

On July 15th a sad accident happened to a party of grenadiers who were practising bombing in a trench, under Lieutenant J. Butler. A grenade exploded prematurely, and 4 soldiers were killed and Lieutenant J. Butler, Second-Lieutenant Reginald Lemare and 5 soldiers wounded. The victims were buried the next day in Houtkerque churchyard.

On July 17th the General Officer Commanding 4th Division presented the ribbon of the Distinguished Conduct Medal to Sergeant Stoner, R.A.M.C., and Corporal W. Bagot.

On July 18th, Lieutenant-Colonel A. R. Burrowes relinquished command of the Battalion on appointment to the staff, and Captain A. B. Incledon-Webber took over temporary command.

The late Commanding Officer endeavoured to express his feelings to all those who had served him so well, in the following words:—

"*Comrades of all ranks:*

"*I have asked you to come here this morning to give me an opportunity of saying good-bye as your Commanding Officer. I have only found one duty as Commanding Officer disagreeable, and that is the administration of justice. If I have at any time treated any man harshly or unjustly, I ask that man's forgiveness. I have asked Captain Webber, and he has kindly given his consent that all regimental punishment now in force shall be remitted, so that every man in the Battalion is a free man from this moment.*

"*It is usual on these occasions to publish a farewell order, but an order is a formal thing. In this great war, in which we are fighting for our existence against a brutal tyranny, I feel that a formal order would be out of place. Besides, the spirit of the Irish Fusiliers is that whilst we do our duty strictly, when not on duty all ranks meet as friends, and it is as to the parting of friends that I would wish to look back on this day.*

"*It is also usual to thank officers, non-commissioned officers and men for their support, but no thanks could express my feelings towards you. This I will say. The officers and soldiers who sleep on the battlefields of France and*

Belgium and you who are present to-day, who by your courage, your patience and devotion to duty are writing a page of history so glorious that the ages will not dim its lustre, are the finest characters God ever made. Luck (whatever that word may mean), I wish you the very best of luck from the bottom of my heart, but I can do more than that.

"*This war, as it has brought us nearer to one another as men, has brought us all nearer to God, and it is to Him I shall continue to pray to give you strength and firmness in the great struggle till right shall triumph over wrong. And it is to Him I shall continue to pray that, when victory comes, as we know it will, He will restore you in health and strength to your loved ones at home. It is not possible to shake hands with you all, but I would esteem it an honour if the officers and those who have served longest will shake me by the hand before I leave.*"

On July 20th the Field-Marshal Commanding-in-Chief inspected the 10th Brigade and expressed his appreciation of the work they had done in the Salient.

On July 21st orders were received to move the next day. When it became known that the move was southwards, great satisfaction was felt at leaving the Salient behind. All superfluous stores were returned, and the Battalion bid farewell to the French villagers. Irishmen have always got on well with the French peasantry, and the Irish Fusiliers were no exception. A really friendly feeling existed, fostered by the soldier's readiness to make himself useful and his proverbial love of children. No language difficulties arose, though it is difficult to believe how sentiments were exchanged. An Irishman walked up to a French woman and said, "Madame, du lait promenade." The lady instantly appreciated the fact that her cows were straying.

The Battalion left Houtkerque at 3 p.m. on July 22nd and entrained at Godewaersvelde, known to the soldiers as "Gerty wears velvet." They detrained at Doullens at 4.45 a.m. on the 23rd, and marched to Freschevillers, and later in the day to billets at Vauchelles. Here the 4th Division became part of the VII Corps, commanded by their former general, Major-General T. D'O. Snow, who sent them the following message of welcome:—

"*Major-General T. D'O. Snow, in welcoming his old friends of the 4th Division to the VII Corps, takes the opportunity of informing the officers, non-commissioned officers and men that he realizes he owes his recent advancement chiefly to the way in which the Division fought and endured at Le Cateau and in the early days of the war. He feels proud at having such tried and trustworthy comrades again in his command.*"

On the evening of July 27th the Battalion moved via Louvencourt, Bertrancourt, and Courcelles-au-Bois to Colincamps, where it was employed on the defences of that village. On the night of the 30th they moved to billets at Mailly-Maillet, where they became support to the line. The 4th Division were in the course of taking over a portion of the line from the French. The 10th Brigade took over from the French 64th Regiment. This was a quiet sector at the time, and, being chalk country, the trenches and dug-outs were good and a pleasing contrast to those of the Salient.

Each soldier at this time had a "smoke helmet," as it was called, for protection against gas. It consisted of a bag soaked in preparation and fitted with eye-pieces; the mouth of the bag was pulled down and the coat buttoned over it.

A Divisional invalid company was formed, called the Divisional Reserve Company, to which men requiring a short rest from active employment could be sent to recuperate.

During this month instructions were issued giving soldiers facilities for investing in War Loan.

AUGUST, 1915.

The first week of this month was spent in providing working parties for the defences, and on the night of the 8th the Battalion relieved the Seaforths for a tour of fourteen days in the trenches east of Mailly-Maillet; the relief was complete by midnight. The Battalion was distributed: Two companies and the machine guns in fire trenches, one company in support and one in reserve. It was arranged for battalions to relieve each other every eight days, in order to equalize time spent in the fire trenches by companies. Although the sector was quiet at this time, there was a good deal of sniping, and, until the men got to know the lie of the land, there were a few casualties from this cause.

On August 10th the trenches were flooded, but the water soon drained away.

On the night of August 12th a patrol, consisting of Lieutenant H. A. H. Warnock and Corporals Stevenson and Murray, encountered an enemy patrol of superior strength. All were wounded, and Lieutenant Warnock and Corporal Stevenson were captured. Lieutenant Warnock died of his wounds on August 16th. Corporal Murray was brought in the next day.

On August 16th the Corps Commander visited the trenches, and on August 17th some delegates from the General Federation of Trade Unions did the same and were given opportunities of conversing with soldiers who had fought in the Ypres Salient.

On the night of August 22nd the Battalion was relieved by the Seaforths, and marched to billets in Acheux, where they became Divisional Reserve.

Up to the end of the month the Fusiliers were employed as working parties on the rear defences, chiefly round Forceville.

The Army Commander, in his remarks on a recent inspection, said he was particularly pleased with the appearance and turn-out of the 4th Division. During the month, steel helmets were issued to all ranks.

The British were brought in touch with the French Camouflage School at Amiens, which led to such important developments later in the war. 'Artillery activity increased towards the end of the month; the Germans also began to supply a paper called the *Gazette des Ardennes*, printed in French and disguised as a French periodical, for purposes of propaganda. Later in the war the enemy sent large numbers of this paper across the lines by means of air balloons made entirely of paper, including the cordage.

The strength of the Battalion on August 30th was 22 officers and 919 other ranks.

SEPTEMBER, 1915.

This was not an eventful month in the part of the line held by the 4th Division. A new system of reliefs was inaugurated, the 10th and 12th Infantry Brigades relieving each other every seven days. This arrangement was presumably made to give the Brigade staffs some relief. The Fusiliers and the 2nd Battalion Lancashire Fusiliers relieved each other in a sector of the line west of Beaumont Hamel, the left company occupying what was known as the Redan, a work about fifty yards from the enemy line. There was a good deal of grenade and trench-mortar fighting about the Redan, and both sides adopted mining tactics.

The Battalion relieved the Lancashire Fusiliers on September 2nd, and were relieved by them on September 9th and went into billets at Mailly-Maillet. These periods out of the line were becoming more and more fully occupied. A number of courses were started. There was a grenadier school at Beaussart, and men were required for tunnelling companies of the Royal Engineers, and for training as machine gunners, snipers, signallers and other duties. There were also new inventions to be tested, such as the West spring catapult, telescopic rifles, and rifle grenades. At the same time route marching and ordinary training were carried out, in addition to large working parties on the second and third defence lines.

On September 16th the Battalion returned to the trenches, and active patrolling was carried on at night, which led to occasional encounters with enemy patrols. The constant display of Very lights was now augmented by rockets of various colours, used by both sides as signals, but chiefly for what were known as S.O.S. signals to call for artillery support when any locality was threatened and communication cut. In heavy bombardments all telephone wires above ground were invariably cut, and even when deep burying was resorted to, alternate lines were necessary.

On September 20th, Lieutenant-Colonel Incledon-Webber proceeded to take up the appointment of Brigade-Major to the 1st Canadian Infantry Brigade, and Major G. Bull assumed command, with the temporary rank of lieutenant-colonel. This temporary rank was given to all officers commanding battalions, and the temporary rank of captain to officers commanding companies.

On September 22nd the Battalion proceeded, on relief, to Forceville, and remained in a state of readiness. On September 25th, Lieutenant-Colonel R. J. Kentish, D.S.O., rejoined, and assumed command of the Battalion.

At 6.30 a.m. on this date the attack of the First Army, in the neighbourhood of Loos and Hulluch, was launched. This attack was made to synchronize with the French attack in Champagne, and the successes of both, which were rapidly conveyed to the troops along the line, were received with lively satisfaction.

The Battalion relieved the 2nd Lancashire Fusiliers on September 29th, and on the 30th had the satisfaction of seeing an enemy aeroplane brought down behind their lines. At this time Major-General Sir Henry Wilson, K.C.B., the popular commander of the 4th Division, left to assume command of the XII Corps, much regretted.

OCTOBER, 1915.

The same routine was continued this month. Night patrolling was carried on with great vigour. Second-Lieutenant C. Williams, Lieutenant N. Russell and Sergeant McMillan distinguished themselves as patrol leaders. They brought in from the German lines an iron plate on which was an announcement of the fall of Novo-Georgevisk. On the night of October 3rd a patrol of four men, under Corporal J. Farrell, of "D" Company, encountered an enemy patrol of eight men, when a bombing fight ensued, and the gallant corporal and two of his men were wounded. For this action, and previous good work, Corporal Farrell was awarded the Distinguished Conduct Medal. On the same night a patrol under Second-Lieutenant C. Williams brought in a newspaper from the enemy lines. There was considerable danger in securing these articles, as the enemy had already begun the laying of booby traps, and, as often as not, the movement of an article caused a bomb explosion.

The enemy somehow always seemed to know the names of the regiments opposed to them. At this time the enemy showed signs of wishing to fraternize, and called the regiment by name. Such overtures were immediately answered by rifle fire.

Occasionally a spy mania swept along the British lines, and at this time one of these epidemics was in full force. The Commanding Officer, whilst making his way up to the line on the night of a relief, was mistaken for a spy. His description was reported to Brigade headquarters, and special patrols were ordered out to search for the supposed spy. He had the satisfaction of receiving the message giving an accurate description of his get-up, which was certainly not strictly of regulation pattern.

On October 4th the Battalion witnessed a very gallant aerial battle, in which the German was eventually shot down.

On October 5th, Major-General the Hon. C. Lambton, the new commander of the 4th Division, visited the trenches and expressed himself as well satisfied with all he saw.

After relief by the 2nd Lancashire Fusiliers, the Battalion proceeded to billets at Verennes on the night of October 6th, where work was diversified with football and other games, "A" Company winning the inter-platoon football match. The evenings were enlivened by the playing of the Drums and the Divisional Band, and with performances given by various troupes of entertainers.

It was about this time that those who had qualified at the Grenade School were distinguished by an embroidered grenade worn on the sleeve of the service jacket.

On October 13th the Fusiliers lost the services of their adjutant, Captain P. Penn, an excellent officer, to whom the Battalion owes much for its general efficiency and well-being. The duties were taken over by Captain W. H. Liesching. On the same night the 2nd Lancashire Fusiliers were relieved in the same sector of the line as before.

On October 14th two platoons of the 8th Battalion Royal Irish Rifles (Ulster Division) were welcomed, on being attached for instruction.

On the night of October 15th patrols reported that they had heard women's voices in the enemy lines. This was not an unusual occurrence.

At this time special snipers' costumes were received from the Camouflage School, to enable the trained snipers to lie concealed in No Man's Land.

On October 18th the Redan suffered a very heavy bombardment, about 600 shells, mostly of heavy calibre, being fired against this work. Much damage was done, except to the actual fire trenches; but thanks to the good work which had been expended on the defences, the casualties were small. On being relieved by the 2nd Lancashire Fusiliers, the Battalion proceeded to Acheux on the night of October 20th, where they remained till the end of the month, carrying out the usual programme of work and sports. A few officers and men were allowed short leave to Paris, Amiens, and Doullens.

On October 25th the Royal Irish Fusiliers, with other troops of the 4th Division, had the honour of being inspected by His Majesty the King. Naturally all did their best in the matter of turn-out. The weather was very inclement, but His Majesty remarked to the Commanding Officer on the good appearance of both officers and men and the strength of the Battalion.

The new armies were now taking the field, and on October 28th the Battalion heard of certain changes in organization necessitated by this fact. The 107th Infantry Brigade (Ulster Division) was to take the place of the 12th Infantry Brigade in the 4th Division, and the 87th had been selected to go to the 107th Brigade to give it the benefit of seasoned troops. The compliment was appreciated, but the Regiment felt much leaving the 10th Brigade, with which they had soldiered since September 30th, 1911.

On October 30th the Irish Fusiliers relieved the Monmouthshire Regiment, and was disposed as follows:—Headquarters, " C " Company and two machine guns at Mailly-Maillet; " B " Company at Auchonvillers; " A " and " D " Companies at Colincamps, with one platoon at La Signy Farm; two machine guns in Elles Square.

PREPARING FOR THE WINTER

NOVEMBER, 1915.

On November 1st Major G. Bull was selected for command of the 12th Battalion Royal Irish Rifles. It is no exaggeration to say that Major Bull carried with him, on leaving the Battalion, the very best wishes of every member. His sterling qualities as a man, his personal bravery as a soldier, and his geniality as a comrade had endeared him to all.

The Battalion had now been issued with winter clothing. All this clothing was of very good quality, and tended much to mitigate the hardships of trench life; in fact, as the duration of the war lengthened, the arrangements behind the lines were so well arranged that the troops were in clover, compared with conditions which obtained in the winter of 1914-15. A regular system of good baths was not the least of these amenities.

The system of giving cards to men who had distinguished themselves still continued, and about this time the following received cards from the Divisional Commander: "A" Company, Company Sergeant-Major Reeve, Company Quartermaster-Sergeant Wilson; "B" Company, Sergeant Branagan, Private Quinlan, Private Pass; "C" Company, Private Ledwidge; "D" Company, Private Kirkham.

The leave roster was most rigorously kept, for it was not possible to grant leave to all who were entitled to it, and on November 3rd there were 105 men in the Battalion who had not been home for over a year.

On November 4th the transfer of the Battalion to the 107th Infantry Brigade was carried out. The Battalion, less the machine guns, which joined later, assembled at Bertrancourt and took over billets at Acheux.

Brigade machine-gun companies were formed at this time, and on November 4th Lieutenant A. Low, the Battalion machine-gun officer, was selected to command that of the 10th Infantry Brigade; he was a keen officer, and had done good work for the Battalion.

Training was also begun on the Lewis guns. This gun, afterwards known as the Light gun, played an important part in infantry fighting subsequently, and at the close of the war every platoon had a Lewis-gun section.

On November 6th about 250 men were entertained at Toutencourt by the 4th Divisional Ammunition Column, whose hospitality was much appreciated. On November 7th the Battalion was selected to attend a special parade at Acheux Park, when the Third Army Commander presented French decorations. The General Officer Commanding 4th Division expressed himself as very pleased with the turn-out of the Battalion.

On this day Lieutenant-Colonel R. J. Kentish, D.S.O., who had been selected for command of the Army School of Instruction at Flixecourt, gave up command to Major R. B. Neill.

The temporary withdrawal of Lieutenant-Colonel Kentish from regimental duty was a great loss to the 87th. No officer could have devoted his life more fully to the welfare of his regiment than Lieutenant-Colonel Kentish. His very successful efforts to improve facilities for sport in the Army, especially at Aldershot, when serving on the staff in that command, had made him one of the best-known officers throughout the service, and his constant care for those under his command had the inevitable result of securing their devotion to himself.

In the evening the 107th Brigade, under command of Brigadier-General W. M. Withycombe, relieved the 10th Brigade in the trenches; the 87th taking over from the 2nd Royal Dublin Fusiliers in their old position, including the Redan.

The remainder of the month passed without any incident of importance. The weather was bad, much wet and some snow, which added greatly to the work of maintaining the defences, and both sides were too much occupied to find time for continuous fighting. The usual bombardments and mutual retaliation went on as usual, and as regards trench mortars and general fighting, as the Fusiliers made it a rule always to give twice as much as they received, the enemy became chary of starting these small affairs. The chief liveliness was always in the neighbourhood of the Redan, and patrolling in the mine-crater area in front of this work was always active.

The General Officers Commanding Division and Brigade visited the trenches on November 13th, and were appreciative of the good work done in keeping the defences in a good state, in spite of the continual falling-in due to the wet and shell fire.

On November 20th Mr. John Redmond visited the Faughs and made them a non-political speech. They relieved the 2nd Royal Dublin Fusiliers on this day, coming from Mailly-Maillet, where they had gone on the night of November 14th.

They were again relieved by the 2nd Royal Dublin Fusiliers on November 26th, and went to Forceville.

There was a story current in the Battalion about this time that the Germans had thrown a piece of paper into one of the trenches, containing news of some enemy success in the eastern theatre of war. The Fusiliers sent back a blank piece of paper, carefully folded, and, after giving time for a number of the enemy to collect, followed it up with a volley of grenades.

On November 27th, Company Sergeant-Major J. Anderson, having been promoted to second-lieutenant, was posted to " D " Company.

So impassable did the trenches become about this time that one senior officer found the best kit was a shirt, trench-coat and pair of boots, and this was his invariable dress when going his rounds.

DECEMBER, 1915.

December opened with very bad weather, which continued throughout the month, and the front line trenches became so bad that it was impossible to

Photo by] [Imperial War Museum

A NIGHT SCENE ON THE WESTERN FRONT.

maintain a continuous line. It was therefore held by groups accommodated in what were really large wooden boxes, communication being carried on at night over the top. In spite of these conditions the men never lost their cheeriness, and, like all Irishmen, the " softer " the weather the happier they seemed.

On December 1st, Lieutenant M. F. J. R. Mahony, the machine-gun officer, left under orders for Serbia, and his place was taken by Second-Lieutenant N. Russell.

On December 2nd the Battalion relieved the 2nd Royal Dublin Fusiliers; so bad were the conditions that it took over four hours to carry out the relief. This tour was a continual fight against the mud, in which the enemy took their share, but our snipers were successful against enemy working parties who showed themselves. Having been relieved by the Royal Dublin Fusiliers on December 8th, the Battalion proceeded to Varennes.

On December 10th Second-Lieutenant E. F. Qualtrough took charge of the new Lewis-gun teams, the old teams having been transferred to the 10th Brigade Machine-gun Company.

On December 13th, Major W. A. V. Findlater, having reported his arrival from England, took over command of the Battalion and proceeded with it to the old trenches until December 17th, when the Battalion went to Acheux after relief by the 2nd Royal Dublin Fusiliers.

About this time the enemy, being somewhat short of artillery in this area, adopted the expedient of moving an organized body of artillery up and down the line and carrying out a programme of bombardments. This formation was known as " Jerry's travelling circus," and, though its visits were unwelcome, they generally met with a warm reception.

The demand for skilled workmen for munition factories at home being urgent, munition investigators visited the troops in France for the purpose of testing tradesmen serving in the ranks, and those found efficient were sent home.

On December 20th Brigadier-General Withycombe met the Battalion when route-marching near Lealvillers, and requested Major Findlater to form them up, which, being done, he addressed them as follows :—

"*Major Findlater, officers, non-commissioned officers and men of the 87th:*

"*It is with great regret that I have to say good-bye to you, on retransfer from my Brigade, but I wish to say how pleased I am at the splendid way in which you have worked while under my command, both in billets and in the trenches, which latter were sometimes in a very bad state, but you have worked cheerfully and well, as only a well-disciplined battalion can. It is discipline which makes a good regiment, and which is going to win the war. I have noticed your very smart appearance when in billets, and your soldierly appearance in the trenches. Good bye.*"

At 6 p.m. on December 21st the Battalion was transferred back to the 10th Brigade. On this day the Battalion heard of Viscount French's Order of the Day bidding farewell to the troops and expressing his heartfelt sorrow at parting from them before victory had been attained.

On December 23rd all the Battalion, except those employed as working parties on the Corps line, were practised in the attack wearing smoke helmets, as the new pattern tube gas-helmet was now called.

On December 24th the Battalion was granted a holiday for Christmas festivities. A strong committee worked hard at the preparations, and after Divine service an excellent Christmas dinner was partaken of in the sucrerie at Acheux. For the good things provided the Battalion was indebted to kind friends at home, especially to Mrs. Churcher, to Miss Kentish (who organized concerts in London to help the funds), and to Mr. Trimble, of the *Armagh Guardian*. In addition, each soldier received a parcel of comforts. After dinner, "The Follies" gave an excellent entertainment, and Lieutenant-Colonel Kentish addressed the men. Greetings were received from, and sent to, old friends, including the General Officers Commanding 4th Division, 10th and 107th Brigades.

On Christmas Day the 87th relieved the 8th Battalion Royal Irish Rifles in a sector south of their former position. The relief was completed between 6 p.m. and 8 p.m.; a good performance, as the trenches were unknown to the Battalion.

Every precaution was taken during the winter months to prevent "trench feet," the dates on which anti-frostbite grease was to be applied, under the supervision of officers, being detailed in orders.

It was early in this month that Captain J. G. Brown relieved Captain O. Hairsine in medical charge of the Battalion.

Nothing of importance occurred during the few days the Battalion occupied this sector, beyond the usual shelling and sniping, and on December 29th the trenches were handed back to the 8th Battalion Royal Irish Rifles and the 87th proceeded to Mailly-Maillet, where they enjoyed one day's rest and bathing.

As the Germans had renewed their gas attacks in the north, strict orders were issued regarding the two protective helmets carried by every officer and man.

At the close of the year the system by which one brigade relieved another in the line was abandoned, and the old arrangement, by which each brigade was permanently responsible for its allotted front, was again adopted.

CHAPTER III—1916.

At the beginning of 1916 the prospects of the Allies were none too bright. The Battle of Loos had had no great results. The withdrawal from the Gallipoli Peninsula and in Serbia, and General Townshend's position in Mesopotamia were all factors on the side of the Central Powers.

On the other hand Vienna was undoubtedly anxious for peace, and was only restrained in this respect by her German ally. Sir Douglas Haig, the new Commander-in-Chief, enjoyed the full confidence of the troops, and was gradually introducing the wearing-down tactics which, in the end, were to break down the highly organized trench systems of the enemy in France and Flanders. The British blockade was beginning to have an appreciable effect on the economic condition of the central Empires, and at home the Government were alive to the fact that very large increases in men, money and munitions were required, and all these were rapidly materializing; the only regret in the ranks of the Irish regiments was that the Military Service Bill was not made applicable to their own country.

Germany, through Sir Roger Casement, had endeavoured to seduce her Irish prisoners of war. This attempt was a failure, but these unfortunate men, at first pampered and made much of, suffered extreme hardships as the penalty for their loyalty. It is satisfactory to know that on one occasion Casement had to run for his life from the enraged soldiers of the Irish Fusiliers.

But the greatest asset at this time, as at all periods of the war, was the cheery optimism of the British fighting man. The silent Navy in their ceaseless watch in the North Sea, the infantry floundering in their water-logged trenches, and the schoolboy airmen, were all imbued with a spirit of cheerful determination to prove themselves superior to all danger, difficulty and hardship. The only incident really resented by all ranks was the existence of labour difficulties at home.

This spirit was shared with our gallant French allies. Germany, feeling the necessity for something big, was commencing what they believed to be an overwhelming attack on the fortress of Verdun. Verdun, to the French, was what Ypres was to the British, and their battle-cry of "Ils ne passeront pas" was an expression of the sentiment which made the troops of both nations truly brothers-in-arms.

January, 1916, found the 87th still in the region west of Bapaume, but on January 1st, in accordance with the new scheme of defence, the 10th Infantry

Brigade took over a new sector of the line. This sector lay to the north of the Mailly-Maillet—Serre road. The 87th took over about 1,000 yards of this line from the 10th Battalion Royal Irish Rifles, the right resting on the above-mentioned road at a bend one mile west of Serre. The fire trenches were held by two companies, the right company occupying trenches 78 to 81 inclusive, and the left company trenches 82 to 86 inclusive. On account of the state of the ground these trenches were held by groups of men. The two remaining companies were in support, and the machine and Lewis guns were distributed in specially prepared emplacements. This relief was completed by 8.45 p.m.

The weather was wet, and about this time the Battalion was completed with one pair of thigh-boots per man. These boots were like fishermen's boots, but made of rubber, and, as their name implied, protected a man right up to his waist, but made movement difficult. Each battalion was also supplied with twenty fire-buckets to assist in bailing out the trenches.

On January 3rd the Battalion lost the services of Captain G. M. H. Wright, who was again severely wounded. Sniping and bombardments by trench mortars and field guns were the order of the day, and the Germans had the advantage in trench mortars, but at this time orders were issued for the formation of a 3.7-in. trench mortar battery within the Brigade. On January 1st the Battalion parted with regret with Sergeant Stoner, R.A.M.C., who had been with them since mobilization, and identified himself in every way with the Regiment. He was selected for duty with a field ambulance. On January 5th the Battalion was relieved by the 1st Royal Warwickshire Regiment, and went to billets at Forceville, where the usual routine of working parties on the Corps line, bathing, etc., was carried out. Whenever a Sunday was spent out of the line, Divine service for all denominations was held.

The Battalion was initiated in the use of iron screw stakes for wire entanglements, a great improvement on the old wooden stakes, as an obstacle could be silently erected, under cover of darkness, and casualties thus avoided. It was a practice of the enemy to attach a wire to the British obstacles and run this back to their own trenches. Many of these wires were found; whether they could be used as telephones, or were merely to give notice when we were working on the wire, was not known.

On January 9th the Battalion relieved the 1st Royal Warwickshire Regiment. In order to ensure hot meals in the trenches, six 5-gallon jacketted food containers were issued as trench stores. By means of hot water, food could be kept hot for twelve hours.

On January 11th, Second-Lieutenant C. R. Williams, the scouting-officer of the Battalion, was seriously wounded. He was an energetic young officer, who had done much good work.

When relieved by the 1st Royal Warwickshire Regiment on the night of January 13th, the Battalion proceeded to Colincamps, where communication with the inhabitants was restricted on account of enteric fever amongst the

Photo by] [*Imperial War Museum*

Portion of country shown in Sketch VI, showing the Redan and Quadrilateral from air photographs taken 30-7-18, 31-7-18 and 10-8-18.

Nº VI

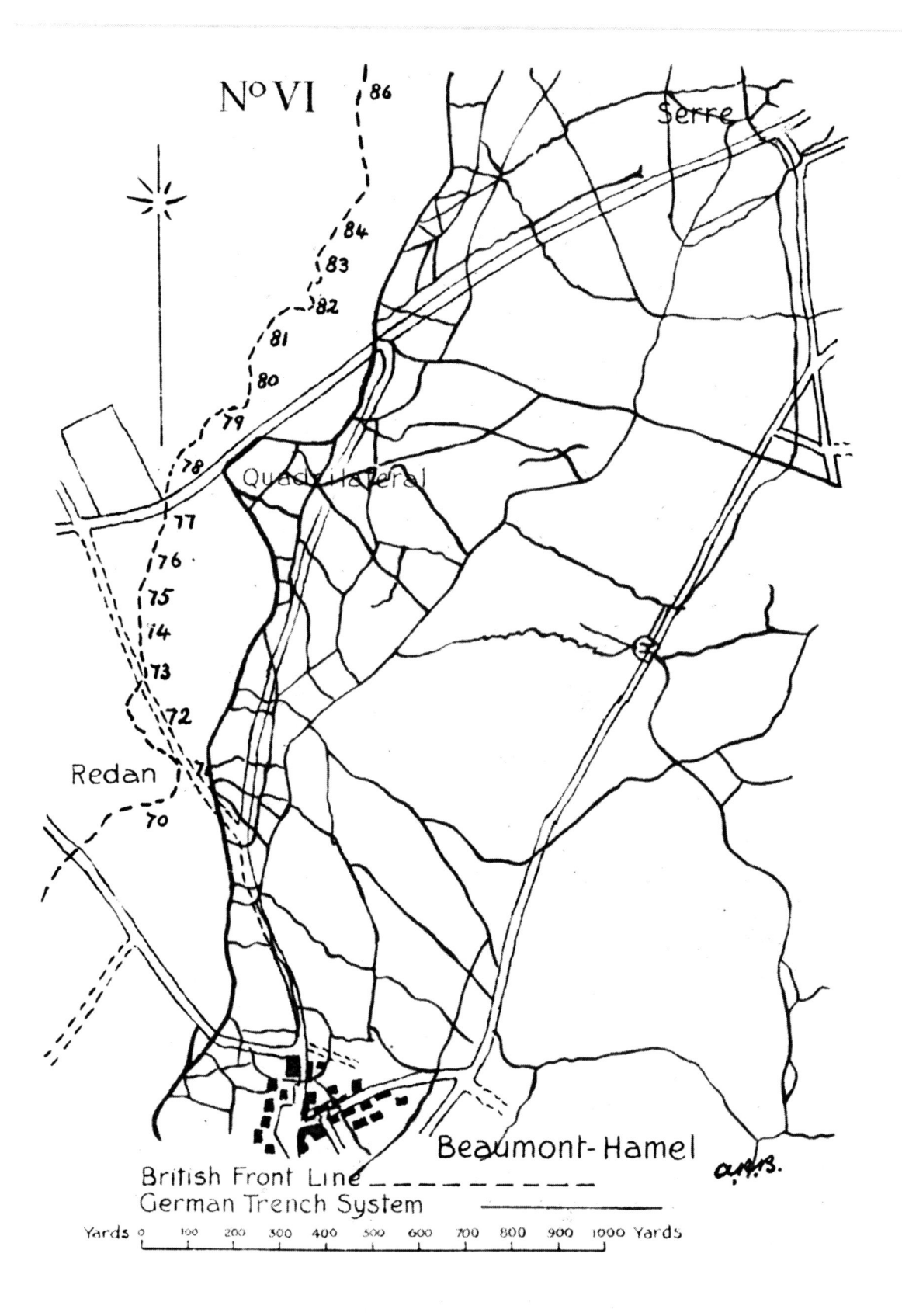

Serre

Quadrilateral

Redan

Beaumont-Hamel

British Front Line — — — — —
German Trench System ——————

Yards 0 100 200 300 400 500 600 700 800 900 1000 Yards

civilians. All ranks who had not been inoculated during the last six months were reinoculated.

A change in the weather from rain to frost was welcomed.

On January 17th the cheering sight of a squadron consisting of twenty-five British aeroplanes returning from the enemy lines was observed. Like the arrival of the guns during an action in open warfare, there is something very encouraging in the sight of a number of aeroplanes in battle formation. In the evening the usual relief of the 1st Royal Warwickshire Regiment took place.

The enemy snipers were very active on January 18th. The casualties on this date included Second-Lieutenant N. Kirkby, severely wounded, who had only joined the previous day. During this tour the enemy shelling was concentrated on specific targets, such as La Signy Farm, but little damage was done.

Trench systems were now becoming so complicated that notice-boards were erected to enable new troops to find their way about. The names were a strange medley. The older trenches, being generally named by the troops who made them, as a rule bore the names of famous battles on the battalion colours, of senior officers, and of places in the recruiting area; but these were mixed with French names, and a main junction was generally called Hyde Park Corner, or after some well-known London street.

Fuel being scarce, these notice-boards sometimes disappeared. An officer of the Battalion had direction and name-plates made of tin from biscuit tins. On remarking to a soldier of the Regiment that they would be useless for "dumming up," he was somewhat disconcerted by the reply that they would be grand things for frying bacon on.

The Battalion was relieved by the 1st Royal Warwickshire Regiment on January 21st, and relieved that unit on January 25th, on which date Major R. G. Shuter, D.S.O., arrived from England and assumed command.

On January 28th news arrived that Company Sergeant-Major S. M. Fynne had been promoted to a commission in the Regiment, dated January 14th, 1916. This well-deserved honour was much belated, solely on account of his severe wounds.

On January 29th the Battalion was relieved by the Royal Warwickshire Regiment, and proceeded to Colincamps, where the usual routine was carried out, including ceremonial drill, and movements executed whilst wearing the smoke and gas-helmets; this was essential, as the enemy were again becoming active with gas attacks. They also made use of rockets at night, a large number of colours being used in combinations. It was not evident what was the meaning of these displays, but the daily news-sheets spoke of a forthcoming attack by the enemy on a large scale, and these rockets may have been practices in signalling for that event.

A Divisional school for junior officers and non-commissioned officers was now started, a very useful means of maintaining the efficiency of the units.

February, 1916.

On February 1st the Battalion relieved the 1st Royal Warwickshire Regiment. During this tour German war-dogs were noticed for the first time. Later in the war the British also used messenger-dogs, but, as the soldiers could not refrain from feeding them in the trenches, they were not always as useful as they might be. These dogs were kept in depôts on the lines of communication, and were always fed to the accompaniment of loud explosions, which rendered them indifferent to shell fire.

On February 4th the Irish Fusiliers were relieved by the 1st Battalion King's Own Regiment, and proceeded to billets at Beaussart. It was at this place that Brigadier-General C. P. A. Hull bade them farewell, on his promotion to command a division. A fine fighting general, he had won the confidence of his troops, who viewed his departure with regret. He was succeeded in command of the 10th Brigade by Brigadier-General C. A. Wilding, C.M.G., of the Inniskilling Fusiliers. On February 5th, Captain R. B. Neill, an excellent officer, was selected as an instructor at the Divisional School.

The 4th Division, less artillery, was now being relieved by the 36th Division, and the Faugh-a-Ballaghs were to enjoy a welcome respite from trench warfare. Accordingly, on February 6th the Battalion, led by their drums, marched from Beaussart, via Bus-les-Artois—Authie—Thièvres, to Halloy, about nine miles behind the firing line, where a comprehensive course of company training was begun.

On February 10th, Major-General the Hon. W. Lambton, commanding the 4th Division, presented the Distinguished Conduct Medal to Private J. Liggett, for gallantry on January 18th, 1916.

The Battalion remained at Halloy for the remainder of the month. The weather was indifferent, frost, snow and thaw alternating, but the fact of not being under fire, and not having to be continually prepared for gas attacks, made life less strenuous.

But it must not be supposed that these periods spent behind the lines were periods of inactivity. The new and complicated forms of training demanded much time, and the training of specialists was being standardized by means of excellent training pamphlets, produced by the various schools of instruction.

What did make training somewhat difficult was the ever-changing personnel and the constant call for officers and other ranks to carry on the numerous services demanded by an army in the field.

Whenever men were required for tunnelling companies, signal service, trench-mortar batteries, etc., demands were naturally made on the infantry, and, as the Irish Fusiliers invariably gave of their best, it made it increasingly difficult to keep the Battalion up to the high state of efficiency to which they had attained.

All this work did not prevent a reasonable amount of recreation, of which football was undoubtedly the favourite. Senior and junior company leagues were formed, and on February 29th "C" Company were beaten by the 7th Argyll and Sutherland Highlanders, in the semi-final of a Brigade league, by 3 goals to nil, after playing two drawn games. There were the usual entertainments, of which "The Follies" took the lead, and Father Hessenauer gave French lessons.

On February 24th all leave was temporarily stopped. The troops did not know the reason when leave was stopped, it was in conformity with the plans of the Higher Commands. But leave was not necessarily stopped on account of active operations. During the Third Battle of Ypres an Australian, who was due for leave on the evening of the day on which his division was to make an attack, fearing he might miss the leave train, went over the top in two complete suits of uniform. He returned safe, but, of course, smothered with mud and dirt. He peeled off the outer suit, and dashed off in time for the train.

March, 1916.

On March 2nd the Battalion marched, via Famechon, Pas and Gaudiempré, to billets at Humbercamp. A sad accident occurred on the march, No. 9807 Private E. O'Rawe being killed by a motor-lorry at Pas. He was a very good soldier, and had been out the whole campaign.

When the Drums, according to custom, played round the billets at dawn of Barrosa Day, March 5th, the ground was covered with snow, but the weather was fine. A comprehensive programme had been prepared. Printed programmes had been obtained from Doullens, and all events were carried through with much success. An inter-platoon rifle match was won by "B" Company, No. 8 Platoon. Then followed a football match between officers and sergeants, in which the latter were the winners. There was the usual five a-side football knock-out tournament, and at 1 p.m. the men sat down to an excellent dinner. The sergeants had their dinner at 7 p.m., the officers attending, and at 8 p.m. the officers had their dinner, the Brigadier being the guest of the evening. The day closed with excellent entertainments by the band of the 4th Division, and the "Barn Owls," the entertainers of the 37th Division.

But the event of the day was the race meeting, held in the afternoon, at which there was a large gathering, including the Corps and Divisional staff. The course was complete with "bookies," etc., the men thoroughly entering into the spirit of the thing. The race of the day was for the "Barrosa Derby," for horses that had been hunted (by shell fire) regularly since August, 1914. After an exciting race, Captain Brown's, R.A.M.C., "The Guardian," by "Editor" out of "Armagh," Company Sergeant-Major Stevenson up, won by a short head. The races were held under the rules of the 87th B.E.F. Committee, which were somewhat out of the ordinary.

This race meeting aroused a good deal of interest amongst the neighbouring troops, and was probably the first of those race meetings and horse shows which became such a feature later in the war.

Altogether, Barrosa Day, 1916, was a great success.

On this date Captain and Adjutant W. Liesching assumed the name of William Carden-Roe. Company training and the usual working parties were resumed at Humbercamp, and on March 14th the Battalion did an attack against practice trenches, in the presence of the Divisional Commander and Brigadier, who expressed themselves pleased. These practice trenches were laid out behind the fighting lines. They were, as a rule, exact copies of some system of enemy trenches in the immediate front. They were traced by means of air photographs, and the practice attacks were carried out in detail, such detail being very thorough and in some cases complicated, as the whole action, from the preliminary bombardment to final consolidation of the objective, was represented.

On St. Patrick's Day the regimental custom of all the officers attending Divine service with the men was carried out, and sprigs of shamrock were distributed to all ranks.

The 4th Division was now in course of relieving the 37th Division, the 10th Brigade relieving the 110th Brigade. Accordingly, on March 19th, the Battalion moved to Berles-au-Bois and relieved the 6th Battalion of the Leicestershire Regiment. The move was made by a circular route, via Laherlière and Bailleulmont, the Battalion moving in smaller bodies as it approached its destination. This was necessary because the village was only one mile behind the firing line, and was in parts under enemy observation, and therefore subject to direct fire. There was, however, ample bomb-proof shelter in the form of cellars and caves in the chalk.

On March 21st the Fusiliers relieved their old friends the Seaforth Highlanders in the line. The trenches were approached from the village by a communication trench known as Hob's Walk, built of what were called " A " and " U " frames because the trench, which was deep and revetted, was strutted with frames of the shape of those letters inverted. The cross-bar of the " A," being placed near the point, formed a support on which the trench boards were laid, whilst a longer bar, near the two feet, kept the sides of the trench from falling in, and also served to catch the heads and loads of those using the trench in the dark.

All four companies were in the fire trenches, finding their own supports.

There were now only 103 steel helmets in the Battalion, and they were used by the sentries. On the day after the relief a soldier on sentry was hit through his steel helmet by a German sniper, but his life was saved.

It was in this sector that the Battalion first had carrier pigeons attached for message work in case of heavy bombardment.

To make identification difficult, units were not addressed by name, but by code letters, the Irish Fusiliers' address being D.1.

On March 25th Major Findlater was ordered to relieve Major Neill at the 4th Divisional School of Instruction, and on the evening of the same day the

Photo by] [*Imperial War Museum*

THE VILLAGE OF MONCHY-AU-BOIS, 1917.

Battalion was relieved by the Seaforth Highlanders, and, amongst other work, began the burying of signal cables. As artillery bombardment increased in intensity it became impossible to rely on cables laid above ground, and, later on, alternative lines of buried cable were employed, as it was not possible to bury them deep enough to be invulnerable to heavy shell fire.

On March 26th Lieutenant-Colonel Shuter proceeded on a few days' leave, and Captain A. P. Faris commanded during his absence. On March 31st the Battalion again relieved the Seaforth Highlanders.

The weather during this month had been severe, and the Battalion were fortunate in being out of the line for the greater part of it; but the weather was now improving, and the trenches taken over, which had formerly been held by the French, had good dug-outs, which meant much for the comfort of the occupants.

A privilege much appreciated, and seldom, if ever, abused in the Battalion, was the "green envelope." Normally, all letters were censored by the company officers, who closed them and initialled them, and the adjutant stamped them with the regimental censor stamp. But a man wishing to write on private family affairs could do so by using a green envelope, which he closed himself, and the letters were only censored at the base.

Incidentally, the letters written by the men of the Regiment, and those received by them, many from people in humble circumstances, disclosed not only a patient and cheerful endurance of their sufferings, but an implicit faith in Divine protection and final victory.

April, 1916.

The first half of April was spent in the usual routine, the Seaforth Highlanders and Irish Fusiliers relieving each other every six days. The sector was a fairly quiet one, and the bombardments were not heavy. There were more casualties in the village of Berles-au-Bois than in the trenches. The sector was about eight miles north of that which the Battalion had held to the north-west of Beaumont Hamel, and was under artillery fire from the villages of Ransart and Monchy-au-Bois. Our patrols and snipers were active, and met with success. On April 7th the strength of the Battalion was 24 officers and 822 other ranks. At this time men were called for to man the new 3-in. Stokes mortar batteries, which proved very serviceable units.

The Battalion was now preparing for a daylight raid, the first of the description carried out by the Expeditionary Force, and, as it proved a very successful one, a description may be not uninteresting, and will illustrate the complicated preparation required to bring off even a small operation of this nature in trench warfare.

The raid was to take place on April 17th, and on April 16th, to use the words of the Battalion diary, Corporal A. Roabuck was given the "privilege" of cutting and rearranging our wire.

The point selected for attack was a German salient opposite a "T" sap which ran out from our trenches, about 50 yards to about 30 yards from the enemy's line, and, as usual, the attack was practised against similar trenches laid out behind the lines.

The raid was under command of Lieutenant N. Russell, and was organized in the following parties:—

No. 1 clearing group, under Lieutenant Russell, in the following order:
  1 Bayonet Man.
  1 Officer.
  1 Bomber.
  1 Support Bayonet Man.
  1 Bomb Carrier.
  1 Bomber.
  1 Bayonet Man.
  1 Bomber.
  1 Bayonet Man.
  1 Wire-cutter and Carrier.

No. 2 clearing group, under Second-Lieutenant W. H. Crotty, consisted of 10 non-commissioned officers and men, of whom two were Parapet Scouts.

There were two blocking groups of 1 non-commissioned officer and 4 men each.

R.E. party of 4 Sappers, under Lieutenant Walker, of the 9th Field Company, Royal Engineers.

Total—3 officers, 33 other ranks.

The programme was as follows:—

At 3.50 p.m. on April 17th the 6-in. howitzers opened on the German trenches.

At 3.55 p.m. the artillery put down a box barrage round the portion of the enemy trenches to be attacked, and two trench-mortar batteries cut the wire opposite the point of entrance.

At 4 p.m. artillery fire ceased on enemy wire and fire trench, and the attackers, led by Lieutenant Russell, rushed forward from the "T" sap-head, the gate, which consisted of two "knife-rests," being opened by wires from our trench.

On reaching the German trench no enemy was in sight, and Lieutenant Russell acted as follows: A blocking party was sent to the left, and Lieutenant Russell's party, supported by that of Second-Lieutenant Crotty, worked to the right.

Ten yards down the trench, Lieutenant Russell found a German officer standing at the entrance to a dug-out; he shot this officer, and the dug-out was bombed. About twenty yards farther on Germans were encountered in the trench, and, at the same moment, the enemy gave the alarm by sounding a bell. Rifle fire and bombing became general, the Germans fighting well, but they

Nº VII

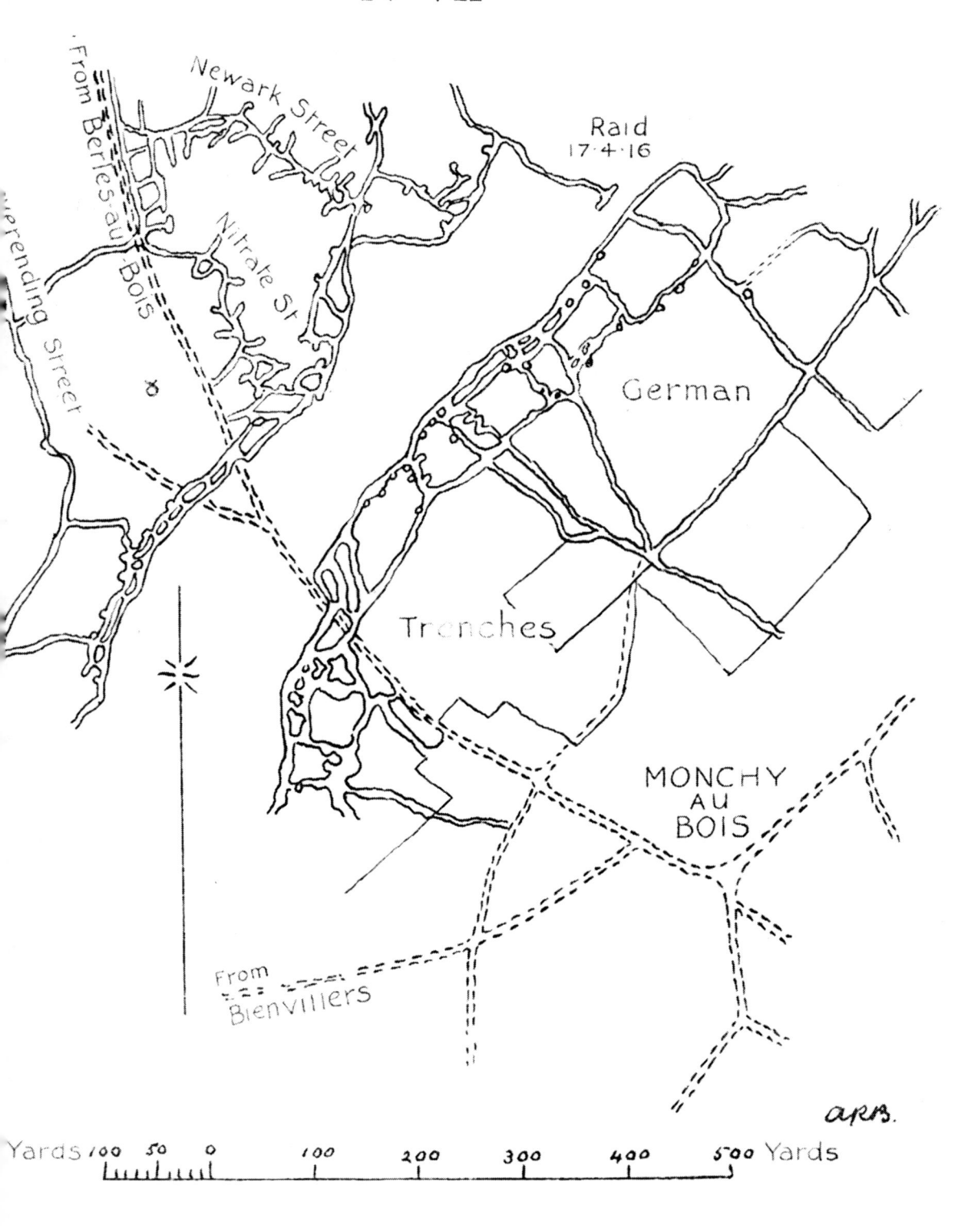

Newark Street
From Berles-au-Bois
Nitrate St
…rending Street
Raid 17·4·16
German
Trenches
MONCHY AU BOIS
From Bienvillers

A.R.B.

Yards 100 50 0 100 200 300 400 500 Yards

were caught in their dug-outs, which were bombed, and they must have suffered heavily. In the meantime, the blocking group which had gone to the left tackled a machine-gun emplacement, killed a German officer and sergeant, and bombed three dug-outs.

At 4.10 p.m. Lieutenant Russell gave the signal to withdraw, to enable the Royal Engineers to do their work, which consisted in laying demolition charges. This was done under cover of the blocking groups, and the whole withdrew to " T " sap-head, the explosions in the German trenches showering debris on the party as they reached their lines. The results of the raid were, 2 German officers and 13 other ranks seen killed. A German deserter later reported their casualties at 63 killed, and there is no doubt the bombing of the dug-outs had great effect. Equipment for identification was brought away. A machine-gun emplacement with fixed tripod, and a suspected mine shaft were blown up by the Royal Engineers. No prisoners were taken. Our only casualty was Private Davis slightly wounded in the hand by a grenade.

The success of the artillery action was largely due to Major McKenzie, of the Royal Garrison Artillery. He stated, with truth, that he could put a shell wherever it was required, and this he was prepared to do at any time of the day or night, except on the Sabbath, on which day his religious scruples forbade him to fire, except in retaliation.

There were one or two amusing incidents. Two men told off to complete the cutting of the enemy wire, found that the artillery had done their work so thoroughly that they had nothing to do. This did not deter them from lying on their backs and going through the motions of using their wire cutters.

As the debris from the explosions in the German lines fell on the retiring raiders, one man exclaimed " Lord save us; 'twould be just my luck to get a Blighty-one before I gets my tay "—referring to a special meal prepared for the party.

For this raid Lieutenant Russell was awarded the Military Cross, and Sergeant F. Baker and Corporal A. Roabuck both received the Military Medal.

The Royal Warwickshire Regiment carried out a raid at the same time.

The Battalion was highly complimented on this most successful daylight raid, and the following message was received, through the VII Corps, from the Commander of the Third Army :—

" The Army Commander has read with interest and pleasure the account of the daring and successful raid carried out in the 4th Division by the 1st Battalion Royal Irish Fusiliers, of the 10th Brigade. Please convey the Army Commander's congratulations to Brigadier-General C. A. Wilding, and to the officers and men who so ably carried out this operation."

The point raided in the German lines was 500 yards north of Monchy-au-Bois, and the success of the raid was not a little due to the excellent and accurate gunnery of the Royal Artillery.

On April 18th the Battalion was relieved by the Seaforth Highlanders.

Both the Corps and Divisional Commanders, when visiting the Battalion, congratulated the raiders of April 17th.

There is no doubt that this daylight raid had a great moral affect on the enemy; he was obviously nervy, and the mere sight of one of the officers, who exposed himself over the parapet, was the cause of an outburst of fire of all descriptions. They evidently feared another raid of the same description.

But beyond this, the enemy's artillery were very active right up to the end of the month, probably due to the presence of their "travelling circus," and the village of Berles-au-Bois was one of their favourite retaliation targets, as our own artillery was also active. It was noticeable what a large proportion of enemy shells were "blind" at this period.

On April 22nd an enemy shell completely destroyed "B" Company's officers' mess in the village; fortunately, the occupants had just taken cover. The night of April 24th saw the Battalion back in the trenches, where they remained until the end of the month, as news was received that the 4th Division was to be relieved by the 37th Division.

On April 29th the enemy displayed a board on his trenches: "Kut capitulated, 13,000 English prisoners." It was practically blown to pieces by rifle fire, and disappeared.

About this time a demonstration was made with a captured *flammenwerfer*, an abominable method of fighting which the Germans had employed against the French. The object of the demonstration was to show that the instrument was powerless against men in the trenches, if they kept down while the operator was dealt with by comrades on their flanks.

The importance of machine guns had brought into existence the famous Machine Gun Corps, and a number of officers were called for to be trained at the central school at Grantham to command the units of the corps.

The Battalion were very pleased to hear that Brevet Lieutenant-Colonel R. J. Kentish, D.S.O., had been selected to command the 76th Infantry Brigade, from April 14th.

MAY, 1916.

The Battalion were now to enjoy a spell out of the line, as the 4th Division was leaving the VII Corps. Accordingly, on May 1st, after being relieved by the 10th Battalion Royal Fusiliers, the Battalion marched to billets at Humbercamp, and the next day, via Gaudiempré, Pas, and Grenas to Halloy, where Lieutenant-Colonel Shuter left the Battalion to take up temporary command of the Brigade.

On May 3rd the Fusiliers occupied huts at Barly, marching through Doullens and Occoches. After a halt on May 4th, Domleger was reached on May 5th, the route laying through Mézerelles, Le Meillard, and Prouville. This village had not before been occupied by British troops, and all ranks were received with great kindness by the inhabitants.

Battalion routine was resumed at Domleger under pleasant circumstances.

On May 8th a kind message of farewell was received from General Snow, commanding VII Corps, to his old division.

While at Domleger the Battalion received a gift of 8,000 cigarettes from J. H. Wilson, late a private in " C " Company, which he had obtained by raffling his gramophone. Samuel Butler, another old soldier of the Regiment and a Mutiny veteran, although in poor circumstances, sent a number of parcels containing pipes, tobacco, newspapers, etc., and what he called " chuck-muks " —a primitive sort of pipe-lighter, as used by our soldiers in the Mutiny. These may seem trivial incidents, but they are only typical of many, and tend to illustrate that intense feeling of comradeship which has always permeated all ranks of the Regiment.

On May 9th a comprehensive course of field training was commenced, and rumours were not wanting of a coming British offensive.

On May 13th Lieutenant-Colonel Shuter resumed command of the Battalion.

On May 18th Brigade athletic sports were held at Mesnil Domquer, at which the representatives of the Fusiliers were very successful and succeeded in winning the Brigade championship and athletic shield, which was presented by Brigadier-General C. A. Wilding.

The programme of training was brought to a close on May 20th. This programme, comprising as it did not only the ordinary duties of the infantry soldier, but the diverse " specialist " training required by the introduction of new weapons and the demands of trench warfare, was strenuous and exacting. One of the new tactical features first practised at this time was the co-operation of infantry with the Air Force.

At 5.30 a.m., May 21st, the Battalion was once more on the move. In spite of the early hour, the greater part of the inhabitants of Domleger, headed by the Curé, turned out to bid farewell to their guests and wish them God-speed. The route lay through Prouville, Fienuillers, Candas, and Beauval to Beauquesne, about fifteen and a half miles, but the march was a trying one on account of the heat.

On May 22nd the Battalion was distributed as follows :—

Headquarters and " B " Company at Bertrancourt; " A " Company at Acheux Wood; " C " Company at Bus-les-Artois; " D " Company at Coigneux, and thus found themselves in rear of their old line near Beaumont Hamel. The reason of this distribution was that the unit had been selected to work on the Corps line, which was expected to take about a fortnight to complete, and they were thus employed up to the end of the month.

On May 24th Lieutenant-Colonel Shuter left the Battalion, on being selected to command the 109th Infantry Brigade. With characteristic modesty, in his farewell order, he attributed his advancement to the high state of efficiency of the Battalion. This may have been one of the reasons, but the universal regret at losing him bore testimony to the extent to which his soldierly qualities and sympathetic care of those under his command had endeared him to all ranks.

He was succeeded in command by Major W. A. V. Findlater, who rejoined from the 4th Divisional School of Instruction.

In the *London Gazette* dated 29th May, the 1st Battalion Royal Irish Fusiliers was one of the units specially mentioned by the Commander-in-Chief for good work in carrying out and repelling local attacks and raids.

A new system of reinforcements was introduced about this time. Up to now reinforcements had been by battalions, with the result that battalions varied in strength. By supplying reinforcements by regiments this was obviated, the only exception being that Territorial reinforcements were still sent to Territorial battalions only.

Also about this time the new box respirator began to be issued. This respirator, with latest improvements, was found to render the wearer immune from the most deadly form of gas attack.

The face of the country had changed much since the Fusiliers had held this part of the line. A net-work of railways, both full and narrow-gauge and light railways, led up to the front. Large numbers of hutted camps had sprung up, and large dumps of ammunition, stores and supplies were established. In fact, the rumours of a coming offensive had become a certainty, and this fact must have been as obvious to the enemy as it was to the civilian inhabitants.

JUNE, 1916.

The Battalion was still employed in working-parties on the Corps line. The chief event at the opening of the month was the Battle of Jutland. The first reports of this great naval engagement were unfortunately misleading, and it was only gradually that the truth of a hard-won victory percolated to the troops at the front; but even when it was believed that the enemy had achieved even a partial success, the dogged spirit of the troops was in no way affected.

On June 5th Captain R. B. Neill was selected to command the 15th Battalion West Yorkshire Regiment. Captain Neill was an officer on the reserve of the Regiment. Throughout the Second Battle of Ypres, and on all occasions of fighting or hard work, he had proved himself the embodiment of all that is best in a company commander.

On this day the Military Service Act was promulgated in Battalion Orders.

On June 8th the Commander-in-Chief's order announcing the death of Lord Kitchener in the loss of *H.M.S. Hampshire* was published. It was with genuine sorrow that the troops heard of the loss of this great organizer. Many remembered the words of Lord Kitchener's message to the original Expeditionary Force which was issued to every soldier, and made fresh resolves to carry out his injunction, "Remember that the honour of the British Army depends on your individual conduct."

On June 11th the Battalion concentrated at Bertrancourt, except "C" Company, who proceeded to Mailly-Maillet. On June 13th the whole Battalion

PREPARATIONS FOR ATTACK

concentrated at Mailly-Maillet, where they were employed on fatigues and in preparing for the coming offensive. On June 14th summer time came into force.

At this time the good news of the Russian "push" did much to stimulate the desire of the troops to get to grips with the enemy.

On the evening of June 18th the Battalion relieved the Seaforth Highlanders in their old sector just north of the Serre road. Captain P. Penn rejoined this day from the General Headquarters School, and took over duties of senior major. Reports in the line were now made by runner only, as it was known that the German listening-sets were capable of picking up telephone messages. On July 19th, 20th and 21st that portion of the line held by "D" Company was subjected to a heavy fire of guns, trench mortars and grenades.

On June 22nd, after relief by the Royal Warwickshire Regiment, the Battalion proceeded to Vauchelles-les-Authie, in order to use the Louvencourt training ground. On June 26th, after an attack on dummy trenches representing the Battalion objective in the coming fight, the Commander of the VIII Corps addressed all ranks, speaking in eulogistic terms of the Regiment and his pride in having it under his command. At night the Fusiliers proceeded to a tented camp at Bertrancourt. The night was very wet, but, like all Irishmen, and, indeed, all British soldiers, the men were in the highest spirits at the prospect of an early action. This was perhaps specially true after a long period of trench warfare, during which the opposing armies lay in close proximity but invisible to each other. The trench line in France and Flanders presented a strange spectacle by day. The terrain had been converted into a tumbled mass of trenches, the prevailing colours being either that of Flanders mud or the white chalk of Picardy. During the intervals of firing not a sound was heard, and it was difficult to believe that this apparent wilderness was indeed thickly inhabited, and that to be seen was to court death. At night the same area, if illuminated, would have disclosed a busy hive of industry. No wonder that the men chafed under such a life, and longed for the time when they could get their enemy in the open and have a stand-up fight.

June 27th. This was X—Y night. The date of an offensive was never stated—it was always referred to as Z day, and other days lettered accordingly. The actual starting time was known as zero hour.

As typical of the work involved in preparation, it may be mentioned that Second Lieutenant C. T. Wilson, with a party of 100 men, marched five miles on this day to an ammunition dump, and from there made five journeys to the trenches carrying trench mortar ammunition, and returned to camp. This fatigue occupied fourteen hours.

On June 28th "Z" day was postponed for forty-eight hours on account of the bad weather. General Lambton, the Divisional Commander, addressed the Battalion. At 9 p.m. on June 30th the Battalion proceeded to their assembly trenches at what was known as the Sunken Road, all ranks being in the highest spirits and the march discipline perfect.

Before dealing with the First Battle of the Somme, which lasted from July 1st to November 18th, it will be well briefly to consider the vast preparation necessary before the actual assault could take place.

In the Russo-Japanese War, the operation order necessary to put a Japanese division into action seldom exceeded three or four lines of print. For this trench warfare battle the first orders received from the Corps were dated June 7th, and from this date onward orders and instructions were frequent and voluminous, so that by zero day the " dossier " was a bulky one. Nor was this to be wondered at when the following are considered :—

    (a) The combination of artillery, infantry, engineers, the air service, the signal service, trench-mortar batteries, gas, the medical service, and all the supply services.

    (b) The moving forward of a completely organized trench system, with its multitude of stores and accessories.

    (c) Necessary preparations for open warfare.

Reference has already been made to the amount of manual labour involved. In addition to all the trench work large dumps of R.E. stores, ammunition and supplies have to be accumulated and protected from shell fire. On this occasion the water supply was a very big and complicated operation.

The plan of the forthcoming battle, from a battalion point of view, was the following :—

After five days of artillery bombardment, on " X—Y " night the assaulting troops moved to their assembly trenches.

Three objectives were allotted to the 11th and 10th Infantry Brigades, who attacked south of the Serre road. First objective, the enemy front line trenches. Second objective, the enemy second line trenches. Third objective, the enemy trenches on the Grandcourt—Serre ridge. Zero hour was 7.30 a.m.

The two first objectives were to be taken by the 11th Infantry Brigade. The method of advance was, that after the artillery had bombarded the immediate objective the barrage lifted, and the infantry assaulted and consolidated their gains.

The task of the 10th Brigade was to leap-frog over the 11th Brigade and assault the final objective, consolidating on the Puisisieux-au-Mont—Beaucourt-sur-Ancre road and establishing strong points.

The formation adopted by the Irish Fusiliers, who were left support battalion in their Brigade, was as follows : Three companies in first line, each company in company column, ninety yards interval between companies and one hundred yards distance between platoons. One company in support in star formation, platoons at two hundred yards distance and interval. All platoons moved in column of fours. The total frontage allotted to the Battalion was 375 yards.

After deducting all carrying-parties, etc., ten per cent. of the remainder of the Battalion were held in reserve, and were not to take part in the fight. Officers were dressed as nearly as possible like their men, and, like them, carried grenades, flares, etc.

JULY, 1916.

First Battle of the Somme.

At 12.35 a.m. on July 1st the Battalion arrived at its assembly trenches on the Sunken Road running slightly west of north from Auchonvillers to the Sucherie. This march was for the greater part of its length across country, by tracks marked with white posts. It was well that it was so, as the enemy subjected all the villages in the vicinity to heavy shelling. The assembly trenches were reached without casualties.

According to programme, the Battalion was the last to leave the assembly trenches, which it was timed to do at 9.30 a.m.

The work of the 10th Brigade was, of course, dependent on the success of the 11th Brigade in their front, and that of the Irish Fusiliers on the success of the battalions in the first line of the 10th Brigade.

At 9.30 a.m. the Battalion movement commenced. At this time a large number of white lights were going up to the front. These were at first mistaken for groups of three white lights, which was the signal that objectives had been reached. They were, unfortunately, single white lights, denoting "held up by wire," and a telephone message was received from headquarters that the Battalion was not to proceed beyond Tenderloin and Mountjoy trenches till further orders. The leading platoons were stopped on this line.

A further message, dated 10.25 a.m., directed that the 10th Infantry Brigade were not to be committed to attack till further orders, as the 29th Division were not attacking Beaumont till 1.50 p.m.

From this time on the Battalion lay under a fairly heavy artillery fire.

At 1.25 p.m. a message, dated 1.15 p.m., was acknowledged. This message directed the Commanding Officer to send one company to reinforce Lieutenant-Colonel J. O. Hopkinson, who, with his Seaforths and details of the 11th Brigade, was holding the Quadrilateral, a salient in the German front line lying in the angle of the road fork south-west of Serre, and from which the enemy were endeavouring to dislodge him with artillery and bombing attacks.

Lieutenant-Colonel Findlater ordered "C" Company, under Captain E. R. Wilson, for this duty.

Captain Wilson endeavoured to advance over the open, and was met with such a heavy rifle and machine-gun fire that the advance failed, Captain Wilson being himself wounded whilst leading the advance.

At 3 p.m the situation report stated that all corps, including the French, except the British VIII Corps had taken their objectives, and that all efforts were to be made to support Lieutenant-Colonel Hopkinson in the Quadrilateral.

About 4 p.m. Lieutenant-Colonel Findlater became aware that "C" Company had failed to reach the Quadrilateral. He therefore ordered "D" Company, under Captain G. W. N. Barefoot, to perform the duty.

Captain Barefoot, leaving two platoons in the British front line trenches as a support, led the remaining two platoons by a circular route, and, approaching the Quadrilateral from the south, succeeded in placing himself under the orders of Lieutenant-Colonel Hopkinson, whose orders were to hold out to the last; the reason being that the Quadrilateral was required as a pivot to form a new line through Serre, which was believed to be in our hands.

At 8.30 p.m. Captain and Adjutant Carden-Roe returned from Brigade headquarters with the following instructions:—

"D" Company were to hold the Quadrilateral at all costs. All troops under Lieutenant-Colonel Hopkinson to be withdrawn. The Battalion to hold a small portion of the original British line. Captain and Adjutant Carden-Roe carried the orders to Lieutenant-Colonel Hopkinson, who withdrew from the Quadrilateral, leaving Captain Barefoot in command.

Owing to heavy shelling, the new dispositions were not complete till 2 a.m. of July 2nd.

In the meantime, at 11.35 a.m. orders were received that Captain Barefoot's company was to be withdrawn from the Quadrilateral, where, as a matter of fact, they were quite happy and had put up a good fight and taken the initiative against the enemy. Second-Lieutenant R. Le Mare, who distinguished himself, was reported to have thrown some hundreds of bombs.

On receipt of these orders, Lieutenant-Colonel Findlater immediately sent runners to Captain Barefoot with orders to withdraw. These orders were repeated by further runners, none of whom succeeded in reaching their destination, and it was not until a message despatched at 8.45 a.m. on July 2nd that success was gained.

At 11.5 a.m. Lieutenant-Colonel Findlater reported that Captain Barefoot had withdrawn, bringing with him all wounded, three prisoners and a quantity of arms and stores. This withdrawal across the open, in daylight and under a heavy fire, was a fine performance, and reflects great credit on Captain Barefoot, who displayed excellent leadership throughout the eighteen hours' bombing fight which he had carried on during his occupation of the Quadrilateral. He himself appears to have returned laden with the spoils of war.

The spirit of this company was typical of all the troops. Many battalions had suffered very severely, and they had not gained their objectives, and as yet had not the comfort of knowing that the Higher Authorities considered that they had done all that was humanly possible.

An eye-witness describes the British trenches, or what was left of them, on the night of July 1st, as crowded with soldiers of many corps, most of them wounded but all cheerful, the able-bodied busy cleaning their arms in readiness for what they described as "getting their own back."

On July 1st the Irish Fusiliers, who were less heavily engaged than the other battalions of the Brigade, lost three officers wounded—Captain E. R. Wilson, Second-Lieutenant C. T. Parker, and Second-Lieutenant W. Johnson, and of other ranks 10 killed, 90 wounded, and 7 missing.

July 2nd was spent in the melancholy task of burying the dead, cleaning up the debris of the battle, and repairing trenches.

On July 3rd trench routine was resumed. The enemy showed distinct nervousness, and on the slightest provocation put down a heavy barrage on our lines.

The Corps Commander issued a bulletin in which he explained that the enemy had expected an attack and had concentrated against the Corps front. The determination with which the troops had attacked had held the enemy forces, and thus materially assisted the attacks further south.

On July 4th the Battalion was relieved by the Lancashire Fusiliers and sideslipped to the south, taking over the Auchonvillers sector from the 2nd Battalion Royal Fusiliers and 1st Battalion Royal Dublin Fusiliers.

At 4 p.m on July 5th one of those instances of chivalry on the part of the enemy, which were, unfortunately, so very rare in this war, took place.

Ever since July 1st British bearer-parties had been working day and night to collect the wounded who still lay in No Man's Land. By night it was difficult to discover men hidden in the shell-torn ground, and by day the enemy lost no opportunity of firing on these Red Cross parties. The incident is best described in the words of an eye-witness.

" A bold scheme was the only one likely to succeed. Accordingly, a large Red Cross flag was brought up to the front line trench and then slowly elevated above the parapet, its bearer still remaining under cover. When, after a few minutes, no shots were fired, two medical officers (one of them Lieutenant-Colonel Fitzgerald, R.A.M.C.) scrambled on to the parapet on either side of the flag. Still the enemy held their fire, and so, after a short pause, the two officers advanced across No Man's Land with the bearer of the flag moving between them. By this time a mass of curious heads appeared above the parapet of the German trench, and a German officer, wearing the Red Cross brassard and carrying a white handkerchief tied on to a walking-stick, hastily sprang out of their lines and advanced across No Man's Land to meet the British party. He was closely followed by several others, all presumably of the medical corps. It was an impressive sight. He waited until our party had come as far as he considered fit, then raised his hand signalling to them to halt. The parties of both sides stiffened to a ceremonious salute, following which he commenced to point out all the British wounded lying close to his lines. A signal from our two medical officers brought forward several stretcher-parties, who at once set about their task. At the same time German parties carried wounded who had been lying close to the parapet of the German trench as far as the middle of No Man's Land, whence they were carried off by the British bearers. And so the great work of humanity went on, until all who could be found were carried back to their new chance of life. Throughout the afternoon not a word was exchanged between the representatives of two great enemy nations. At last it all came to an end. The German officers gravely saluted and turned about; the British officers returned the salute with a feeling of gratitude."

As if to vindicate his character for "frightfulness" after this episode, the enemy subjected the front line trenches to heavy bombardment for three hours, commencing at 11 p.m.

On July 6th the Battalion suffered from shell fire, one stray shell falling amongst a fatigue party and another wrecking the orderlies' dug-out at Battalion headquarters. Amongst those killed was No. 11072 Lance-Corporal W. Taylor, a most promising young soldier who, from the commencement of the war, had been employed on the perilous duty of a runner, and by his courage and genial nature had endeared himself to all ranks.

The rainfall was so heavy that the trenches were flooded and in a very bad state.

On July 7th a smoke-bomb attack, for which all preparation had been made, had to be postponed as the wind was adverse. Battalion headquarters was again subjected to heavy shelling. In the evening the Battalion was relieved by the Seaforth Highlanders, and went into bivouac near Forceville, where equipment was completed and some training carried out. On July 8th the Corps Commander visited the Battalion and made a stirring speech, in which he explained how the vigorous attack of the VIII Corps had assisted the attacks made further south. The Anzac Corps sent a message of congratulation to the VIII Corps, which ended, "They are indeed heroes, and their name will live for ever." The troops were also cheered by the reports telling of the good progress made in the battle.

From July 10th dates the receipt of the order that gas masks were to be worn at all times when in the danger zone.

On the night of July 12th the Battalion furnished large parties to carry gas cylinders up to the front line for a demonstration, combined with artillery bombardment, to make the enemy believe a serious attack was intended. On July 14th the Battalion relieved the Seaforth Highlanders in the Auchonvillers sector by daylight.

On July 15th the British bombardment was almost continuous, but the enemy's retaliation was negligible. Active patrolling at night was carried on, especially in the neighbourhood of Beaumont Hamel. Signal wires were discovered in No Man's Land, by means of which the enemy endeavoured to gain information by intercepting telephone conversations.

The 4th Division was now to be withdrawn from the Somme battle, and as a preliminary the 12th Brigade relieved the 10th Brigade in the line, the Duke of Wellington's Regiment relieving the Royal Irish Fusiliers in the trenches on July 17th, the latter unit proceeding to Bertrancourt in Divisional Reserve, where the Brown line of entrenchments was situated; the Green, or second line of entrenchments being further east.

On July 20th the Battalion marched with the remainder of the Brigade, via Louvencourt, Vauchelles, Marieux and Beauquesne, to Beauval; only one man was unable to complete the march. "B" Company, under Captain J. K. Boal, did not accompany the Battalion, having been detailed for work with the 252nd Tunnelling Company, Royal Engineers, but rejoined the Battalion the next day.

After two days' rest and training, the Battalion paraded at 4 a.m. on July 23rd and marched to Candas, where it entrained, and at 3.15 p.m. detrained near Poperinghe and marched to "M" Camp, about two miles west of that town. This camp was considered the best quarters the Battalion had occupied since leaving England.

At 7.45 p.m. on July 26th the Battalion paraded and proceeded by train to Vlamertinghe and took post in reserve at the Château des Trois Tours, which some of them knew well. The 10th Brigade were relieving the 1st Guards Brigade, and here the 3rd Coldstream Guards were relieved.

Only one night was spent at the château, and on July 27th the Battalion relieved the 2nd Battalion Coldstream Guards in the left sub-sector of the line in the neighbourhood of Morteldje Estaminet and Turco Farm, with Battalion headquarters at La Belle Alliance, just east of that portion of the line occupied by the Battalion in 1915.

This sector was, of course, comparatively quiet after the Battle of the Somme, but the trenches were bad and not continuous, and the water supply was still a difficulty, all having to be carried up in tins.

On July 31st the Battalion was relieved by the Seaforth Highlanders and withdrew to the Château des Trois Tours, except one and a half companies which remained on the canal bank, which was now honeycombed with dug-outs, the canal itself being reduced by shell fire to little more than a broad, muddy ditch.

AUGUST, 1916.

The weather at this time was very fine, but owing to the fact that no movement was allowed except under cover of the woods surrounding the château, in order not to attract the unwelcome attentions of the enemy aircraft, little training could be carried on.

During the night of August 3rd the Battalion was relieved by the 2nd Battalion Lancashire Fusiliers, and moved to "J" Camp, north of Poperinghe, where their duty was to be in readiness to man what was known as the "L" line in case of a serious attack. On August 6th, Captain and Adjutant W. Carden-Roe having been selected as chief instructor at the 4th Divisional School, the duties of adjutant were taken over by Captain W. Scott.

At about 1 p.m. on August 10th the Battalion received orders to relieve the

1st Battalion Somerset Light Infantry as left support battalion to the line, as the 10th Brigade were relieving the 11th Brigade, and proceeded to Magenta Farm, about fifteen hundred yards north of Brielen. The Battalion were here in touch with the French troops holding the line on the left of the British.

On the night of August 14th the Battalion moved forward into the front line trenches on the extreme left of the British Army, relieving the Seaforth Highlanders. This relief was carried out by alternative platoons, by order of the Divisional Commander.

On August 15th "A" Company was much annoyed with enemy trench-mortar bombs of a light description, which were christened "trench prawns." They could not be seen coming, and made no noise. The company had twelve men wounded this day. The enemy patrols were active in this sector, but showed little inclination to fight, always dispersing when our men attacked them.

On the night of August 18th the Seaforths and Irish Fusiliers again changed places, and on the 20th the Battalion was relieved by the 15th Battalion Royal Welch Fusiliers, of the 113th Infantry Brigade, and entrained at the Asylum Station, Ypres, and proceeded to "L" Camp.

On the afternoon of August 23rd the Battalion proceeded by train to the Asylum Station, and thence took up the left sub-sector of the line lying to the north-east of Hill 60, the scene of much bitter fighting. They relieved the 43rd Canadian Regiment. The relief was not complete until 2 a.m. on the 24th, when the companies were posted as follows: From right to left—"D" Company, "C" Company, "A" Company; "B" Company was in reserve.

On August 26th "A" Company and "C" Company were subjected to an intense bombardment, the object of which was believed to be the destruction of our trench-mortar emplacements in the locality. Second-Lieutenant W. W. Dyson and 14 other ranks were killed, and Second-Lieutenant T. F. H. Graves and 8 other ranks were wounded. "A" Company trenches were flattened out and other defences were much damaged. "B" Company relieved "A" Company the following night.

This shelling, but of less intensity, was continued on the two following days, and on the night of August 28th the Battalion took the place of the Seaforth Highlanders in Brigade Support. On the night of the 31st the Australians began to relieve the 10th Brigade, and, after handing over to the 3rd Australian Regiment, the Battalion went by train to Brandhoek, and took over what was known as Toronto Camp.

August was not an eventful month for the Irish Fusiliers, but it must be borne in mind that the constant changes of quarters, and taking over of new sectors of the line, entailed an immense amount of labour on all ranks.

What gave real satisfaction to the man in the trenches was the fact that the expenditure of high-explosive shells was more than eleven thousand times what it was in September, 1914.

Some Members of Parliament do not seem to have been perturbed by the previous shortage, though one Honourable Member was seriously concerned about an alleged shortage of sausage skins on the home front.

September, 1916.

The first half of September was uneventful. The Battalion moved to " L " Camp on September 4th, where training and routine were carried out. On September 5th the Divisional Commander inspected a platoon, under Lieutenant Reeve, selected to form part of a demonstration company at the VIII Corps School, and expressed himself as very pleased with physique and turn-out. Amongst other work, the Battalion supplied large working parties at night for burying signal cable in the Salient.

On September 11th a party of 1 officer and 20 other ranks represented the 4th Division at the presentation of medals to Belgian interpreters by the Army Commander at Bailleul.

The good news from the Somme had had a cheering influence. Especially were the men of the Regiment glad to hear of the gallant action of their countrymen in taking the village of Guillemont.

The 4th Division having been selected for further service in the Somme battle, the Corps Commander paid an informal visit to the Irish Fusiliers on September 16th, to bid them farewell on leaving the VIII Corps. In the course of his address he spoke in eulogistic terms of the Battalion.

At 7.45 a.m. on September 17th the Battalion entrained at Proven and proceeded, via Calais and Boulogne, to Longueau, south-east of Amiens, where it detrained at 8.45 p.m., and marched north to Coisy and remained there till the 24th. Little training could be done, as the weather was bad. All ranks were now in possession of steel helmets. The tube gas helmets were withdrawn, the box respirator being sufficient for all purposes. On September 24th the whole Brigade marched via Allonville to Corbie, practising a brigade attack on the village of Querrieu on the way. The Irish Fusiliers billeted at Corbie. On September 25th the Battalion moved to Mericourt l'Abbé, the Brigade practising an attack. On the 26th the Battalion bathed in the river Ancre.

The 4th Division now formed part of the XIV Corps. Officers and men were trained in communication with aeroplanes, practising with the pilots and observers told off to work with the Division in action.

On September 29th Brigadier-General R. J. Kentish visited the Battalion, on his way home to take up an important staff appointment. He had lately visited the 7th, 8th and 9th Battalions of the Regiment, and told how these young battalions were ably maintaining the high reputation of the Regiment.

On September 30th the Battalion moved to Daours, west of Corbie, the Brigade, as usual, practising an attack during the march.

October, 1916.

On October 1st summer time came to an end, the clocks being put back one hour.

On October 2nd a practice attack was carried out as against the village of Le Transloy, which indicated where the 4th Division was to be thrown into the line, and on October 5th a full divisional exercise was carried out.

On October 7th the Battalion marched via Corbie and Mericourt to Méaulte, and the next day to Hansel Camp, situated in what was No Man's Land before July 1st, about twelve hundred yards south of Mametz, on which date the fighting strength of the Battalion was reported as 24 officers and 825 other ranks.

The situation when the 87th again found themselves engaged in the Battle of the Somme was as follows: The British had, since July 1st, taken 26,735 prisoners. They had engaged 38 German divisions, of which 29 had been withdrawn in an exhausted or broken state. They had driven back the enemy to his fourth line of defence, which in this sector was situated west of the Bapaume—Le Transloy road, and they had, at all events temporarily, considerably lowered the *moral* of the enemy forces.

At 6.30 a.m. on October 9th the Battalion was clear of the camp, and proceeded to the south-east corner of Trones Wood, where a guide was met and a halt was made for dinner; and at 1 p.m., moving by platoons, proceeded via Guillemont and Ginchy to a trench junction about 1,000 yards south south-west of Les Bœufs, where Battalion headquarters were established.

The 10th Brigade, which was now the extreme right of the British line and in touch with the French, took over from the 168th British Brigade. The Irish Fusiliers, who had the Royal Warwickshire Regiment between them and the French, took over from Queen Victoria's Rifles and the Kensington Rangers, in trenches on the eastern side of Les Bœufs, which had been captured on September 25th, "C" and "A" Companies in front line, the other two in support. This relief must have been visible to the enemy, for he put down a moderate barrage from which the Battalion suffered some casualties.

During the whole of October 10th the lines were under intermittent bombardment, the losses being 3 killed, 13 wounded, and 4 missing. The Brigadier personally gave orders to prepare to attack on October 12th. This involved great labour in getting up ammunition and stores, and though 200 men of the Royal Dublin Fusiliers helped, the task was not accomplished till 1 a.m. on the 11th. There was also considerable work in removing the wounded left from previous fighting.

During the night October 10th to 11th the trenches were partially cleared, to enable the British heavy artillery to deal with the trenches immediately in front of the Irish Fusiliers. This naturally provoked retaliation, and the Battalion lost 6 killed, 28 wounded, and 4 missing. An explanation is necessary as to how soldiers in trenches can be missing. When trenches are shelled by heavy ordnance firing high explosives, the results are so great that the whole trench is obliterated, and soldiers are often buried or blown to atoms. On this day Second-Lieutenant R. F. Pepper was twice dug out after being buried by shell fire.

From 3.10 p.m. to about 5 p.m. the artillery carried out what was called a Chinese bombardment, or bombardment with the sole object of making the enemy believe that an assault was about to be launched against them.

At 9.30 p.m. orders were issued for an assault next day. This entailed a great deal of work and also movement to get the companies to their starting-off lines. Chiefly through the able and hard work of Captain and Adjutant W. Scott, these arrangements were all complete by 4 a.m. on October 12th.

Two German deserters gave themselves up to Lieutenant Reeve's company on this day.

Owing to casualties, it was found necessary to send for the 10 per cent. reserves left at the transport lines, and these arrived about 6.30 a.m. on October 12th.

The object of the attack on October 12th was to establish a position from which the enemy's main line at Le Transloy could be assaulted, but it was not a success from the Battalion point of view. Suffice it to say that the Royal Warwickshire Regiment were on the right and the 12th Infantry Brigade on the left of the Irish Fusiliers.

At 2.5 p.m., zero hour, the barrage started and the soldiers leapt from their trenches. Unfortunately, in their eagerness, they followed too closely on the barrage, suffering casualties. This caused a momentary halt, but long enough to enable the enemy to get their machine guns into action at a strong point about 500 yards due east of Les Bœufs. This strong point had not been thoroughly dealt with by the artillery. It was also given in orders as being on the dividing line between the Irish Fusiliers and the Royal Warwickshire Regiment, so that neither unit was entirely responsible for dealing with it. Officers and men made repeated attempts to advance, but this was impossible, and the result of the day's fighting was that the Brigade Commander ordered the old front line to be consolidated and held. This was done, and it was ascertained by patrolling that the Germans were also in their forward positions. The estimated strength of companies at the close of the day was:—

"A" Company—no officers, 39 other ranks; "B" Company—3 officers, 61 other ranks; "C" Company—1 officer, 50 other ranks; "D" Company—1 officer, 59 other ranks.

The following officers were killed: Lieutenant H. J. C. Penrose-Fitzgerald, killed on the German parapet in hand-to-hand fighting; Lieutenant E. E. Hyde, Second-Lieutenants J. J. Boyer, T. H. L. Dease, E. R. Gilmer, R. F. Pepper.

October 13th was spent in reorganizing and repairing trenches. The Seaforth Highlanders were ordered to relieve the Irish Fusiliers about 5 p.m., but this was delayed on account of the enemy artillery bombardment, for which he received ample retaliation. After 7 p.m. the Battalion, which had been expecting an enemy counter-attack all day and the previous night, moved back to the support position about Battalion headquarters, bringing with them the wounded and as much salvage as they could carry, and leaving trench guides to help the Seaforths.

On October 14th it was possible to estimate casualties fairly accurately. Only nine officers remained at duty, of whom four belonged to Battalion headquarters. The total casualties from October 9th to October 14th, both dates included, were about 385.

At 6.30 p.m. on this day the Seaforth Highlanders and Royal Dublin Fusiliers attacked the strong point which had held up the attack on October 12th, but, after a very gallant attempt and severe fighting, they were compelled to withdraw to their original lines.

On October 16th the strength of the Battalion in the trenches was 8 officers and 419 other ranks. The whole Battalion was employed in digging trenches from 6 p.m. to 12 midnight, when, having been relieved by the 12th Rifle Brigade, they moved to the bivouac vacated by that unit. The next few days were very wet, and were spent in replacing deficiencies, erecting shelters, and digging-parties. On October 20th was the first frost of autumn, and the weather turned cold.

On October 22nd the Battalion received orders to act as Brigade Support, the Brigade itself being in support of the 4th Division, in an attack which was to take place the next day. Accordingly, by 7 a.m. on October 23rd, the Battalion found itself in assembly trenches in the neighbourhood of the Battalion headquarters during the recent fighting, but farther west on the Ginchy—Les Bœufs road. A German aeroplane dropped three bombs on their bivouac just after they had left it. The weather was foggy, and zero was put off from 11.30 a.m. to 2.30 p.m. The attack was successful, and the Battalion was not called into action. The French had captured Sailly-Saillisel a few days before, and this, no doubt, was an aid to the British, as the village flanked the enemy strong point which had given so much trouble on the two former occasions.

By 5 a.m. on October 24th the Battalion reached Bernafay Wood, to the west of Trones Wood, which it left at 9.45 a.m., and reached Sandpit Camp, near Méaulte, at 3.30 p.m. Only one man fell out, but the troops were very weary, and the help afforded by the Brigade staff, in providing lorries for carrying the men's packs, was very welcome. On October 27th the Battalion moved to billets in Corbie.

On October 30th, after waiting three hours in pouring rain, the Battalion entrained at Corbie at 5.15 p.m., and detrained at Airaines about 10 p.m. and marched via Hallencourt to Bailleul, south of Abbeville, which was reached about 2 a.m. on the 31st. The transport, which had left Corbie by road on October 29th, arrived at Bailleul about 4 p.m. on October 30th.

NOVEMBER, 1916.

On November 2nd the Battalion marched to billets as follows: Headquarters, "A" and "C" Companies, Grébault Mesnil; "B" Company, Longuemort; "D" Company, "Hamicourt." The whole of this month was spent in training, but the weather was bad, being very wet for the earlier portion and turning cold towards the end of the month. On November 6th the General Officer Commanding 4th Division visited the Battalion and expressed himself pleased with the training. On November 8th a presentation of medals was made by Lieutenant-General Sir J. Du Cane, commanding the XV Corps, near St. Maxent-en-Vimeu, a recipient from the Battalion being No. 10985 Sergeant P. C. Nicholson, awarded the Military Medal for gallantry on October 12th, 1916. As usual on these occasions, the troops present on parade marched past the recipients after the ceremony.

On November 12th, Lieutenant-Colonel W. A. V. Findlater having been summoned to a long conference at the Fourth Army School at Flixecourt, Captain W. N. Barefoot, M.C., assumed command.

News was received on November 13th that No. 8084 Private H. Adams, a stretcher-bearer of "D" Company, had been awarded the Distinguished Conduct Medal. On November 14th "C" Company moved to Onicourt. Lieutenant-Colonel Findlater returned on November 19th.

On November 21st the Emperor Francis Joseph of Austria-Hungary died, aged 86 years.

On November 26th the following non-commissioned officers and men who were still with the Battalion were presented with Military Medals by the General Officer Commanding 4th Division, for acts of gallantry performed during 1915. The ceremony took place at Ercourt: 6923 Sergeant S. McMillan, 8973 Sergeant G. Craig, 10033 Sergeant C. Austin, 10387 Sergeant H. Goode, 10372 Sergeant J. T. Bridges, 9820 Sergeant J. Lennon, 10678 Sergeant P. Evans, 6124 Lance-Corporal A. Crawford, 10071 Private J. Fraser, 7239 Private T. Parker, 7232 Private J. Dougan, 9431 Private W. Radcliffe, 6668 Private W. Mitchell, and 7574 Company Sergeant-Major (now Lieutenant) G. Reeve.

On the last day of the month the Battalion commenced to fill in the trenches on their training grounds, preparatory to a move back to the trenches.

The main Battle of the Somme was now over. In spite of his resort to gas, liquid-fire and other methods foreign to the accepted laws of civilized warfare, the enemy had been forced to give way before the repeated blows of the Allies, and the troops were now preparing for another winter of trench warfare. The Battalion was very healthy.

DECEMBER, 1916.

December opened with cold weather, denoting an early winter. A battalion formed from dismounted men of the Household Cavalry, and known as the Household Battalion, now formed part of the 10th Infantry Brigade.

The British were now in process of taking over a portion of the line from the French lying south of the last sector held by the 4th Division, and on December 1st the transport of the 10th Brigade left by road for this new area. The fighting portions of units were moved in what were known as tactical trains, and on December 3rd the Irish Fusiliers left Oisemont at 2.30 p.m., and detrained at Mericourt l'Abbé and marched via Treux to Morlancourt, and the next day to Camp 112 near Bray-sur-Somme. On December 5th the Commanding Officer and party proceeded to Maurepas, the headquarters of the XX French Corps and the 11th French Division, to reconnoitre the new line.

On December 6th a further move was made to Bronfay Farm, and the next day to a camp at Maurepas Station.

On December 8th the Battalion marched to Fregicourt, where it was met by guides from the 1st Battalion 79th French Regiment, and took over about 900 yards of trench from that unit, situated south of Saillisel and east of the main Bapaume—Peronne road, having the 1st Battalion Royal Warwickshire Regiment on their right. Three companies were in fire trenches and one in support. The relief was complete by 10 p.m., with only one casualty.

As tight putties and boots had been found to be conducive to trench feet, the men took sand-bags to replace putties in the trenches, the trousers being tucked into the socks. December 9th was very wet and the trenches fell in, and there being no materials for repairs, they got into a very bad state, being knee-deep in mud and water. As usual on these occasions, the spirits of the men rose in proportion.

On December 10th there was a good deal of shelling, the headquarters dug-outs being considerably knocked about. At night the battalion was relieved by the Seaforth Highlanders and one company of the Duke of Wellington's Regiment. This was due to the whole Division side-slipping farther south. The Battalion moved to a supporting position about 1,000 yards behind the line, and spent the night drawing trench stores and thigh boots, which were badly wanted.

There were no shelters in the support trenches, and on account of the wet and cold all ranks suffered considerably; the men's hands were so swollen that they could not work, and rheumatism became very prevalent. Nevertheless, a good deal of work was done in digging trenches and clearing mud. Dug-outs could not be provided owing to lack of material. Fortunately the enemy appeared to be in much the same situation, so that shelling, though of course continuous on both sides, was not heavy. On December 13th the Battalion relieved the Seaforths in the fire trenches, which had now become so bad that they could only be held by scattered posts with Lewis guns. The strength of the Battalion in the trenches was reduced by sickness to 247.

On December 14th the enemy subjected the sector to heavy bombardment for about three quarters of an hour. This was attributed to "wind up," as both sides were only too anxious to work on their defences.

On December 15th, after being relieved by the 1st Battalion East Lancashire

Regiment, the Battalion was conveyed in lorries to Camp 107, near Bronfay Farm, a sea of mud. The weather continued very bad whilst the Battalion was in this camp, and they were chiefly employed on drainage work.

On December 17th the Irish Fusiliers heard with genuine sorrow of the death of Brigadier-General G. Bull, D.S.O., who died of wounds on December 11th whilst in command of the 8th Infantry Brigade. Brigadier-General Bull was the personification of all that is best in a soldier and a man, and the fact that he enjoyed the esteem and affection of his fellow soldiers to the full is the greatest tribute to his merits, for that esteem and affection are never bestowed except where deserved.

On December 22nd Lieutenant-Colonel Findlater proceeded on leave, and Major W. J. J. S. Haskett-Smith assumed command of the Battalion.

On December 23rd the 10th Brigade relieved the 12th Brigade in the line, the Irish Fusiliers being detailed as support battalion and relieving the King's Own Regiment in Frégicourt, where it was employed in improving the accommodation, and working parties.

A truly wretched Christmas Day was only marked by an increase of artillery fire, both sides being very active.

The Battalion relieved the Seaforth Highlanders in the left sub-sector on December 27th. As few men as possible were kept in the posts, the companies being distributed as far back as Combles. Battalion headquarters were close to the ruined chapel at Sailly-Saillisel.

The trenches were still very bad, and little more could be done beyond constant pumping and bailing. On December 30th the 25th Brigade of the 8th Division relieved the 10th Brigade. After handing over to the 1st Battalion Royal Irish Rifles, the Royal Irish Fusiliers marched to Maurepas, and thence proceeded by lorry to Camp 111, where the Brigade was in Corps Reserve.

December, 1916, was perhaps one of the worst months spent in the trenches. In addition to the bad weather conditions, the fact that a new trench line was being established on a terrain already badly cut up in the hard fighting of the Somme battle, made conditions very uncomfortable. On the other hand, the troops enjoyed amenities which were lacking earlier in the campaign. The periods actually spent in the fire trenches were short. Steps were taken to provide thigh-boots and relays of socks. The constant application of whale oil to the feet, under the superintendence of officers, did much to reduce the numbers suffering from trench feet.

Troops out of the line were accommodated in hutted camps, and the provision of divisional canteens enabled the men to provide themselves with many small comforts.

At this time the system of calling upon units to provide candidates for commissions was introduced. These non-commissioned officers were interviewed by the Brigade Commander, and, if considered suitable, were sent to Cadet Schools. A Works Battalion was also formed in the Division from selected men, and Captain T. J. Jenkinson was detailed to command the company found by the 10th Brigade.

The work of salvage on the battleground was considerable, and a complete organization for dealing with this particular problem came into being. As an example, the following is a list of salvage sent to the rear by one company of the Irish Fusiliers in December, 1916:—

Fourteen and a half pairs gum-boots, 8 rolls wire netting, 12 rolls concertina wire, 20 French rifles, 16 English rifles, 50 shovels, 10 sets of equipment, 9 boxes small arms ammunition, 6 petrol tins, spare barrel and cleaning rod of Lewis gun.

As regards the general situation at the end of the year, Germany, after concentrating all the troops she could spare against Rumania, had succeeded in crushing that small nation, and made this an opportunity to put out peace feelers, which met with no response from the Allies.

At this time the war was costing the British Government more than five and a half millions a day.

CHAPTER IV—1917.

JANUARY, 1917.

ON January 1st, Captain A. J. Trousdell, who returned from the 11th Brigade, took over command from Major W. J. J. S. Haskett-Smith, who proceeded to join the Machine Gun Corps. Company training was commenced.

Major E. G. S. Truell, Connaught Rangers, took over command of the Battalion on January 6th.

January 7th was appointed for the observance of Christmas Day, and, after the usual religious services, dinner was served in the company huts, rations being augmented by an issue of plum puddings and other extras. The officers visited the rooms, and in the afternoon a football competition was won by " D " Company.

On January 14th the Corps Commander presented ribbons to the following: Captain H. A. MacMullen, Military Cross; No. 8084 Private H. Adams, Distinguished Conduct Medal.

Captain Trousdell left the Battalion on January 16th, on appointment to the General Staff of the 33rd Division.

The British were now taking over still more of the line from the French, the 4th Division relieving the 18th French Division.

The movements of the Irish Fusiliers are not quite clear during this operation. They may or may not have moved from Camp 111, near Bray, on January 16th, to a tented camp about one mile distant, but on the night of January 17th they occupied a tented camp near Suzanne, on the north bank of the River Somme, the weather being very cold. The relief was delayed twenty-four hours on account of the troops on both flanks also being relieved.

On January 19th the Battalion proceeded via Curlu to dug-outs near Brigade headquarters, south-east of Hem Wood, where they remained till January 21st, when they relieved the Seaforths in the left sub-sector of trenches lying south of Bouchavesnes and east of the Bapaume—Peronne road. This was a difficult relief on account of the number of posts, and was not complete till 3.30 a.m. on January 22nd.

On January 18th, Father J. H. McShane relieved Father J. Hessenauer as chaplain of the Battalion.

On the night of January 23rd the Battalion was relieved by the 1st Battalion Somerset Light Infantry, after a short but bitterly cold tour in the trenches. The instructions at this time were that the enemy were to have no peace, and he was kept constantly under fire of all descriptions. The Battalion only lost 1 man killed and 4 wounded during this tour. After relief the Fusiliers marched to Camp 18, south-west of Vaux, and the next day via Suzanne and Bray to Camp 112. Bombs were dropped on the camp at night, and 1 man was wounded and 3 horses killed.

Whilst in this camp the Battalion was employed on working parties and making a camp for the Royal Flying Corps, also on training of all sorts, including the training of raiding parties. The recreations included football and cross-country running. News was received of a successful attack by the 29th Division just south of Le Transloy, and also of successful fighting against the Turks in Mesopotamia. A new preventative against trench feet was introduced. In spite of the severe weather the Battalion was very healthy, the numbers admitted to hospital seldom exceeding two per diem.

February, 1917.

On February 8th Brevet Lieutenant-Colonel A. B. Incledon-Webber D.S.O., rejoined the Battalion and assumed command. On February 10th the 4th Division, being in process of relieving the 8th Division in the Bouchavesnes north sector, the Fusiliers proceeded by lorry from Camp 18 to Maurepas, and thence by march route to the line, relieving the 2nd Battalion Northamptonshire Regiment in the left sub-sector just north of St. Pierre Vaast Wood, two companies in the fire trenches and two in support. These trenches could not be approached by day. At this time the men did not take their packs into the trenches, but each man took his greatcoat, one blanket, and ground sheet.

This sector was quiet, but the policy of giving the enemy no peace, and the constant destructive shoots by our artillery, naturally provoked enemy retaliation. In this the enemy was materially assisted by his good observation from Mont St. Quentin, north of Peronne. Active patrolling was carried on at night by both sides, using white clothing while the snow was on the ground. The enemy aircraft also became more active; his own men had complained bitterly of their supineness while the British airmen flew low over their trenches. Precautions against gas attack were continuous, the enemy employing new forms of gas. Each company had a gas non-commissioned officer specially trained to supervise and see that all apparatus was in working order.

As in all the chalk country, water was a difficulty. Wells had to be sunk, and water was carried up in tins on pack animals from the various water points.

On February 16th the Battalion was relieved by the 1st Battalion Rifle Brigade, and moved to reserve at what was known as Asquith Flats, south of Le Forest, where they were employed on carrying parties for the Royal Engineers and other work. The next day the weather broke, and a thaw set in with sleet and rain. For this reason it became necessary to keep as many lorries off the roads as possible, and reliefs to and from the back areas were carried out by route march. On February 20th the Battalion marched to Camp 18, and the next day to Camp 13, near Chipilly.

As the 4th Division was now about to move to the Third Army area, on February 23rd the officers and other ranks who had been attached to the Tunnelling Company and Works Battalion rejoined headquarters.

On February 27th an accident occurred at bombing practice, due to a defective fuze, 3 officers and 2 other ranks being wounded, of whom Second-Lieutenant G. B. P. Kiddell died of his wounds.

Instructions were issued by which personnel on leave could be recalled by telegram. This was probably due to the fact that there were signs of a withdrawal on the part of the enemy. Not only did the information given by deserters point to this probability, but the enemy were known to have blown craters in the main roads passing through his lines.

The weather improved towards the end of the month, and the usual programme of training was carried out. The number of Lewis guns per battalion was increased to sixteen.

March, 1917.

From March 1st the 4th Division were in General Headquarters Reserve, prepared to move by rail at forty-six hours' notice.

On March 3rd the final in the football competition for the Divisional Commander's Cup was played at Sailly Laurette, between the Irish Fusiliers and the R.A.M.C., the latter winning by three goals to one.

The Battalion moved by route march to billets in Corbie on March 4th, the next day to Coisy, and on March 6th, via Bellevue and Talmas, to Beauval. On March 7th the route was continued, via Doullens, Hem, Mezerelles and Frohen-le-Grand to Villers l'Hôpital.

As it had not been possible to celebrate Barrosa Day on March 5th, leave was obtained to treat March 10th as a holiday.

The Battalion having been detailed with the Household Battalion to furnish working parties for the XVII Corps, proceeded on March 12th, via Bonniers and Frevent, to Rebreuve on the River Canche, and the next day to Savy, via Rebreuviette, Berlencourt and Ambrines.

On March 14th the Battalion moved by Aubigny and Capelle-Fermont, and pitched camps in the neighbourhood of Acq. The tents were camouflaged to conceal them from air reconnaissance.

The work consisted in improving ammunition dumps, the men operating in shifts and working by night as well as day.

Instructions were received about this time for the recovery of fat and bones from the cook-houses of the Army. This became a fine art, and there was considerable rivalry between units to be head of the list in the saving of by-products. So enormous in amount did the by-products of the cook-houses alone become, that trains were required to remove it. Fat and dripping were especially valuable for the munition works at home.

The Battalion remained at work till March 23rd, when it was relieved in the morning by the 8th Battalion Durham Light Infantry, and moved back to Savy.

On March 24th a move was made by Villers Brulin and Frévillers to Magnicourt-en-Comté, on which day summer-time was taken into use, and on March 26th the Battalion billeted in Diéval, midway between St. Pol and Bruay, where it was to prepare for active operations.

During the month the enemy commenced his withdrawal to the famous Hindenburg line, which he had prepared with immense labour and in a highly scientific manner. During this move the enemy did not neglect to violate the laws of civilized warfare. The setting of traps may be forgiven, but the poisoning of wells, as at Barleux, near Peronne, and the deliberate attempt to spread the germs of glanders, and possibly other diseases, are acts which can only be justified in a German mind.

APRIL, 1917.

Whilst at Diéval the Battalion was in active preparation for the coming attack, and on March 1st a Brigade exercise took place adjacent to Monchy Breton. Numerous secret orders and instructions were received, and a new terror to young officers, in the shape of the "Bab" code, was introduced. The name was not a suitable one. The code was a very clever means of sending information during an action, without fear of the enemy being able to decipher the messages, but it was complicated, and it is difficult to believe that the inventor had ever himself been in the position of a platoon commander fighting in the enemy trenches; but it was under similar circumstances that the code was to be used.

On April 6th the Divisional Commander inspected the Battalion. The dignity of the inspection was somewhat marred by an irate French lady, who strongly objected to her meadow being used for this purpose, and expressed herself strongly to the inspecting officer. Colonel A. R. Burrowes also visited the Battalion on this date.

On April 7th the Battalion marched to "X" hutments, half a mile south of Ecoivres, by Monchy Breton, Chelers, Tinques, Savy and the main Arras road, where they rested on April 8th, preparatory to the Battle of Arras, which commenced the next day.

The Irish Fusiliers, leaving their details at Camp "X," marched from that place at 6 a.m. on April 9th, the fighting strength being 20 officers and 617 other ranks, the position of assembly being about one mile east of St. Nicholas and north of Arras.

The course of the action proceeded exactly according to schedule, and the Battalion reached their objective, known as the Brown line and just west of the German fourth line of defence, which they commenced to consolidate at 4.30 p.m., and continued this work throughout the following night and day without being disturbed.

BATTLE OF ARRAS

On April 10th the 10th Brigade received orders to attack the Greenland Hill position the next day.

April 11th was a snowy morning. A conference of commanding officers was held at 2.30 a.m., to settle details, and at 9 a.m. the Fusiliers left the Brown line and proceeded to their position of assembly, a sunken road running north and south and situated to the north of Fampoux. This movement was complete by 11 a.m., but, unfortunately, it was observed by an enemy aeroplane, and the position was heavily shelled.

The objective allotted to the Battalion was about 520 yards of front, and included the Château south of the famous Chemical Works, and passing north across the railway to a cross-roads 250 yards north of it. This involved an advance of over 2,000 yards.

Lieutenant-Colonel Incledon-Webber disposed his companies as follows: " D " Company on the right, " C " Company on the left, " A " Company in support, " B " Company in reserve and carrying company; he also had one section of a machine-gun company attached. The 2nd Battalion West Riding Regiment were on the right and the Seaforth Highlanders on the left.

At 12 noon the action commenced, and the troops advanced with great gallantry, but were at once met with heavy machine-gun fire from the north, south, and the buildings at the Chemical Works. In spite of losses the attackers pressed on, and one platoon of " D " Company succeeded in getting within 200 yards of the Railway Station, but as their officer was wounded, and the 12th Brigade on the right were unable to advance, they withdrew, and, with some men of the West Riding Regiment, established themselves in a trench about 600 yards short of the objective and just short of the railway, the embankment being manned and used as a defensive flank. On the left, " C " Company did not succeed in advancing quite so far; they suffered severely, and Captain W. A. Verschoyle was killed, whilst gallantly leading a bombing party, in an endeavour to put an enemy machine gun out of action which was holding up troops on our left.

All the officers of the two leading companies having become casualties, Company Sergeant-Major R. Neville took command, established the line, and got in touch with the units on his flanks.

Captain H. A. MacMullen, M.C., commanding " A " Company, although wounded early in the day, refused to leave his company until 12 midnight, an act which was typical of this excellent officer's conduct at all times of stress and danger. The Battalion lost 11 officers and 307 other ranks during the action. So soon as it was known that the attack had failed, a further attack was ordered for 3 p.m., but the orders to the artillery did not reach them in time, so it did not materialize. During the night " B " Company relieved " C " and " D " Companies.

On April 12th the enemy continued to bombard Fampoux and its vicinity with great vigour. At 5 p.m. two brigades of the 9th Division made an attack on the same objective. Elements succeeded in crossing the line held by the Irish Fusiliers, but were compelled to withdraw. Apparently the enemy defences had not yet been adequately dealt with by the artillery.

The Battalion was relieved by the 5th Battalion Cameron Highlanders, and withdrew to the Brown line.

At 6 a.m. on April 13th the Battalion reached its position in the Brown line, the strength being 7 officers, 1 medical officer, and 292 other ranks. The Divisional Commander visited the Battalion and complimented it on the part it had taken in the operations. During the night the enemy put over a large number of gas shells. Five men suffered from gas, 1 man was killed and 8 wounded. Second-Lieutenant W. M. Livingston died of wounds received from a gas shell this night.

On April 14th the Battalion moved to the Blue line, being quartered in a railway cutting west of Athies, where it was joined by the reserve details. The Battalion paraded at 9 p.m. on April 16th, and meeting guides at Le Point du Jour, took over about 1,000 yards of the line from the 1st Battalion Hampshire Regiment, astride of the Fampoux—Gavrelle road. The line consisted of a series of posts, which they proceeded to improve and connect up during the next three days, under considerable bombardment from the enemy's guns, but being cheered by the good news of progress on the front as a whole. The Canadians had seized the famous Vimy Ridge, the Hindenburg line had been broken south-east of Arras, and the French had made great progress on the Chemin des Dames.

On April 20th, after relief by the 4th Battalion Middlesex Regiment, the Fusiliers again moved to the Blue line in Brigade Reserve, marching by l'Abbayette and St. Laurent Blangy. The next day the Battalion was moved by bus to billets in the village of Dernier, fifteen miles west of Arras, where the usual work of reorganizing and training was carried on until April 28th, on which day they marched via Ambrines, Villers-sire-Simon, Izel-les-Hameau and south of the Bois d'Habarcq to "Y" hutments, near Etrun, and the next day to billets in Arras.

On April 30th the 10th Brigade relieved the 101st Brigade in the line, the Fusiliers being in reserve with the Seaforth Highlanders in the railway cutting south of the River Scarpe and south of Fampoux.

The chief political event of this month was the entrance of America into the war on the side of the Allies, and, though it was well understood that a long period must elapse before the American armies could be trained and transported across the Atlantic, the moral effect was considerable.

The Germans stated, with truth, that they had placed in front of their new lines a strip of country, varying from twelve to fifteen kilometres in breadth, which they had reduced to a wilderness.

Nº VIII

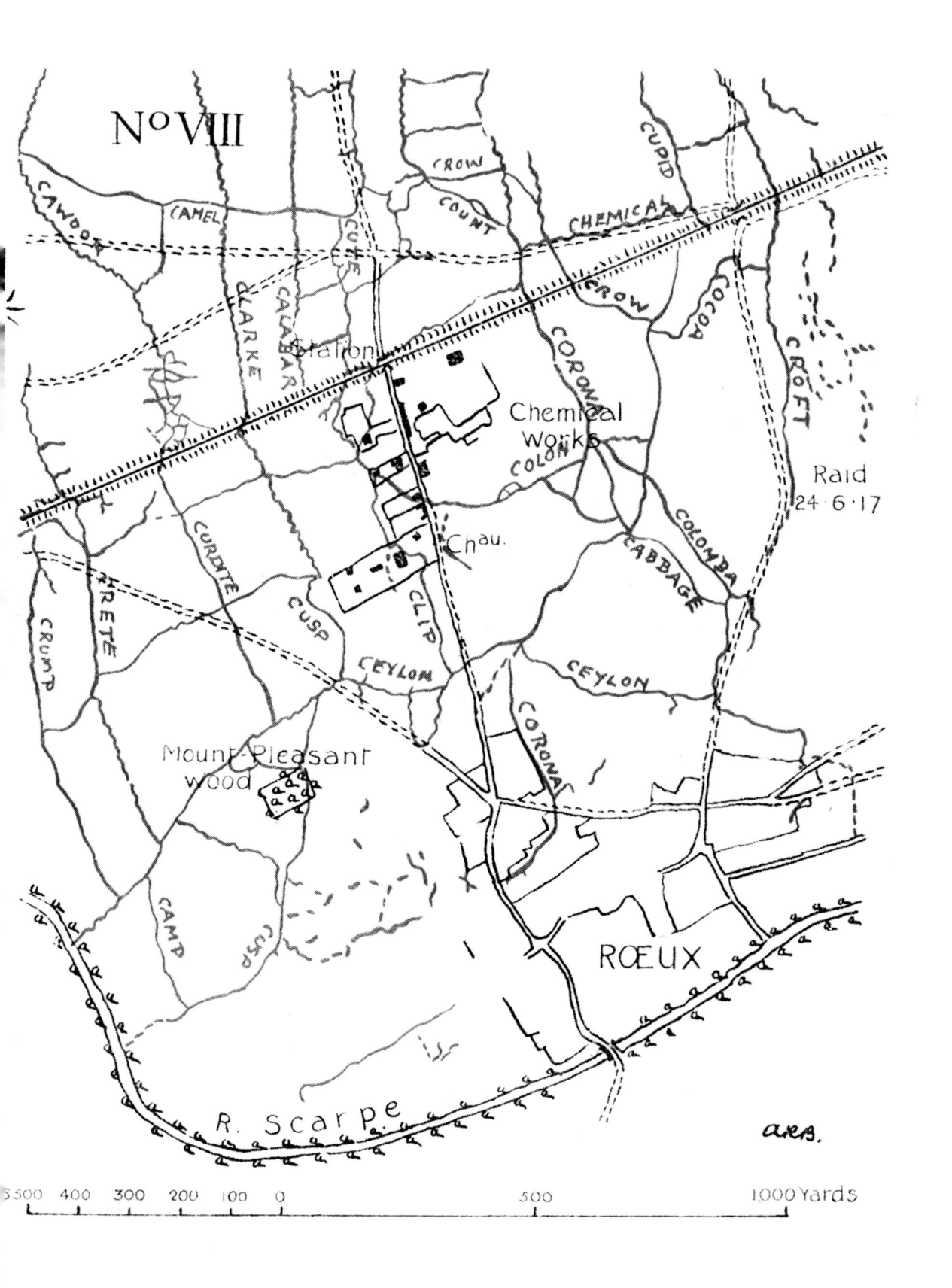

THE BATTLE CONTINUED

May, 1917.

May 1st was spent on working parties and digging shell slits, or "feathers," in the railway embankment, for protection from bombardment.

At 2.30 p.m. on May 2nd orders were received for an attack the next day, and all were busy in preparation. At 10.10 p.m. the Battalion—18 officers and 392 other ranks—proceeded to their assembly positions in trenches about 1,000 yards south-west of the Chemical Works.

Major E. G. S. Truell, Connaught Rangers, left the Battalion to assume command of the 12th Battalion Manchester Regiment.

The attack on May 3rd was not successful. The objective of the Third Army was the line Plouvain—Fresnes-les-Montauban, the 4th Division being on the right and extending as far south as the River Scarpe.

The Division had three objectives, known as the Black, Blue, and Red lines. The objective of the Irish Fusiliers, who were a support battalion in the 10th Brigade, was a portion of the Red line just south of Plouvain, and their success was, of course, contingent on the other two objectives being secured.

Zero was at 3.45 a.m., and, according to plan, the Fusiliers advanced at 4.15 a.m. in two waves, "A" Company on the right, "B" Company on the left, No. 9 Platoon as "moppers up." "D" Company was in reserve, and three platoons of "C" Company were attached to the Seaforth Highlanders. At about 4.25 a.m. the Battalion came under heavy machine-gun fire from the Chemical Works and other buildings which had not been captured, and became mixed up with details of the Duke of Wellington's Regiment and the King's Own Regiment. Second-Lieutenant G. Reeve, although wounded, reorganized these troops, and dug in on a line west of the Chemical Works as far north as the railway line, and held this position throughout the day. He was recalled at 10.10 p.m., and withdrew, bringing his wounded with him.

About 2 p.m. Second-Lieutenant P. Munro took out a patrol, and, in spite of heavy fire, gained touch with Second-Lieutenant Reeve, whose position up to that time was unknown.

After dark, Second-Lieutenant W. H. Crotty established five posts in front of the line, and captured a machine gun, which he brought back to our lines.

The next day was fine and hot. The Battalion held a position south of the Château at the Chemical Works, which the enemy persistently shelled with guns and howitzers of all calibres.

After dark, Second-Lieutenant Crotty's posts were withdrawn, and the Battalion was relieved by the Hampshire Regiment and Seaforth Highlanders, and proceeded to the reserve position in the railway cutting south of the Scarpe. On the roll being called, it was found that the following officers, some of whom were reported wounded and missing at the time, had been killed in action: Captain J. K. Boal (an officer who had given his very best to his regiment),

Lieutenant G. C. S. Armstrong, Second-Lieutenant H. M. Bussey, Second-Lieutenant F. G. McGibney, and Second-Lieutenant H. H. Sheridan; in addition, 6 officers were wounded, and there were 126 casualties amongst other ranks, leaving a trench strength of 6 officers and 236 other ranks.

The Battalion remained in the railway cutting till May 7th, on which date they lost 13 killed and 16 wounded from shell fire and relieved the Household Battalion in the front line immediately north of the River Scarpe. There was a good deal of shelling on both sides, some of it provoked by a "Chinese" attack on the part of the British. On May 10th the enemy devoted his attention to the bridges over the river, and succeeded in temporarily cutting off the Fusiliers from support. This was serious, as at the time the forward positions had been evacuated to assist the fire of our heavy guns. However, the enemy made no attempt to advance, and, under darkness, the troops took up assembly positions in the trenches, preparatory to an attack on May 11th, strict orders being issued to ensure concealment.

May 11th was fine and warm, and was spent by the troops resting and preparing for the coming attack. Captain R. B. Neill, who was in command, in the absence of Lieutenant-Colonel Incledon-Webber on leave, disposed his companies in the following order from south to north: "B," "A," "C" and "D," and issued a stirring appeal to his men to make a real success of their advance. The objective of the 10th Brigade was the Black line, and this included the Chemical Works, which had so long withstood the British attacks. The immediate object of the Fusiliers was to form a defensive flank north-west of the village of Roeux, and for this purpose Captain Neill was given the services of one section of the 10th Machine Gun Company and all spare men of that unit. At 7.30 p.m., zero hour, the troops advanced, the Irish Fusiliers supported by the Royal Warwickshire Regiment, and the Household Battalion, whose objective was east of the Chemical Works, by the Seaforth Highlanders, whose special duty was to "mop up" the buildings. The advance was preceded by a creeping barrage, and all went well. The enemy massed for counter-attack about Hausa Wood, north-east of Roeux, but this concentration was dealt with by our artillery, and at 8.15 p.m. Second-Lieutenant F. P. Kiely, who was acting as intelligence officer, was able to report that all companies were on their objectives and digging in. The position of the most advanced parties was ascertained by the lighting of green flares when called for by the contact aeroplanes. "D" Company, on the left, were compelled to withdraw about 150 yards by our artillery fire, but they returned to their objective on May 12th. The Household Battalion were also successful, but as a gap had occurred between them and the Fusiliers, two companies of the Royal Warwickshire Regiment were sent forward to fill it. This brilliant success was marred by the death of Captain H. E. Herrick, killed in action. This gallant officer had only rejoined the Battalion a few days before, having recovered from his serious wounds received in the Second Battle of Ypres. He was a great

ROYAL IRISH FUSILIER JUST COME FROM THE CHEMICAL WORKS, ROEUX.

Sketch by Sir William Orpen.

loss to the Regiment, both as an officer and a comrade. Amongst the wounded were Second-Lieutenant B. J. Eyre and Captain J. G. Brown, R.A.M.C. Casualties were slight, and the Battalion took about 56 prisoners, mostly of the 360th Regiment.

On May 12th the attack was continued by other troops, and the Battalion underwent a heavy bombardment whilst consolidating the ground won the day before. After dark they were relieved by the 1st/5th Seaforth Highlanders, of the 152nd Brigade, and moved back to the railway embankment.

On May 13th the Battalion marched to Arras, and from thence proceeded in buses to Houvin Houvigneul, six miles south south-east of St. Pol, the strength being 6 officers and 156 other ranks. Captain R. G. Abrahams, R.A.M.C., joined for duty.

On May 14th the details from the Divisional Depôt Battalion rejoined.

On May 15th the Divisional Commander inspected the Battalion, and congratulated them on the part they had taken in the recent operations.

The Corps Commander sent the following message to the General Officer Commanding 4th Division :—

"*Hearty congratulations to you and your Division on their fine work during the last fortnight. Their recent success will result in the capture of positions which have blocked us for the past month.*"

On May 16th, General Allenby, commanding the Third Army, inspected the 10th Infantry Brigade, and expressed his satisfaction at their appearance and congratulated them on their recent performances.

A course of training was commenced on May 17th, attention being paid to gas drill. At this time every officer and man was provided with a box respirator, a P.B. helmet, and a pair of rubber sponge goggles.

The Battalion was employed up to the end of the month in ordinary routine and training, interspersed with sports. A Battalion meeting was held on May 22nd and 23rd, and the Fusiliers obtained second place in a Brigade sports meeting held on May 26th.

On May 25th, General Sir C. Fergusson, commanding the XVII Corps, presented medal ribbons to the following :—

Distinguished Conduct Medal: Company Sergeant-Major R. Neville. Military Medal: 4517 Sergeant J. Hughes, 9810 Corporal C. Robinson, 16971 Private J. Reilly, 10400 Corporal J. Boyd, 9610 Corporal G. H. Powell, 8085 Private P. Bannon, 6175 Private H. Barton.

June, 1917.

On the afternoon of June 1st the 4th Division held a horse show, at which Captain M. J. W. O'Donovan, on "Hill 60," won the jumping competition. The standard attained at these periodical shows was very high. All classes of military vehicles and turn-outs were shown, and there was much rivalry between units. The shows did much to keep up a high standard of cleanliness and efficiency, which won the admiration of our French colleagues.

On June 7th was received the cheering news of the great success of the Second Army at Messines and Wytschaete, when the British exploded the biggest land mine used in the war.

On June 9th, Lieutenant-Colonel Incledon-Webber, D.S.O., took over temporary command of the 10th Infantry Brigade from Brigadier-General A. G. Pritchard, and Major R. B. Neill assumed command of the Battalion, each company of which at this time was formed into two platoons only.

On June 10th the 10th Brigade was paraded for inspection by the Divisional Commander, Major-General the Hon. W. Lambton, who presented the following decorations for gallantry:—

Bar to Military Medal: 6923 Sergeant S. McMillan. Military Medal: 3383 Lance-Corporal G. Irwin, 2741 Lance-Corporal M. Lawless, 11221 Lance-Corporal J. Sweeney. Major A. Low was this day appointed Divisional machine-gun officer.

On June 11th Captain G. W. N. Barefoot and Second-Lieutenant W. D. Bradley left the Battalion to take up their duties on the staff of the Divisional forward area.

Training was continued up to June 12th, when the Battalion left Houvin Houvigneul by bus for Arras, where they billeted north of the cathedral, the strength being 20 officers and 473 other ranks.

On June 17th the Battalion moved to a camp at Blangy Château, east of Arras, where they remained till June 20th, on which day they moved to the Blue line Lancaster and Stirling Camps, in the railway cutting adjacent to the Chemical Works, and the scene of their hard fight on April 11th.

On June 21st Lieutenant-Colonel Incledon-Webber resumed command of the Battalion.

On the night of June 22nd, the Battalion relieved the 1st Battalion Royal Warwickshire Regiment in a section of the front line north of Roeux, and between that place and the railway line. Three companies were in what was called Croft trench, and one in support. "D" Company of the 3rd/4th Queen's Regiment were attached for instruction.

At 10.15 p.m. on June 24th the Battalion carried out a successful raid against the enemy system of organized shell holes in front of our lines, with the object of finding out how he held his lines, and gaining other information. The objective embraced an area of 170 yards by 75 yards, lying about 50 yards due north of the most easterly buildings of the village of Roeux.

The party consisted of Captain G. M. P. Hornidge (in command), Second-Lieutenants N. E. L. Fitt, F. P. Kiely, T. Houston, and about 60 other ranks with two Lewis guns.

The raiders were told off into sections, each section having its allotted task, and moved in two lines, a Lewis gun on each flank. The time allowed for the raid was fifteen minutes. No equipment was worn, but each rifleman carried 35 rounds in his right hand pocket. Box respirators were worn at the alert position, and white bands on both arms.

The artillery barrage was good, and the men, well led, advanced with great dash. The enemy fled from several of his first-line shell holes, but more fighting took place at the second line. Little had been done to improve the shell holes, which were about twelve feet in diameter and in some cases eight feet deep. Enemy reinforcements coming up were dealt with by the Lewis guns, and considerable casualties were inflicted. Five prisoners were secured and brought back. Our casualties were: Second-Lieutenant F. P. Kiely killed, Second-Lieutenant N. E. L. Fitt died in German hands two days later, 5 other ranks wounded, and 9 other ranks reported missing.

Captain G. M. P. Hornidge and Second-Lieutenant T. Houston were awarded the Military Cross, and 10086 Sergeant M. Conway, 10542 Sergeant D. Barry, and 23551 Private P. McAleavey the Military Medal. The last named, who had handled his Lewis gun with skill and gallantry, was unfortunately killed whilst on a working party on the night of July 11th following.

The General Officer Commanding, 4th Division, sent his congratulations the next day.

At 2 a.m. on June 26th, Livens projectors were fired from Croft trench, and that night, after relief by the 10th Lancashire Fusiliers, the Battalion withdrew to Lancaster Camp on the railway.

On June 28th the Battalion moved to Dingwall Camp.

The instructional pamphlets, such as "The Training of a Platoon in the Attack," which were issued this year, were most useful. They were adapted to all formations up to a division, and conduced to the rapid training of units withdrawn exhausted from the line.

This month saw the arrival of the first American soldiers in France.

JULY, 1917.

On July 1st the Battalion completed the construction of a rifle range and bayonet-fighting course in the Roclincourt Valley, north of Arras.

When out of the trenches, all time that could be spared was spent in training. This at first sight may appear unnecessary, but the complicated nature of that training must be borne in mind, and that the personnel were constantly changing. Also young officers were not nearly so highly trained as the old Regular officers. For example, it was found that the matter of writing messages in action had to be thoroughly studied. In this respect the Fusiliers were good, and little information proved valueless on account of the common mistakes of leaving out the time and place.

About this time both the British and the enemy introduced body armour for the use of infantry patrols, etc. The German armour consisted of two layers of steel with a space between them.

On July 4th the Battalion relieved the 1st Royal Warwickshire Regiment in trenches in front of Roeux. Only one battalion of the Brigade was in front line, and two companies only in the fire trenches.

On July 5th Major R. B. Neill left the Battalion, having been selected to command the 2nd Battalion Royal Munster Fusiliers.

On July 8th "A" Company succeeded in establishing a post well forward to the north-east of Roeux. The enemy were holding a line of organized shell holes, and these forward posts were useful to keep him in check.

In addition to active patrolling, there was a good deal of trench mortar activity, and as the enemy had caused considerable annoyance, especially at night, a fight was organized on July 9th and the enemy was severely dealt with. Our casualties were: Second-Lieutenant D. J. Henry and 5 other ranks killed, and 10 other ranks wounded.

On July 10th the Battalion was relieved by the Household Battalion, and became support battalion in their old position at the railway cutting south of Fampoux, except "C" Company, which remained in close support of the Household Battalion. Here the men were employed on working parties.

On July 14th the Divisional Commander inspected the men who took part in the last raid.

On July 16th the Battalion was relieved by the Royal Warwickshire Regiment, and proceeded to Dingwall Camp, near Blangy, just east of Arras, where training was continued.

On July 26th, Captain R. G. Abrahams, R.A.M.C., was compelled to go sick, and was relieved by Captain R. Ryan.

On July 28th the 2nd Seaforth Highlanders were relieved at the railway cutting, one company proceeding to Crump trench. This was probably for the last time, as news was received on July 31st that the 87th were to leave the 4th Division. This was also the opening day of the third great Battle of Ypres, and the initial successes were made known to the troops.

During this month the enemy aircraft, following the British example, and no doubt urged on by the complaints of their infantry, became very active, flying low over the forward trenches and firing on the garrisons. The British aircraft could, of course, not prevent this, and they were dealt with by rifle and machine-gun fire.

AUGUST, 1917.

On August 1st, the Seaforth Highlanders having taken over duty as support battalion at the railway cutting, the Fusiliers moved to Stirling Camp. Two 24 centimetre shell-cases from Roeux were presented to the Mayor of Arras as a token of good feeling. On this day the Irish Fusiliers received orders to entrain at Arras the next day, on transfer to the 36th, or Ulster, Division.

Accordingly, at 9 a.m. on August 2nd, the Divisional Commander visited the Battalion and expressed his extreme regret that they were leaving the 4th Division. This feeling was mutual and only natural, the Battalion having done all its training before the war in the 4th Division, and having served with it throughout the campaign.

In the afternoon the Battalion proceeded to the railway station at Arras, being played there by the pipes of the Seaforth Highlanders, the drums of the Household Battalion, the drums of the Warwickshire Regiment, and the 4th Divisional Band. At the station a large number of senior officers were assembled to bid them farewell, including the Corps Commander (Sir C. Fergusson) and the Divisional Commander (Major-General the Hon. W. Lambton).

The train left Arras at 4.54 p.m., being played out of the station by the pipers of the Seaforth Highlanders, a compliment which was much appreciated. The two battalions had been close friends for many years, the officers being perpetual honorary members of each others' messes, and this friendship had been cemented by three years' close association in the field and in the trenches, the two battalions constantly relieving each other.

The following letter was received from the General Officer Commanding, 4th Divisional Artillery :—

"*I wish to express, on behalf of the officers, non-commissioned officers and men of the 4th Divisional Artillery, our deep regret at the departure of the Royal Irish Fusiliers to another division, after having had the honour of serving with them so long.*

"*The Gunners feel that they are losing a battalion the covering of which has always been an easy and grateful task.*

"*We wish all ranks of the Battalion the best of luck, and hope we may serve together again before long.*

(Sd.) "C. A. SYKES, *Brigadier-General*,
"*Commanding 4th Divisional Artillery.*"

The Irish Fusiliers detrained at Abeele, on the Belgian frontier, at 4 a.m. on August 3rd, and, in heavy rain, marched to camp near Poperinghe, coming under the orders of the 36th Division as divisional troops. The 36th Division belonged to the XIX Corps of the Fifth Army. The Battalion thus commenced the fourth year of the war in their old haunts.

On August 6th the Battalion marched west to Howe Camp, in No. 3 Area, around Watou, and commenced a course of training. The Rev. J. H. McShane, M.C., returned to the 4th Division; he was replaced by the Rev. J. J. Noblett.

On August 8th Major P. E. Kelly left the Battalion, having been selected to command the divisional troops.

Nothing of importance occurred till August 18th, when the Battalion moved to the Winnezeele area to a camp near Droglandt, and was attached to the 109th Infantry Brigade. On August 20th, orders were received that the Ulster Division was to move south and join the IV Corps of the Third Army at Bapaume.

The Battalion left Caestre at 4 p.m. on August 23rd, and detrained at Bapaume at 10 a.m. the next morning, and thence by march route to Barastre, where they came under the orders of the 107th Brigade, the strength being 29 officers and 692 other ranks.

The 107th Brigade were to take over from the South African Brigade what was known as the Trescault sector, about eight miles south-west of Cambrai.

Two battalions were in the line, one in Brigade Reserve at Metz-en-Couture, and one in Divisional Reserve at Ytres.

August 26th being the anniversary of the Battle of Le Cateau, a census was taken of all those who had fought in the battle and were still present with the Battalion. There are 112 names on this roll—6 officers and 106 other ranks—a large proportion of whom were soldiers recovered from wounds.

On August 27th the Battalion moved forward to Neuville, and the next day relieved the 2nd Battalion South African Regiment in Brigade Reserve at Metz-en-Couture. This village had been systematically destroyed by the Germans in their retreat, and the troops were employed in clearing the debris and erecting shelters, and also on working parties in the forward area and trenches.

September, 1917.

On September 3rd the Battalion relieved the 10th Royal Irish Rifles, and part of the 11th Royal Irish Rifles, in the left sub-sector south of Havrincourt, three companies being in the trenches and one in support. This was a quiet sector, and both sides were busy consolidating; but active patrolling took place at night, and there were many minor encounters.

During the night of September 9th they were relieved by the 10th Royal Irish Rifles, and proceeded to Equancourt, where they came into Divisional Reserve, moving by light railway, a luxury to which they were not accustomed.

At 2.45 p.m. on September 12th, the Corps Commander, Lieutenant-General Sir C. L. Woollcombe, K.C.B., inspected the Battalion, and requested the Commanding Officer to make known to all ranks his appreciation of the turn-out and appearance of the men.

On September 15th the Battalion proceeded by light railway to Trescault, and relieved the 10th Royal Irish Rifles in trenches close to that village. The sector was still quiet, with rather more shelling, and, on relief by the same unit, the Fusiliers proceeded to Metz-en-Couture on the night of September 21st.

On September 22nd Major S. U. L. Clements assumed temporary command, Lieutenant-Colonel Incledon-Webber proceeding on leave.

Whilst at Metz-en-Couture the Battalion found large working parties. The village was intermittently shelled, and on September 27th the Battalion lost

6 killed and 7 wounded from heavy gun-fire, and the same night relieved the 10th Royal Irish Rifles in the trenches close to Trescault.

On September 29th, Captain A. E. Thompson was relieved by Captain L. H. Seville in medical charge of the Battalion.

This was an uneventful month in this part of the line, but good news was received of the advance of the Second and Fifth Armies in the Third Battle of Ypres, and the 36th Division was by no means idle. One means of annoying the enemy was a programme of systematic shoots by night on his tender spots. These shoots were carried out not only by the artillery, but by Stokes guns, Vickers guns, and the Lewis guns of the infantry.

In changing from the 4th to the 36th Division, the Fusiliers had changed their divisional sign from a ram's head to the red hand of Ulster. These signs were painted on all vehicles instead of the official title. Some of them were very ingenious, and a collection of these signs would be interesting from an artistic point of view.

October, 1917.

On the 1st of this month, Brigadier-General R. J. Kentish, now in command of the Senior Officers' School at Aldershot, visited the Battalion.

On October 3rd, on being relieved by the 10th Royal Irish Rifles, the Battalion proceeded to Equancourt. The weather, from being fine, now broke, and this gave much work to do in keeping the billets and camps in order, as well as preparations for the coming winter.

On October 5th, in spite of the wet weather, a very enjoyable day was spent at Ruyaulcourt with the 9th Battalion Royal Irish Fusiliers, also belonging to the Ulster Division. Sports were keenly contested, "The Wayfarers" concert party provided an excellent entertainment, and the Battalion returned to their camp at 10 p.m.

On October 8th, Lieutenant-Colonel A. B. Incledon-Webber, who had returned from leave on October 7th, left the Battalion, having been selected to command the 37th Infantry Brigade, with temporary rank of Brigadier-General. He had maintained the Battalion in a high state of efficiency. He bade farewell to the Battalion in the following words:—

"Fusiliers: I have been appointed to command the 37th Infantry Brigade, and leave here this afternoon. I came out with the Battalion in 1914, and, with the exception of fifteen months, have been with it ever since. As far as war can be made pleasant, the pleasantest times that I have spent during the campaign have been with the Battalion. The loyalty, endurance and behaviour of all ranks, both in action and billets, has made my period of command a very pleasant and easy one, and I shall always regard with pride the fact that I have had the honour to command so fine a battalion. In spite of all we have gone through since 1914, the best traditions of the Regiment are maintained, as I trust they

always will be. I wish all ranks the best of luck and all the success they deserve, and I look forward to the time when, this grim business being brought to a satisfactory issue, I may be permitted to return."

Major S. U. L. Clements, who assumed command, led the hearty cheers with which the Battalion received the parting words of their late commander.

The next day the Fusiliers relieved the 10th Royal Irish Rifles in the same sub-sector. The trenches were wet and dirty, and a special issue of rum was made on October 10th. This issue of rum in the trenches, which seems such a small thing when writing in a comfortable house, was looked upon at the time as a real blessing. Efforts were not wanting at one time, by individuals who had no experience of life in the trenches, to do away with the issue of rum. It is quite possible that a cup of hot cocoa would be a much better stimulant, but how was it to be got? The writer can affirm from experience, that the issue of a tot of rum in the early morning, after a night of hard work in the wet and cold of muddy trenches, has kept many a good soldier in the ranks.

After being relieved by the 10th Royal Irish Rifles on October 15th, the Battalion proceeded to Metz-en-Couture, where they were employed as working parties, half the Battalion working by day and the other half by night.

The next tour in the trenches commenced on October 21st, and on the 24th Second-Lieutenant A. C. Watson captured a wounded prisoner of the 84th Infantry Regiment. Second-Lieutenant Watson went out with a patrol, which occupied a German post and was waiting for the enemy to come on. One of the enemy advanced first to reconnoitre, and, becoming suspicious, it was necessary to fire on him. He was wounded and brought in; the remainder of the enemy retired.

However, the next day the enemy was able to cry quits, for a patrol of Fusiliers, consisting of 1 officer and 10 other ranks, after attacking a German post of about 30 men and inflicting casualties on them, lost 3 men while withdrawing to our own lines. Search was made for many hours, but no trace could be found.

October 27th found the Battalion back at Equancourt, and on this day Captain W. A. Foley was severely wounded by a bullet which must have been fired at a range of not less than 2,200 yards. He died five days later, deeply regretted throughout the Battalion.

At 1.30 p.m. on October 31st the Battalion moved to a new camp, near the Bois de Vallulart.

NOVEMBER, 1917.

The night of November 2nd found the Fusiliers again relieving the 10th Royal Irish Fusiliers in the front line. The enemy were now active. An enemy patrol, which attacked one of the sap-heads in front of our line, was driven off, and a wounded prisoner of the 84th Infantry Regiment secured by "C" Company.

Photo by] [Imperial War Museum

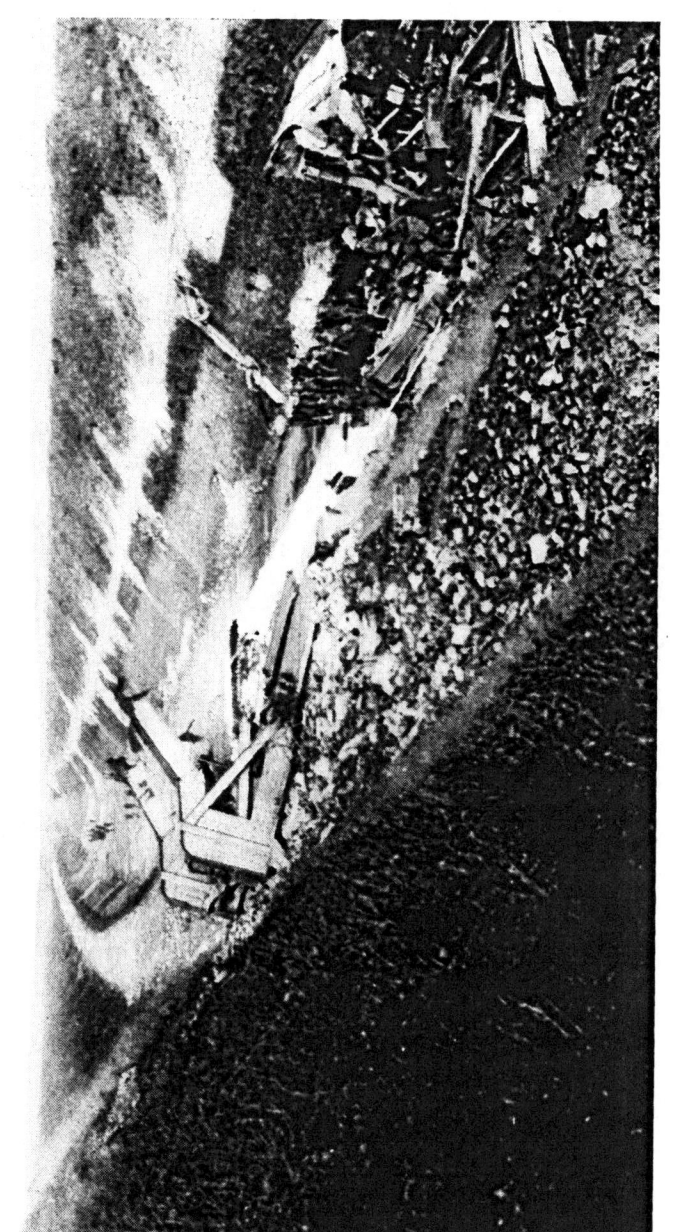

CANAL DU NORD NEAR MOEUVRES, 28-11-17.

The enemy artillery, following our example, bombarded not only the line, but tender spots in rear of it, and on November 3rd the Battalion had 7 men wounded by shell fire at the ration dump. The sap-heads were also bombarded.

On November 4th work was commenced on a support line, which had to be completed in four days.

The Battalion was employed at Metz-en-Couture from November 7th to November 13th, when it again relieved the 10th Royal Irish Rifles, and, subsequently, a portion of the 8/9th Royal Irish Rifles to the north.

During the three following days, parties of officers proceeded north to Demicourt, to view enemy trenches from that place. This was a sure indication of an attack, and in truth, whilst further north the British troops were fighting their way up the Passchendaele Ridge, literally through seas of mud, farther south the troops were about to enter upon the Battle of Cambrai.

On November 17th the Battalion was relieved by the 2nd/7th West Yorkshire Regiment, and proceeded to Metz-en-Couture, but left, by order, eleven men in each of the four saps and what was known as Mons post.

After a night of continuous effort, in which these small posts repulsed all attacks, the enemy, early on the morning of November 18th, having put a box barrage round E sap, succeeded in rushing that post, and six Fusiliers were missing. Later in the day the Battalion moved to a tented camp near Ytres.

On November 19th the Divisional Commander addressed the officers of the 107th Infantry Brigade, and explained the plan for the Battle of Cambrai, which was to commence the next day. The general idea was that the Third Army, in assuming the offensive, should attack with the III Corps on the right and the IV Corps on the left. The attack was to be a surprise, and it was intended to break through with the aid of tanks, and thus create a gap through which the cavalry were to advance in front of the IV Corps and capture Bourlon village and wood, with Cambrai as their second objective. The 107th Brigade were to be in reserve on zero day, and continue the attack on the day following.

Early on November 20th the Fusiliers moved from Ytres to a concentration area near the Slag Heap, south of Hermies, where battle equipment was completed. This movement was completed by 8.30 a.m. Although the attack had been successful, no orders reached the 107th Brigade till 1.30 p.m., when they moved to Square Copse, 1,000 yards west of Havrincourt and close to the Canal du Nord, then under construction. Here the Battalion lay, under very heavy rain, from 3.15 p.m. to 8 p.m., when it marched in rear of the Brigade to old enemy trenches and dug-outs west of Havrincourt. Although the distance was only about two miles, it took seven and a half hours to cover the ground. The night was wet and dark, the bridge over the Canal du Nord only admitted of men passing in single file, and the trenches in the old German lines were almost impassable, on account of mud.

On this day Lieutenant-Colonel M. J. Furnell reached the Details, *en route* to take command of the Battalion.

As Bourlon village had not been captured, the attack which the 107th Brigade was to have made on November 21st did not take place, but the Brigade moved forward at 3.30 p.m. to the old Hindenburg support line, north and south of the Graincourt—Demicourt road. The Fusiliers were again at the rear of the column, and did not reach their position till 8 p.m., marching by compass the last part of the route.

November 22nd was fine. The 15th Royal Irish Rifles, supported by the 10th Royal Irish Rifles, attacked and captured German trenches to the west of Graincourt, then held them against counter-attacks. The Irish Fusiliers, following up this attack, found themselves at 7 p.m. in trenches north of the Bapaume—Cambrai road.

At 10.30 a.m. on November 23rd the 107th Brigade renewed the attack, this time with the aid of eleven tanks, but the tanks made little progress, probably due to the fact that no time had been available for reconnoitring the ground. The 87th, who were still in the trenches east of the Canal du Nord and north of the Bapaume—Cambrai road, were given as an objective an enemy trench running north-east from Lock No. 4 to a point 300 yards north-west of Quarry Wood. The assembly positions were to be a portion of the Hindenburg support line, which faced south on the opposite side of the canal to the village of Moeuvres. The companies were detailed from right to left as follows:— "A," "D," "C." "B" Company, in support, was to move in rear of the centre.

Five tanks were detailed to work with the Battalion, of which two were to deal with Quarry Wood. It will be seen that the direction of the attack was due north.

About 12.30 p.m. the Battalion moved forward towards the assembly positions, but, on coming over a slight rise of ground, they were met by heavy machine-gun fire and rifle fire, and it became evident that not only were the assembly trenches strongly held by the enemy, but that a strong point known as Round trench, in front of the right of the attack, and Lock No. 5 on the left, were also occupied. All these positions were supposed to have been captured by tanks during the morning.

In spite of heavy losses, the Fusiliers proceeded to attack the Round trench and Lock No. 5. Captain and Adjutant Scott, two other officers, and about thirty other ranks, of whom six were wounded, actually succeeded in reaching the wire in front of these posts, but the Battalion withered away under the close and accurate fire of the enemy. Major O'Donovan, who was wounded early in the action, saw the Germans sniping the wounded soldiers as they endeavoured to crawl to the shelter of shell holes, and heard these men shouting to the stretcher-bearers not to come near them. The line was advanced to Round trench and Lock No. 5, and about 10 p.m. the 10th Royal Irish Rifles took over Round trench, and the 8/9th Royal Irish Rifles took over Lock No. 5.

The casualties in this attack were 8 officers and 225 other ranks. Lieutenant-

Nº IX

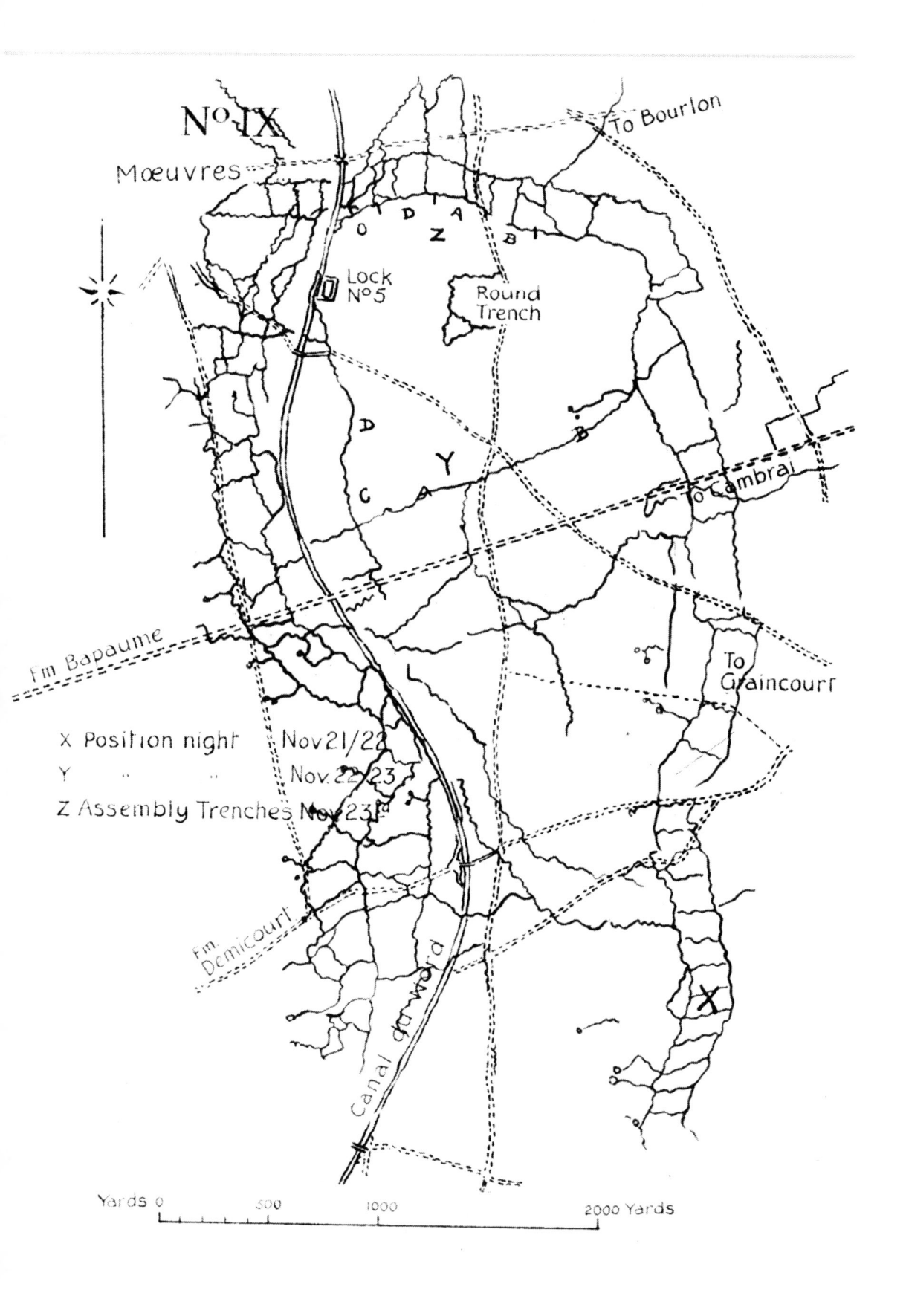

Mœuvres

To Bourlon

Lock Nº 5

Round Trench

To Cambrai

Fm Bapaume

To Graincourt

X Position night Nov 21/22
Y   "   "   Nov 22/23
Z Assembly Trenches Nov 23rd

Fm Demicourt

Canal du Nord

Yards 0   500   1000   2000 Yards

Colonel Clements was wounded, but remained at duty. Major O'Donovan was a very serious loss to the Battalion. It was in this action that Captain and Adjutant W. Scott earned the Distinguished Service Order.

At 1 a.m. on November 24th, a conference of commanding officers was held at Brigade headquarters, with a view to renewing the attack. With this object the Battalion relieved the Royal Irish Rifles in trenches 2,000 yards east southeast of Moeuvres. The attack was to be launched at 3.30 p.m., this time with artillery preparation, but, probably owing to the difficulties of co-ordination, the barrages were not effective, strong points were not dealt with, and the barrage continued for forty minutes after zero hour, causing casualties to be inflicted on our own troops. Consequently, the Battalion, which was now reduced to below 200 of all ranks, did not attack.

November 25th was again wet. Orders were received to consolidate, and this was done, the trenches being deepened by two feet.

On November 26th the Battalion was relieved by a company of the 1st King's Royal Rifle Corps, and moved to the Slag Heap, north of Hermies. It was a very rough night, with sleet and wind. The move was not complete till 4 a.m. on November 27th.

During these first days of the Battle of Cambrai, the Battalion suffered the following casualties: Killed, 1 officer and 130 other ranks; wounded, 8 officers and 201 other ranks; missing, 1 officer and 5 other ranks; total, 346. This was more than any other unit in the Brigade. Second-Lieutenant A. C. Watson and the Rev. Father Donohoe especially distinguished themselves during this period.

On the evening of November 27th, the 107th Brigade, after being relieved by the 99th Brigade, concentrated in camps about Barastre.

On November 28th orders were received for the Brigade to move to the Fosseux area.

At 9.45 a.m. on November 9th the Battalion entrained at Ytres, for Rivière, from whence it marched north to billets at Berneville, south-west of Arras.

November 30th was spent in the inevitable task of reorganizing the Battalion. But there was to be little rest. The enemy could not take the bold attack of the Third Army lying down, and was already making his counter-stroke felt. Orders were received that the 107th Brigade were to be prepared to move back to the line at the shortest notice, and early in the afternoon definite orders were received to proceed, via Wailly and Moyenneville, to Courcelles-le-Comte, and by 12 midnight, November 30th—December 1st, the whole of the Brigade was concentrated at the latter place.

December, 1917.

On December 1st the 36th Division was transferred to the V Corps, and the 107th Brigade continued its march back to the line, via Achiet-le-Grand to Beaulencourt, south-east of Bapaume.

On December 2nd the march was continued, via Le Transloy, Rocquigny and Bus, to Lechelle, and the next day to Divisional Reserve trenches about three quarters of a mile east of Trescault, the weather being very cold, but dry. The details went to Manancourt.

On December 8th the 107th Brigade relieved the 109th Brigade in the right Brigade sector, the Irish Fusiliers relieving the 9th Inniskilling Fusiliers in Brigade Reserve about one mile south-east of Ribecourt, where they were employed up to December 13th on working parties.

Owing to the numerical weakness of the Battalion, it was formed into two companies, and two companies of the 10th Royal Irish Rifles were attached, the composite battalion thus formed being under command of Lieutenant-Colonel M. J. Furnell, and this battalion, on the night of December 13th, relieved the 11/13th Royal Irish Rifles in trenches about three quarters of a mile south of Marcoing. This was an outpost position, and some of the posts were isolated. It was under orders of the 108th Brigade, and the Composite Battalion remained under the orders of the 108th Brigade till it rejoined the 107th Brigade on December 18th.

Meanwhile, the 36th Division was being relieved by the 63rd Division, and on the night of December 16th the Fusiliers were relieved by the 1st/4th King's Shropshire Light Infantry, and proceeded to billets in Metz-en-Couture. The 107th Brigade group was moving to the Etricourt area, and, apparently, the transfer of the 36th Division to the V Corps did not take effect till the completion of the moves, but they were to come under the orders of the III Corps.

On December 17th the 87th marched to Etricourt, where the details and transport rejoined.

On December 18th the Battalion moved by train to Mondicourt, and marched from there to Ivergny, six miles north of Doullens. The transport, which moved by road, did not rejoin till December 20th, the roads being much blocked by snow. A short march was made on December 20th to Sus St. Leger, where the Battalion remained till December 27th, being employed in clearing the roads. The men were given dinners on Christmas Day in the estaminets.

On December 26th intimation was received that the 36th Division was to be transferred from the III Corps command, in the Third Army, to the XVIII Corps, in the Fifth Army. Accordingly, on December 27th, the Battalion marched to Mondicourt and entrained for Corbie, and, on arrival at that place, went into billets at Fouilloy, just south of that place, where they were busy training till the end of the year, the weather continuing very cold.

CHAPTER V—1918.

January, 1918.

The beginning of 1918 found the Battalion still at Fouilloy, south of Corbie, sadly depleted after their experiences in the Battle of Cambrai, but busy reconstructing the Battalion, special attention being paid to the training of specialists, which by this time formed a considerable portion of the unit. The hard weather continued, but this was not allowed to interfere with route marching and games calculated to keep all ranks fit and ready for the next effort.

On January 7th, the 36th Division having been again warned for duty in the line, the 87th marched to Vauvillers, via Villers Bretonneux and Harbonnières.

On January 9th the Battalion continued its march, via Chaulnes and Nesle, to Voyennes, where they obtained good billets, very different to the short halt at this place in the early morning of August 28th, 1914, on the retreat from Le Cateau. Here training was continued till January 11th, when the 36th Division moved forward into the area of the French III Corps. The 87th marched, via Matigny and St. Sulpice, to Fluquières and Roupy, on the St. Quentin—Ham road. This day the weather broke and changed to rain.

On January 12th, the 87th, reinforced by one company of the 10th Royal Irish Rifles, relieved the 1st Battalion of the French 24th Regiment in the left sub-sector of the line south of St. Quentin. The French were most friendly; they provided guides on the eastern outskirts of Roupy, and also entertained the officers to lunch and dinner. Trench stores were taken over from the French, and their artillery continued to cover the sector till the night of January 16th/17th. They also left details in the line for twenty-four hours. This was a very quiet sector, but, as the trenches were not revetted, they became bad on account of the wet weather.

The Battalion was relieved by the 10th Royal Irish Rifles on January 18th, and again relieved this unit on January 24th. During this tour in the trenches the Battalion captured two German prisoners of war who had escaped from a French prisoners' camp at Roye.

The Battalion was again relieved by the 10th Royal Irish Rifles on January 30th, and became Brigade Reserve. During the month the Battalion received a welcome reinforcement of 295 other ranks. Already there were rumours of a great German offensive.

February, 1918.

Up to February 5th the Battalion was employed on working parties, and on that night relieved the 10th Royal Irish Rifles in the trenches, but only remained one night, as they proceeded to Brigade Reserve on the night of February 7th.

The reason for this was that the number of battalions in a British infantry brigade was being reduced from four to three, and the 87th were under orders to proceed to the 108th Brigade, in place of the 2nd Royal Irish Rifles, who exchanged to the 107th Brigade.

Accordingly the 87th moved, on February 8th, to the reserve position of the 108th Brigade at Essigny Station, the 108th Brigade being on the right of the 107th Brigade, and consisting of, besides the 87th, the 12th Royal Irish Rifles and the 9th (North Irish Horse) Royal Irish Fusiliers, under command of Brigadier-General R. J. Griffith, C.B., C.M.G., D.S.O.

On February 9th the Battalion relieved the 9th (North Irish Horse) Royal Irish Fusiliers in the support line.

On February 11th the 87th received a draft of 9 officers and 241 other ranks from the 7/8th Royal Irish Fusiliers, on the reduction of that battalion.

On February 15th the Battalion relieved the 12th Royal Irish Rifles in the right sub-sector of the Brigade line, and on February 16th took over an extra piece of the line from the 8th Rifle Brigade, of the 41st Infantry Brigade.

The Battalion front consisted of about 1,700 yards, a large extent of ground for one unit to hold; in consequence, it was held as an outpost line. The right rested on a wood known as Dragon Wood, lying to the east of the St. Quentin —Vendeuil road, and north of the Itancourt—Urvillers road; thence it ran slightly north of west along the high ground south of the valley which terminates at the village of Grugies.

As this was the sector in which the Battalion was stationed when the enemy made his great effort in the following month, it will be well to consider the principles on which the defence was organized. It was unfortunate that just at this time it should have been found necessary to reduce the infantry of the British Expeditionary Force by one quarter. The three battalions allotted to an infantry brigade did not admit, in this instance, of two men per yard of the front to be held. Distribution was in depth, one battalion being detailed for the forward (or outpost) zone, of which two companies were in the outpost line, one company counter-attack company, and one company passive resistance company. Farther to the rear, one battalion occupied the battle zone, which was strengthened with field redoubts; and, still further to the rear, was the third battalion, in reserve. This system came into force on February 22nd, when the Irish Fusiliers handed over a portion of the outpost line to the 15th Royal Irish Rifles. It was well known to the troops by this time that the Germans were preparing for a great offensive, but they awaited it with the habitual calm of the British soldier, and were at least as much concerned with a new educational scheme which was launched from Headquarters about this time.

On February 23rd the Battalion was relieved by the 12th Royal Irish Rifles, and moved back into the battle zone, with headquarters at Essigny Station, where a great deal of work was done on entrenchments.

Up to the end of the month the Battalion was employed in strengthening the defences, and from this time great activity was noticed behind the enemy lines. The success of the enemy in other theatres of war, and, notably, the collapse of Russia, enabled him to augment greatly his armies on the western front, and it was known that very large additions had been made to his artillery.

On February 28th the strength of the Battalion was 51 officers and 1,195 other ranks, but it must be borne in mind that considerable numbers, both of officers and men, were absent from headquarters on various duties, courses, leave, etc.

March, 1918.

On March 1st the Fusiliers relieved the 12th Royal Irish Rifles in the forward zone, thus holding the right of the 36th Division at the bend in the line north of Urvillers, the 41st Brigade being on their right and the 107th Brigade on their left. At 1.50 p.m. on March 1st, the Germans, apparently under the impression that our lines were not held, advanced two patrols of 20 to 30 men each, one against Sphinx Wood, on the right of the Battalion, and one against a ruined house on the Vendeuil road, on the left of the Battalion. They were scattered by fire, and our patrols, advancing into the open, captured 1 non-commissioned officer and 3 men near Sphinx Wood, and 1 officer and 3 men near the ruined house.

On March 6th the Battalion was relieved by the 9th (North Irish Horse) Royal Irish Fusiliers, and proceeded to billets at Grand Séraucourt.

As "Barrosa" Day had been spent in the line, leave was obtained to celebrate it on March 11th, when several guests were entertained, and the men had a holiday.

On March 15th the Battalion relieved the 12th Royal Irish Rifles in the dug-outs about Essigny Station, and became garrison for the battle zone, the 12th Royal Irish Rifles being in the forward area and the 9th (North Irish Horse) Royal Irish Fusiliers in reserve.

Up to March 20th, inclusive, the sector was a very quiet one. There were, of course, the usual bursts of artillery fire, and aircraft were active on both sides, the enemy doing a good deal of night-bombing in back areas, but otherwise there was a calm well understood by all. It was on March 20th that the troops were officially warned of a German attack being expected the next morning.

The night of March 20th/21st was very quiet, the stillness being only broken by the British artillery shelling places likely for the assembly of enemy troops.

As daylight broke the whole country was shrouded in mist, so thick that it was not possible to distinguish objects at a few yards distance.

It was at 4.30 a.m. that the stillness was suddenly broken by the commencement of a terrific bombardment by artillery of all calibres and trench mortars, in which a good proportion of gas shells was employed, especially against artillery positions.

The writer was at this time at the remains of Nobescourt Farm, not far from Roisel, the farm which the 87th had placed in a state of defence the day after Le Cateau. The thunder of the bombardment, enhanced by the stillness of the air and thick mist, was indescribable, perhaps sublime is the word most appropriate.

The long-expected German offensive had begun, and the troops of the Fifth Army braced themselves to meet it. Much has been said and written about the Fifth Army, but there is no doubt that these troops, largely outnumbered and in face of an enemy who was greatly aided by the morning mists which continued for some days, played an heroic rôle in this great battle. This fact becomes more and more evident as the narratives of the various units are made public.

By 5 a.m. all communications with the 12th Royal Irish Rifles in the forward area were cut. It was impossible to repair them in such a storm of shells, and the exceptionally thick mist precluded the use of visual signalling. This gallant battalion fought on to the end, and sacrificed itself in delaying the enemy infantry attacks, which surged forward like huge waves, overwhelming the isolated defended posts like sand castles on the beach.

From now on Brigade headquarters was dependant for information on reports from the 1st Royal Irish Fusiliers. A summary of these reports gives the following narrative of the progress of the fight.

At 7.30 a.m. the Battalion were in their battle positions, with headquarters in Station Redoubt. A few minutes later a heavy barrage was put down on the railway cutting and the redoubts near Essigny Station.

At 12.25 p.m. the message reporting that the enemy had broken through the forward zone was received at Brigade headquarters.

At 12.47 rifle fire was reported in front of the left company, and at 1.5 p.m. the enemy were reported attacking the battle zone in force.

At this time the line of redoubts was intact, and was repelling assaulting troops with great gallantry. The Battalion also reported at this time that the 41st Brigade, on their right, had been forced back slightly, but that they, the Irish Fusiliers, were holding out.

About 1 p.m. the fog lifted, and it was then seen that the right of the Battalion was completely turned, and that the troops on the right were withdrawing south of Essigny. Indeed, at this time the enemy was endeavouring to force his way up the railway cutting from the south, but was kept in check by Lewis-gun fire.

At 2.30 p.m. the enemy were in Fay Farm, one and a half miles south of Essigny, and well in rear of the position held by the Fusiliers.

And so the day wore on. Considering his distinct advantages, the enemy's success had not been great on the front held by the 108th Brigade. But at 6.40 p.m. the enemy had seized the quarries, 1,500 yards north-east of Grand Seraucourt. The Battalion was thus in danger of being completely surrounded. But they fought on.

At 8.45 p.m. orders were received from Brigade headquarters to withdraw west of the St. Quentin Canal, and this was carried out during the hours of darkness, without serious molestation.

So far as the 108th Brigade is concerned, the result of the first day's fighting was largely due to the following tactical consideration.

It will be remembered that the front of the 36th Division faced almost due north, and that the 1st Royal Irish Fusiliers were in that sector which formed the angle at which the line bent southward. Here was the head of the above-mentioned Grugies Valley, running nearly east and west and forming excellent cover from view, but at the same time an avenue of approach should the enemy force an entrance to the south of the 36th Division. Moreover, the line of advance of the attackers was from east to west, and thus on the flank of the 36th Division.

This is exactly what happened, and there is no doubt that the 12th Royal Irish Rifles were first attacked by enemy troops, who, having forced an entrance further south, advanced eastward down the Grugies Valley. As the enemy attack progressed to the southward, the same thing happened in the battle zone held by the Royal Irish Fusiliers, and, as the troops were tied down in small bodies to their defended posts, they were surrounded and overwhelmed by superior numbers.

The casualties reported on this day were: Killed, 10 other ranks; wounded, 1 officer and 55 other ranks; missing, 9 officers and 275 other ranks, a large proportion of those reported missing being killed and wounded.

The 1st Royal Irish Fusiliers crossed the canal at Grand Seraucourt and took up a position about Happencourt, the 108th Brigade being ordered to hold a line from half-way between Tugny and Artemps to the cemetery at Happencourt.

The bridges over the canal were blown up by the Royal Engineers, who behaved in a most gallant manner.

This line was held, in spite of heavy artillery and trench-mortar bombardment, but, in consequence of the enemy's break through farther north, the 36th Division were ordered to recross the Somme Canal, and form a defensive flank facing north. This was done, and, after dark on March 22nd, the 1st Royal Irish Fusiliers were in position about Sommette Eaucourt, with the 9th (North Irish Horse) Royal Irish Fusiliers on their right. Both these battalions were now reduced to about 250 men. The 12th Royal Irish Rifles had disappeared, having carried out their orders and fought to the last in the forward zone. The morning of March 23rd was again foggy, and soon after dawn the enemy captured Ham and advanced on Brouchy, to the left rear of the position held by the 1st Royal Irish Fusiliers. At 10 a.m. he was reported on the right rear. By 2 p.m. it became necessary to draw back the left flank, which now rested on Brouchy, but by 8 p.m. the enemy had captured Cugny, almost due east of Brouchy, and the front of the 36th Division had been forced into the shape of an acute angle, pointing northwards, the 1st Royal Irish Fusiliers being near the point. During this day's fighting the Battalion suffered about 100 more casualties, amongst these Captain and Adjutant W. Scott, D.S.O., M.C., who was wounded and had to be evacuated. The loss of so excellent a staff officer at such a time was keenly felt.

The night was fairly quiet, and the enemy did not renew the attack in the morning, but during the night he had occupied Golancourt, thus again threatening the left flank, or rather western face of the triangle. It was not till 11 a.m. on March 24th that the Germans renewed their attack in force, but they did so in such numbers as to drive the British troops southwards to the village of Villeselve, on to French troops who were now coming up in support. After severe fighting the enemy succeeded in entering the village, but were driven back by a gallant charge of cavalry of the 3rd Cavalry Division, which the remnants of the 1st Royal Irish Fusiliers, with their comrades of the 9th Battalion, followed cheering, and about 150 prisoners were taken. But the enemy were too strong, and eventually the British were driven to the north of Berlancourt, which the enemy shelled heavily at 9 p.m. The 108th Brigade, covered by the 9th (North Irish Horse) Royal Irish Fusiliers, withdrew to Crisolles, where the troops were reorganized, and at 11 p.m. the 36th Division came under the orders of the 62nd French Division, and eventually withdrew to Sermaize, where some rest was obtained.

At 9.30 a.m. on March 25th the 108th Brigade marched northwards to Beaulieu, and then west to Avriecourt, in hopes of rest, but at 5 p.m. they set out for Erches, which was not reached till 2 a.m. on March 26th, where six hours sleep was obtained.

It is useless to attempt to describe the appearance of the troops on this march, in their worn-out state, or the sad plight of the French civilians, young and old. Only those who have witnessed these spectacles can realize the misery.

At 10 a.m. on March 26th the 108th Brigade took up a position facing north-east, between the villages of Andechy and Erches, the 1st Royal Irish Fusiliers advancing to the former village. They were without artillery support. At 11 a.m. the 1st Royal Irish Fusiliers came under machine-gun fire, and at 1 p.m. the enemy appeared in force. So rapid was his advance that Brigadier-General Griffith was wounded in fighting his way clear, and the Commanding Officer of the 1st Royal Irish Fusiliers who, with the G.S.O.1 of the Division and Major J. G. Brew of the 9th Battalion, was returning to the front in a motor car from a conference, ran into a party of enemy troops and was taken prisoner.

All day long the soldiers of the 1st Royal Irish Fusiliers, acting with the greatest steadiness, repulsed the attacks of the enemy, but by 8 p.m. the enemy launched his main attack, and having captured the village of Guerbigny, directly in rear, the Battalion was surrounded. Nevertheless, they held out, and, so far as can be ascertained, it was not before 11.20 a.m. on March 27th that they were finally overwhelmed. Of those who were present at Andechy, only 1 officer and 19 other ranks got away. This sacrifice was not in vain. Like the isolated bodies of infantry in the Battle of Le Cateau, and the 12th Royal Irish Rifles in the forward zone on March 21st, they had served to stem and to delay the greatly superior forces of the enemy.

Lieutenant-Colonel S. U. L. Clements, D.S.O., who was in command of the Battalion at Andechy, had been told by the Brigade-Major of the 109th Infantry Brigade that he, Lieutenant-Colonel Clements, was expected to hold on for twenty-four hours, to enable the French to detrain at Montdidier.

Lieutenant-Colonel Clements made several attempts to procure food and ammunition, which were not forthcoming, and, when the remnants of the Battalion were finally surrounded, they were without food or ammunition and were completely isolated, the troops on their left having withdrawn. The messengers sent to inform Lieutenant-Colonel Clements of this withdrawal failed to reach him.

North of the Regiment, the remains of the 1st and 2nd Battalions Royal Irish Rifles, under an Irish Fusiliers officer, Lieutenant-Colonel McCarthy-O'Leary, did gallant work. This officer was twice wounded.

The value of the resistance of the troops in the neighbourhood of Andechy was specially mentioned by the Commander-in-Chief in his despatches.

On the morning of March 28th the remains of the 36th Division were near Sourdan, and at 8 a.m. the remnants of the 108th Brigade, now numbering 14 officers and 321 other ranks, were sent to Couillemelle to cover the British and French artillery, the enemy having captured Montdidier. But the German attack had reached its high-water mark, and troops sent to Cantigny, east of Couillemelle, found French troops solidly established.

On the march to Taisnil, which was resumed at midnight, March 29th, the tired troops had the satisfaction of meeting heavy columns of French moving forward.

On March 30th the 108th Brigade moved to Saleux, where it entrained at 5 a.m. on March 31st and proceeded to Eu, via Gamaches, and, on detrainment, the 1st Royal Irish Fusiliers marched to Ault.

On March 31st the total strength of the Battalion was 22 officers and 461 other ranks, showing that the casualties during the month were 29 officers and 734 other ranks. The reader is again reminded that the total strength is that of the whole Battalion in France, not of those actually present with the unit.

Thus ended the First Battle of the Somme, 1918, so far as the 87th were concerned. A peculiar trait in the character of the British fighting-man was much in evidence during this German victory—I mean the infinite capacity to take everything as in the day's march. Curiously enough, the only Battalion order available for the month of March is that for the 20th, the day before the great attack, when, it will be remembered, the troops were warned. From this order it is impossible to detect anything out of the ordinary—the customary duties, working parties, and bathing parties are detailed as usual. On another part of the front the writer saw troops of a division in retreat—the line had been broken, these men showed no signs of fear; there was no hurry; except that they were not, of course, in formed bodies, they might have been returning from a field day. Certainly, every man was not a hero, but the troops were not beaten troops, and they undoubtedly looked upon the retreat as a temporary reverse only.

In their new quarters on the coast, it was hoped that the 36th Division would have time to reorganize and train for their next effort. How short that time was will be seen in the diary for the month which follows.

APRIL, 1918.

On April 1st the Battalion was commanded by Captain N. E. V. Dicks, M.C. How weak it was will be realized when it is stated that the fighting portion of the 108th Brigade, including transport, was only a little over 300. But during this month heavy drafts were received. These were mostly very young and partially-trained soldiers, but right well did they carry on the traditions of the Regiment.

Preparations for refitting were in progress, when orders were received to proceed by rail to the Ypres Salient. The Battalion entrained at Eu on April 3rd, and detrained at Rexpoede at 2 a.m. on April 4th and marched to billets at Herzeele, nine miles to the west of Poperinghe.

On April 6th, the Battalion, with other units, was inspected by the commander of the II Corps, and Captain H. A. MacMullen, M.C., on return from leave, assumed command.

On April 9th the Germans began what is known officially on the British side as the Battle of Messines. At Givenchy the British held well, but farther north the line was broken, and Armentières fell. This was followed by Estaires, and, later on, Bailleul. And yet, on the whole, this great assault was a German failure.

The Allies had now an asset which they had not previously enjoyed. The Allied armies were directed by one man, Marshal Foch, and therefore co-ordination and mutual support were not only better, but much quicker in materializing.

The 108th Brigade were placed at the disposal of the II Corps, and on this date proceeded by metre-gauge railway to Poperinghe, and suffered considerable casualties when detraining, as the enemy was shelling the station. They proceeded to Siege Camp, south-east of Elverdinghe, where they were in Corps Reserve. At 12 noon on April 10th the 108th Brigade received orders to proceed forthwith by bus, via La Clytte, to Kemmel, under orders of the 19th Division, the Battalion taking over huts and trenches on the Kemmel—Lindenhoek road.

At 12.30 a.m. on April 11th, orders were received to proceed to Messines. The 1st Royal Irish Fusiliers took up a position on the Messines—Wytschaete road between Four Huns' Farm and the Pick-house, with the South African Brigade on their left, where they were heavily shelled. At 3.30 p.m. the enemy attacked in force, and at first met with some success, but a gallant charge of Fusiliers and South Africans drove him back with loss. The General Officer Commanding, 19th Division, sent the following message: "Heartiest congratulations to 108th Brigade, Royal Irish Fusiliers, and South Africans, on their fine success."

At 7 p.m. the attack was renewed with heavy bombardment, and the Battalion reported that troops on their left had been driven back, but that they were holding on, and intended to do so. But at 8.40 p.m. the enemy had gained possession of Hill 63, to the south, and well known to the Battalion in the winter of 1914-15. The right flank was thus turned, and they were being fired into from that direction. So, although they had been supported by two companies of the 12th Royal Irish Rifles, they withdrew by order to a north and south line east of Wulverghem, which was reached by 4 a.m. the next day.

April 12th was fairly quiet, but the Battalion had lost so heavily that it was organized in one company and attached to the 9th Royal Irish Fusiliers, under Lieutenant-Colonel P. E. Kelly.

At 6.40 p.m. the enemy renewed the attack, but were repulsed by a charge led by Lieutenant-Colonel Kelly, the men leaving their trenches and meeting the enemy as he advanced. Captain C. Drew and Second-Lieutenant M. W. Taylor, M.C., were killed, and Captain MacMullen was again wounded. The line remained intact.

April 13th was a day of desultory fighting, in which the enemy made minor attacks, all of which were repulsed. But in the evening news arrived from the right that the enemy was in Neuve Eglise, and thus that flank was again threatened. It was a repetition of the Somme battle.

The following message was received from the Corps Commander:—

"*IX Corps Commander wishes to congratulate all ranks on the magnificent fighting qualities which they are displaying under arduous conditions against heavy odds. Reinforcements are coming up to our assistance, and the enemy has suffered heavy losses in his attempt to break through the British Armies.*"

At 12.30 a.m. the 9th Royal Irish Fusiliers, including the 87th, were relieved by the 7th Battalion Sherwood Foresters and withdrew to Kemmel shelters, but they had little rest. At 11.45 a.m. they were ordered forward again, the 1st Royal Irish Fusiliers being sent to Beehive dug-outs, about 1,500 yards north of Wulverghem, in close support of the front line. Although no infantry assault was delivered this day, the enemy bombardment was intense.

At 5.30 a.m. on April 15th the continuous bombardment was followed up by attack, and the left of the line was driven back a few hundred yards. The 87th and men of the 12th Royal Irish Rifles, under Major Holt-Waring, who was killed, succeeded in stopping the advance, but failed to drive the enemy back.

Congratulatory messages were received this day from the Army, Corps, and Divisional Commanders.

On April 16th the 108th Brigade, still under orders of the 19th Division, withdrew to reserve at Clydesdale Camp, about 1,200 yards east of La Clytte.

Little rest was obtained on April 17th, for the enemy shelled the camp all day, and the troops had to seek what shelter they could in the neighbouring ditches.

At midnight, April 17th/18th, orders were received to form the remains of the 108th Brigade, now numbering about 400 rifles, into a composite battalion, under Lieutenant-Colonel P. E. Kelly, and they were sent back to Kemmel Hill. Here the 87th alone suffered 45 casualties from shell fire, and Captain Despard, of the 9th Royal Irish Fusiliers, the sole remaining captain of the Brigade, was killed. All day the men suffered heavy shell fire, and at 8.30 p.m. were withdrawn. The French were arriving in force, and had taken over the Kemmel defences.

The remnants of the Brigade marched all night to rejoin the 36th Division, the 1st Royal Irish Fusiliers arriving at Hôpital Farm, south-west of Elverdinghe, at 5.30 a.m. on April 19th.

If the reader will study the times and movements noted in the above narrative, he cannot fail to be impressed with the fact that few soldiers, and especially such young soldiers, can ever have been through such an ordeal and come through it with better credit to themselves.

On April 19th, Major T. A. Lowe, M.C., 2nd Royal Irish Regiment, took command of the Battalion, strength, 2 officers and about 60 other ranks, Captain N. E. V. Dicks, M.C., from the details, assuming the duties of adjutant. A large draft was received, and companies were reorganized, all being under command of second-lieutenants.

On April 20th the Divisional Commander addressed the Battalion.

Fighting now gave place to digging new lines of defence west of the canal, and at the same time all the intricate details of refitting had to be attended to.

On April 26th, Mount Kemmel having fallen and the enemy having made progress towards Locre and La Clytte, the 108th Brigade were ordered to man their defences, the 1st Royal Irish Fusiliers occupying the Green (or outpost) line south of Elverdinghe. The remainder of the Brigade were in the Yellow

A MESSAGE FROM H.M. THE QUEEN

line, or line of resistance. The 41st Division were on the right of the 87th, and the 1st Battalion Carabineers (Belgian Army) were on their left.

The remainder of the month was spent in working on the outpost line, and in training.

The following letter from Her Majesty the Queen is doubtlessly a treasured possession in many homes:—

"*Windsor Castle.*

"*To the men of the Navy, Army and Air Force:*

"*I send this message to tell every man how much we, the women of the British Empire at home, watch and pray for you during the long hours of these days of stress and endurance.*

"*Our pride in you is immeasurable, our hope unbounded, our trust absolute. You are fighting in the cause of Righteousness and Freedom, fighting to defend the children and women of our land from the horrors that have overtaken other countries, fighting for our very existence as a people at home and across the seas. You are offering your all, you hold back nothing, and day by day you show a love so great that no man can have greater. We, on our part, send forth with full hearts and unfaltering will the lives we hold most dear. We, too, are striving in all ways possible to make the war victorious. I know that I am expressing what is felt by thousands of wives and mothers when I say that we are determined to help one another in keeping your homes ready against your glad home-coming. In God's name we bless you, and by His help we, too, will do our best.*

"MARY R.

"*April 26th, 1918.*"

May, 1918.

On May 1st the 87th were relieved in the outpost line by the 12th Royal Irish Rifles, and went back to Border Camp for work on the main line of defence in the new system of trenches, the routine being one company at training and three companies working.

On May 5th Lieutenant A. E. McM. Cuming, M.C., rejoined from the 107th Brigade, where he had done excellent work as intelligence officer, and was appointed scout officer. The next day, Captain C. C. Canning, 11/13th Royal Irish Rifles, joined the Battalion, and was appointed adjutant. On May 8th the Battalion was ordered to select twenty men per company for attachment to the 9th (North Irish Horse) Royal Irish Fusiliers, and on May 10th the Battalion relieved the 9th Battalion in the Green line (outposts), and up to May 17th did one hour's training and five hours' working daily.

Sir Oliver Nugent, in giving up command of the 36th Division, which he had held so long, published the following farewell order:—

"*I want you to wish officers and men the best of luck and honour. The spirit of discipline and self-respect, the determination to win and the pride of race which is our birthright, have made us unconquerable up to now, and will surely give us the final victory. Good-bye, and good fortune to you and your command."*

On the night of May 17th the Battalion again went into the line, relieving the 15th Royal Irish Rifles in the left sub-sector north of Wieltje, in the neighbourhood of the famous Mouse-trap Farm, known in the Second Battle of Ypres as Death-trap Farm. The relief was complete by 1.30 a.m. on May 18th, the 87th having the 18th (Belgian) Brigade on their left. The line was comparatively quiet, but Mouse-trap Farm had a special attraction for the German gunners.

On May 20th Lieutenant Cuming captured a German sergeant-major single-handed, for which he received the Military Cross.

On May 21st Brigadier-General Griffith handed over command of the 108th Brigade to Brigadier-General E. Vaughan, D.S.O.

On this day the 87th are given credit for raiding an enemy strong point near Juliet Farm and securing identification in the person of an acting sergeant-major, 84th Landwehr Infantry Regiment, with a loss of only 1 missing and 2 slightly wounded, but this is not mentioned in the Battalion war diary.

The Battalion held a post on the road 600 yards north north-east of Mouse-trap Farm, known as O.W. Test Point because the signal service had formerly used it as a test point for their wires. At 10.20 p.m. on May 23rd the enemy put a box barrage on this post, and at 10.30 p.m. a party of between 20 and 30 Germans were seen coming from Cheddar Villa, farther south. The garrison of the post drove them off with rifle fire and grenades, and four men were seen to fall. Our casualties were 2 other ranks killed, Acting-Captain R. G. Stirling and 13 other ranks wounded during the bombardment.

On May 27th a party of two officers (Lieutenant A. E. McM. Cuming, M.C., and Second-Lieutenant J. Dixon, M.M.) and No. 5 Platoon raided another strong point, but the enemy fled.

On May 29th the Battalion was relieved by the 2nd Royal Irish Rifles, and entrained at Zouave Siding, north of Ypres, for Steentje Camp, about mid-way between Poperinghe and Elverdinghe, the Brigade being in reserve.

JUNE, 1918.

The Battalion, which now numbered 28 officers and 824 other ranks, was about to enjoy a period of peace and training, which was badly wanted, to fit it for the strenuous times still to come. The 108th Brigade was relieved in Divisional Reserve by a Belgian brigade, and proceeded to training camps in the vicinity of Proven.

On June 2nd the Battalion was inspected by Major-General C. Coffin, V.C., C.B., D.S.O., the new Divisional Commander, who presented the following ribbons :—

Military Cross : Lieutenant A. E. McM. Cuming, D.C.M. ; 8740 Company

Photo by] [*Imperial War Museum*

SCENE IN YPRES SALIENT, 15-2-18.

Sergeant-Major C. Jones. Second bar to Military Medal: 20165 Lance-Corporal W. M. M. McCall.

On June 3rd, the Battalion, having been relieved by the 2nd Battalion (Belgian) Grenadiers, moved to Pekin Camp, where they were employed on the defence lines east of Poperinghe, there being four distinct lines of trenches between Ypres and Poperinghe.

On June 13th the Battalion moved to Road Camp, where training was continued, and on June 14th the 108th Brigade was inspected by General Sir Herbert Plumer, commanding Second Army, and Lieutenant-General Sir Claud Jacob, commanding II Corps.

On June 19th an assault at arms was held.

On the same day the 87th moved still farther west for musketry training, one half going to Mont des Recollets, just east of Cassel, and the other half still further west to Rubrouck. They returned to Road Camp on June 24th, and the next day entrained at Proven for Cormette musketry camp, west of St. Omer, whence they returned to Pekin Camp, in the Proven area, on June 30th, by which date the strength of the Battalion had increased to 39 officers and 1,018 other ranks.

July, 1918.

July 1st was observed as a holiday in the 36th Division, for the purpose of holding a horse show. The cooks' vehicles of the Battalion secured second place in their class. This was the end of the period of peace, for the Division was due again to enter the line. They did so in good spirits. It was felt that this time there would be no drawing back. It is true that the enemy had made a great assault against the French, leading to the Second Battle of the Marne, but all along the front, from Switzerland to the sea, he appeared to have shot his bolt. Moreover, the British were in good physical condition, and all losses in guns and munitions had been more than made good. The enemy might bombard Paris with "Big Bertha," but on the battle front he was inferior in artillery. The British were again taking over from the French in the big salient made by the German offensive on the River Lys. The enemy held Bailleul, Meteren, and Merris, well known to the 1st Royal Irish Fusiliers.

The movement began on July 2nd, when the 108th Brigade got as far as Road Camp, and the next day marched via Steenvoorde to Le Carreaux, the 87th taking over billets from the 2nd Battalion 79th (French) Regiment, the 36th Division being in reserve to the XVI (French) Corps. It was destined to take over the St. Jans—Cappel sector on the north-west corner of the German salient.

On July 6th the Battalion took over the reserve position on Mont Noir from the 3rd Battalion 23rd (French) Regiment.

On the night of July 12th/13th the Battalion took over the left sub-sector from the 9th (North Irish Horse) Royal Irish Fusiliers, known as the Croix de

Poperinghe sub-sector. The right rested on the Bailleul—Locre road, and ran in an east north-east direction for 1,100 yards. There were no regular trenches—it was an outpost line only. Enemy activity was generally confined to artillery and machine-gun fire at night, but he was very active behind the lines with night-bombing.

On July 18th, after a preliminary heavy bombardment, the enemy put down a box barrage, taking in the front and support lines held by the 87th. At 3.10 a.m. he raided in parties all along the front. He was driven back everywhere, except on the left of "C" Company, which was left company of the line, where 1 officer and 6 other ranks succeeded in entering. One non-commissioned officer was killed before they were ejected, but no identification was obtained. Our losses were: Captain R. W. Kingham, M.C., and Second-Lieutenant J. Dixon wounded, 2 other ranks killed, 16 other ranks wounded, and 8 other ranks missing. The missing are easily explained by those who have been in an intense bombardment.

The enemy repeated his bombardment the next morning, July 19th, but no infantry action followed.

At dawn on July 22nd an enemy aeroplane visited the lines held by the Battalion, and, flying low, fired on the men in the trenches. He was engaged by the Battalion anti-aircraft Lewis guns, and, though seen to be hit, managed to return over to his own lines.

On the night of July 23rd/24th the Battalion was relieved by the 2nd Battalion Royal Inniskilling Fusiliers, and withdrew to Divisional Reserve, Battalion headquarters being in the Curé's house at Boeschepe, and the companies in farmhouses and dug-outs between that place and Mont Noir, where they were employed till the end of the month in training and digging on what was known as the Blue line, about Mont Noir.

On the last day of the month the enemy obtained a direct hit on Battalion headquarters billet; fortunately, there were no casualties. The total casualties amongst other ranks for July were 5 killed and 41 wounded, the strength of the Battalion on the last day of the month being 38 officers and 965 other ranks.

By the end of July the final expulsion of the enemy from French soil had begun, and the Second Battle of the Marne was a great victory for the French. Moreover, the Americans, now in force, were making their presence felt.

AUGUST, 1918.

The beginning of this fateful month found the 87th still in Divisional Reserve and working at night on the defences. The 4th of the month saw the commencement of the fifth year of the war, but not without reasonable hope that it would be the last. It was known that His Majesty the King was visiting the troops, and this fact added to the high spirits of the men.

On the night of August 8th/9th the Battalion moved forward into Brigade

GENERAL VIEW OF BAILLEUL, 1-9-18.

[Photo by Imperial War Museum]

Reserve, relieving the 1st Battalion Royal Inniskilling Fusiliers, and continued work on the forward trenches.

It was on August 8th that the British Fourth Army, in conjunction with the French, commenced their great attack, astride of the Amiens—Roye road, which initiated the great final advance to victory.

On August 12th the 87th relieved the 12th Royal Irish Rifles in the left sub-sector which they had held previously. It was with sorrow that the troops saw the little town of Bailleul destroyed. Bailleul had all through the war been a haven of rest for the troops, and it was sad to see it destroyed by British artillery. Even the cottages on the outskirts, where the soldiers had watched the Flemish women working at their lace pillows, were demolished, and the fine old church, which had sheltered the 87th after the action at Meteren, was indistinguishable in the heaps of rubble.

At 5 p.m. on August 13th, Lieutenant R. O. Eaton and No. 41825 Private C. H. Tasker entered the enemy trenches 250 yards in front of the extreme left of the Battalion, and found six Germans, who showed fight. Lieutenant Eaton killed one with his revolver, and they returned with a notice posted up in the enemy lines. For this exploit Lieutenant Eaton received the Military Cross and Private Tasker the Military Medal.

The next day, August 14th, Lieutenants J. I. Smith and A. L. Dobbyn, with Sergeant Downey, penetrated the enemy lines opposite the right of the sub-sector, and had a fight, in which they killed several of the enemy and obtained an identification, 118 I.R., 58 Division, and returned without casualties.

The enemy attempted a raid on August 22nd, but was driven back. On this day the brigade on the left had advanced about a quarter of a mile, and the 1st Royal Irish Fusiliers were ordered to establish three posts north-west of La Bourse, to link up with them.

Ou August 24th the 108th Brigade took their first step forward in the final advance. The objective was, roughly, the road running north-east from La Bourse. The troops detailed were the 9th Royal Irish Fusiliers, "B" and half of "A" Company 1st Royal Irish Fusiliers, under Captain H. Haughey. The 87th objective was astride of the Bailleul—Locre road, and included what was known as Tomlin Farm and another strong point. They were on the left of the 9th Royal Irish Fusiliers, "B" Company being lent to that unit.

At 3 a.m. the troops were in assembly positions, cocoanut matting being provided to hide them from hostile aeroplanes. Zero was at 7 a.m., when the barrage was put down, the Battalion having crawled through their own wire at 6.45 a.m.

The troops rushed forward, and by 7.20 a.m. the 87th had overcome all opposition and were consolidating their position, many of the enemy having been killed. Covering parties were sent out with Lewis guns, who dealt with the retreating enemy.

Our losses were: Lieutenants T. O. J. Kavanagh and T. E. Bunting and 7 other ranks killed, 37 other ranks wounded, and 1 other rank missing. Lieutenant Bunting was a worthy son of that fine old soldier, Major T. E. Bunting, D.C.M.

The 87th took 25 prisoners, 3 machine guns, and a considerable amount of equipment.

The success was largely due to the dash of the troops and the element of surprise.

The Second Army Commander sent the following message: "Army Commander congratulates troops on success of this morning's operations"; to which the Divisional Commander also added his commendations.

The enemy made a feeble counter-attack from the direction of the Asylum about 7.30 p.m., which was easily broken up.

On the night of August 24th/25th the Battalion was relieved by the 1st Battalion Royal Inniskilling Fusiliers, and withdrew to the neighbourhood of Mont des Cats, and on August 29th to St. Sylvestre Cappel, but returned to Mont des Cats the next day.

The enemy having retired from Bailleul, the 108th Brigade were ordered to support the 109th Brigade, who were now on the north-west slopes of the Revelsberg Ridge, east of Bailleul. Accordingly, at 11.30 a.m. on August 31st, the 87th moved to Hoogenacker, and thence to the northern slopes of the Revelsberg, which they reached at 5 p.m. and bivouacked, the headquarters in a shack built by themselves and the men under hedges and in shell-holes.

The whole casualties for the month were: Officers, 2 killed, 1 wounded; other ranks, 13 killed, 80 wounded, 1 missing. Strength, 38 officers and 902 other ranks.

September, 1918.

The feeling of elation, natural to troops pursuing a retreating enemy, was enhanced by the deeper feeling that this time the enemy were withdrawing not to return, and that the end of the great struggle was in sight. The few who had been with the Battalion in the early days, and remembered Bailleul as it then was, a haven of rest and comfort, must have been impressed by the sad change which had come over the old town. Nothing remained of the fine old church which had sheltered the whole Battalion after the action of Meteren, and of the town itself nothing remained but heaps of rubble, through which passages had been cleared for the movement of troops.

On September 1st the 108th Brigade were ordered to relieve the 109th Brigade, passing through them. The 87th were directed to relieve the 2nd Royal Inniskilling Fusiliers, about Neuve Eglise. Accordingly, the Battalion moved at 10 p.m., and Battalion headquarters were established north of Neuve Eglise, south-east of Stampkotmolen.

At 3 a.m. on September 2nd telephonic orders were received to attack, the objective being from White Gates, the north-west entrance of the Château grounds on Hill 63, to North Midland Farm, on the Wulverghem—Messines road. The 12th Royal Irish Rifles were on the right, their objective including Red Lodge, an old Battalion headquarters in the winter of 1914-15. The advance was made in artillery formation, "A" Company (Captain Kingham, M.C.) and "D" Company (Captain Cuming, M.C.) leading, "B" Company (Captain Lennon, M.C., D.C.M., M.M.) in support, and "C" Company (Captain Jenkinson) in reserve. At 6.30 a.m. the Battalion, which had now extended, was held up by machine-gun fire, especially by that of guns located in Neuve Eglise, but, after artillery preparation, this village was captured by a company of the 12th Royal Irish Rifles. After dark, the advance was continued to the old British General Headquarters line, which was taken with slight opposition, and where the Battalion was in touch with the 12th Royal Irish Rifles on the Neuve Eglise—Wulverghem road.

On September 3rd the frontage allotted to the 108th Brigade was reduced, and did not extend farther south than White Gates. At 9.30 a.m. the Battalion advanced in artillery formation and made rapid progress, but, on reaching St. Quentin Cabaret, it was found necessary to extend into line south-east of that place. The enemy retired fighting and the advance now became slow, but by 2.30 p.m. "C" and "B" Companies were on their objectives. At 3.30 p.m. enemy shelling was heavy, and troops on the left withdrew from the high ground about North-Midland Farm. "C" Company therefore withdrew slightly in conformity with this movement. During the night the whole Brigade front was taken over by the 9th (North Irish Horse) Royal Irish Fusiliers, and the 87th withdrew to the old General Headquarters line.

At 12.30 p.m. on September 4th the Battalion was moved forward to a position south-east of Petawawn Farm to support the 9th (North Irish Horse) Royal Irish Fusiliers, who had been counter-attacked as the British were now approaching positions which the enemy desired to hold. In the evening, "C" Company, under Lieutenant Michie, was sent to fill a gap near La Plus Douve Farm.

At 4 a.m. on September 5th, verbal orders were received to attack on the line Irish Farm—Stinking Farm, in conjunction with the 9th (North Irish Horse) Royal Irish Fusiliers. The night was very dark, but the commanders of "B" and "D" Companies, detailed for this duty, made a personal reconnaissance, and at 5 a.m. the attack was launched. West of La Plus Douve Farm a heavy belt of wire was encountered, in which the enemy had left booby traps which caused some casualties, and, as dawn broke, a heavy fire was opened from Stinking Farm, which the enemy had retaken after a counter-attack. This fire was so heavy that movement was impossible. This night the 108th Brigade, which had been fighting for four days in bad weather and with no shelter, was relieved by the 107th Brigade, the 87th moving to the northern slopes of the Revelsberg.

From September 1st to September 5th the Battalion lost 22 other ranks killed, 4 officers and 95 other ranks wounded, and 9 other ranks missing.

On September 8th the Battalion marched, via Bailleul—St. Jean Cappel, to the neighbourhood of Berthen, where they were visited by Sir Horace Plunkett.

On September 20th a night march was made to the Terdeghem area, via Godewaersvelde, avoiding Steenvoorde and on the following night to the Watou area. The reason for these marches, and the secrecy with which they were carried out, was that the 36th Division had been selected to form part of the composite army—British, French and Belgian—which, under the supreme command of His Majesty the King of the Belgians, was to have the honour of driving the enemy from his positions about Ypres and on the Belgian coast.

A certain amount of training was possible, and full advantage was taken in preparations for what all ranks realized would be strenuous fighting.

Captain W. Scott rejoined on September 24th, and resumed his duties as adjutant.

The 36th Division, which was in reserve to the II Corps, was ordered to concentrate on the nights of September 27th and September 28th, and, in accordance with the scheme, the 87th was moved by light railway to Orilla Camp, near Vlamertinghe, and at 3 p.m. on September 28th marched to a position north-west of Ypres. At 4 a.m. on September 29th the Battalion was again on the move, and, passing through Ypres and the Menin Gate, halted at the famous White Château on the Menin road. At 8 a.m. they were ordered to Westhoek in support of the 109th Brigade, experiencing some difficulty on account of congestion on the road. Thence they moved south-east to Glencorse Wood, and at 3 p.m. to Black Watch Corner, at the south-west end of the Polygone de Zonnebeke, where shacks were built for the night. This procedure was reminiscent of marches in the Peninsular War, where the soldiers took pride in the rapidity with which they were able to build shelters for the night.

The plan for the day was that the 109th Brigade of the 36th Division was introduced between the two other divisions of the Corps at Becelaere, the objective of the 109th Brigade being Terhand, which it captured at 3.45 p.m.

The objective for the 108th Brigade, on September 30th, was the great Menin—Roulers road from Kezelberg northwards. They were ordered to pass through the troops of the 109th Brigade, which they did at 7.30 a.m. The 9th (North Irish Horse) Royal Irish Fusiliers were on the right, the 12th Royal Irish Rifles on the left, and the 1st Royal Irish Fusiliers, who had come up through Terhand, were in reserve. The key to the position was some rising ground immediately east of Vijfwegen, known as Hill 41. It was surmounted with farm buildings and covered with hedges suitable for defence, and very strongly held, especially with machine guns.

The Allied troops had now driven the enemy from the devastated area, and this success involved a serious handicap to further operations. It must be

Nº X

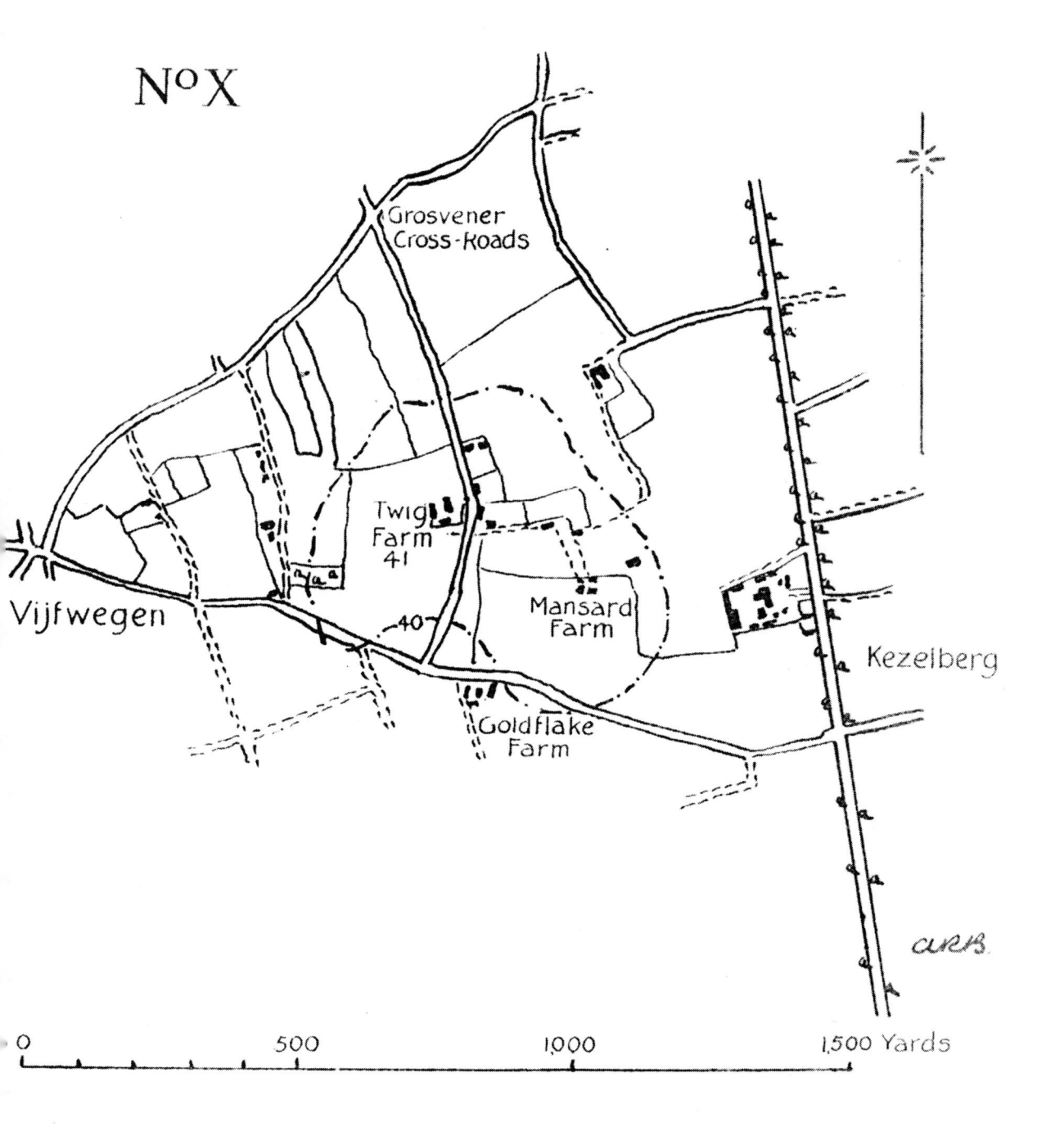

remembered that the only means of bringing artillery and stores of all sorts across the devastated area was by means of the plank roads which had long replaced the remains of the original highways. These plank roads, being under constant shell fire, were in a bad state. Moreover, all traffic being confined to these well-known tracks, they formed an easy target, not only to artillery but for bombing aeroplanes. The enemy took full advantage of his opportunities, especially at night.

October, 1918.

Although the 108th Brigade had reached the main Menin—Roulers road both south and north of Hill 41, on the last day of September they had not succeeded in taking the hill itself, in spite of gallant attempts. The 1st Royal Irish Fusiliers were ordered to attack the hill from the west at 6.15 a.m. on October 1st. " C " Company, under Captain V. J. Lynch, M.C., and " D " Company, under Lieutenant R. O. Eaton, M.C., were detailed for the task, " A " Company, under Captain R. W. Kingham, M.C., being in support. In spite of heavy resistance from trench mortars and machine guns, Twig Farm, on the summit, was captured, but such was the concentrated fire of the enemy that it was impossible to advance farther. Twenty-three prisoners were captured in the farm. At 11.30 a.m. the enemy counter-attacked Twig Farm, but was driven off. After heavy artillery preparation, the enemy again attacked at 6.30 p.m., but this attack was driven off by " C " Company, and the Battalion established a line on the hill, including Twig Farm. It is regretted that no details are forthcoming of this gallant action, in which the Battalion sustained heavy losses. The losses in officers were as follows: Killed, Lieutenant W. R. Graham, Lieutenant P. Browne, Second-Lieutenant H. G. Skitt, and Second-Lieutenant H. W. Cunningham; wounded, Lieutenant A. R. Crosbie, Second-Lieutenant R. O. Eaton, M.C., Second-Lieutenant P. J. Lowe, Second-Lieutenant J. Cullen, M.C., and Captain R. W. Kingham, M.C.

On being relieved by the 2nd Royal Inniskilling Fusiliers, the Battalion withdrew to the west of Terhand.

On October 2nd and 3rd the Battalion were in the vicinity of Becelaere, where they were heavily shelled, but on October 4th they again moved forward, to a support position at Dadizeele. This day the Commanding Officer, Lieutenant-Colonel T. A. Lowe, M.C., was wounded, but remained at duty.

On October 7th the Battalion relieved the 12th Royal Irish Rifles in the left sub-sector on Hill 41. By this time the British had succeeded in bringing up considerable artillery across the devastated area. The enemy had also been largely reinforced in that arm, and the shelling on both sides was heavy. Nor were the enemy infantry inactive, especially in his endeavours to retake Hill 41. Twig Farm on the crest, Mansard Farm to the east, and Goldflake Farm on the south all changed hands. Mansard Farm was finally rushed on October 12th, when 1 prisoner and 1 light trench mortar were captured.

This day was the eve of another grand attack, and the 108th Brigade were withdrawn from the line to Divisional Reserve, north of Terhand, the 1st Royal Irish Fusiliers being relieved by the 2nd Royal Inniskilling Fusiliers. On October 14th they moved to Vijfwegen, where they were in reserve to the 109th Infantry Brigade. So well had the battle gone, that the Divisional Reserve moved on October 15th, through Moorseele and Gulleghem to the north of Heule.

It was on October 10th that Major P. E. Kelly was killed, whilst in command of the 9th (North Irish Horse) Royal Irish Fusiliers. He had been visiting the line, and was standing at one of his company headquarters, when he was killed by a shell. The Brigadier rightly gauged Major Kelly's character when he wrote: "I deeply deplore his loss, as he was a gallant and fearless officer and full of energy and keenness, and was popular with all ranks."

The next task of the 108th Brigade was to force the passage of the River Lys at Courtrai. This was accomplished on October 16th, under cover of a smoke screen, but the 87th took no active part, being in reserve. The bridgehead thus established (the enemy had destroyed the fine permanent bridges) was not used because, in order to spare the town of Courtrai from bombardment, the main attack was to be made farther north, which also had the advantage of threatening the enemy in the great industrial districts of Lille and Roubaix. The 36th Division were detailed to take part in this attack, and were relieved by the 41st Division for this purpose. The 87th moved to Drie Masten to refit, and on October 17th were paraded to hear a complimentary speech from the Divisional Commander, Major-General C. Coffin, V.C., C.B., D.S.O.

On October 18th Lieutenant-Colonel T. A. Lowe, M.C., received the honour of the Distinguished Service Order as an immediate award.

The 36th Division had now the post of honour on the left of the British Army and next to the 133rd (French) Regiment.

The Division was ordered to cross the Lys between Bavichove and the point where the Roulers Canal joins the river. For this purpose the 36th Division relieved the 3rd Belgian Division on the left bank of the River Lys on October 18th.

The actual forcing of the river passage, which was accomplished in spite of considerable opposition, was carried out by the 107th and 109th Brigades on the night of October 19th/20th. On October 20th the 108th Brigade were brought up to renew the attack, and the 1st Royal Irish Fusiliers relieved the 9th Royal Inniskilling Fusiliers at Dries, a hamlet of Desselghem, between the Lys and the main Courtrai—Ghent road.

On October 21st the Battalion attacked from Spriete, at 7.30 a.m., in conjunction with the 107th Brigade on their right. The French did not advance. In spite of this, and the fact that they were not supported by artillery and much worried by machine-gun fire in a country where there was little cover from view, the Battalion had by 9 a.m. established itself near Spitaal and south of that place.

Unfortunately, the Battalion lost Captain A. E. McM. Cuming, M.C., who was wounded, and died on October 26th.

On October 22nd the attack was renewed, but the 108th Brigade were not to advance till the French came up. After heavy fighting, they joined up at Spitaal.

On October 23rd an enemy runner was captured when carrying orders for a retirement. At 8 a.m. the Battalion was formed up on the Deerlyck—Waereghem road about Evangelleboom, and advanced, covered by a screen of scouts. By 12 noon they had advanced as far as Engelhoek without opposition, but by 4 p.m. the enemy was located at Heirweg, a hamlet about half way between Courtrai and Audenarde. He was driven out by a very daring attack on the part of one of the companies of the Battalion. The enemy were, however, too strong, and, by means of a vigorous counter-attack, drove the company out of the hamlet. Second-Lieutenant J. M. Denny was killed, and Second-Lieutenant T. R. Coghlan, who was reported wounded and missing, died of wounds the next day. This was the last time the 1st Royal Irish Fusiliers was in close action with the enemy. An international post was established at the level-crossing at Heirweg with the 41st Chasseurs.

On the evening of October 24th the Battalion was relieved by the 12th Royal Irish Rifles, and moved to Brigade Reserve at Leemput.

At 9 a.m. on October 25th the Battalion took up a position of readiness in support of the 12th Royal Irish Rifles and 9th (North Irish Horse) Royal Irish Fusiliers, who were attacking. Captain A. G. Porter was wounded, and died on October 29th. At night the Battalion was accommodated in cellars, to protect them from shell fire, but the enemy used much gas.

On October 27th the 108th Brigade was relieved by the 101st Infantry Brigade, and moved to Hulste, 5,000 yards north of Courtrai. Although they did not know it at the time, this was the end of the war for the Battalion. Like all infantry units in the 36th Division, they were greatly reduced in strength. The casualties reported for the month of October were 5 officers and 40 other ranks killed; 9 officers and 234 other ranks wounded; and 1 officer and 99 other ranks missing.

The men were much in need of a rest after their strenuous exertion, and especially after the gas-shelling to which they had been constantly subjected.

That the work of the division was appreciated at Headquarters was testified by a letter of appreciation received by the Divisional Commander from Lieutenant-General Sir C. W. Jacob, commanding II Corps.

November, 1918.

On November 1st the Battalion were at Lauwe, east of Menin, busy as usual at training, and receiving drafts to prepare for a renewal of the contest, which was not to be. On November 3rd they moved to Luingne, near Mouscron, and the next day they welcomed Lieutenant-Colonel H. W. D.

McCarthy-O'Leary, D.S.O., M.C., who, after distinguishing himself as the leader of a battalion of the Royal Irish Rifles, now came to assume command of his own Battalion, Lieutenant-Colonel T. A. Lowe, a deservedly popular commanding officer, being given a hearty send-off.

New billets were taken over in Mouscron on November 7th, where the Battalion was to remain for some time.

The entry in the official war diary of the Battalion for November 11th reads as follows: "Armistice signed. Brigade parade in the morning. Officers played 12th Royal Irish Rifles at Rugby."

The services of the 36th Division in the last phase of the war are well epitomized in the following message received from the Corps Commander shortly before the Division was withdrawn from the line on October 27th:—

"*To Major-General C. Coffin, V.C., D.S.O., commanding 36th Division:*

"*The 36th (Ulster) Division has been fighting continuously since the 28th September in the operations in Flanders. The spirit, dash, and initiative shown by all ranks has been splendid, and beyond all praise. The leadership displayed by yourself and your Brigade and other commanders could not have been bettered. The conditions under which the men have had to fight have been, and are still, very trying, but nothing seems to stop your gallant Division.*

"*I have also been much struck with the good staff work of the Division, and it is very creditable to all concerned.*

"*Will you kindly express to the commanders, staffs, and all ranks of the Division my heartiest congratulations and thanks for their work.*

"*When the history is written of what the Division has done in Flanders during the past month, it will prove to be a record of magnificent fighting and wonderful progress; for, during this period, an advance has been made of about twenty-five miles over the worst country, and under the heaviest machine-gun fire ever experienced in this war. This advance has entailed constant fighting, but the 36th has overcome every obstacle, and has proved itself one of the best fighting divisions in the Army, well commanded and well staffed. My best wishes to you all.*"

"C. W. JACOB, Lieutenant-General,
"Commanding II Corps."

Wormhoudt
Poperinghe
Ypres
Courtrai
Harlebeke
Ledeghem
Cassel
Steenvoorde
St Omer
Bailleul
Hazebrouck
Armentières
Quesnoy
Tourcoing
ROUBAIX
LILLE
Mouscron
Tournai
Aire
Merville
Estaires
Laventie
Haubourdin
Lannoy
Norrent Fontes
Lillers
Béthune
La Bassée
Seclin
Cysoing
Orchies
St Amand
Heuchin
Houdain
Lens
Carvin
Marchiennes
VALENCIENNES
St Pol
Douai
Denain
Aubigny
ARRAS
Vitry en Artois
Arleux
Bouchain
Frevent
Avesnes le Comte
Beaumetz
Croisilles
Marquion
CAMBRAI
Solesmes
Doullens
Pas
Marcoing
Le Cateau
Bapaume
Bertincourt
Clary
Acheux
Albert
Combles
Le Câtelet
Villers
Bohain

Scale
0 5 10 Miles
Railways
Roads
Franco-Belgian boundary
PARIS
ST DENIS
SOISSONS
Compiègne
Montdidier
Noyon
Chauny
La Fère
Coucy
Anizy
Vailly
Braisne
Pierrefonds
Villers Cotterets
Crepy
Senlis
Creil
Pont Ste Maxence
Clermont
Liancourt
St Just en-Chaussée
Breteuil
Moreuil
Ailly sur-Noye
Roye
Nesle
Ham
St Simon
Guiscard
Lassigny
Ressons
Ribecourt
Estrees St Denis
Mouy
Neuilly en Thelle
Luzarches
Ecouen
Gonesse
Montmorency
Dammartin en Goele
Nanteuil-le Haudouin
Betz
Oulchy
Neuilly
Château-Thierry
Meaux
Claye
Lagny
Crecy
Coulommiers
Rebais
Montmirail
La Ferte-Gaucher
La Ferte sous Jouarre
Noisy le Sec
Montreuil
Vincennes
Charenton
Sceaux
R. Oise
R. Aisne
R. Marne
R. Ourcq

CHAPTER VI—The Armistice and After.

The Armistice was welcomed by the troops in the field in a very sober manner. Indeed, in the forward lines the men were too weary, and the weather conditions were too bad, for exuberant demonstrations. Perhaps, also, the feeling of relief and thankfulness was too deep for outward expression. At all events, amongst the fighting men there were no scenes of wild enthusiasm such as took place behind the lines and at home.

One of the first steps taken was to establish a line of outposts, with examining-posts on every road leading in the direction of the enemy, and all intercourse was forbidden.

The 36th Division was not one of those selected to take part in the triumphant advance to the Rhine.

A feature of this advance was that the troops which took part had the appearance of going to a big review at Aldershot, rather than that of troops who had been in the field for years. New clothing was issued to the men, only the best horses and vehicles were allowed to proceed, and all harness and equipment were brought up to a pitch of cleanliness only known in the British Army.

The 87th experienced what may be called the " shock " of the Armistice in their billets at Mouscron. The fact that it was possible to sleep without a gas-mask, the relaxation of the censorship, the comparative unimportance of the two identity discs worn by every man, one of which was to be buried with him if he fell—these were things which it was difficult at first to realize.

But all this made no outward difference to routine. The Battalion orders contain the same detail of duties, training and recreation. But the Battalion staff were soon busy with other than ordinary routine work.

Education to fit the soldiers for return to civil life was taken up very earnestly. The Battalion had an education officer, who, with a representative from each company, formed an educational committee, and classes were started in elementary subjects.

Demobilization, when it commenced, involved very heavy work, and the Battalion were fortunate in having the services of Captain W. Scott, D.S.O., M.C., as adjutant.

There was some discontent about the manner in which demobilization was carried out. The soldier's idea was that the man who had served longest should be discharged first, and the War Office had worked out a scheme on these lines. But conditions at home demanded that this scheme should be modified, and the principle on which it was actually carried out was that the men who could most easily be absorbed in civil life were discharged first. The first class to go were the miners, then what were called pivotal men, and "one-man business" men. The machine was a marvel of organization, and worked very smoothly.

It is impossible to speak of demobilization without thinking of the women at home, and their fortitude and patience throughout the long years of war. This applies to all ranks of society. The spirit of endurance and faith which permeated the letters addressed to the Irish Fusiliers was the same whether they came from a stately mansion or the humblest Irish cabin.

Nor can one refrain from again expressing the heartfelt thanks of all ranks to those women and children who throughout the war worked so hard to provide comforts. The ladies who so ably organized the workers will for ever hold a warm place in the hearts of those who enjoyed the fruits of their labours.

Amongst the mothers at home, Mrs. Camlin, of Cellars Street, Armagh, was a proud woman. She had five sons serving in the Royal Irish Fusiliers, and two in other corps.

The returned prisoners of war who passed through the lines were a sad sight. Irishmen who were prisoners of war suffered much, and the men of the Irish Fusiliers were no exception.

At first petted and made much of, this treatment was reversed when it was found useless to endeavour to tamper with their loyalty. Reference has been made before to the reception accorded to Sir Roger Casement when he endeavoured to seduce Irish soldiers incarcerated at Limburg.

Many of the Irish Fusiliers who were prisoners of war owe their lives to Mr. Delmege Trimble, of the *Armagh Guardian*, who organized a food supply by parcel post. His O.B.E. was a worthy recognition of his good work. On May 5th, 1920, a silver cup, inscribed as under, was sent to Mr. Trimble:—

"Presented to Delmege Trimble, Esq., O.B.E., by all ranks of the Royal Irish Fusiliers, in appreciation of his untiring efforts on behalf of the Regiment during the Great War, 1914—1918."

Several men of the Battalion, of whom No. 8365 Private Charles McDonald was one, succeeded in making their escape, and No. 7958 Private G. McCollum is credited with never having done any work for the Germans. At the time of the Armistice he was under sentence of six years' imprisonment, "to be served after the war," for refusing to work.

On November 18th special thanksgiving services were held for the termination of the war.

On December 5th the 87th had the great honour of being selected out of the Fifth Army to furnish a Guard of Honour for His Majesty the King. Accordingly the next day, the guard, under command of Captain C. S. Tuely, with Lieutenant C. G. McClean and Second-Lieutenant C. B. Camlin, proceeded by bus to Lille.

His Majesty, accompanied by H.R.H. the Prince of Wales and H.R.H. the Duke of York, arrived on December 7th, and that morning the 87th took over the guard on His Majesty's quarters from the details of the Brigade of Guards.

His Majesty left Lille on December 9th, and, before doing so, made a very thorough inspection of the guard, speaking to many of the men. After the inspection, His Majesty congratulated Captain Tuely on the appearance of the men, saying "that it was a pleasure to inspect such a guard."

One day H.R.H. the Prince of Wales entered the guard-room and chatted to the men. He told Captain Tuely that he thought the sentries were very good indeed.

The guard returned to Mouscron by bus on the evening of December 9th, having been highly complimented on the manner in which they had performed their duties.

On December 10th the Battalion won a cross-country race, having nine men in the first sixteen men home.

A very happy Christmas was spent, good fare being provided for the men by officers past and present.

JANUARY, 1919.

On January 4th, 1919, Lieutenants N. A. Rattray and G. W. R. Templer, who had been sent to Armagh with the usual escort, returned with the Regimental Colours.

FEBRUARY, 1919.

On February 6th the Brigadier-General carried out his annual peace-time inspection. He expressed great satisfaction, and congratulated all ranks.

The Battalion was still at Mouscron, busy with education, but, by February 19th, it was so depleted by demobilization that there were no men available for parades.

MARCH, 1919.

On St. Patrick's Day the Cadre of the 87th, under command of Lieutenant-Colonel H. W. D. McCarthy-O'Leary, D.S.O., M.C., left Mouscron for the rest camp at Dunkerque. On March 31st the Cadre reached Southampton, and proceeded to the New Barracks, Gosport. The strength was 7 officers and 51 other ranks, including No. 7233 Private J. Dougan, who had not been absent from the Battalion a single day throughout the campaign.

The next few months were spent in hard work reconstructing the Battalion, Lieutenant-Colonel F. A. Greer, C.M.G., D.S.O., being in command, and Captain M. J. W. O'Donovan, M.C., being adjutant.

SEPTEMBER, 1919.

The 87th, having been ordered to proceed to Persia, embarked at Tilbury, Thursday, September 18th, on board the s.s. *Nevasa*.

October, 1919.

Bombay was reached on October 10th, and the next day the Battalion transhipped to the s.s *Barala,* and reached Basra on October 17th, when it again transhipped to river boats and proceeded to Kut-el-Amara, where it remained about a fortnight, thus having an opportunity to visit the scene of fighting.

November, 1919.

The Battalion left Kut-el-Amara about November 7th, and proceeded by rail to Fuaraitu, then the railhead. The journey was continued in two parties by lorry, and Kasvin was reached on November 13th and 14th, and the Battalion went into a camp consisting of mud huts.

March, 1920.

In order to impress the inhabitants by a display of force, the Battalion marched through Kasvin on March 26th, with bayonets fixed and in open order. The townspeople were much interested in the military music.

April, 1920.

Major and Brevet Lieutenant-Colonel H. C. H. Orpen-Palmer left the Battalion to take up the appointment of Military Attaché at Pekin.

May, 1920.

The band and drums proceeded by lorry to Teheran, to play during the race week. So far as is known, this was the first occasion on which a British military band has visited the Persian capital. Their playing was much appreciated, and the inhabitants subscribed a sum of £500 for the benefit of the Regimental Old Comrades Association.

On May 18th a Bolshevist force invaded Enzeli, on the Caspian Sea. There was no fighting, our troops withdrawing to Resht and remaining in observation.

June, 1920.

On June 1st the Shah of Persia passed through Kasvin on his way from the United Kingdom. A Guard of Honour, consisting of 2 officers and 50 rank and file, with band and Regimental Colour, under Captain C. S. Tuely, received him at Sultanabad.

The summer heat being great, serge clothing was discarded for drill clothing.

On June 14th, Lieutenant-General Sir Aylmer Haldane, K.C.B., D.S.O., Commanding-in-Chief, Mesopotamia, inspected the Battalion and expressed himself as very pleased with all he saw. He reminded the Battalion of the old days at Shorncliffe, and commented on the *esprit de corps* of all ranks.

In addition to routine training, the senior and junior cross-country races for the Southey Shield were held this month.

JULY, 1920.

In order to watch the Bolshevists, two platoons of "A" Company and the Battalion scouts, under Lieutenant G. W. R. Templer, were sent on July 7th to support a troop of the Guides Cavalry at Kamisa, where they remained about three weeks.

AUGUST, 1920.

Owing to the Bolshevist menace, it was decided to withdraw detachments and take up an outpost position round Kazvin. Lieutenant-Colonel F. A. Greer, C.M.G., D.S.O., was appointed Outpost Commander, and the Battalion held one section, under Brevet Lieutenant-Colonel R. C. Dobbs, D.S.O. But the situation soon underwent a rapid change. The Arabs had revolted and cut the Baghdad railway, thus severing connection between north and south.

On August 19th the Fusiliers were withdrawn from the outpost position and ordered to proceed by motor to Quaritu, which was now the railhead from the north. The Battalion proceeded in two parties. The first left Kazvin on August 25th, and arrived at Quaritu on August 27th. The heat and dust were very trying, and the lorries were closely packed.

The Colours and heavy baggage were left under escort at Hamadan.

On arrival at Quaritu the Battalion was ordered to Khanikin Road Station, to form part of a column under Lieutenant-Colonel F. A. Greer.

The duty of this column, which was called "Greercol," was to work south, repairing the railway line and bridges, to meet a stronger column which was working up from the south.

Lieutenant-Colonel Greer divided his column into two portions—one to proceed by rail, the other, under Brevet Lieutenant-Colonel Dobbs, called the "Road Column." This latter column consisted of Battalion Headquarters, "C" Company, and "D" Company (the machine-gun company) less one section, the 13th Pack Battery less one section, 100 rifles of the 79th Carnatic Infantry, one section of a light armoured motor battery, and the transport of all units.

On August 30th Lieutenant-Colonel Dobbs moved his column to Khanikin town, a distance of about seven miles, and on August 31st issued orders for the next day as follows:—The objective was Mirjana, a distance of about twenty miles. Any hostile force met with was to be dispersed. The light armoured motor battery was to act as advanced guard, and the Carnatic Infantry as rearguard and baggage guard.

Lieutenant-Colonel Greer, with the remainder of his troops, was to proceed by rail to Mirjana.

SEPTEMBER, 1920.

At 2 a.m. on September 1st Lieutenant-Colonel Dobbs moved off through the town of Khanikin. The route lay across an absolutely barren desert, and at sunrise, about 5 a.m., the advanced guard were about one mile short of the

Fasilah Pass, where opposition was expected. Captain H. A. MacMullen, M.C., commanding "C" Company, advanced in attack formation, and was soon engaged with the enemy, who were holding a ridge distant about 600 yards, and who waved a flag striped black, red and white. As the target was a poor one, the Fusiliers held their fire. This encouraged the Arabs, who advanced to about 200 yards, when they were met with such an effective rifle and machine-gun fire that they fled, and, on arrival at the summit of the pass, could be seen galloping away on their horses. Our casualties were 2 other ranks killed, Second-Lieutenant H. V. Gough and 1 other rank wounded. In this small action, Captain and Adjutant M. J. W. O'Donovan, M.C., and Captain H. A. MacMullen, M.C., especially distinguished themselves.

The enemy strength was about 200, and his casualties estimated at about 20.

The column was reformed, and an advance made to the Qizil Pass, where a second body of the enemy was located, but was quickly driven off by the guns of the pack battery.

From the top of Qizil Pass, Mirjana was clearly visible, and communication was opened, but it was not till 4 p.m. that the column arrived at their destination, after a very trying march on account of the sweltering heat, the water in the water-bottles being so hot that it was scarcely drinkable. The rail column had already arrived, not having met with opposition.

The next few days were employed in visits to the neighbouring villages and impressing the inhabitants.

On September 6th a reconnaissance, under Lieutenant-Colonel Dobbs, proceeded by train towards Kadarah. The train was attacked by mounted Arabs, who pursued it on its return, but they were easily driven off.

On September 10th the whole force proceeded to Kadarah, where a large iron bridge over the River Kadarah was found to have been destroyed. A temporary diversion was completed in two days, "C" Company performing a large part of the heavy work of carrying material, etc.

On September 16th, the railway being now open, Lieutenant-Colonel Greer proceeded to Table Mountain Station, and conferred with the commander of the southern column.

On September 17th the Irish Fusiliers proceeded by rail to Quaraghan, and, the railway from Quaritu to Baghdad being now complete, the next task was to open the line to Kingarban. Armoured trains were employed and blockhouses built, in much the same way as during the South African War.

OCTOBER, 1920.

On October 3rd the Battalion moved by rail to Sharaban, and camped near the station. Sharaban is a considerable village, and as the country is well watered by streams and irrigation canals, the ground is fruitful, the village itself being surrounded with well-stocked gardens. The camp, which was a perimeter one, consisted of bivouac tents and a few Indian E.P. tents.

On October 12th "Greercol" was broken up, and the Battalion became a unit in the 75th Brigade, commanded by Brigadier-General J. A. H. Beatty, C.M.G., D.S.O.

The rebels having shown some activity at Tel-el-Ibara, a mixed column, under Lieutenant-Colonel Greer, including the whole of the Royal Irish Fusiliers except the garrison of Sharaban town and camp, proceeded to that place on October 15th and burnt the rebels' camp, returning the next day.

On October 29th a strong column, under Brigadier-General Beatty, marched from Sharaban to visit villages and dictate terms of peace, also to collect fines in the shape of rifles and ammunition. The column marched very light, the men in shirt sleeves, blankets on carts, and with two days' emergency rations only. The tribesmen were notified of the route to be taken, and ordered to provide goats, sheep, flour and forage on payment. If not produced, these supplies would be requisitioned without payment.

Bal-ad-Ruz was reached on October 30th, where Brigadier-General Beatty dictated terms to the Sheiks.

November, 1920.

On November 1st the column marched about eighteen miles to Marut Post, whence all wheeled transport was sent back to Sharaban.

On November 3rd Amraniyah was reached, after a march of about fifteen miles, and on November 4th a further march of about twelve miles brought the column back to Sharaban. No opposition was met with during the trek, but full military precautions were taken both on the march and in bivouac.

As fines in arms had not been fully complied with, on November 25th a small column, under Lieutenant-Colonel Greer, marched to Abaniyah, where it halted till November 29th whilst the Political Officer collected fines, and on that date marched to Barganiyah, burning *en route* a village which had not paid its fine. The column returned to Amaniyah on November 30th. The burning of the village had a salutary effect, and fines came in in a satisfactory manner.

During the month the heavy baggage and band and drums arrived from Hamadan. The baggage, which was in charge of Persian transport, suffered considerably *en route*.

By Army Order No. 509 of November, 1920, the title of the Regiment was changed to "Royal Irish Fusiliers (Princess Victoria's)" thus restoring the title given when the 87th and 89th Regiments were amalgamated in 1881.

December, 1920.

Lieutenant-Colonel Greer's column returned to Sharaban on December 3rd, but another punitive campaign was in prospect, and on December 10th, with other units, it marched to Abijisra, and the next day to Baqubah, where it joined a column under Brigadier-General Beatty. The route of this column lay by Daltawah—Dijman—Chaikannah, on the Adhiam river, which was crossed by a suspension bridge—Khansaurah to Sammarah, which was reached on December 27th. This march was rendered trying by reason of heavy rains and alternate heat and cold. Sammarah is a walled city, situated on the Baghdad—Mosul railway and the River Tigris. It boasts a large mosque, with gilded dome, and is held very sacred by Moslems.

On December 31st the movement of the Battalion to a new camp near the station, by ferry across the Tigris commenced.

JANUARY, 1921.

The movement across the Tigris was not completed till January 6th, and soon after orders were received that the Irish Fusiliers were to join a strong column, under Brigadier-General Dent, C.M.G., D.S.O., concentrating at Kut-el-Amara. This was one of two heavy columns destined to demonstrate in the country of the Muntafik, the most powerful tribe in Mesopotamia, hitherto friendly. The Irish Fusiliers were the only British infantry in Brigadier-General Dent's column, and were selected for their good marching qualities.

The Battalion entrained on January 10th and proceeded, via Baghdad, to Kut, which place was reached on January 12th, and where it joined the "Kut" column, as it was called. The other infantry units were: 45th Sikhs, 94th Russell's Infantry, 108th Rajputs, and 1st/10th Gurkha Rifles.

The itinerary of this column was as follows:—

January 16th, to camp on Shatt-al-Garraf, or Hai River, 10 miles; January 17th, to camp on Shatt-al-Garraf, or Hai River, 13 miles; January 18th, to two miles south of Hai village; January 19th, halt; January 20th, to Iman-Saiyad-Jawwad, 11 miles; January 21st, to Qalat-Sikar, 12 miles; January 22nd, march; January 23rd, to Karradi, 12 miles.

At Karradi the 24th Brigade column, the other of the two heavy columns, was met.

The halt on December 19th was a forced halt because many of the mahalas, or large flat-bottomed native boats, on which the supplies and baggage were carried, had stuck in the mud of the Hai River.

The return march was commenced on January 24th, but, on reaching Hai village, so many mahalas were stuck in the mud that it was found necessary to split the column into two, and the Irish Fusiliers returned to Kut with the second half.

FEBRUARY, 1921.

On February 1st the Battalion reached their old camp at Kut. In addition to the vagaries of the Hai River, which apparently flows alternately into the Tigris and Euphrates, this march demanded hard work, as perimeter camps were formed each night, which entailed much trench-digging and sentry work for the infantry.

On February 4th orders were received to entrain immediately for Baghdad, which was reached the next day.

LT.-COL. F. A. GREER, C.M.G., D.S.O., RELINQUISHES COMMAND

On February 10th, on completion of his period of command, Lieutenant-Colonel F. A. Greer, C.M.G., D.S.O., bade farewell to the Battalion in a soldierly speech. Lieutenant-Colonel Greer had served with the Royal Irish Fusiliers for more than thirty years, and was typical of the fine stamp of officer trained in the Regiment. He had reorganized and trained the Battalion after the Great War, and his officers and men fully appreciated how much they owed to his whole-hearted devotion to their welfare. Lieutenant-Colonel Greer had attained his ambition in reaching the command of the Faugh-a-Ballaghs, a regiment in which, to use his own words, " he had never received a discourteous word from any non-commissioned officer or man."

Brevet Lieutenant-Colonel R. C. Dobbs, D.S.O., assumed temporary command.

Between February 15th and February 22nd the Battalion moved to Shergat, the railhead of the Mosul Railway. Here it was found possible to establish an officers' regimental mess, canteens and recreation tents for the men, and other amenities of a standing camp. The camp itself lay close to the railway and under the foot-hills, which were steep. The barbed-wire entanglements not only took in the camp, but a portion of ground on the brow of the hills where an outpost position was established, the defence of which was shared with the 1st/3rd Gurkha Rifles. Duties at Shergat were heavy, but it was found possible to do a certain amount of military training.

On Sunday, February 13th, with suitable ceremonial, the stand of Colours, which were presented to the 87th by Lady Nicolay on March 5th, 1838, at Port Louis, Mauritius, were deposited in Armagh Cathedral. These Colours were given to the Regiment when at Swebo, in Burmah, by Major-General Wolfe-Murray, whose father was in command of the 87th when the present Colours were presented at Umballa in 1860.

MARCH, 1921.

During this month, in order to obtain a better site for the column and to avoid dust-storms, it was decided to move the camp farther west to the high ground already mentioned. This involved much labour, as the wire entanglements had to be pushed farther out so as to embrace the new camp, new strong points had to be made, and the buildings necessary for a standing camp erected. In addition, the water pipe-line, which came from the river, had to be extended, and a pumping station provided.

A draft of 95 non-commissioned officers and men, under command of Lieutenant E. Sirrell, joined from the United Kingdom.

APRIL, 1921.

The work of preparing the new camp, training and outpost duty were continued this month, but, on April 25th, Lieutenant-Colonel H. C. W. Wortham, C.M.G., D.S.O., assumed command of his old battalion, of which he had been adjutant, and brought with him the welcome news that the Fusiliers would shortly move to Egypt. As the new camp would not now be required, all the work had to be undone, and the business of packing and returning stores was commenced.

During its stay in Mesopotamia the Battalion had been organized in three companies and a machine-gun platoon. This was very convenient for column work, but it was now advisable to resume a normal organization. "D" Company was reconstituted by taking platoons No. 4, 8 and 9, one from each company. Each of the four companies then organized their three platoons into four. Lieutenant A. Low, M.C., was specially selected to command "D" Company. The Machine-gun Platoon was retained.

May, 1921.

On May 1st the new "D" Company acted as such for the first time.

At 2 p.m. on May 7th an urgent telegram was received that the Battalion was to entrain as soon as possible for Basrah. So expeditiously was the work done that the first of the two trains left Shergat at 7.10 a.m. on May 8th.

On arrival at Baghdad the same evening, orders were received to hand in all animals and vehicles and entrain at once in a train which was waiting at the same platform. Lieutenant-General Sir Aylmer Haldane came to say good-bye.

At 5 a.m. on May 9th the Battalion left Baghdad, and arrived at Makina, the station for Basra, at 10.20 a.m. on May 10th. It was not without a good deal of heart-burning that the Irishmen parted with their horses and mules.

It was not a very comfortable journey—sixteen men in each of the small iron trucks. Halts were made for meals, and military precautions were taken, as it was reported that there was unrest amongst the Muntafik tribes.

On May 12th and 13th there were heavy rains, most unusual for the season of the year, and the camp was flooded.

On May 18th, Major and Quartermaster T. E. Bunting, D.C.M., with the baggage guard, embarked on the s.s. *Varsova*. The embarkation of the Battalion was delayed because the ship's fittings were not yet complete.

On the morning of May 20th, the Battalion, with kits and light baggage, embarked in forty-five minutes, the strength being 21 officers and 863 other ranks, and at about noon the ship cast off and proceeded slowly down the Shatt-el-Arab. Anchor was dropped at Abuflus, to take on board native cooks, etc., for the voyage. Great credit is due to the quartermaster's department for the efficient way in which these rapid moves were carried out.

The first part of the voyage was very hot, but the provision of ice and four bottles of soda-water per man helped to overcome the discomfort.

Coal and water were taken on board at Aden on May 27th. Time on board was taken up with the usual routine of a transport and a novices' boxing competition.

The work done by the Battalion in Persia and Mesopotamia received the commendation of all the general officers under whom it served, and it left with a high reputation. Amongst the honourable awards, the following were mentioned in despatches in September of this year:—

Lieutenant-Colonel F. A. Greer, C.M.G., D.S.O., Brevet Lieutenant-Colonel R. C. Dobbs, D.S.O., Private J. English, and Private (Acting-Sergeant) A. L. Fry.

JUNE, 1921.

At 10 a.m. on June 1st the s.s. *Varsova* arrived at Suez and tied up at No. 1 quay, Port Tewfik, where instructions were received that the Battalion would be quartered at Abbassia, Cairo, and the advance party, under Major T. E. Bunting, D.C.M., and Lieutenant Austin, M.M., proceeded to take over barracks. After cleaning ship and bidding farewell to the ship's company, who had done all in their power to make the voyage a pleasant one, the Battalion disembarked on June 2nd and proceeded in two trains to Abbassia main barrack, which was reached in the early morning of June 3rd, and where it was met by Major-General Sir G. F. Gorringe, K.C.B., K.C.M.G., D.S.O., commanding the field troops in Egypt. A hot meal was ready for the men, and the 2nd Battalion The Middlesex Regiment hospitably entertained the officers and members of the sergeants' mess.

On June 11th, Lieutenant-General Sir W. Congreve, V.C., K.C.B., General Officer Commanding-in-Chief in Egypt and Palestine, inspected the Battalion on parade, and expressed himself as well pleased.

As there was a total absence of recreation grounds, the Battalion set to work to make them, and a hockey ground was in use by June 21st. The Battalion also made a 30 yards range in barracks, under the supervision of the Royal Engineers.

JULY, 1921.

The 30 yards range was completed.

On July 12th Battalion orders were issued in print for the first time since the war, the Battalion having purchased a printing press.

On July 27th the Battalion temporary transport stables caught fire by a spark from a passing engine, and were completely destroyed. There were no casualties, but several mules were badly burned before they could be got out.

AUGUST, 1921.

This month was spent in routine training. A platoon was furnished for the School of Musketry at Zeitoum, and the Battalion signallers worked in conjunction with the 47th Squadron, Royal Air Force.

On August 30th the senior cross-country race for the Garrard Cup was held. The teams had trained hard for the race, and very keen interest was taken, a fine contest being won by "C" Company. The first man home was Lance-Corporal Mansfield.

SEPTEMBER, 1921.

Training was continued during the first part of the month, including night operations, and the Battalion found a permanent gun-crew for No. 2 Armoured Train.

On September 10th, Colonel E. M. Morris, C.B., C.M.G., commanding the Cairo Brigade, visited the barracks and expressed himself pleased.

Owing to unrest in Egypt, the Battalion was ordered to hold itself in readiness to proceed to Tanta at twenty-four hours' notice, and, on September 24th, Major-General Sir George Gorringe witnessed a practice entrainment, when the Battalion, complete with vehicles, animals and stores, entrained in thirty minutes.

The whole Battalion was employed in levelling, wiring, and pitching a camp for the married families of the garrison.

OCTOBER, 1921.

On October 7th a draft of 122 other ranks joined from home, under command of Lieutenant N. E. V. Dicks, M.C.

On October 20th, Talana Day was celebrated for the first time since the war.

NOVEMBER, 1921.

On November 4th twenty married families arrived, and were accommodated in the new married families' camp.

Armistice Day, November 11th, was celebrated by special parade services. On the same day the Battalion furnished a Guard of Honour at Cairo Station to receive His Excellency the Viscount Allenby, the High Commissioner. Captain A. Faris, M.C., commanded the guard, and His Excellency expressed himself as very pleased with the turn-out and bearing of the men.

In the evening of November 28th, Lieutenant H. Stewart, of the Royal Army Temperance Association, delivered an address which was much appreciated, and about 100 members of the Battalion joined the Association.

On November 19th Field-Marshal Sir Henry Wilson opened the War Memorial to the 36th (Ulster) Division. The memorial is a replica of the famous Helen's Tower, and stands on the site of the Schwaben redoubt at Thiepval. The memorial tablet outside the building was unveiled by General Weygand, Marshal Foch's Chief of the Staff. The tower itself was dedicated by the Primate, and the Duchess of Abercorn hoisted the Union Jack and the Tricolor. An avenue of trees, brought from Ulster, was planted, Lieutenant-Colonel R. G. Shuter, D.S.O., planting one on behalf of the Regular battalions of the Royal Irish Fusiliers.

DECEMBER, 1921.

On December 7th, Major-General Gathorne-Hardy, who had succeeded Lieutenant-General Sir G. Gorringe in command of the 10th Division, paid his first visit to the Battalion.

AN ESTABLISHMENT OF PIPES AUTHORIZED

On December 8th heavy rain commenced, which continued for thirty-six hours, flooding out the barracks and the married families' camp, where a large fatigue party was required to re-erect the tents and dig drains.

In consequence of an increase in unrest, the Battalion Headquarters, the Machine-gun platoon, and two companies were ordered on December 23rd to entrain for Tanta, which place was reached at 9.30 p.m., and the troops billeted in the Secondary Schools.

Duty in aid of the civil power is not a pleasant way of spending Christmas. The duty consisted of constant picquets and patrols, but Christmas dinner was served as the men came off duty.

On December 30th Lieutenant-Colonel Wortham assumed command of the Cairo Brigade, Colonel E. M. Morris having reported sick, and Brevet Lieutenant-Colonel Dobbs assumed command of the Battalion.

It was during the year 1921 that an establishment of pipers was authorized for all Regular Irish Battalions. The pipes adopted were the "Brian Boru," or Irish war pipes. A special uniform was also approved for the pipers. The 87th was the first Irish regiment to adopt the bagpipes, pipers having been specially enlisted on the raising of the Regiment in 1793.

January, 1922.

The situation in Cairo and the Provinces having improved, on January 17th the whole Battalion, which was by this time at Tanta, returned to Abbassia and quarters in the New Barracks, which had been taken over by the details from the 2nd Battalion Middlesex Regiment. These barracks were a great improvement on the Main Barracks.

February, 1922.

On February 12th Captain P. Penn joined with a draft of 12 men from the 2nd Battalion.

Training and tactical exercises were in full swing when, on February 25th, the Battalion was dismayed on receiving instructions to embark about March 15th for the United Kingdom, for disbandment.

The division of Ireland into Ulster and the Free State, and the demand for economy at home, necessitated large reductions in the Army. In addition to the junior battalions of several English regiments, all Irish battalions whose recruiting areas were in the Free State were ordered to be disbanded. This decision, which was communicated to the troops in A.O. 78 of 1922, included the Royal Irish Fusiliers, although their Depôt and one of their recruiting counties, Armagh, was in Northern Ireland.

March, 1922.

The first part of the month was spent in preparation for the move home. Barrosa Day and St. Patrick's Day were celebrated with the time-honoured customs, and in as good heart as the circumstances permitted. Lieutenant-General Sir W. N. Congreve, Major-General Gathorne-Hardy, and Colonel E. M. Morris all came to say farewell to the Battalion, and did so with kindly words. Lieutenant-Colonel Wortham assumed command on March 10th.

At 9 p.m. on March 21st the Battalion entrained for Port Said, having been relieved by the 2nd Battalion Highland Light Infantry. The band of the 9th Lancers played the Battalion to the station, and a large number of friends assembled at the station to bid good-bye and testify to the popularity of the Battalion.

At 8 a.m. on March 22nd, the Battalion, strength 14 officers and 726 other ranks, commenced to embark on the s.s. *Huntsend*. This was completed in two and a quarter hours, a very good performance, as the ship lay off, and all stores and baggage had to be embarked by lighter.

Gibraltar was reached on March 31st, when the ship berthed, and coal and water were taken on board.

The Irish Women's Association presented a lasting memorial of all they had done for the Regiment during the war, in the shape of a handsome silver bowl, which they desired might be used as an Inter-Company Challenge Cup. Most appropriately, it was received by the Regiment on St. Patrick's Day.

APRIL, 1922.

After a rough voyage, the s.s. *Huntsend* arrived in Southampton Water on the morning of April 5th, where she was met by Brigadier-General F. F. Hill, C.B., C.M.G., D.S.O., who brought the welcome news that the Regiment had been saved, but that the 1st and 2nd Battalions would probably be amalgamated.

The ship berthed about noon, and later in the day the Battalion proceeded by train to Shorncliffe, where they were met by the staff of the 10th Brigade, and were played to the Napier Barracks by the bands and drums of The Buffs and East Yorkshire Regiment.

The Battalion soon settled down to training, but garrison duty was heavy, and as many men as possible were sent on furlough. It was unfortunate that all furlough to Ireland was stopped at this period.

On April 26th, Colonel W. Dugan, C.M.G., D.S.O., commanding the 10th Infantry Brigade, inspected the Battalion, and expressed himself pleased with the appearance and turn-out of the men.

MAY, 1922.

On May 13th, Lord Horne, Commanding-in-Chief Eastern Command, inspected the Battalion and barracks. He expressed himself as pleased with all he had seen, and the fine appearance of the men. On the afternoon of the same day the Commanding Officer took 12 officers and 200 other ranks to Dover to witness the arrival of their Majesties the King and Queen from France, where they had been to inspect the war cemeteries. The whole of the 2nd Battalion, stationed at Dover, were also present, and the Regiment was allotted accommodation on the Western Mole.

As the Royal Yacht slowly steamed into Dover Harbour, the Regiment welcomed their Colonel-in-Chief with immense cheers, which His Majesty acknowledged from the bridge. The cheering was continued until the Royal yacht had passed well into the harbour and alongside the quay.

On May 15th the Commanding Officer received the following letter from the Equerry-in-Waiting to His Majesty:—

"*Buckingham Palace,*
"*15th May, 1922.*

"*I must send you a line to let you know how pleased the King was to hear the ringing cheers of the men of his Regiment, who had come over from Shorncliffe of their own free will to welcome their Majesties back from France. The King did not fail to observe them on the Mole at Dover.*

(Sg.) "CLIVE WIGRAM, *Colonel,*
"*Equerry.*"

On May 16th the Battalion had an opportunity of entertaining and expressing personal gratitude to Mr. Delmege Trimble, O.B.E., of Armagh, for all he had done for them in the war.

During the month instructions were received that all men serving on a four years' agreement whose time expired before March 31st, 1923, were to be discharged forthwith. This was with a view to reducing the establishment preparatory to the amalgamation of the Regular battalions.

JUNE, 1922.

On June 8th, welcome authority was received for men to proceed to Ireland on furlough.

On June 11th the Battalion furnished band and full Guard of Honour to escort the Colours of the 1st Battalion Connaught Rangers from Risboro Barracks to the station, *en route* to be handed over to His Majesty the King at Windsor Castle. A Guard of Honour of 50 other ranks was also furnished at the station on this sad occasion.

On June 26th, Captain C. S. Tuely and two drummers proceeded to London with a wreath from all ranks of the Battalion, to attend the funeral of Field-Marshal Sir Henry Wilson at St. Paul's Cathedral. A telegram of condolence was also sent to Lady Wilson. It was only on June 16th that the Field-Marshal had addressed the officers of the Regiment at the annual dinner of the Faugh-a-Ballagh Club, and the melancholy news of his assassination came as a shock to all ranks.

JULY, 1922.

During the first days of July the annual Battalion athletic meeting was held, and, in spite of very inclement weather, all events were keenly contested.

From July 8th to 21st the Battalion was employed in marking for the National Rifle Association at Bisley. The work done was much appreciated by the staff, and a letter to this effect was received by the Commanding Officer.

On July 19th a conference was held in London, at which the following were present :—

The Secretary of State for War, General Sir Archibald Murray (Colonel of the Royal Inniskilling Fusiliers), Major-General Vezey (Director of Organization), Lieutenant-Colonel R. G. Shuter, D.S.O. (commanding 2nd Battalion Royal Irish Fusiliers), Lieutenant-Colonel H. C. Wortham, C.M.G., D.S.O. (commanding 1st Battalion Royal Irish Fusiliers), and Lieutenant-Colonel C. Ridings, D.S.O., O.B.E. (2nd Battalion Royal Inniskilling Fusiliers).

This conference foreshadowed the following reductions: The Royal Inniskilling Fusiliers to be reduced to one battalion by the disbandment of their 2nd Battalion; the Royal Irish Fusiliers to be reduced to one battalion by the amalgamation of the 1st and 2nd Battalions; the Depôts to remain for the present.

Army Order No. 341 of 1922 cancelled that portion of Army Order No. 78 of 1922 referring to the disbandment of the Corps of The Royal Irish (Princess Victoria's), and stated that His Majesty had approved of the amalgamation of the 1st and 2nd Battalions, The Royal Irish Fusiliers (Princess Victoria's).

The period of negotiations which led to this happy result was one of extreme anxiety to the Regiment. Officers past and present naturally did all that the Regulations of the Service admitted to save the life of the Regiment. Sir James Craig, the Prime Minister of Northern Ireland, lent his active support, and he was ably assisted by Members of Parliament, the Lord Lieutenant of Armagh, and the leading inhabitants. Generals under whom the Regiment had served, and was still serving, strongly recommended its retention, and members of the Army Council were at all times sympathetic. But, apart from the popularity of the Regiment, and its record, there is no doubt that its admitted efficiency went far to enlist the active sympathy of those who worked on its behalf.

The real difficulty to be overcome was that the Government had decided that only five Regular Irish battalions were to remain on the Active List, viz., Irish Guards one battalion, Royal Inniskilling Fusiliers two battalions, Royal Ulster Rifles two battalions. It was not until the Royal Inniskilling Fusiliers, through their Colonel, General Sir Archibald Murray, G.C.M.G., K.C.B., C.V.O., D.S.O., expressed the opinion that the line battalions to be retained should be the four battalions taken in order of seniority of the date of their origin, namely, 27th (Royal Inniskilling Fusiliers), 83rd and 86th (Royal Ulster Rifles), and the 87th (Royal Irish Fusiliers) that the question was solved.

This generous action on the part of the Royal Inniskilling Fusiliers, the senior Irish regiment, has placed the Royal Irish Fusiliers under a debt of

**MEMORIAL TO OFFICERS WHO GAVE THEIR LIVES.
NOW IN THE OFFICERS' MESS.**

THE BEGINNING OF A NEW ERA

gratitude which they can never repay, and which should prove a bond of friendship for all time.

On July 30th a party of 50 from the Old Comrades Association, London branch, with their families, made their annual visit to the Regiment.

August, 1922.

The Battalion held an aquatic meeting at the Folkestone Swimming Baths on August 28th, which proved a great success.

September, 1922.

On September 12th, Colonel-Commandant W. Dugan, C.M.G., D.S.O., carried out his annual inspection, and expressed his satisfaction in very complimentary terms, especially remarking on the appearance of the Battalion and its steadiness on parade, and on the state of the interior economy.

On September 27th, Major-General Sir C. D. Shute, K.C.B., commanding the 4th Division, inspected the Battalion on parade and in barracks, and especially asked that his appreciation should be conveyed to all ranks.

October, 1922.

This month was spent in winding up the affairs of the Battalion, closing accounts, handing in equipment, etc. Surplus personnel were either discharged or drafted to other corps, whilst those remaining were sent in parties to the new battalion being constituted at the Grand Shaft Barracks at Dover.

November, 1922.

On November 15th the last party of the 1st Battalion Royal Irish Fusiliers joined the new battalion at Dover. There were many sore hearts amongst those who had perforce to continue their careers in other corps. They left with the good wishes of their comrades, and the sympathy of all went out to Lieutenant-Colonel H. C. Wortham, who, being the junior Commanding Officer, could not be absorbed. His heart was in the Regiment for which he had done so much. The authorities showed their appreciation of his merit by immediately giving him another command.

Thus ended a phase in the history of the Faugh-a-Ballaghs, but, reconstituted from two battalions than which no better ever served in the British Army, they may look forward to the future with hope and determination to make it vie with their glorious past.

APPENDIX I.

ROLL OF HONOUR AND NOMINAL ROLL OF OFFICERS WHO SERVED WITH THE 1ST BN. ROYAL IRISH FUSILIERS IN THE FIELD BETWEEN AUGUST 23RD, 1914, AND NOVEMBER 11TH, 1918, WITH THE APPROXIMATE DATES ON WHICH THEY ACTUALLY JOINED THE BATTALION.

An asterisk (*) against an officer's name indicates that he disembarked with the Battalion on August 23rd, 1914.

As far as possible, officers who were wounded have a W. against their names. Of these 279 officers, 69, or 1 in 4, gave their lives.

Name	Date	Status	Name	Date	Status
Abbott, L. J. W.	30/11/14	K. in a. 17/5/15	Connar, R. L.	20/12/17	W.
Anderson, J.	27/11/15	—	Cooke, C. E.	3/11/14	K. in a. 25/5/15
Arlott, M. J.	1918	—	Cooke, J. A.	19/10/18	—
Armstrong, G. C. S.	21/3/17	K. in a. 3/5/17	Craiger-Watson, G.	15/5/17	W.
Ashley, M.	4/7/17	K. in a. 23/11/17	Creighton, J. L.	5/9/16	—
Atkinson, M. S. H.	27/5/15	—	Crilley, F. L.	4/5/18	—
Barefoot, G. W. N.	*	W.	Crosbie, A. R.	1918	W.
Barton, C. E.	10/5/15	—	Crotty, W. H.	10/2/17	W.
Barwood, H. P.	28/5/15	—	Crymble, C. R.	23/9/14	K. in a. 20/11/14
Beckingsale, B. L.	—/4/17	K. in a. 21/3/18	Cullen, G. S. Y.	16/7/16	K. in a. 11/4/17
Best, W. J.	27/10/16	W.	Cullen, J.	23/10/17	D. of w. 3/10/18
Bishop, C. L.	23/4/18	—	Cuming, A. E. McM.	30/7/17	D. of w. 26/10/18
Black, C. M.	24/3/17	W.	Cunningham, W.	23/4/18	K. in a. 1/10/18
Boal, J. K.	28/7/15	K. in a. 3/5/17	Darling, J.	1918	D. of w. 26/10/18
Boyd, T. W.	23/4/18	—	Darling, O. R.	20/6/16	—
Boyer, S. J.	26/3/16	K. in a. 12/10/16	Davison, D. A.	26/12/14	W.
Bradley, W. D.	27/4/17	W.	Deane, G. A.	16/5/17	D. of w. 11/4/18
Brennan. R.	22/6/15	W.	Dease, T. H. L.	7/6/16	K. in a. 12/10/16
Bridges, J.	19/12/17	W.	Deeming, H.	26/10/16	W.
Brinckman, D.	10/5/15	K. in a. 10/6/15	Dempsey, P. H. D.	27/4/17	W.
Browne, P.	1918	K. in a. 1/10/18	Denny, J.	3/10/18	K. in a. 23/10/18
Bull, G.	*	D. of w. 11/12/16	Dicks, N. E. V.	24/11/15	W.
Bunting, T. E.	*	W.	Dixon, J.	23/4/18	W.
Bunting, T. E., jun.	23/4/18	K. in a. 24/8/18	Dobbyn, A. L.	14/8/18	(present)
Burrowes, A. R.	*	—	Dobson, J.	16/12/16	D. of w. 4/5/17
Burrowes, A. B.	10/10/16	—	Domegan, C.P.	19/5/17	Drowned 10/10/18
Bussey, H. M.	27/4/17	K. in a. 3/5/17	Donagh, P. A.	19/10/18	—
Butler, J.	12/6/16	W.	Drew, C.	8/9/15	K. in a. 12/4/18
Butler, L. W.	25/7/16	K. in a. 20/11/17	Drury, W.	9/9/16	W.
Canning, C. C.	6/5/18	—	Duncan, D.	23/4/18	—
Carbery, M. B. C.	*	K. in a. 18/10/14	Dyson, W. W.	27/6/16	K. in a. 26/8/16
Carden-Roe (Liesching), H. W.	*	W.	Eaton, R. O.	1917	W.
Chalmers, J. L.	16/5/17	K. in a. 27/3/18	Elkan, C. J.	*	—
Churcher, D. W.	*	—	Emerson, R. L.	18/10/18	—
Clements, S. U. L.	30/7/17	W.	Eyre, B. J.	25/10/16	W.
Cockburn, G. E. G.	14/11/14	W.	Falle, T. de C.	5/6/18	—
Coddington, A. F.	15/2/18	—	Faris, A. P.	11/12/15	W.
Coghlan, T. R.	19/10/18	D. of w. 24/10/18	Fforde, E. H.	20/9/14	—
Coles, H. H. E. Q.	15/2/18	—	Findlater, W. A. V.	13/12/15	—
Colhoun, W. A.	12/3/17	W.	Fitt, N. E. L.	—/5/17	Died 26/6/17
			Fitzgerald, L. de V.	*	K. in a. 16/9/18

Flood, W. J. L.	...	2/4/16	—	Le Mare, Reginald	8/7/15	—
Foley, W. A.	...	12/6/16	D. of w. 1/11/17	Lemon, G. H.	—/5/17	—
Forsyth, A. J.	...	4/10/18	—	Lennon, J.	30/10/17	—
Fraser, A. D.	...	9/9/18	—	Leonard, J. S.	26/10/16	—
Furnell, M. J.	...	20/11/17	—	Lindsay, R. H.	23/4/18	—
Fynne, M.	...	12/7/16	W.	Livingston, W. M.	20/6/16	D. of w. 15/4/17
Galvin, B. St. J.	...	15/2/18	—	Low, A.	17/3/15	W.
Gilmer, E. R.	...	4/7/16	K. in a. 12/10/16	Lowe, P. J.	1918	W.
Girvin, W. H.	...	29/12/16	W.	Lowe, T. A.	19/4/18	—
Glover, R. E.	...	13/11/17	—	Luttman-Johnson, K.	5/11/18	—
Glover, S. G.	...	12/6/16	—			
Gough, G. F.	...	4/2/15	W.	Lynch, V. J.	31/8/18	(present)
Graham, M. B.	...	13/12/16	—	Lynden-Bell, D. P.	26/12/14	K. in a. 25/4/15
Graham, W. R.	...	14/6/18	K. in a. 1/10/18	Macmanus, O. B.	18/6/16	W.
Graves, T. F. H.	...	20/7/16	W.	Macmorrow, J.	20/6/16	—
Gray, H.	...	15/2/18	—	MacMullen, H. A.	*	W.
Gray, R. A.	...	*	—	Mahony, M. F. J. R.	26/5/15	—
Grundy, F. W. D.		26/1/17	D. of w. 26/2/17	Mansfield, E. F. H.	11/2/15	—
Hall, T. F.	...	—/2/18	—	Mansfield, R. G. H.	10/5/15	—
Hamill, W. J.	...	26/3/16	W.	Massy - Westropp, J. F. R.	*	W.
Hamilton, N. F. V.		23/4/18	—			
Harris, C. M.	...	2/11/16	W.	McCarthy, G. W.	23/4/18	—
Harris, E. E.	...	17/3/17	W.	McCartney, J. R. F.	5/11/18	—
Harrison, L. J.	...	6/11/17	D. of w. 17/4/18	McCarthy - O'Leary, H. W. D.	5/11/18	W.
Hartley, B.	...	13/11/17	—			
Haskett-Smith, W. J.		1/12/16	—	McClean, C. G.	3/10/18	—
Haswell, T. S.	...	6/11/17	W.	McClenaghan, H. E. St. G.	30/7/17	—
Haughey, H.	...	16/12/16	—			
Hayes, J. P. H.	...	1916	—	McClure, J.	11/8/17	D. of w. 24/11/17
Henry, D. J.	...	13/12/16	K. in a. 9/7/17	McCracken, E. T.	1/11/18	(present)
Henry, J. C.	...	28/3/15	—	McGibney, F. G.	15/1/17	K. in a. 3/5/17
Henry, W. E.	...	28/3/15	K. in a. 1/5/16	McMonagle, D. B. C.	14/6/18	—
Henry, T.	...	23/4/18	—	McKenny, C. N.	4/7/17	—
Hepburn, W. J.	...	19/10/18	—	Michie, J. J.	—/12/16	W.
Herrick, H. E.	...	*	K. in a. 11/5/17	Millar, A. J.	27/10/14	K. in a. 25/4/15
Hill, G. V. W.	...	*	W.	Millerd, J. A.	15/1/15	—
Hogg, W. F.	...	5/6/18	—	Minniece, T. L.	23/4/18	—
Honor, A. C.	...	15/2/18	W.	Mitchel, V.	2/4/16	—
Hornell, J.	...	22/4/17	W.	Moore, R. M.	6 11/17	—
Hornidge, G. M. P.		21/5/17	W.	Morris, —	25/4/18	(present)
Houston, T.	...	16/5/17	W.	Moss, H. W.	9/9/18	—
Hyde, E. E.	...	17/8/16	K. in a. 12/10/16	Mott, J. E.	4/7/16	K. in a. 23/12/17
Incledon-Webber, A. B.		*	W.	Munro, P.	22/4/17	W.
				Murphy, W.	1/10/14	—
Jackson, R. V.	...	13/9/16	—	Neat, C. E. W.	15/2/18	—
Jenkinson, T. S.	...	10/12/16	W.	Neill, R. B.	2/7/15	W.
Jeudwine, R. W. R.		23/11/14	—	Nelson, F. W.	16/5/17	—
Johnston, W.	...	2/4/16	W.	Neville, W. W.	15/2/18	—
Joule, A.	...	—/12/16	W.	Nicholson, P. C.	23/10/17	W.
Kavanagh, T. O. J.		23/4/18	K. in a. 24/8/18	O'Brien, J. C. P.	*	W.
Kavanagh, V. H.		*	W.	O'Connell, J. F. H.	15/2/18	—
Kelly, P. E.	...	27/6/17	K. in a. 10/10/18	O'Donohoe, J. C.	20/6/16	W.
Kennedy, A. B.	...	15/2/18	W.	O'Donovan, M. J. W.	*	W.
Kentish, R. J.	...	29/9/14	W.	O'Driscoll, M. J. L.	10/8/17	—
Keogh-Cullen, E.		19/7/16	—	Olphert, A. V.	*	W.
Kiddell, G. B. P.		17/11/16	Died 27/2/17	O'Toole, D.	6/11/17	K. in a. 23/11/17
Kiely, F. P.	...	22/4/17	—	O'Toole, W.	22/12/16	—
King, C. H.	...	14/6/15	W.	Oulton, W. P.	6/4/15	W.
Kingham, R. W.		20/6/17	W.	Owens, L. C. C.	9/7/15	—
Kirkby, N.	...	15/10/15	W.	Page, F. T.	8/5/17	—
Knowles, P. R.	...	19/6/18	—	Parker, C. T.	8/9/15	W.
Lee, H. S.	...	2/6/17		Parkhill, E. J.	3/10/17	—
Lee, S.	...	28/10/16		Pascoe, F. G. B.	6/2/17	—
Le Mare, Ralph	...	29/4/15	—	Patterson, D. K.	25/10/14	—

Name	Date	Status
Penn, P.	5/9/14	—
Penrose, E. J. McN.	*	K. in a. 25/4/15
Penrose-Fitzgerald, H. J. C.	21/10/15	K. in a. 12/10/16
Pepper, R. F.	7/6/16	K. in a. 12/10/16
Phibbs, W. G. B.	*	Died 8/11/14
Pickett, C. W.	23/4/18	W.
Pollock, J.	17/3/17	W.
Pope, J. H.	8/5/16	D. of w. 11/4/17
Pople, D.	—/5/17	—
Porter, A. G.	3/10/18	D. of w. 29/10/18
Power, R. P.	9/9/14	—
Precha, P.	15/2/18	—
Qualtrough, E. F.	28/9/15	—
Rattray, N. A.	18/5/16	W.
Reeve, G.	10/11/15	W.
Robinson, T.	1/10/14	—
Rogers, A. J.	19/12/17	—
Russell, N.	28/7/15	—
Samuels, A. M.	23/9/14	K. in a. 13/10/14
Sander, R. H.	23/4/18	—
Schroeder, E. D.	7/6/18	—
Schute, F. G.	22/6/15	—
Scott, H. T.	3/2/17	—
Scott, W.	9/7/15	W.
Sheridan, H. H.	16/1/17	K. in a. 3/5/17
Shersby, G.	6/11/17	W.
Shine, H. P.	27/1/15	K. in a. 25/5/15
Shuter, R. G.	27/10/14	W.
Simpson, E. A.	6/11/17	—
Sinclair, D. J. O.	3/9/18	—
Skitt, H. G.	23/4/18	K. in a. 1/10/18
Sloan, N. E. W.	25/10/16	W.
Smith, J. I.	7/8/18	—
Smith, L. B. S.	—/6/16	—
Steavenson, A. F. T.	10/5/15	—
Stirling, R. I. G. L.	23/4/18	W.
Stokes, H. F.	*	—
Synott, F. W.	24/3/15	—
Taylor, M. W.	15/2/18	K. in a. 12/4/18
Taylor, O. T.	23/4/18	—
Templer, G. W. R.	6/11/17	—
Thompson, T. J. C. C.	31/8/18	K. in a. 24/3/18
Trousdell, A. J.	4/5/16	—
Truell, E. G. S.	6/1/17	—
Tuely, C. S. T.	*	W.
Turner, H.	19/1/15	W.
Tyrrell, J. M.	10/5/15	Killed 20/6/18
Upton, G. N. R.	14/10/15	—
Vanston, H. W. F. M.	18/6/15	Died 4/9/17
Verdon, E. H.	28/6/17	—
Verschoyle, W. A.	10/5/15	K. in a. 11/4/17
Vint, F. W.	16/5/17	—
Wadden, G.	3/11/14	—
Wainwright, W.	1918	—
Wakefield, R. O. B.	*	D. of w. 28/8/14
Walkington, E. K.	5/6/18	W.
Warnock, H. A. H.	25/6/15	D. of w. 16/8/15
Warren, H. N. W.	23/4/18	—
Watson, A. C.	24/11/15	—
Watson, J. L. A.	12/10/18	W.
West, A. F.	25/10/14	—
White, H. A.	12/3/17	D. of w. 22/11/17
White, R. M.	23/4/18	—
Wilkinson, R. J.	20/7/16	Died 2/7/18
Williams, C. R.	8/9/15	W.
Wilson, C. T.	19/11/15	—
Wilson, E. R.	18/5/16	W.
Wilson, L.	23/4/18	—
Wilson-Slator, H. B.	*	—
Wingfield, R. A.	10/2/16	—
Winter, B. L. V.	27/5/17	—
Wolsey, S. G.	25/5/17	—
Wortham, H. C. W. H.	*	—
Wright, G. M. H.	9/9/14	W.
Yates, H. W. M.	*	—

Army Chaplains' Department.

The Rev. Father J. Carden (Hessenauer), M.C., C.F.
The Rev. Father P. Donohoe, C.F.
The Rev. Father J. H. McShane, C.F.
The Rev. Father J. J. Noblett, C.F.
The Rev. Father G. Ryan, C.F.

Royal Army Medical Corps.

Captain R. G. Abrahams.
Captain J. G. Brown.
Captain O. Hairsine, M.C.
Captain A. S. Littlejohns, D.S.O.
Lieutenant K. C. Middlemiss.
Captain R. Ryan.
Captain L. H. Seville.
Lieutenant C. W. Sparks, M.C.
Captain A. E. Thompson.

APPENDIX II.

Roll of Honour—Other Ranks.

Reprint from "Soldiers Died in the Great War," 1914–1919, Part 68.
(Authority, H.M. Stationary Office, No. C/56/3/19a, dated 29 : 2 : 1924.)

EXPLANATION OF ABBREVIATIONS.

" b."	"born."	" k. in a."	" killed in action.
" e."	" enlisted."	" F. & F."	" France & Flanders "
" d."	" died."		(including Italy).
" d. of w."	" died of wounds."		

N.B.—When the place of enlistment is followed by the name of another place in brackets, the latter represents the deceased soldier's place of residence.

Abell, Harry, b. Battersea, S.W., Surrey, e. Woolwich, Kent (Fulham, S.W., Middx), 41879, Pte., k. in a., F. & F., 9/10/18, formerly 026107, R.A.O.C.
Adams, William John, b. Crewe, Cheshire, e. Whitehall, S.W., Middx (Crewe), 42043, Pte., k. in a., F. & F., 17/7/18.
Adamson, George, b. Portadown, Co. Armagh, e. Portadown (Belfast), 6105, Pte., k. in a., F. & F., 25/4/15.
Adamson, Joseph, b. Gilford, Co. Down, e. Belfast, 8746, Pte., d., F. & F., 6/6/18.
Alderman, Frank, b. Winchester, e. Winchester, 9634, Pte., k. in a., F. & F., 12/4/15.
Alderson, Benjamin, b. Whitehaven, Cumberland, e. Workington, Cumberland (Whitehaven), 10286, Pte., k. in a., F. & F., 1/7/16.
Allen, David, b. Mintburn, Co. Tyrone, e. Armagh (Mullin, Co. Monaghan), 24898, Pte., d. of w., F. & F., 2/10/17.
Allen, James Griffin, b. Shankill, Belfast, e. Belfast, 7563, Pte., k. in a., F. & F., 16/2/17.
Allen, John, b. Trim, Co. Meath, e. Dublin, 16754, Pte., d., F. & F., 25/11/16.
Allison, William, b. Ballymena, Co. Antrim, e. Belfast (Drogheda, Co. Louth), 7864, Pte., d., Home, 14/11/14.
Anderson, Charles William, b. Islington, N., Middx, e. Hounslow, Middx (Blackstock Road, N., Middx.), 41968, Pte., k. in a., F. & F., 27/4/18, formerly 685549, 3/22 London Regt.
Anderson, Joseph John, b. Erith, Kent, e. Stratford, E., Essex (Leyton, N.E., Essex), 23514, L/Cpl., k. in a., F. & F., 11/4/17, formerly 5171, Middlesex Regt.
Andrews, Horace Edgar, b. Kildare, e. Bandon, Co. Cork, 22767, Pte., k. in a., F. & F., 23/11/17.
Armstrong, William, b. Dunmurry, Co. Antrim, e. Belfast (Monaghan), 12311, Pte., k. in a., F. & F., 23/11/17.
Armstrong, William Henry, b. Portadown, Co. Armagh, e Porta down, 7599, Pte., k. in a., F. & F., 11/3/15.
Aston, David Alexander, b. Portadown, Co. Armagh, e. Portadown, (Tandragee, Co. Armagh), 5737, Pte., k. in a., F. & F., 19/6/16.
Bailey, Frank, b. Swindon, Wilts, e. Southampton (Cheriton, Kent), 9336, Pte., k. in a., F. & F., 24/3/18.
Bailie, Matthewson, b. Shankill, Belfast, e. Belfast (Milford, Co. Armagh), 9721, Sgt., d., F. & F., 6/6/18.
Baker, John, b. Dundalk, Co. Louth, e. Dublin (Potton, Beds), 6796, Pte., k. in a., F. & F., 18/10/14.
Ball, John David Sullivan Leonard, b. Chatham, e. Dublin (Tunbridge Wells, Kent), 9869, L/Sgt., d. of w., F. & F., 3/10/14.
Ballantyne, John, b. Newtownstewart, Co. Tyrone, e. Glasgow (Cowcaddens, Glasgow), 8050, Pte., k. in a., F. & F., 6/7/16.
Bannan, James, b. Templeport, Co. Cavan, e. Glasgow (Pollockshaws, Glasgow), 27419, Pte., k. in a., F. & F., 21/3/18.
Banyard, Arthur Cecil, b. Cherry Hinton, Cambs, e. Cambridge, 22222, Pte., k. in a., F. & F., 3/5/17, formerly 7288, Bedford Regt.

Barlow, James, b. Forkhill, Co. Louth, e. Armagh (Forkhill), 11453, Pte., d. of w., F. & F., 23/5/15.
Barnard, Leonard, b. Acton, W. Middx., e. Fulham, S.W., Middx. (Colnbrook, Bucks), 18928, Pte., d. of w., Home, 12/10/15, formerly 11777, Huss. of the Line.
Barnes, Albert John, b. Blackheath, Kent, e. Kingston-on-Thames (Sydenham, S.E., Surrey), 50036, Pte., k. in a., F. & F., 1/10/18, formerly 636237, 20th London Regt.
Barrett, John ,b. Dublin, e. Dublin, 11397, Pte., k. in a., F. & F., 12/10/16.
Bartley, Michael, b. Donegal, e. Glasgow (Newferry, Cheshire), 8579, Pte., d. of w., F. & F., 15/10/14.
Barton, James, b. Ardee, Co. Louth, e. Edinburgh (Leith), 11709, Pte., k. in a., F. & F., 25/4/15.
Barugh, Thomas William, b. Bombay, e. Leeds, 7919, Pte., k. in a., F. & F., 27/8/14.
Bates, Thomas, e. Widnes, Lancs (Runcorn, Cheshire), 49839, Pte., d. of w., F. & F., 27/8/18, formerly 62174, Ches. Regt.
Beagan, Francis, b. Clones, Co. Monaghan, e. Londonderry (Govan, Glasgow), 8210, Pte., k. in a., F & F., 24/5/15.
Beattie, Francis John, b. Gilford, Co. Down, e. Belfast (Pendleton, Manchester), 3425, L/Cpl., k. in a., F. & F., 23/11/17.
Behan, Walter, b. Widnes, Lancs, e. Warrington (Widnes), 18814, Pte., d. of w., F. & F., 2/4/18.
Beirne, Patrick, b. Balbriggan, Co. Dublin, e. Dublin (Balbriggan), 24512, A/Cpl., k. in a., F. & F., 11/4/17.
Bell, James, b. Shankill, Belfast, e. Belfast, 5993, Pte., k. in a., F. & F., 26/6/15.
Bell, John George, b. Portadown, Co. Armagh, e. Portadown, 7036, Pte., k. in a., F. & F., 10/6/15.
Bell, Moses, b. Donaldstown, Co. Down, e. Lurgan (Donaldstown), 5760, Pte., k. in a., F. & F., 25/4/15.
Bennett, Ernest Henry, b. Ashill, Norfolk, e. Norwich (Ashill, Norfolk), 19075, Pte., k. in a., F. & F., 7/5/17, formerly 146746, R.F.A.
Bergin, Denis, b. Drumcliffe, Co. Sligo, e. Dublin (Cheriton, Kent), 11101, Pte., k. in a., F. & F., 12/10/16.
Bew, Charles George, b. Westbourne Park, W., Middx., e. New Kent Road, S.E., Surrey, 9329, Pte., k. in a., F. & F., 26/10/16.
Blades, George, b. Louth, Lincs, e. Louth (Alvingham, Lincs), 40148, Pte., k. in a., F. & F., 21/3/18, formerly 50639, 3rd Notts & Derby Regt.
Bolton, Albert, b. Nelson, Lancs, e. Burnley (Nelson), 41833, Pte., k. in a., F. & F., 21/3/18, formerly T/1st/5186, R.A.S.C.
Bolton, Cecil Arthur Reginald, b. Leeds, e. Leeds, 27566, Pte., k. in a., F. & F., 21/3/18, formerly 31909, W. Yorks Regt.
Bonner, Peter, b. Templemore, Co. Londonderry, e. Maryhill, Glasgow (Londonderry), 21597, Pte., k. in a., F. & F., 12/10/16.
Bonscy, Arthur Albert, b. Cranleigh, Surrey, e. Guildford, 19039, Pte., k. in a., F. & F., 24/3/18, formerly 146757, R.F.A.

150

APPENDICES

Boston, Alfred, e. Shorncliffe, Kent, 11011, Pte., k. in a., F. & F., 9/7/17.
Boughton, Albert, b. Dublin, e. Dublin (Drumcondra, Dublin), 10936, Pte., d. of w., F. & F., 27/4/15.
Boughton, Robert, b. Fairview, Dublin, e. Dublin (Buncrana, Co. Donegal), 6066, Sgt., d. of w., F. & F., 13/4/17.
Bowler, Laurie, b. Shirland, Derbyshire, e. Wakefield (Banbury, Oxon), 41874, Sgt., k. in a., F. & F., 21/3/18, formerly 07829, 18th K.R.R.
Bowman, Henry, b. Gateshead, Durham, e. Gateshead, 23480, Pte., k. in a., F. & F., 13/4/18, formerly 30077, Manchester Regt.
Boyd, James, b. Shankill, Belfast, e. Belfast, 10400, Sgt., d. of w., F. & F., 11/10/18, M.M.
Boyle, Edward James, b. Belfast, e. Belfast (Liverpool), 9062, Sgt., d. of w., F. & F., 18/12/17.
Boyle, George, b. Tassagh, Co. Armagh (Belleeks, Co. Armagh), 20115, Pte., k. in a., F. & F., 12/10/16.
Boyle, Henry, b. Belfast, e. Cavan (Castlerea, Co. Roscommon), 10309, Pte., k. in a., F. & F., 18/10/14.
Boyle, James, b. Shankill, Belfast, e. Belfast, Co. Down (Belfast), 7152, Pte., k. in a., F. & F., 21/3/18.
Boyle, James, b. Belfast, e. Belfast, 12653, Pte., k. in a., F. & F., 11/4/17.
Boyle, John, b. Govan, Glasgow, e. Glasgow, 18951, Pte., k. in a., F. & F., 21/3/18.
Boylen, James, b. South Bank, Yorks, e. South Bank, 41678, L/Cpl., k. in a., F. & F., 2/9/18, formerly 017555, R.A.O.C.
Brady, Charles, b. Dublin, e. Belfast (Dublin), 5848, Pte., k. in a., F. & F., 10/6/15.
Brady, Edward, b. Glasgow, e. Glasgow (Johnstone, Renfrewshire), 10601, Pte., k. in a., F. & F., 12/4/17, D.C.M.
Brady, Thomas, b. Clones, Co. Monaghan, e. Monaghan (Clones), 25042, Pte., k. in a., F. & F., 11/4/17.
Brennan, Joseph, b. Dublin, e. Dublin, 40115, Pte., k. in a., F. & F., 11/4/17, formerly 24720, Hussars of the Line.
Brien, William, b. Kilclooney, Co. Galway, e. Ballinasloe (Caledon, Co. Tyrone), 24876, L/Cpl., k. in a., F. & F., 11/4/17.
Brigdell, Gerald George, b. Limerick, e. Hamilton, Lanarks (Glasgow), 11393, Pte., k. in a., F. & F., 23/11/14.
Briggs, Arthur, b. Manchester, e. Liverpool (Manchester), 27734, Pte., k. in a., F.&F., 21/3/18, formerly 9482, Dragoons of the Line
Broad, Frederick, b. Barton Stacey, Hants, e. Aldershot (Barton, Stacey), 25234, Cpl., k. in a., F. & F., 21/3/18, formerly 24528, Hussars of the Line.
Brock, Francis, b. Penzance, Cornwall, e. Dublin (Penzance), 10478, Sgt., k. in a., F. & F., 12/10/16.
Brophy, George, b. Dublin, e. Dublin, 9339, Pte., d. of w., F. & F., 17/9/14.
Brophy, John, b. Ballyraggett, Co. Kilkenny, e. Maryborough (Ballyraggett), 11703, Pte., d. of w., F. & F., 11/6/15.
Brown, George, b. Gt. Yarmouth, Norfolk, e. Gt. Yarmouth, 17821, L/Cpl., k. in a., F. & F., 11/4/17, formerly 7157, 5th Lancers.
Brown, James, b. Shankill, Belfast, e. Belfast, 7538, Pte., k. in a., F. & F., 7/5/17.
Brown, Robert, Henry, b. Lurgan, Co. Armagh, e. Armagh (Portadown), 6133, Pte., d. of w., F. & F., 4/4/16.
Browne, William, b. Ballysillan, Co. Antrim, e. Clones (Crumlin, Co. Antrim), 9093, Pte., k. in a., F. & F., 6/7/16.
Browning, George Albert, b. Shankill, Belfast, e. Belfast, 29472, Pte., d. of w., F. & F., 5/9/18.
Brownlee, Albert, b. Portadown, Co. Armagh, e. Portadown, 6370, Cpl., d. of w., F. & F., 23/4/18.
Bryan, Daniel, b. Kingstown, Co. Dublin, e. Dublin, Kingstown), 11302, Pte., d. of w., F. & F., 26/4/15.
Buckley, Thomas Henry, b. Annaghmore, Co. Armagh, e. Armagh (Loughgall, Co. Armagh), 5516, Pte., d., F. & F., 10/2/17.
Bull, Arthur Henry, b. Camden Town, N.W., Middx., e. Holloway, N., Middx. (Islington, N., Middx.), 41955, Pte., d., F. & F., 9/4/18.
Burke, Edward, b. Hulme, Manchester, e. Manchester (Old Trafford, Manchester), 6240, Pte., k. in a., F. & F., 25/4/15.
Burns, Alexander, b. Markethill, Co. Armagh, e. Newry (Durham), 26109, Pte., k. in a., F. & F., 27/9/17.
Burns, Samuel, b. Bessbrook, Co. Armagh, e. Newry (Bessbrook), 11122, Pte., k. in a., F. & F., 27/8/17.
Burrells, Alfred Albert, b. Islington, N., Middx., e. Whitehall, S.W., Middx. (Lower Edmonton, N., Middx.), 50040, Pte., k. in a., F. & F., 3/9/18, formerly 636000 20th London Regt.
Butt, James, b. Swansea, e. Pontypridd, Glam. (Treforest, Glam.), 41716, L/Cpl., d. of w., F. & F., 2/10/18, formerly A/1005, R.A.S.C.
Byrne, Benjamin, b. Dublin, e. Dublin, 13860, Pte., k. in a., F. & F., 12/10/16.
Byrne, John, b. Dublin, e. Dublin, 7654, Pte., k. in a., F. & F., 25/4/15.

Byrne, Patrick, b. Dublin, e. Dublin, 6252, Pte., k. in a., F. & F., 25/4/15.
Byrne, Patrick, b. Termonfeckin, Co. Louth, e. Drogheda, Co. Louth (Termonfeckin), 10201, Pte., k. in a., F. & F., 27/5/15.
Byrne, Simon, b. Barrindarrig, Co. Wicklow, e. Bray, Co. Wicklow (Kilbridge, Co. Wicklow), 21740, Pte., k. in a., F. & F., 3/5/17.
Byrne, William Joseph, b. Dublin, e. Dublin, 11265, k. in a., F.&F., 18/10/14.
Caffrey, John, b. Dublin, e. Dublin, 10532, Cpl., k. in a., F. & F., 13/2/18.
Calwell, Arthur James, b. Dublin, e. Dublin, 10501, C.S.M., k. in a., F. & F., 3/5/17.
Camp, Albert, b. Southwark, S.E., Surrey, e. Southwark, S.E. (Walworth, S.E., Surrey), 18647, Pte., k. in a., F. & F., 6/7/15.
Campbell, Alexander, b. Shankill, Belfast, e. Belfast, 3385, Pte., k. in a., F. & F., 30/4/16.
Campbell, James, b. Kilclooney, Co. Galway, e. Ballinasloe, Co. Galway, 10955, Pte., k. in a., F. & F., 10/12/16.
Campbell, John, b. Newry, Co. Down, e. Newry, 19861, Pte., k. in a., F. & F., 11/4/18.
Campbell, Michael, b. Drumcree, Portadown, Co. Armagh, e. Portadown, 6184, L/Cpl., d. of w., F. & F., 24/10/16.
Campbell, Patrick, b. Monaghan, e. Monaghan, 23689, Pte., k. in a., F. & F., 1/10/18.
Canavan, Patrick, b. Ballyclare, Co. Antrim, e. Belfast, 8372, Pte., d. of w., F. & F., 10/5/15.
Carlon, John, b. Glasgow, e. Glasgow, 20824, Pte., d. of w., F. & F., 10/10/16.
Carmichael, Andrew, b. Ballyclare, Co. Antrim, e. Belfast (Ballyclare), 8318, Pte., k. in a., F. & F., 25/4/15.
Carney, Thomas, b. Widnes, Lancs, e. Warrington (Widnes), 6251, Pte., d., F. & F., 25/6/18.
Carragher, John, b. Ballybay, Co. Monaghan, e. Cavan (Ballybay), 3407, Pte., k. in a., F. & F., 19/11 17.
Carroll, William, b. Lambeth, S.E., Surrey, e. London (St. Albans, Herts), 9690, Pte., d. of w., F. & F., 7/7/18.
Carroll, William, b. Dundrum, Co. Dublin, e. Dublin, 18958, L/Cpl. k. in a., F. & F., 18/4/18, formerly 13136, Hussars of the Line.
Carson, Hugh, b. Cambusnethan, Lanarks, e. Hamilton (Wishaw, Lanarks), 17563, Pte., k. in a., F. & F., 4/7/15.
Carson, William, b. Donaldstown, Co. Down, e. Lurgan, Co. Armagh (Donaldstown), 5749, Pte., d. of w., F. & F., 27/4/15.
Carton, James, b. Drogheda, Co. Louth, e. Drogheda, 6656, Pte., d. of w., F. & F., 17/8/16.
Carty, Edward, b. Dublin, e. Dublin, 7074, Pte., k. in a., F. & F., 18/10/14.
Casey, James, b. Blanchardstown, Co. Dublin, e. Dublin (Castleknock, Co. Dublin), 11010, Pte., k. in a., F. & F., 12/10/16.
Casey, John, b. Balbriggan, Co. Dublin, e. Dublin (Balbriggan), 22910, Pte., k. in a., F. & F., 12/10/16, formerly 3/23894, R. Dublin Fus.
Casey, Michael, b. Carrickmacross, Co. Monaghan, e. Monaghan (Carrickmacross), 24390, Pte., d. of w., F. & F., 23/4/17.
Casey, William, b. Blanchardstown, Co. Dublin, e. Dublin (Kilburn, N.W., Middx.), 9189, Sgt., k. in a., F. & F., 12/10/16.
Cassidy, James, b. Ross, Co. Meath, e. Monaghan, 20636, Pte., d. of w., F. & F., 10 9/18.
Cassidy, Thomas, b. Belturbet, Co. Cavan e. Cavan Belturbet), 2821, Pte., k. in a., F. & F., 11 4/17.
Cathcart, George, b. Ballinrobe, Co. Mayo, e. Galway (Ballinrobe), 8849, Sgt., k. in a., 11/4/17.
Caulfield, Stephen, b. Kilclooney, Co. Galway, e. Ballinasloe, 11115, Pte., k. in a., F. & F., 11/4/17.
Chambers, Bernard, b. Newry, e. Newry, 5316, Pte., k. in a., F. & F., 25/4/15.
Chappell, Bertie, b. Houghton Regis, Beds, e. Luton, Beds (Dunstable, Beds), 19077, Pte., k. in a ,F & F. , 1/7/17, formerly 146482, R.F.A.
Charles, George, b. Killinkere, Co. Cavan, e. Cavan (Bailieborough, Co. Cavan), 9131, L/Cpl. d. of w., Home, 6/11/16.
Cheney, Edward Emerson, b. Enniskillen, e. Glasgow (Belfast), 8409, Pte., k. in a., F. & F., 25/4/15.
Clail, William, b. Cavan, e. Cavan, 24857, Pte., d. of w., F. & F., 17/5/17.
Clanachan, James, b. Dundrum, Co. Dublin, e. Newry (Blacklion, Co. Cavan), 8412, Pte., k. in a., F. & F., 7/12/14.
Clarke, Thomas, b. Drogheda, Co. Louth, e. Drogheda, 5895, Pte., d. of w., F. & F., 9/5/15.
Clarke, William, b. Bessbrook, Co. Armagh, e. Armagh (Newry, Co. Down), 5598, Pte., k. in a., F. & F., 7/12/14.
Cleary, William, b. Forfar, e. Hamilton (Dundee), 11016, Pte., d. of w., F. & F., 10/10/14.
Coffey, Peter, b. Multyfarnham, Co. Westmeath, e. Mullingar (Rathowen, Co. Westmeath), 9636, Pte., k. in a., F. & F., 21/10/14.

Coghlan, Christopher, b. Dublin, e. Dublin 11392, Pte., d. of w., F. & F., 3/5/15.
Collins, Francis, b. Langloan, Lanarks, e. Glasgow (Coatbridge, Lanarks), 8049, Pte., d. of w., F. & F., 17/9/14.
Collins, George, b. Doncaster, Yorks, e. Longmoor (Twyford, Hants), 18931, Pte., k. in a., F. & F., 23/11/17, formerly H/19119, Hussars of the Line.
Colrain, Bartholomew, b. Maryhill, Glasgow, e. Rutherglen, Glasgow, 17759, Pte., d. of w., F. & F., 7/7/15.
Conaty, Michael, b. Ballinagh, Co. Cavan, e. Cavan (Kilmaleck, Co. Cavan), 11707, Pte., k. in a., F. & F., 25/4/15.
Condron, Thomas, b. Dublin, e. Glasgow, 24941, Pte., k. in a., F. & F., 11/4/17.
Conlan, Alexander, b. Largey, Co. Cavan, e. Belfast (Templepatrick, Co. Antrim), 6315, Pte., d., Home, 28/2/16.
Conlan, Bernard, b. Clones, Co. Monaghan, e. Clones, 5685, L/Cpl. k. in a., F. & F., 24/6/17.
Conlan, Francis, b. Clones, Co. Monaghan, e. Clones, 10515, Pte., d. of w., F. & F., 26/8/16.
Conlon, John William, b. Tydavnet, Co. Monaghan, e. Monaghan, 20701, Pte., d. of w., F. & F., 8/5/17.
Conlon, Patrick, b. Armagh, e. Armagh, 12267, Pte., k. in a., F.& F., 10/10/16.
Connolly, Charles, b. Dublin, e. Dublin, 11214, Pte., d. of w., F. & F., 8/1/15.
Connolly, George, b. Frenchpark, Co. Roscommon, e. Boyle (Frenchpark), 40091, Pte., k. in a., F. & F., 11/4/17.
Connolly, James, b. Whitehaven, Cumberland, e. Belfast, 3793 Pte., k. in a., F. & F., 24/6/17.
Connolly, Patrick, b. Dublin, e. Dublin, 7957, L/Sgt., k. in a., F. & F., 1/7/16.
Connolly, Thomas, b. Kilmore, Co. Cavan, e. Cavan (Drumconnick, Co. Cavan), 20670, Pte. k. in a., F. & F., 1/7/16.
Connor, James, b. Cootehill, Co. Cavan, e. Cootehill, 7971, Pte., d., Home, 21/5/15.
Connor, John, b. Shankill, Belfast, e. Lurgan, Co. Armagh (Belfast), 4716, Pte., k. in a., F. & F., 14/10/14.
Conway, Frederick, b. Dublin, e. Dublin, 10662, Cpl., k. in a., F. & F., 9/7/17.
Conway, Michael, b. Longford, e. Armagh (Longford), 10086, Sgt., k. in a., F. & F., 23/11/17, M.M.
Coogan, James, b. Widnes, Lancs, e. Warrington, Lancs (Widnes), 17566, Pte., k. in a., F. & F., 14/12/16.
Coogan, John, b. Armagh, e. Finner Camp, Co. Donegal (Armagh), 4024, Pte., k. in a., F. & F., 25/4/15.
Cooke, Patrick James, b. Bristol, e. Bristol, 10645, Cpl., k. in a., F. & F., 21/3/18.
Cooke, Richard, b. Kirkham, Lancs, e. Belfast (Whitehouse, Co. Antrim), 6698, Pte., k. in a., F. & F., 6/11/14.
Coombes, Thomas. b. Liverpool, e. Liverpool, 15306, Pte., k. in a., F. & F., 30/3/18.
Cope, Thomas, b. Dublin, e. Dublin, 7042, Pte., k. in a., F. & F., 20/11/14.
Copeland, John, b. Shankill, Belfast, e. Belfast (Ballymacarrett, Belfast), 6484, Pte., k. in a., F. & F., 26/4/15.
Corbally, Patrick, b. Drogheda, Co. Louth, e. Drogheda, 2902, Pte., k. in a., F. & F., 25/8/16.
Cordner, Thomas, b. Portadown, Co. Armagh, e. Armagh (Portadown), 11254, Pte., k. in a., F. & F., 9/11/14.
Corps, Frederick Freeman, b. Stoke, Devon, e. Plymouth (Devonport), 49897, Pte., k. in a., F. & F., 1/10/18.
Corps, John Thomas, b. Sherburn, Co. Durham, e. Shirehampton, Glos. (Hetton-le-Hole, Co. Durham), 25151, Pte., k. in a., F. & F., 24/8/18, formerly 65990, R.A.S.C. (Remount), M.M.
Corr, James, b. Shankill, Co. Armagh, e. Armagh (Lurgan), 6187, Pte., k. in a., F. & F., 12/10/16.
Corrigan, Patrick, b. Shankill, Belfast, e. Belfast, 7134, Pte., k. in a., F. & F., 25/4/15.
Cosgrave, John, b. Dublin, e. Dublin, 10940, Pte., k. in a., F. & F., 11/4/17.
Costello, Edward, b. Roscommon, e. Leeds (Roscommon), 10588, Pte., k. in a., F. & F., 12/10/16.
Costigan, William, b. Dublin, e. Dublin (Salford, Manchester), 11340, Pte., k. in a., F. & F., 27/8/14.
Coulahan, Arthur Herbert, b. Dublin, e. Dublin, 11449, Pte., k. in a., F. & F., 6/7/15.
Coupland, William, b. Annan, Dumfriesshire, e. Carlisle (Gretna, Carlisle), 41834, Pte., d., F. & F., 29/4/18, formerly T/4/055824, R.A.S.C.
Courtney, James, b. Clones, Co. Monaghan, e. Dublin (Clones), 3471, Pte., d. of w., F. & F., 4/12/14.
Cox, Frederick Charles, b. Ilsington, Devon, e. Newton Abbot, Devon (Ilsington), 41646, Cpl., k. in a., F. & F., 16/4/18, formerly S/4/11300, R.A.S.C.

Coyle, Edward, b. Urney, Co. Cavan, e. Cavan, 11205, Pte., k. in a., F. & F., 27/8/14.
Coyle, Robert, b. Ballyjamesduff, Co. Cavan, e. Cavan (Springburn, Glasgow), 24611, Pte., k. in a., F. & F., 23/11/17.
Craig, Edmund, b. Shankill, Co. Armagh, e. Portadown, Co. Armagh (Lurgan, Co. Armagh), 11310, Pte., k. in a., F. & F., 30/4/16.
Craig, George, b. Rathfriland, Co. Down, e. Belfast (Banbridge, Co. Down), 8973, Sgt., k. in a., F. & F., 11/5/17, M.M.
Craig, John, b. Killeshandra, Co. Cavan, e. Cavan (Killeshandra), 2522, Pte., k. in a., F. & F., 11/4/17.
Craig, John, e. Glasgow (Cambuslang, Lanarks), 22570, Pte., k. in a., F. & F., 13/2/18.
Crangle, John, b. Shankill, Belfast, e. Belfast, 16377, Pte., d. of w., F. & F., 30/4/15.
Crawford, Alexander, b. Paisley, e. Glasgow (Paisley), 9971, Pte. k. in a., F. & F., 12/10/14.
Crimlage, Francis, b. Strabane, Co. Tyrone, e. Carrickfergus, Co. Antrim (Dungannon, Co. Tyrone), 3334, Pte., k. in a., F. & F., 12/10/16.
Crimmins, Patrick, b. Ennis, Co. Clare, e. Tipperary (Dublin), 18385, Pte., k. in a., F. & F., 24/8/18, M.M.
Croley, William, b. Dublin, e. Dublin, 11334, L/Cpl., k. in a., F. & F., 11/4/17.
Cromwell, Henry James, b. Ballymena, Co. Antrim, e. Randalstown, Co. Antrim (Harryville, Co. Antrim), 21647, Pte., k. in a., F. & F., 12/10/16.
Crorken, Thomas, b. Brookeborough, Co. Fermanagh, e. Armagh (Fivemiletown, Co. Tyrone), 25051, Pte., k. in a., F. & F., 15/3/18.
Crowther, Harold, b. Oldham, Lancs, e. Shaw, Lancs (Oldham), 41905, Pte., k. in a., F. & F., 2/9/18, formerly 11914, R.A.S.C.
Crowther, William, b. Wexford, e. Dublin, 10767, Cpl., k. in a., F. & F., 22/10/14.
Cunningham, Francis Joseph, b. Nowshera, India, e. London (Wandsworth, S.W. Surrey), 10441, Pte., k. in a., F. & F., 7/10/18.
Cunningham, John, b. Lildallen, Co. Cavan, e. Cavan (Ardlogher, Co. Cavan), 26883, Pte., d. of w., F. & F., 17/7/18.
Cunningham, Michael, b. Newry, Co. Down, e. Newry, 8353, Pte., k. in a., F. & F., 18/10/14.
Daily, John, b. Tartlachan, Co. Tyrone, e. Hamilton, Lanarks (Coatbridge, Lanarks), 24896, Pte., k. in a., F. & F., 18/7/18.
Daly, James, b. Peshawur, India, e. Armagh, 9719, L/Sgt., k. in a., F. & F., 26/10/14.
Dalzell, James, b. Drumcree, Co. Armagh, e. Portadown, Co. Armagh, 5505, Sgt., d. of w., F. & F., 12/5/15.
Dalzell, William, b. Rathfriland, Co. Down, e. Armagh (Castlewellan, Co. Down), 8678, L/Cpl., d. of w., F. & F., 2/6/15.
Darby, Patrick, b. Johnstone, Co. Meath, e. Navan, Co. Meath, 24805, &tc., d. of w., F. & F., 28/3/18.
Davies, John David, b. Welshpool, e. Manchester (Middleton, Lancs), 41652, Pte., k. in a., F. & F., 14/4/18, formerly T./3/023051, R.A.S.C.
Delaney, John, b. Ballywalter, Co. Down, e. Newtonards, Co. Down (Portaferry, Co. Down), 21940, Pte., d. of w., F. & F., 14/4/17, formerly 4151, R. Irish Rif.
Delaney, Joseph Francis Patrick, b. Clonagown, Queen's Co., e. Maryborough, Queen's Co., 17043, L/Sgt., k. in a., F. & F., 21/3/18, formerly 1702, R. Irish Rif.
Dempsey, James, b. Mountmellick, Queen's Co., e. Naas, Co. Kildare (Dublin), 6450, Pte., k. in a., F. & F., 25/4/15.
Dempsey, John, b. Rathmines, Dublin, e. Dublin, 11420, Pte., d., F. & F., 3/11/14.
Dempster, Samuel, b. Greenock, Renfrews, e. Belfast, 7237, Pte., k. in a., F. & F., 25/4/15.
Devaney, Joseph, e. Glasgow, 6324, Pte., d., F. & F., 21/3/15.
Devin, James, b. Dunleer, Co. Louth, e. Dundalk, Co. Louth (Dunleer), 17520, Pte., k. in a., F. & F., 7/5/17.
Devlin, John, b. Annaclone, Co. Down, e. Newry, Co. Down (Rathfriland, Co. Down), 8242, Pte., k. in a., F. & F., 4/4/15.
Devlin, Patrick, James Joseph b. Belfast, e. Belfast, 21054, Pte., k. in a., F. & F., 29/10/16, formerly C/2509, Connaught Rangers.
Diamond, Thomas, e. Dublin, 40122, Pte., k. in a., F. & F., 11/4/17, formerly 24826, Hussars of the Line.
Dickson, Moses, b. Gilford, Co. Down, e. Portadown, Co. Armagh (Laurencetown, Co. Down), 5960, Pte., k. in a., F. & F., 9/5/15.
Dingle, John, b. Dublin, e. Dublin, 9340, Pte., d., F. & F., 3/11/14.
Dixon, Frederick, b. Walsall, Staffs, e. Wednesbury, Staffs (Caldmore, Staffs), 8742, Pte., d. of w., F. & F., 17/10/16.
Dobbin, Michael, b. Dublin, e. Dublin, 49792, Pte., k. in a., F. & F., 1/10/18, formerly 13984, Hussars of the Line.
Docherty, Edward, b. Leith, e. Glasgow, 8666, Pte., d. of w., F. & F., 28/4/15., formerly 7264, R. Innis. Fus.

APPENDICES

Dodds, Michael, b. Magherasaul, Co. Down, e. Lisburn, Co. Antrim, 3466, Pte., k. in a., F. & F., 9/4/17.
Dogherty, Patrick, b. Shankill, Co. Antrim, e. Bridge End, Belfast (Belfast), 28897, Pte., k. in a., F. & F., 1/10/18.
Doherty, James, b. Falcarragh, Co. Donegal, e. Ludden Camp, Co. Donegal (Falcarragh), 6426, L/Cpl., d. of w., F. & F., 24/3/18.
Doherty, John Francis, b. Strabane, Co. Tyrone, e. Newry, Co. Down, 24244, Pte., d. of w., F. & F., 30/6/18.
Dolan, William John, b. Belturbet, Co. Cavan, e. Cavan (Belturbet), 3381, Pte., k. in a., F. & F., 21/3/18.
Donaghy, Edward, b. Belfast, e. Belfast, 23452, Pte., k. in a., F. & F., 11/4/17.
Donaghy, Henry, b. Athlone, Co. Westmeath, e. Portadown, 10509, Pte., k. in a., F. & F., 12/10/16.
Donaghy, Patrick James, b. Belfast, e. Belfast, 3846, Pte. k. in a., F. & F., 15/4/17.
Donegan, John, e. Cavan, 20412, Pte., k. in a., F. & F., 7/5/17.
Donnan, John, b. Shankill, Belfast, e. Belfast, 42411, Pte., k. in a., F. & F., 1/10/18, formerly 19/33 R. Irish Rif.
Donnelly, Daniel, b. Dungannon, Co. Tyrone, e. Belfast, 8752, Pte., k. in a., F. & F., 14/11/14, formerly 8222, E. Lancs Regt.
Donnelly, James, b. Dublin, e. Naas, Kildare (Dublin), 8374, Pte., d. of w., F. & F., 17/9/14.
Donnelly, Patrick, b. Dublin, e. Dublin, 11339, Pte., k. in a., F. & F., 27/8/14.
Donnelly, Patrick, b. Banbridge, Co. Down, e. Belfast, 24050, A/Cpl., k. in a., F. & F., 11/4/17.
Donohoe, Thomas, b. Belturbet, Co. Cavan, e. Glasgow, 8537, Pte., d., F. & F., 27/5/16.
Doogan, Thomas, b. Monaghan, e. Monaghan, 19985, L/Cpl., k. in a., F. & F., 2/10/17.
Dooley, Thomas, e. Enniskillen (Omagh, Co. Tyrone), 29262, Pte., d. of w., F. & F., 1/10/18.
Doonan, Francis, b. Keshcarrigan, Co. Leitrim, e. Belfast (Keshcarrigan), 3550, Pte., d., F. & F., 31/7/18.
Dooris, Thomas, b. Linwood, Renfrews, e. Johnstone, Renfrews, 26917, Pte., d. of w., F. & F., 2/9/18.
Doran, John, b. Belfast, e. Glasgow (Belfast), 25977, Pte., k. in a., F. & F., 27/9/17.
Douglas, William John, b. Portadown, Co. Armagh, e. Belfast, 25189, Pte., k. in a., F. & F., 1/10/18.
Douthwaite, Arthur Henry, b. Newington, Kent, e. Woolwich (New Cross, S.E., Kent), 19013, Pte., k. in a., F. & F., 3/5/17, formerly 146909, R.F.A.
Dowie, James, b. Shankill, Belfast, e. Belfast, 10047, Pte., k. in a. F. & F., 26/8/14.
Downey, Daniel, b. Newry, Co. Down, e. Newry, 5622, Pte., k. in a., F. & F., 2/4/16.
Downing, William Morris, b. Sketty, Glam., e. Swansea, 41651, Pte., d., Home, 28/3/18, formerly T/2/10164, R.A.S.C.
Doyle, Daniel, b. Belfast, e. Belfast, 3848, Pte., k. in a., F. & F. 11/4/17.
Doyle, James, b. Newry, Co. Down, e. Newry, 6041, Pte., k. in a., F. & F., 27/8/16.
Drabwell, Charles, e. Stratford, E., Essex (Somertown, N.W., Middx.), 11109, Pte., k. in a., F. & F., 11/5/17.
Dragonett, Michael, b. Belfast, e. Dundalk (Belfast), 24770, Pte., k. in a., F. & F., 11/4/17.
Drennan, James Arthur, b. Donaghadee, Co. Down, e. Belfast (Donaghadee), 22820, Pte., d. of w., F. & F., 14/4/17.
Duffy, Patrick, b. Ballinrobe, Co. Mayo, e. Ballinrobe, 9565, Pte., d. of w., F. & F., 7/7/16.
Duffy, Patrick James, b. Ballybay, Co. Monaghan, e. Armagh (Monaghan), 11110, Pte., k. in a., F. & F., 7/5/17.
Duffy, Thomas, b. Arva, Co. Cavan, e. Cavan (Arva), 8092, Pte., k. in a., F. & F., 27/8/14.
Dugdale, William, b. Dundalk, Co. Louth, e. Galway (Dundalk) 16892, L/Cpl. k. in a., F. & F., 23/11/17, formerly 1398, Conn. Rangers.
Duggan, John, b. Raheny, Co. Dublin, e. Dublin (Raheny), 9918, Pte., d. of w., F. & F., 28/12/16.
Duggan, William, b. Armagh, e. Armagh (Poplar, E., Middx.), 27655, Pte., d., Home, 6/11/18.
Dundas, William Henry, b. Belleek, Co. Fermanagh, e. Ballyshannon, Co. Donegal (Belleek), 41399, Pte., k. in a., F. & F., 1/10/18, formerly 620, N. Irish Horse.
Dungey, George, b. Whitfield, Kent, e. Canterbury (Faversham, Kent), 8777, L/Cpl., d. of w., F. & F 4 5/ 7
Dunlop, James, b. Ballycastle, Co. Antrim, e. Belfast, 5813, Pte., k. in a., F. & F., 25/4/15.
Dunn, William, b. Dublin, e. Luton, Beds (Allenwood, Co. Kildare), 19726, Pte., k. in a., F. & F., 5/4/18.

Dunne, Edward Patrick, b. Tinahely, Co. Wicklow, e. Waterford (Ballytruckle, C. Waterford), 8950, Pte., k. in a., F. & F., 6/7/15.
Dunne, John, b. Dublin, e. Dublin, 11354, Pte., k. in a., F. & F., 26/10/14.
Dunne, Martin, b. Dublin, e. Dublin, 11119, Pte., k. in a., F. & F., 21/10/14.
Dunne, Philip, b. Cavan, e. Cavan, 28993, Pte., d. of w., F. & F., 1/10/18.
Durkin, Anthony John, b. Dublin, e. Dublin, 11322, Pte., d. of w., F. & F., 4/5/15.
Dynes, Frederick, b. Lurgan, Co. Armagh, e. Lurgan, 5424, Sgt., k. in a., F. & F., 25/4/15.
Edginton, Harry, e. West Norwood, S.E., Surrey, 19109, L/Cpl., k. in a., F. & F., 9/4/18, formerly 146851, R.F.A.
Edmunds, Hezekiah, b. Dowlais, Glamorgan, e. Merthyr, Glamorgan (Dowlais), 3632, Pte., k. in a., F. & F., 31/7/16, formerly 50388, R.G.A.
Edwards, Charles Edward, b. London, e. West London, 41994, Pte., k. in a., F. & F., 22/10/18, formerly 67153, R.W. Surrey Regt.
Edwards, Herbert, b. Liverpool, e. Liverpool, 41801, Pte., k. in a. F. & F., 21/3/18, formerly S/3/023024, R.A.S.C.
Elder, Frederick Henry, b. Marylebone, N.W., Middx., e. Whitehall, S.W., Middx. (Lisson Grove, N.W., Middx.), 41945, Pte., d. of w., F. & F., 28/5/18, formerly 685484, London Regt.
Eldridge, Willie Austin, b. Bournemouth, Hants, e. Kingston-on-Thames, Surrey (East Sheen, S.W., Surrey), 41653, Pte., k. in a., F... F., 14/4/17, formerly T/2/029670, R.A.S.C.
Elliott, William, b. Banbridge, Co. Down, e. Lurgan, Co. Armagh (Banbridge), 11924, Pte., k. in a., F. & F., 12/10/16.
Ellis, James Proctor, b. Slingsby, Yorks, e. Malton, Yorks (Walthamstow, Essex), 26854, C.S.M.A./R.S.M., k. in a., F. & F., 11/4/17, formerly 6310, G. Guards.
Elwood, Henry, b. Belfast, e. Perth (Belfast), 42319, Pte., d. of w., F. & F., 2/11/18, formerly 11072, R. Irish Rif.
Ennis, Michael, b. Brannockstown, Co. Meath, e. Navan (Rathmolyon, Co. Meath), 15951, Sgt., k. in a., F. & F., 12/10/16.
Ervine, John, b. Banbridge, Co. Down, e. Newry (Banbridge), 5912, Pte., k. in a., F. & F., 25/4/15.
Evans, Evan, b. Porth, Glam., e. Tonyrefail, Glam. (Trebanog, Glam.), 17193, Pte., k. in a., F. & F., 9/12/16, formerly 14018, K.S.L.I.
Evans, Michael, b. Newry, Co. Down, e. Newry (Camlough, Co. Armagh), 25197, Pte., k. in a., F. & F., 11/4/17.
Faloon, James, e. Lurgan, Co. Armagh (Portadown, Co. Armagh), 22122, Pte., k. in a., F. & F., 11/4/17.
Fanning, Francis, b. Dundalk, Co. Louth, e. Newry (Dundalk), 8067, Pte., k. in a., F. & F., 25/4/15.
Farleigh, Alfred Richard, b. Ynishir, Glams, e. Cardiff (Canton, Glam.), 13764, L./Cpl., k. in a., F. & F., 3/5/17.
Farrell, James, b. Oldcastle, Co. Meath, e. Liverpool (Tue Brook, Liverpool), 9499, Pte., k. in a., F. & F., 25/4/15.
Farrell, Owen, b. Drogheda, Co. Louth, e. Drogheda, 11505, Pte., k. in a., F. & F., 25/4/15.
Farrell, Patrick, b. Mount Nugent, Co. Cavan, e. Cavan (Mt. Nugent), 2533, Pte., k. in a., F. & F., 25/4/15.
Farrell, Thomas, b. Newbliss, Co. Monaghan, e. Cambuslang, Glasgow (Newton, Glasgow), 12802, Pte., k. in a., F. & F., 11/4/17.
Farrelly, Francis, b. Cootehill, Co. Cavan, e. Cootehill (Stradone, Co. Cavan, 11019, Pte., k. in a., F. & F., 12/10/16.
Farthing, John James, b. Newcastle, Northumberland, e. South Shields, Co. Durham (Newcastle-on-Tyne), 40114, L./Cpl, k. in a., F. & F., 11/5/17, formerly R/4/062563, R.A.S.C.
Faul, Patrick, b. Inniskeen, Co. Monaghan, e. Dundalk, Co. Louth (Inniskeen), 26857, Pte., k. in a., F. & F., 21/3/18.
Fifield, James William, b. Westminster, S.E., Middx., e. Piccadilly, W., Middx. (Old Pye St., S.W.), 40123, Pte., k. in a., F. & F., 18/4/17, formerly 24635, Hussars of the Line.
Figes, Charles Henry, b. Islington, N., Middx., e. London (Hackney Wick, E., Middx.), 9404, Pte., d., Home, 4/11/14.
Fitton, Alfred, b. Whitefield, Manchester, e. Manchester (Whitefield), 20775, Pte., k. in a., F. & F., 11/4/17, formerly 24137, R.F.A.
Fitzpatrick, James, b. Shankill, Co. Armagh, e. Lurgan, 10611, L/Cpl., k. in a., F. & F., 22/10/18.
Fitzpatrick, Patrick, b. Templemore, Co. Tipperary, e. Glasgow (Templemore), 17259, Pte., k. in a., F. & F., 21/3/18.
Fitzsimons, Charles, b. Shankill, Co. Armagh, e. Lurgan (Belfast), 8077, Pte., k. in a., F. & F., 5/6/17.
Fitzsimons, Robert, b. Lurgan, Co. Armagh, e. Armagh (Lurgan), 10398, Pte., k. in a., F. & F., 26/8/16.
Fleming, Peter, b. Ballybot, Co. Armagh, e. Belfast, 3594, Pte., k. in a., F. & F., 21/3/18.

Flynn, William, b. Shankill, Belfast, e. Belfast, 7189, Pte., d. of w., F. & F., 20/10/14.
Flynn, William, b. Govan, Lanarks, e. Glasgow, 18941, Pte., d. of w., F. & F., 14/10/16, formerly 13032, Hussars of the Line.
Foley, James, b. Dublin, e. Dublin, 7709, Pte., k. in a., F. & F., 25/4/15.
Follis, Samuel, b. Shankill, Co. Armagh, e. Finner Camp, Co, Donegal (Lurgan, Co. Armagh), 4749, Pte., k. in a., F. & F., 11/4/17.
Foote, George Francis, b. Islington, N., Middx., e. Charing Cross, S.W., Middx. (Caledonian Rd., N., Middx.), 17491, Pte., k. in a., F. & F., 6/4/18.
Foreman, Ernest, b. Belfast, e. Belfast, 29480, Pte., k. in a., F. & F., 14/4/18, formerly 4494, 1/6th Seaforth High.
Fowler, James Walter, b. Lambeth, S.E., Surrey, e. Lambeth, S.E., Surrey, 49875, Cpl., k. in a., F. & F., 22/10/18, formerly 8040, 9th County of London Regt.
Fox, Albert Victor, e. Sherborne, Dorset (Newport, Mon.), 41920, Pte., k. in a., F. & F., 11/4/18, formerly T/4/159773, R.A.S.C.
Fox, James, b. Raphoe, Co. Donegal, e. Londonderry, 8704, Pte., k. in a., F. & F., 25/4/15.
Fox, John, b. Shankill, Co. Armagh, e. Portadown, Co. Armagh (Lurgan, Co. Armagh), 5844, Pte., k. in a., F. & F., 25/4/15.
Fox, Patrick, b. Ballinamuck, Co. Longford, e. Cavan (Arva, Co. Cavan), 8312, Pte., k. in a., F. & F., 27/8/16.
Fox, Samuel, b. Portadown, Co. Armagh, e. Portadown, 11664, Pte., d. of w., F. & F., 12/12/16.
Foy, Patrick, b. Clones, Co. Monaghan, e. Cavan (Newtownbutler, Co. Fermanagh), 17863, Pte., k. in a., F. & F., 11/4/17.
Fraser, Ebenezer, b. Hillsborough, Co. Down, e. Cavan (Belturbet, Co. Cavan), 3047, Pte., d. of w., F. & F., 22/5/15.
Fraser, James, b. Lochee, Forfarshire, e. Glasgow (Lochee), 10071, L/Cpl., k. in a., F. & F., 11/4/17, M.M.
Frazer, Robert Martin, b. Ennis, Co. Clare, e. Galway (Ennis), 8272, Pte., d. of w., F. & F., 4/5/15.
Freeburn, David, b. Portadown, Co. Armagh, e. Finner Camp, Co. Donegal (Belfast), 4106, Pte., d. of w., F. & F., 25/5/15.
Freeland, John, b. Clones, Co. Monaghan, e. Cavan (Rockcorry, Co. Monaghan), 3387, Pte., k. in a., F. & F., 24/6/17.
Freeman, Sidney Wilfred, b. Glinton, Hunts, e. Nottingham, 43241, Pte., k. in a., F. & F., 21/3/18, formerly 35780, Notts & Derby Regt.
Fryer, Frederick George, b. Portsmouth, e. Portsmouth, 49902, Pte., k. in a., F. & F., 13/10/18, formerly 8/3501, Hants Regt.
Fulton, Wilson, b. Knocknamuckly, Co. Down, e. Lurgan, Co. Armagh (Donaldstown, Co. Down), 10882, A/Sgt., k. in a., F. & F., 11/4/17.
Furse, Frederick, b. Launceston, Cornwall, e. Launceston (Ashwater, Devon), 13661, Pte., k. in a., F. & F., 26/8/16, formerly 15802, D.C.L.I.
Gainfort, Percival William, b. Sandyford, Co. Dublin, e. Dublin (Rathmines, Dublin), 9989, Sgt., k. in a., F. & F., 9/9/15.
Gallagher, Thomas James, b. Belfast, e. Belfast, 20937, Pte., k. in a., F. & F., 3/5/17, formerly 43619, Connaught Rangers.
Galligan, Philip, b. Larah, Co. Cavan, e. Cavan (Crossdoney, Co. Cavan), 23453, L/Cpl., k. in a., F. & F., 23/11/17.
Gamble, David, b. Conlig, Co. Down, e. Belfast, 8290, Pte., d., F. & F., 23/8/16.
Gammell, Patrick, b. Kilquade, Co. Wicklow, e. Dublin (Kilcool, Co. Wicklow), 29418, Pte., k. in a., F. & F., 18/4/18.
Gannon, Patrick, b. Dublin, e. Dublin, 10085, Sgt., k. in a., F. & F., 25/4/15.
Gardner, George, b. Larne, Co. Antrim, e. Belfast (Larne), 42418, L/Cpl., k. in a., F. & F., 1/10/18, formerly 8/1260, R. Irish Rif.
Garland, John, b. Tandragee, Co. Armagh, e. Armagh (Tandragee), 20529, Pte., k. in a., F. & F., 21/3/18.
Gartland, Robert John, b. Newry, Co. Down, e. Newry, 27852, L/Cpl., d., F. & F., 20/6/18.
Gash, David, b. Cardiff, Glam., e. Cardiff (Canton, Glam.), 15629, L/Sgt., k. in a., F. & F., 11/4/17, formerly 7591, Lancs Fus.
Gawley, Andrew, b. Mintburn, Co. Tyrone, e. Armagh (Caledon, Co. Tyrone), 24906, Pte., d. of w., F. & F., 13/4/17.
Gaynor, Michael, b. Leixlip, Kildare, e. Cavan (Ballinagh, Co. Cavan), 3361, Pte., k. in a., F. & F., 12/10/16.
Geddis, Robert, b. Rathfriland, Co. Down, e. Newry, Co. Down (Rathfriland), 7887, Pte., d. of w., F. & F., 18/9/14.
Gee, Henry Thomas, b. Birmingham, e. Birmingham, 49903, Pte., k. in a., F. & F., 1/10/18.
Geoghegan, Richard, b. Dublin, e. Dublin, 25901, Pte., k. in a., F. & F., 11/4/18.
Gerrity, Francis William, b. Longford, e. Manchester, 20667, Pte., k. in a., F. & F., 21/3/18.
Gibbens, Thomas, b. Ashford, Kent, e. Southampton (Eastleigh, Hants), 9333, Pte., k. in a., F. & F., 25/4/15.

Gibbons, Albert, b. Notting Hill, W., Middx., e. Hounslow, Middx. (Chiswick, W., Middx.), 41966, Pte., k. in a., F. & F., 23/5/18, formerly 685547, London Regt.
Gibbons, Neil, b. Letterkenny, Co. Donegal, e. Londonderry, 20724, Pte., d. of w., F. & F., 13/10/16.
Gibbons, Patrick, b. Kilmore, Co. Mayo, e. Belmullet, Co. Mayo, 24084, Pte., k. in a., F. & F., 16/8/17.
Gibney, Bernard, b. Listowel, Kerry, e. Tralee, Co. Kerry (Granard, Co. Longford), 24640, Pte., k. in a., F. & F., 9/4/17.
Gilbert, Joseph, b. Balbriggan, Co. Dublin, e. Dublin (Balbriggan), 11226, Pte., k. in a., F. & F., 2/5/15.
Gill, Roland, George b. Wormley, Essex, e. Shoreham-by-Sea, Sussex (Wimbledon, S.W., Surrey), 45055, Pte., d. of w., Home, 24/9/18, formerly G/8573, E. Kent Regt.
Gilliland, David, b. Lisburn, Co. Antrim, e. Holywood, Co. Down (Belfast), 3783, Pte., d. of w., F. & F., 30/4/18, formerly 7248, R. Irish Rif.
Gilliland, James, b. Ballybay, Co. Managhan, e. Cavan (Monaghan), 24142, Pte., k. in a., F. & F., /4/18.
Gillin, Joseph, b. Ballycastle, Co. Antrim, e. Ballymoney, Co. Antrim (Ballycastle), 15896, Pte., k. in a., F. & F., 1/7/16.
Gilmore, Felix, b. Glasgow (Calton, Glasgow), 18693, Pte., k. in a., F. & F., 17/7/18.
Gilmore, Peter, b. Portadown, Co. Armagh, e. Portadown, 3930, Pte., d. of w., F. & F., 14/4/17.
Girvan, John, b. Derryadd, Co. Armagh), e. Lurgan, Co. Armagh Portadown, Co. Armagh), 8429, Pte., k. in a., F. & F., 15/9/16.
Glenville, Alfred, b. Bristol, e. Camberwell, S.E., Surrey (Deptford, S.E., Kent), 43328, Pte., d. ,F. & F., 29/5/18, formerly 352936, City of London Regt.
Godby, Cecil Francis Edwin, b. Weston-super-Mare, Somerset, e. Taunton (Weston-super-Mare), 49933, Cpl., d. of w., F. & F., 2/10/18, formerly 30727, Som. L.I.
Godfrey, Edgar Cecil, b. Kensal Rise, N.W., Middx., e. Hounslow, Middx. (Kensal Rise, N.W.), 50037, Pte., k. in a., F. & F., 30/9/18, formerly 636186, 20th London Regt.
Godfrey, John Francis, b. West Gorton, Lancs, e. Manchester (Abbey Hey, Lancs), 15029, Pte., k. in a., F. & F., 12/10/16, formerly 6753, Lancs Fus.
Godley, Robert, b. Stockport, Ches., e. Salford, Manchester, 17324, Sgt., k. in a., F. & F., 23/5/18.
Godwin, Charles Blair, b. Willesden, N.W., Middx., e. London (Frenchay, Som.), 10274, Sgt., k. in a., F. & F., 27/8/14.
Goldie, Barney, b. Aberdeen, e. Belfast, 3517, Pte., d. of w., F. & F., 22/10/16.
Goodman, John, b. Dundalk, Co. Louth, e. Dundalk, 24239, Pte., d., Home, 12/7/17.
Gorman, Patrick, b. Portadown, Co. Armagh, e. Glasgow (Partick, Glasgow), 17632, Pte., d. of w., F. & F., 17/10/16.
Gorman, Peter, b. Street, Co. W. Meath, e. Mullingar (Hamilton, Lanarks), 7640, Pte., k. in a., F. & F., 25/4/15.
Gracey, Joseph, b. Newry, Co. Down, e. Newry (Dundalk), 8119, Pte., k. in a., F. & F., 4/9/18.
Gradidge, Albert Frederick, b. Ealing, Hants, e. Caxton Hall, S.W., Middx. (Southampton), 18773, Pte., k. in a., F. & F., 26/8/16, formerly 24196, Hussars of the Line.
Graham, Albert, b. Shankill, Co. Armagh, e. Lurgan, Co. Armagh, 8692, Pte., k. in a., F. & F., 25/4/15.
Graham, Albert, b. Portadown, Co. Armagh, e. Armagh (Portadown), 11984, Pte., k. in a., F. & F., 12/10/16.
Graham, David, b. Greencastle, Co. Antrim, e. Belfast (Greencastle), 6809, Pte., k. in a., F. & F., 21/10/14.
Graham, Henry, b. Portadown, Co. Armagh, e. Portadown, 7513, Pte., k. in a., F. & F., 12/10/16,
Graham, John, b. Newry, Co. Down, e. Hamilton, Lanarks (Kilkeel, Co. Down), 10696, Pte., k. in a., F. & F., 26/4/16.
Graham, William, b. Bessbrook, Co. Armagh, e. Newry, Co. Down (Markethill, Co. Armagh), 5311, Sgt., k. in a., F. & F., 6/7/15.
Gray, Bernard, b. Cavan, e. Cavan, 3299, Pte., k. in a., F. & F., 12/4/15.
Gray, John, b. Cavan, e. Cavan, 20278, Pte., k. in a. F. & F., 11/4/17.
Gray, Patrick, b. Cavan, e. Cavan, 19855, Pte., d. of w., F. & F., 26/5/18.
Gray, William, b. Dundalk, Co. Louth, e. Warrington, Lancs (Dundalk), 7541, Pte., k. in a., F. & F., 25/4/15.
Gray, William, b. Paisley, Renfrew, e. Paisley, 42353, Pte., k. in a., F. & F., 1/10/18, formerly 20223, R. Irish Rif.
Green, Thomas, b. Dublin, e. Dublin, 26913, Pte., k. in a., F. & F., 26/4/18.
Greenaway, Francis, b. Portadown, Co. Armagh, e. Armagh (Portadown), 6119, Pte., d. of w, F. & F., 28/4/15.
Greene, Joseph, b. Shankill, Belfast, e. Belfast, 24242, Pte., k. in a., F. & F., 21/3/18.

APPENDICES

Greenwood, George, b. Bromley, Kent, e. Woolwich (Bromley Common, Kent), 9323, Pte., k. in a., F. & F., 25/4/15.
Grey, William, b. Ballinasloe, Co. Galway, e. Dublin (Wicklow), 16166, Pte., k. in a., F. & F., 9/4/18.
Gribben, Thomas, b. Downpatrick, Co. Down, e. Downpatrick (Killyleagh, Co. Down), 8228, Pte., k. in a., F. & F., 25/4/15.
Gribbons, James, b. Clones, Co. Monaghan, e. Cavan (Clones), 3298, Pte., d., Home, 26 11/16.
Ground, Alfred, b. Armagh, e. Belfast, 8616, Pte., d. of w., F. & F., 24/6/15.
Gunn, Thomas, b. Drumsnat, Co. Monaghan, e. Monaghan (Smithborough, Co. Monaghan), 27967, Pte., k. in a., F. & F., 21/3/18.
Haddock, Samuel, b. Shankill, Co. Armagh, e. Portadown, Co. Armagh (Lurgan, Co. Armagh), 11309, Pte., d. of w., F. & F., 27/1/15.
Haggarty, Peter, b. Anderston, Lanarks, e. Glasgow (Maryhill, Glasgow), 24944, Pte., d. of w., F. & F., 25/11/17.
Hagger, William Henry, b. Stepney, E., Middx., e. Leicester (Wokingham, Berks), 9475, Cpl., k. in a., F. & F., 11/4/17.
Hall, James Milroy, b. Lanark, e. Glasgow (Springburn, Glasgow), 50052, Pte., k. in a., F. & F., 30/9/18, formerly 100288, R.F.C.
Hall, John William, b. Colne, Lancs, e. Colne, 17454, Pte., k. in a., F. & F., 12/10/16.
Halloran, Michael, b. Ballinrobe, Co. Mayo, e. Ballinrobe, 9763, Pte., k. in a., F. & F., 10/4/17.
Halpin, William, b. Waterford, e. Waterford, 16203, Pte., d of w., F. & F., 25/8/16, formerly 1190, R. Irish Regt.
Hampson, John, b. Killoe, Co. Longford, e. Armagh (Killoe), 8483, Pte., d. of w., F. & F., 1/11/14.
Hanley, William, b. Foxford, Co. Mayo, e. Ballina, Co. Mayo (Foxford), 16646, Pte., k. in a., F. & F., 1/1/18, formerly 478, Conn. Rangers.
Hanna, William, b. Shankill, Belfast, e. Newtownards, Co. Down (Skerries, Co. Dublin), 29416, Sgt., k. in a., F. & F., 5/4/18.
Hannah, William, b. Ballymoney, Co. Antrim, e. Hamilton, Lanarks (Mossend, Lanarks), 42324, Pte., d. of w., F. & F., 3/10/18, formerly 22198, 3rd R. Irish Rif.
Hanvey, William, b. Portadown, Co. Armagh, e. Armagh (Portadown), 11158, Pte., d. of w., F. & F., 8/11/14.
Haraghy, John, b. Shankill, Belfast, e. Belfast, 24226, Pte., k. in a., F. & F., 10/7/17.
Harding, Ernest Victor, b. Fernhurst, Surrey, e. Guildford, Surrey (Haslemere, Surrey), 45828, Pte., k. in a., F. & F., 11/4/18, formerly 4647, 5th Battn. R.W. Surrey Regt.
Hardwick, Henry, b. Bayswater, W., Middx., e. London (Reading, Berks), 9686, A/Sgt., k. in a., F. & F., 24/6/17.
Hardy, Charles John, b. Wareham, Dorset, e. Guildford, Surrey (Wareham), 49978, Pte., k. in a., F. & F., 2/9/18, formerly 1701, R.W. Surrey Regt.
Harkness, Cecil, b. Boveva, Co. Londonderry, e. Londonderry (Dungiven, Co. Londonderry), 40103, Pte., k. in a., F. & F., 11/4/18, formerly 31753, Hussars of the Line.
Harrigan, John, b. Glasgow, e. Glasgow, 23404, Pte., k. in a., F. & F., 11/4/17.
Harte, Michael, b. Glenfarne, Co. Leitrim, e. Glasgow (Manor(hamilton, Co. Leitrim), 18388, Pte., k. in a., F. & F., 9/12/16.
Hay, Samuel, b. Calton, Glasgow, e. Glasgow (Calton), 18285, Pte., k. in a., F. & F., 26/8/16.
Hayden, Christopher, b. Longford, e. Longford (Birmingham), 9013, Pte., d., F. & F., 5/4/15.
Hyaden, Christopher, b. Dublin, e. Dublin, 11284, Cpl., k. in a., F. & F., 11/4/17.
Hayden, Michael, b. Dublin, e. Dublin, 20184, Pte., d., F. & F., 1/7/18.
Hayes, William, b. Portadown, Co. Armagh, e. Portadown, 6042, Pte., k. in a., F. & F., 12/10/16.
Healy, William, b. Dublin, e. Dublin, 7609, Pte., k. in a., F. & F., 25/4/15.
Heaney, John, b. Ballyhorden, Co. Armagh, e. Armagh, 22744, Pte., k. in a., F. & F., 12/10/16.
Heath, George David, b. Birmingham, e. Birmingham, 49993, Pte., k. in a., F. & F., 2/9/18, formerly 37956, D.C.L.I.
Heathman, Harold, b. Camberwell, S.E., Surrey, e. Lambeth, S.E. Surrey (Denmark Hill, S.E., Surrey), 50019, Pte., d. of w F. & F., 2/9/18, formerly 557149, London Regt.
Henderson, Thomas, b. Govan, Glasgow, e. Glasgow (Partick, Glasgow), 17574, Pte., k. in a., F. & F., 30/4/16.
Hennessy, Patrick, b. Dalkey, Co. Dublin, e. Kingstown, Co. Dublin (Dalkey), 24482, Pte., d. of w., F. & F., 10/5/17.
Henson, Henry Frederick, b. St. Peter's, Middlesex, e. Aldershot, Hants (Battersea, S.W., Surrey), 10379, Pte., k. in a., F. & F., 25/4/15.
Herrning, John, b. St. Pancras, N.W., Middx., e. Hampstead, N.W. Middx. (Willesden Green, N.W., Middx.), 41740, Pte., d. of w., F. & F., 13/4/18, formerly S/4/146950, R.A.S.C.

Herron, Joseph, b. Ballymacarrett, Co. Down, e. Belfast, 42364, L/Cpl., k. in a., F. & F., 1/10/18, formerly 8/12292, 8th R. Irish Rif.
Hetherington, Richard, b. Mountrath, Queen's Co., e. Maryborough, Queen's Co. (Mountrath), 8135, Cpl., k. in a., F. & F., 18/9/14.
Hewitt, Edward James, b. Norwich, e. Birmingham (Minworth, Birmingham), 41749, Pte., k. in a., F. & F., 11/4/18, formerly S/4/055632, R.A.S.C.
Hewitt, James, b. Portadown, e. Belfast (Portadown), 14306, Pte., k. in a., F. & F., 4/9/18.
Higgins, John, b. Kilkenny, e. Dublin (Plasmarl, Glam.), 17093, Pte., k. in a., F. & F., 21/3/18.
Hill, Charles Victor, b. Chelsea, S.W. Middx., e. West London (Fulham, S.W. Middx.), 42059, Pte., k. in a., F. & F., 1/10/18, formerly 77405, R.W. Surrey Regt.
Hill, Denis, b. Dublin, e. Dublin (Saltcoats, Ayrshire), 7299, Pte., k. in a., F. & F., 25/4/15.
Hill, Edward, b. Shankill, Co. Armagh, e. Portadown, Co. Armagh (Lurgan, Co. Armagh), 9987, L/Cpl., k. in a., F. & F., 12/10/16.
Hill, James, b. Shankill, Belfast, e. Lurgan, Co. Armagh (Belfast), 2669, Sgt., k. in a., F. & F., 11/5/17.
Hill, James, b. Sydenham, Co. Down, e. Belfast (Lurgan, Co Armagh), 42425, Pte., k. in a., F. & F., 1/10/18, formerly 8074 R. Irish Rif.
Hincks, Denton Stanley, b. Liverpool, e. Bootle, Lancs (Litherland, Liverpool), 29441, Pte., k. in a., F. & F., 1/10/18.
Hodd, Frederick Walter, b. Eastbourne, Sussex, e. New Kent Rd., S.E., Surrey (Peckham, S.E., Surrey), 9328, Sgt., k. in a., F. & F., 10/6/15.
Holden, Joseph, b. Strabane, Co. Tyrone, e. Londonderry (Glasgow), 8306, Pte., d. of w., F. & F., 25/4/15.
Holland, Edward, b. Dublin, e. Dublin, 21376, Pte., d. of w., Home, 9/2/20, formerly 22934, R. Dublin Fus.
Holland, Harry, b. Birmingham, e. Birmingham, 49811, Pte., k. in a., F. & F., 2/9/18, formerly 6506, Oxf. & Bucks L.I.
Holland, James, b. Carlow, e. Manchester (Dublin), 27777, Pte., d. of w., F. & F., 22/4/18.
Holloran, Stanley Herbert, b. Marylebone, N.W., Middx., e. Hammersmith, W., Middx., (Shepherd's Bush, W., Middx.), 41942, Pte., d., F. & F., 25/10/18, formerly 685487, 22nd London Regt.
Holmes, Albert, b. Belfast, e. Armagh (Belfast), 11097, L/Cpl., k. in a., F. & F., 3/5/17.
Holmes, William John, b. Armagh, e. Armagh (Belfast), 5812, L/Cpl., k. in a., F. & F., 3/5/17.
Hooke, Patrick, b. Dublin, e. Navan, Co. Meath, 20038, Cpl., k. in a., F. & F., 10/4/18.
Hope, Walter, b. Northampton, e. Northampton, 9302, Pte., d., F. & F., 31/10/18.
Hopper, Samuel William, b. Borham, Norfolk, e. Holt, Norfolk (Saxlingham, Norfolk), 45029, Pte., k. in a., F. & F., 13/10/18, formerly 20862, Norfolk Regt.
Hopps, Frederick Arthur, b. Leeds, e. Leeds, 41860, Pte., k. in a., F. & F., 2/9/18, formerly T/4/250970, R.A.S.C.
Horne, Vincent Edward, b. Chelsea, S.W., Middx., e. Fulham, S.W., Middx., 45838, Pte., k. in a., F. & F., 14/4/18, formerly 4288, 2/5th E. Surrey Regt.
Horrigan, Vincent, b. Dublin, e. Dublin, 40124, Pte., k. in a., F. & F., 19/4/17, formerly 24553, Hussars of the Line.
How, Frederick Henry, b. Islington, N., Middx., e. St. Paul's Churchyard, E.C., Middx. (Forest Gate, E., Essex), 14900, Cpl., d. of w., F. & F., 23/10/18, formerly 14417, D.C.L.I.
Howard, John Richard, b. Langham, Norfolk, e. Norwich (Willesden Green, N.W., Middx.), 10684, Pte., k. in a., F. & F., 23/6/15.
Howes, Ambrose Arthur, b. Wymondham, Norfolk, e. Wymondham, 18991, Pte., k. in a., F. & F., 11/4/17, formerly 146467, R.H.A.
Hubbard, Percy, b. Peterborough, Northants, e. Leicester (Armagh), 8864, C.S.M., k. in a., F. & F., 23/11/17.
Hughes, Edward, b. Lurgan, Co. Armagh, e. Glasgow (Lurgan), 24798, Pte., d. of w., F. & F., 13/4/17.
Hughes, Joseph, b. Drumcree, Co. Armagh, e. Portadown, Co. Armagh, 18568, Pte., d. of w., F. & F., 2/5/16.
Hughes, Peter, b. Dundalk, Co. Louth, e. Dundalk, 20688, Pte., k. in a., F. & F., 15/2/17.
Hughes, William James, b. Bushey, Herts, e. Watford, Herts (Bushey), 22307, Pte., d. of w., F. & F., 14/8/18, formerly 19105, Beds Regt.
Humphreys, William, b. Shankill, Co. Armagh, e. Portadown (Belfast), 5176, Pte., k. in a., F. & F., 25/4/15.
Hunter, Thomas, e. Clydebank, Glasgow (Coa, Co. Fermanagh), 49776, Pte., d. of w., F. & F., 30/10/18, formerly 92382, R. Innis. Fus.
Hurst, Thomas, b. Shankill, Co. Armagh, e. Lurgan, Co. Armagh, 11504, Pte., d. of w., F. & F., 25/5/15.

Hyde, James, b. Clones, Co. Monaghan, e. Belfast, 11229, Pte., k. in a., F. & F., 25/4/15.
Hyland, Joseph, b. Dublin, e. Dublin (Liverpool), 11056, Pte., k. in a., F. & F., 2/9/18.
Hylands, Frank, b. Larne, Co. Antrim, e. Larne, 3394, Pte., d. of w., F. & F., 14/10/16.
Hylands, Thomas, John b. Donaghcloney, Co. Down, e. Finner Camp, Co. Donegal (Lurgan, Co. Armagh), 4760, Pte., k. in a., F. & F., 22/12/14.
Irwin, George, b. Belturbet, Co. Cavan, e. Cavan (Belturbet), 3383, L/Cpl. ,d. of w., F. & F., 1/6/18, M.M.
Irwin, John, b. St. Patrick's, Co. Armagh, e. Belfast (Lisburn, Co. Antrim), 21250, Pte., k. in a., F. & F., 22/10/18, formerly 2412, Leinster Regt.
Jackson, John, b. Shankill, Co. Armagh, e. Lurgan, Co. Armagh, 5231, Pte., k. in a., F. & F., 12/4/15.
Jagger, Ernest, b. Halifax, Yorks, e. Halifax (Hipperholme, Yorks.). 41882, Pte., k. in a., F. & F., 2/9/18, formerly 024834, R.A.O.C.
Jardine, George, b. Alexandria, Dumbarton, e. Dumbarton (Alexandria), 6334, Pte., k. in a., F. & F., 12/10/16.
Jebb, John, b. Monaghan, e. Monaghan (Glasgow), 8786, Pte., k. in a., F. & F., 18/9/14.
Jebb, Ralph, b. Ballybay, Co. Monaghan, e. Monaghan, 12240, Pte., k. in a., F. & F., 12/10/16.
Jenkins, John, b. Cardiff, Glam., e. Cardiff (Roath, Glam.), 13565, Cpl., k. in a., F. & F., 12/10/16.
Johnson, George, b. Widnes, Lancs, e. Warrington (Widnes), 14903, Pte., k. in a., F. & F., 3/5/17, formerly 7626, Lancs Fus.
Johnston, Patrick, b. Cookstown, Lanarks, e. Armagh (Lislea, Co. Armagh), 25208, Pte., k. in a., F. & F., 11/4/17.
Johnston, Robert, b. Carlisle, Cumberland, e. Carlisle, 8773, Pte., k. in a., F. & F., 21/10/14.
Johnston, Samuel, b. Carrickfergus, Co. Antrim, e. Lurgan, Co. Armagh (Carrickfergus), 11201, Pte., d., Home, 30/11/14.
Johnston, William Robert, b. Ballymena, Co. Antrim, e. Belfast, 8166, Pte., d., F. & F., 11/12/15.
Jones, David, Carson, b. Cloverhill, Co. Cavan, e. Cavan (Cloverhill), 9560, Sgt., d. of w., F. & F., 20/10/14, D.C.M.
Jones, Henry Ronald, b. Pontrilas, Hereford, e. Newport, Mon. (Pontrilas), 41751, Pte., k. in a., F. & F., 18/4/18, formerly S/4/064811, R.A.S.C.
Jones, Percy, b. Northwich, Ches., e. Widnes, Lancs (Ditton, Lancs), 20831, Pte., k. in a., F. & F., 18/4/18.
Jones, Wallace John, b. Plymouth, e. Newton Abbot, Devon (Thorverton, Devon), 49911, Pte., k. in a., F. & F., 2/9/18, formerly 3648, Hamps Regt.
Judkins, Arthur Lewis, b. Tamworth, Staffs, e. Stafford (Little Haywood, Staffs), 17456, Pte., k. in a., F. & F., 23/11/17.
Juett, George Henry, b. Plaistow, E. Essex, e. Stratford, E., Essex (Highgate Hill, N. Middx.), 22719, Cpl., k. in a., F. & F., 3/5/17.
Kadwill, Edward George, b. Faversham, Kent, e. Chatham, 9370, Sgt. k. in a., F. & F., 12/10/16.
Kane, Henry, b. Belfast, e. Armagh (Belfast), 8361, Pte., d. of w., F. & F., 21/12/14.
Kane, James, b. Paisley, Renfrews, e. Armagh (Belfast), 25043, Pte., d. of w., F. & F., 14/5/17.
Kane, Thomas, b. St. Joseph's, Co. Antrim, e. Belfast, 23638, Pte., d., F. & F., 29/6/18.
Kavanagh, Alfred, b. Portarlington, Queen's Co., e. Monaghan (Portarlington), 11069, Pte., k. in a., F. & F., 21/10/14.
Kavanagh, James, b. Ballybrack, Co. Dublin, e. Bray, Co. Wicklow (Enniskerry, Co. Wicklow), 20000, Pte., k. in a., F. & F., 21/3/18.
Kavanagh, John, b. Kilcullen, Co. Kildare, e. Naas, Co. Kildare (Kilcock, Co. Kildare), 7223, Sgt., k. in a., F. & F., 26/8/16.
Kavanagh, Joseph, b. Dublin, e. Dublin (Govanhill, Lanark), 6696, Pte., k. in a., F. & F., 17/11/14.
Kavanagh, Peter, b. Dublin, e. Dublin, 25900, Pte., k. in a., F. & F., 3/5/17.
Kay, Frederick, b. Longton, Staffs, e. Liverpool, (Stoke-on-Trent), 8806, Pte., k. in a., F. & F., 7/5/17.
Keating, Thomas, b. Dublin, e. Dublin (Inchicore, Dublin), 20190, Pte., k. in a., F. & F., 11/4/18.
Keefe, Patrick, b. Dublin, e. Drogheda (Dublin), 11058, Cpl., k. in a., F. & F., 12/10/16.
Keenan, Bernard, b. Enniskillen, Co. Fermanagh, e. Enniskillen, (Buncrana, Co. Donegal), 30404, L/Cpl., k. in a., F. & F., 1/10/18.
Keenan, Martin, b. Kildare, e. Naas, Co. Kildare (Abbeyleix, Queen's Co.), 6766, Pte., k. in a., F. & F., 12/10/16.
Keinzley, James, b. Portadown, Co. Armagh, e. Portadown, 5726, Pte., d., Home, 20/3/15.

Kelcher, James, b. Bermondsey, S.E., Kent, e. Camberwell, S.E., Kent (Bermondsey, S.E.), 41941, Pte., d. of w., F. & F., 29/7/18, formerly 683832, London Regt.
Kelledy, Thomas, e. Dundalk, Co. Louth, 18481, Pte., k. in a., F. & F., 12/10/16.
Kelly, Daniel, b. Kellogs, Co. Donegal, e. Blantyre (Stonefield, Lanarks), 13253, Pte., k. in a., F. & F., 12/10/16.
Kelly, Edward, b. Newtownmountkennedy, Co. Wicklow, e. Wicklow (Newtownmountkennedy), 7617, Pte., d. of w., F. & F., 26/10/14.
Kelly, James, b. Newtown Hamilton, Co. Armagh, e. Armagh (Newtown Hamilton), 10774, Pte., d., F. & F., 18/6/18.
Kelly, James, b. Dublin, e. Dublin, 11506, Pte., k. in a., F. & F., 6/7/15.
Kelly, James Patrick, b. Armagh, e. Armagh, 8173, Sgt., d. of w., F. & F., 31/3/15.
Kelly, John, b. St. Helens, Lancs, e. St. Helens, 15004, L/Cpl. k. in a., F. & F., 12/10/16.
Kelly, Joseph, b. Navan, Co. Meath, e. Drogheda (Wilkinstown, Co. Meath), 6625, Pte., d. of w., F. & F., 18/10/14.
Kelly, Michael, b. Limerick, e. Dundalk, Co. Louth, 25299, Pte., d., F. & F., 18/6/18.
Kelly, Patrick, b. Newry, Co. Down, e. Newry, 6095, Pte., k. in a., F. & F., 21/3/18, M.M.
Kelly, Patrick, b. Bray, Co. Wicklow, e. Monkstown, Co. Dublin (Bray), 6303, Pte., k. in a., F. & F., 9/11/14.
Kenlock, Sydney, b. Beckles, Lancs, e. London (Wembley, Middx.), 15677, Pte., k. in a., F. & F., 11/4/17, formerly 6730, Lancs. Fus.
Kennedy, Joseph, b. Dublin, e. Dublin (Salford, Manchester) 12322, Pte., k. in a., F. & F., 12/10/16.
Kent, Ernest Jacob, b. Bungay, Suffolk, e. Norwich (Ditchingham, Norfolk), 41752, Pte., k. in a., F. & F., 18/4/18, formerly S/4/064775, R.A.S.C.
Keogh, John, b. Dublin, e. Dublin, 8553, Pte., d. of w., F. & F., 30/11/14.
Keppel, Joseph, b. Skibbereen, Co. Cork, e. Kinsale, Co. Cork (Skibbereen), 18595, Pte., d. of w., F. & F., 26/6/18.
Kerr, Patrick, b. Addiewell, Midlothian, e. Bathgate (Addiewell), 24030, Pte., k. in a., F. & F., 24/3/18.
Kerr, Thomas Robert Samuel, b. Dromore, Co. Down, e. Belfast (Dromore), 8126, L/Sgt., k. in a., F. & F., 3/5/17.
Kershore, John, b. Battersea, S.W., Surrey, e. Kingston-on-Thames, Surrey (Battersea, S.W.), 9554, Pte., d., Home, 12/9/15.
Keys, Ellis, b. Hammersmith, W., Middx., e. East Ham, E., Essex (Forest Gate, E., Essex), 42039, Pte., d. of w., F. & F., 8/6/18.
Kierans, Patrick, b. Clones, Co. Monaghan, e. Cavan (Clones), 2994, Pte., k. in a., F. & F., 21/3/18.
Kiernan, Edward, b. Mullingar, Co. West Meath, e. Mullingar, 7626, Pte., k. in a., F. & F., 25/4/15.
Kiernan, Edward, b. Rathkeale, Co. Limerick, e. Glasgow (Rathkeale), 24038, Pte., k. in a., F. & F., 14/2/17.
King, Robert, b. Darwen, Lancs, e. Liverpool (Darwen), 18757, Pte., k. in a., F. & F., 26/8/16, formerly 37146, R.A.M.C.
Kirk, Frank, b. Belfast, Co. Antrim, e. Belfast, 8642, Sgt., k. in a., F. & F., 2/5/15.
Kirkham, John, b. Leek, Staffs, e. Leek, 8809, Pte., d., Home, 9/4/18, D.C.M.
Knight, Albert, b. Aldershot, Hants, e. Dover (Aldershot), 29574, L/Cpl., k. in a., F. & F., 9/4/18.
Knights, Frederick, b. Southampton, Hants, e. Winchester (Swaythling, Hants), 49913, Pte., k. in a., F. & F., 26/5/18.
Knott, John, b. Kilnhurst, Yorks, e. Mexborough, Yorks (Kilnhurst), 43150, Pte., k. in a., F. & F., 3/5/17, formerly 5950, Connaught Rangers.
Knowles, Reginald, b. Aldershot, Hants, e. Stratford, E., Essex (Leytonstone, N.E., Essex), 41703, Cpl., k. in a., F. & F., 11/4/18, formerly 26940, Northants Regt.
Koszegi, Frank, b. New York City, U.S.A., e. Buffalo, N.Y. (New York City), 29616, Pte., k. in a., F. & F., 2/9/18.
Laird, Samuel, b. Raphoe, Co. Donegal, e. Glasgow, 9495, Pte., d. of w., F. & F., 1/5/16.
Lalor, William, b. Abbeyleix, Queen's Co., e. Maryborough (Abbeyleix), 43109, Pte., k. in a., F. & F., 11/4/17, formerly 11137, Connaught Rangers.
Lamb, James, b. Portadown, Co. Armagh, e. Finner Camp, Co. Donegal (Portadown), 4626, Pte., k. in a., F. & F., 21/3/18.
Lambert, James, b. Dublin, e. Dublin, 24830, L/Cpl., k. in a., F. & F., 21/3/18.
Lambert, John, b. Wexford, e. Wexford, 16498, Pte., k. in a., F. & F., 12/10/16, formerly 1840, R. Irish Regt.
Lamburn, William Clifford, b. Mountain Ash, Glam., e. Mountain Ash, 41659, Pte., d. of w., F. & F., 24/8/18, formerly T/3/027409, R.A.S.C.

APPENDICES

Langley, George, b. Shankill, Co. Armagh, e. Lurgan, 11945, Pte., k. in a., F. & F., 1/7/16.
Lappin, Thomas, b. Portadown, Co. Armagh, e. Cambuslang, Glasgow (Newton, Glasgow), 11862, Pte., k. in a., F. & F., 9/6/15.
Larkin, Henry, b. Newry, Co. Down, e. Newry, 7771, Pte., k. in a., F. & F., 26/8/16.
Larkin, John, b. Dundalk, Co. Louth, e. Dundalk, 6158, Pte., k. in a., F. & F., 25/4/15.
Larkin, Patrick, b. Dundalk, Co. Louth, e. Ayr (Stevenston, Ayrshire), 25060, Pte., k. in a., F. & F., 11/4/17.
Laverty, Daniel, b. Coatbridge, Lanarks, e. Dunfermline, Fife, 16332, Pte., d. of w., F. & F., 19/4/17.
Lavery, Felix, b. Shankill, Co. Armagh, e. Portadown (Lurgan, Co. Armagh), 3910, Pte., d. of w., F. & F., 4/10/18.
Lavery, Francis, b. Tandragee, Co. Armagh, e. Armagh (Tandragee), 20571, Pte., k. in a., F. & F., 3/5/17.
Lavery, John, b. St. Paul's, Co. Durham, e. Belfast, 20013, Pte., k. in a., F. & F., 11/4/17.
Lavery, Owen, b. Newry, Co. Armagh, e. Newry, 5087, Pte., k. in a., F. & F., 25/4/15.
Leah, John William, b. Bradford, Manchester, e. Manchester (Bradford, Manchester), 23478, Cpl., k. in a., F. & F., 2/9/18, formerly 3631, Manchester Regt.
Leathem, George, b. Shankill, Co. Armagh, e. Lurgan, Co. Armagh, 5245, Pte., k. in a., F. & F., 9/8/15.
Leddy, Bernard, b. Cavan, e. Clones (Cavan), 6374, Pte., d. of w., F. & F., 26/5/15, D.C.M.
Leddy, Joseph, b. Cavan, e. Cavan, 20080, Pte., k. in a., F. & F., 16/10/18.
Lee, Michael, b. Dublin, e. Dublin, 11446, Pte., k. in a., F. & F., 26/8/14.
Lenehan, John, b. Carbury, Co. Kildare, e. Armagh (Carbury), 10346, Pte., k. in a., F. & F., 12/10/16.
Lennon, James, b. Shankill, Co. Armagh, e. Lurgan, Co. Armagh, 5979, Pte., k. in a., F. & F., 3/5/17.
Lennon, John, b. Crossmaglen, Co. Armagh, e. Dundalk, Co. Louth, 7092, Pte., d., F. & F., 7/5/17.
Letsome, Maurice, b. Ashton-under-Lyne, Lancs, e. Newcastle-on-Tyne (Haswell Plough, Co. Durham), 24680, L/Cpl., d., F. & F., 26/4/18.
Lewis, Charles George, b. Kensington, W., Middx., e. Kensington (Notting Hill, W., Middx.), 45829, Pte., k. in a., F. & F., 6/5/18, formerly 5143, County of London Regt.
Lewis, John, b. Belfast, e. Belfast, 25056, Pte., k. in a., F. & F., 21/10/18.
Lewis, Robert, b. Bridgeton, Glasgow, e. Glasgow, 23712, Cpl, k. in a., F. & F., 3/5/17.
Linney, Ernest Harry, b. Hinckley, Leics, e. Hinckley, 41811, Pte., k. in a., F. & F., 2/9/18, formerly S/4/042517, R.A.S.C.
Little, Andrew, b. Leith, Midlothian, c. Belfast (Glasgow), 6190, Pte., k. in a., F. & F., 4/9/18.
Livingstone, James, b. Shankill, Co. Armagh, e. Lurgan, Co Armagh, 11317, Pte., k. in a., F. & F., 26/10/14.
Lloyd, Benjamin, b. Portadown, Co. Armagh, e. Portadown (Tandragee, Co. Armagh), 6031, Pte., k. in a., F. & F., 3/5/17.
Logue, William John, b. Ballymacarrett, Co. Down, e. Belfast, 24123, Pte., k. in a., F. & F., 11/4/17.
Long, Henry, e. London (Upper Edmonton, N., Middx.), 9768 Pte., k. in a., F. & F., 6/4/16.
Lucas, Andrew, b. Maryhill, Glasgow, e. Milngavie, Glasgow (Glasgow), 41755, L/Cpl., d. of w., Home, 9/12/18, formerly S/22414, R.A.S.C.
Lundy, John, b. Newry, Co. Down, e. Belfast (Newry), 18731, Pte., k. in a., F. & F., 24/3/18, formerly 41594, R.A.M.C.
Lunn, Samuel, b. Shankill, Armagh, e. Lurgan, Co. Armagh, 5503, Pte., k. in a., F. & F., 12/10/16.
Lynn, William, b. Coalisland, Co. Tyrone, e. Portadown, Co. Armagh (Coalisland), 5700, Sgt., k. in a., F. & F., 17/7/16.
Lyons, Leonard Bernard, b. Maidstone, Kent, e. Leicester (Battersea, S.W., Surrey), 10271, Sgt., d. of w., F. & F., 19/9/14. formerly 6305, R. Fus.
Lyons, Michael, b. Maryborough, Queen's Co., e. Cootehill, Co. Cavan, 7985, Pte., d. of w., F. & F., 28/4/15.
Lyster, John, b. Kingstown, Co. Dublin, e. Kingstown, 8265, Pte., d. of w., F. & F., 18/9/14.
Lyttle, David, b. Cloverhill, Co. Cavan, e. Cavan (Cloverhill), 23911, Pte., k. in a., F. & F., 9/7/17.
Macken, Patrick, b. Dublin, e. Dublin, 42357, Pte., k. in a., F. & F., 1/10/18 formerly S/4/090283, R.A.S.C.
Mackin, Francis, b. Armagh, e. Coatbridge, Lanarks, 24264, Pte., k. in a., F. & F., 11/4/17.
Mackin, James, b. Crossmaglen, Co. Armagh, e. Dundalk (Crossmaglen), 17864, Pte., k. in a., F. & F., 14/4/18.
Magee, Edward, b. Belfast, e. Belfast, 8507, Pte., k. in a., F. & F., 27/8/14.

Magee, Thomas, b. Dublin, e. Leeds, 7403, Pte., k. in a., F. & F., 26/10/14.
Magill, John, b. Shankill, Co. Armagh, e. Portadown, Co. Armagh (Lurgan, Co. Armagh), 5260, Pte., d. of w., F. & F., 27/4/15.
Magill, William, b. Belfast, e. Belfast, 8391, Pte., k. in a., F. & F., 21/11/14.
Maguire, John, b. Shankill, Belfast, e. Belfast, 23900, Pte., k. in a., F. & F., 11/4/17.
Maguire, John, b. Laragh, Co. Monaghan, e. Wallasey, Ches. (Birkenhead, Ches.), 29242, Pte., d. of w., F. & F., 25/8/18.
Maguire, Michael, b. Glasgow, e. Glasgow, 24466, Pte., d. of w., F. & F., 18/5/17.
Mahaffey, Joseph, b., Shankill, Co. Armagh, e. Lurgan, Co. Armagh, 6612, Pte., k. in a., F. & F., 21/11/14.
Mahoney, James, b. Ballymacarrett, Co. Down. e. Belfast, 13519, L/Cpl, k. in a., F. & F., 3/5/17.
Maidens, John, b. Doncaster, Yorks, e. Carrickfergus. Co. Antrim (Doncaster), 3335, Pte., k. in a., F. & F., 26/8/16.
Malcolm, William, b. Holywood, Co. Down, e. Belfast (Craigavad, Co. Down), 8204, Pte., k. in a., F. & F., 25/4/15.
Malcomson, Richard, b. Monaghan, e. Belfast, 8261, Cpl., k. in a., F. & F., 24/5/15.
Malcomson, William, b. Portadown, Co. Armagh, e. Finner Camp, Co. Donegal (Portadown, Co. Armagh), 4142, Pte., k. in a., F. & F., 25/4/15.
Mallon, Joseph, b. Shankill, Belfast, e. Ballykinlar Camp, Co. Down (Belfast), 9207, Pte., d. of w., F. & F., 27/9/14.
Manning, Percy, b. Waterford, e. Dublin, 11248, Pte., d. of w., F. & F., 8/11/14.
Markey, Felix, b. Donaghmoyne, Co. Monaghan, e. Armagh (Broomfield, Co. Monaghan), 24811, A/Cpl., k. in a., F. & F., 23/1/17.
Martin, Albert, b. Wandsworth, S. W., Surrey, e. London (St. Neots, Hunts), 9530, Sgt., k. in a., F. & F., 11/10/18.
Martin, Bernard, b. Newcastle-on-Tyne, e. West St., E., Middx. (Newcastle-on-Tyne), 24002, Pte., k. in a., F. & F., 27/9/17.
Martin, Bermard, b. Scrabby, Co. Cavan, e. Cavan (Gowno, Co. Cavan), 28676, Pte., d., F. & F., 29/6/18.
Martin, Daniel, b. Cavan, e. Cavan, 11471, Pte., k. in a., F. & F., 12/10/16.
Martin, David, b. Newry, Co. Down, e. Newry (Belfast), 7636, Pte., d., F. & F., 27/5/16.
Martin, Francis, b. Monaghan, e. Lisburn (Belfast), 27811, Pte., d. of w., F. & F., 28/11/17.
Martin, John, b. Dundalk, Co. Louth, e. Armagh (Dundalk), 8463, Pte., d. of w., F. & F., 10/5/15.
Martin, John, b. Shankill, Co. Armagh, e. Lurgan, Co. Armagh 10261, Cpl., d. of w., F. & F., 15/7/16.
Martin, Patrick, b. Ballyjamesduff, Co. Cavan, e. Cavan (Ballyjamesduff), 24086, Pte., k. in a., F. & F., 12/10/16.
Martin, Patrick, b. Ballyjamesduff, Co. Cavan, e. Cavan (Ballyjamesduff), 24086, Pte., k. in a., F. & F., 12/10/16.
Martin, Samuel Alexander, b. Londonderry, e. Londonderry, 8706, Pte., d. of w., F. & F., 20/7/16.
Mason, Jospeh William, b Stockport, Ches., e. Ashton-under-Lyne, Lancs, 15558, Pte., k. in a., F. & F., 12/10/16.
Mason, Richard, b. Whitby, Yorks, e. Middlesbrough, Yorks (Folkestone, Kent), 11243, Sgt., k. in a., F. & F., 16/8/16, formerly 3502, Northumberland Fus., M.M.
Masterson, Michael, b. Milltown, Co. Cavan, e. Monaghan (Milltown), 23713, Pte., k. in a., F. & F., 4/9/18.
Matthews, Edward, b. Dundee, Forfar, e. Dundee, 20434, Pte., k. in a., F. & F., 12/10/16.
Maxfield, William George, b. Bridgend, Glam., e. Bridgend (Gilfach, Goch, Glam.), 17767, Pte., d., F. & F., 7/11/18.
Meagher, Edward, b. Dublin, e. Dublin, 7022, C.S.M., k. in a., F. & F., 14/4/18.
Meagher, Joseph, b. Dublin, e. Curragh, Camp, Co. Kildare (Dublin), 11294, Pte., k. in a., F. & F., 10/10/16, formerly 8699, R. Irish Regt.
Meagher, Thomas, b. Widnes, Lancs. e. Warrington, Lancs (Widnes), 17442, Pte., k. in a., F. & F., 12/10/16.
Meehan, Francis, b. Drogheda, Co. Louth, e. Drogheda (Blackburn, Lancs), 10107, Pte., k. in a., F. & F., 5/4/18.
Meehan, Patrick, b. Castletown, Co. Meath, e. Armagh (Navan, Co. Meath), 18688, Pte., k. in a., F. & F., 11/4/17.
Mehegan, Michael Aloysius, b. Athlone, Co. W. Meath, e. Dublin, 24410, Cpl., k. in a., F. & F., 26/6/17.
Mellor, Henshaw, b. Denbigh, e. Northwich, Ches. (Davenham, Ches.), 47736, Pte., k. in a., F. & F., 1/10/18, formerly S/3/030611, R.A.S.C.
Mercer, James, b. Holmwood, Surrey, e. London (Fulham, S.W., Middx.), 9279, Pte., k. in a., F. & F., 27/8/14.
Metson, Sidney, b. Great Leights, Essex, c. Ilford, Essex (Brentwood, Essex), 18997, Pte., k. in a., F. & F., 23/11/17, formerly 146861, R.F.A.

Millar, Samuel, e. Lisburn, Co. Antrim, 13044, Pte., k. in a., F. & F., 29/7/16.
Miller, Robert, b. Shankill, Belfast, e. Belfast, 17574, Pte., k. in a., F. & F., 23/11/17.
Miller, Thomas, b. Shankill, Belfast, e. Belfast, 12405, Pte., k. in a., F. & F., 24/3/18.
Mills, John, b. Portadown, Co. Armagh, e. Lurgan (Portadown), 8527, Pte., k. in a., F. & F., 25/4/15.
Mitchell, Hedley Percival, b. Holsworthy, Devon, e. Taunton (Weston-super-Mare, Som.), 49789, Pte., d. of w., F. & F., 25/5/18, formerly 41739, R. Innis. Fus.
Mohan, Francis, n. Ballybay, Co. Monaghan, e. Dundalk (Ballybay), 17685, Pte., d. of w., F. & F., 9/7/15.
Moloney, William, b. Dublin, e. Dublin, 18955, Pte., d. of w., F. & F., 2/7/16, formerly 13215, Hussars of the Line.
Monaghan, Francis, b. Portadown, Co. Armagh, e. Portadown, 6394, Pte., k. in a., F. & F., 26/6/17.
Monaghan, John, b. Dublin, e. Dublin, 9727, Pte., k. in a., F. & F., 16/7/16.
Monaghan, Peter, b. Drogheda, Co. Louth, e. Drogheda, 11437, Pte., k. in a., F. & F., 1/7/16.
Montgomery, Samuel, b. Lisburn, Co. Antrim, e. Belfast, 2482, Pte., k. in a., F. & F., 2/9/18.
Montgomery, Thomas, b. Conlig, Co. Down, e. Clandeboye, Co. Down (Conlig), 42345, Pte., d. of w., F. & F., 30/9/18, formerly 1533, R. Irish Rif.
Mooney, Martin, b. Philipstown, King's Co., e. Tullamore, King's Co. (Philipstown), 42402, Pte., k. in a., F. & F., 1/10/18, formerly 5471, R. Irish Rif.
Moore, Francis, b. Armagh, e. Belfast, 15748, Pte., d. of w., F. & F., 11/1/16.
Moore, George, b. Dublin, e. Dublin, 23912, Pte., k. in a., F. & F., 12/10/16.
Moore, John, b. Tullylish, Co. Down, e. Portadown, Co. Armagh (Gilford, Co. Down), 24400, Pte., k. in a., F. & F., 11/4/17.
Moore, Joshua, b. Portadown, Co. Armagh, e. Portadown, 5868, Pte., k. in a., F. & F., 8/12/15.
Moore, Robert James, b. Shankill, Co. Armagh, e. Lurgan, Co. Armagh, 8403, Pte., k. in a., F. & F., 29/11/14.
Moorehouse, George, b. Nuns Cross, Co. Wicklow, e. Dublin (Enniskerry, Co. Wicklow), 49806, L/Cpl. k. in a., F. & F., 1/10/18, formerly 23536, R. Innis. Fus.
Moran, John, b. Dublin, e. Dublin, 11005, Pte., k. in a., F. & F., 22/2/15.
Morris, James, b. Donegal, e. Cavan (Carrigallen, Co. Leitrim), 7828, Pte., k. in a., F. & F., 6/5/15, formerly 7558, Conn. Rangers.
Morris, William, b. Kingstown, Co. Dublin, e. Kingstown (Dalkey, Co. Dublin), 20243, Pte., k. in a., F. & F., 26/8/16.
Morrison, Robert, b. Shankill, Belfast, e. Belfast, 42398, Pte., k. in a., F. & F., 1/10/18, formerly 22437, R. Irish Rif.
Morrow, James Stewart, b. Knockbride, Co. Cavan, e. Cotehill, Co. Cavan (Knockbride), 7683 Pte., k. in a., F. & F., 18/10/14
Morrow, Robert, b. Carland, Co. Tyrone, e. Dungannon (New Mills, Co. Tyrone), 10531, Pte., d. of w., F. & F., 26/4/15, V.C.
Moss, William, b. Hoxton, N., Middx., e. Shoreditch, N., Middx. (Hoxton, N.). 42056, Pte., k. in a., F. & F., 1/10/18.
Motherwell, William, b. Liverpool, e. Cardiff, Glam. (Roath, Glam.), 41841, Pte., d., F. & F., 29/8/18, formerly T/2/13586, R.A.S.C.
Mount, James Alfred, b. Edmonton, N., Middx., e. Chatham, Kent (Hoo, Kent), 9369, L/Cpl., k, in a., F. & F., 12/10/16.
Muir, Alexander, b. Belfast, e. Newry (Belfast), 26002, Pte., d. of w., F. & F., 1/10/17.
Mulgrew, Edward, b. Shankill, Belfast, e. Belfast, 24691, Pte., k. in a., F. & F., 24/3/18.
Mulholland, John, b. Dundalk, Co. Louth, e. Newry (Dundalk), 5393, Pte., k. 8n a., F. & F., 25/4/15.
Mulholland, Robert, b. Shankill, Belfast, e. Belfast, 23575, Pte., k. in a., F. & F., 9/7/17.
Mullen, Patrick, b. Dublin, e. Dublin, 11436, Pte., k. in a., F. & F., 26/8/14.
Mullen, Thomas, e. Dublin (Drogheda, Co. Louth), 17059, Pte., k. in a., F. & F., 12/10/16.
Mulligan, Patrick, b. Cootehill, Co. Cavan, e. Cavan (Cootehill), 23801, Pte., k. in a., F. & F., 23/11/17.
Munro, James, b. Coatbridge, Lanark, e. Glasgow (Coatbridge), 10935, Pte., k. in a., F. & F., 26/8/14.
Murdoch, Ross, b. Ballymacarrett, Co. Down, e. Newtownards, Co. Down (Belfast), 12568, Pte., k. in a., F. & F., 12/10/16.
Murfitt, Albert, b. Cambridge, e. Stratford E., Essex (Canning Town, E., Essex), 42029, Pte., d. of w., F. & F., 15/10/18, formerly TR/77410, 11th T.R. Battn.
Murphy, Henry, b. Dundalk, Co. Louth, e. Dundalk, 8032, Pte. k. in a., F. & F., 14/10/15.

Murphy, Hugh, b. Lanark, e. Glasgow, 20517, Cpl., k. in a., F. & F., 11/4/18.
Murphy, James, b. Dalry, Ayrshire, e. Glasgow, (Kilbirnie, Ayrshire), 19988, Cpl., k. in a., F. & F., 11/4/17.
Murphy, James, A., e. Belfast, 21176, Pte., k. in a., F. & F., 24/8/18, formerly 2554, Connaught Rangers.
Murphy, James Joseph, b. Glasgow, e. London, 11210, Pte., k. in a., F. & F., 12/4/15.
Murphy. Joseph, b. Ditton, Lancs, e. Warrington, Lancs (Ditton), 6257, Pte., k. in a., F. & F., 14/2/17.
Murphy, Michael, b. Newry, Co. Down, e. Newry, 5542, Pte., k. in a., F. & F., 12/10/16.
Murphy, Patrick, b. Dublin, e. Dublin, 8942, Pte., d., F. & F., 6/1/15.
Murray, Andrew, b. Shankill, Co. Armagh, e. Portadown, Co. Armagh (Lurgan, Co. Armagh), 5122, Pte., k. in a., F. & F., 25/4/15.
Murray, James, b. Portadown, Co. Armagh, e. Portadown, 5481, Pte., k. in a., F. & F., 11/4/18.
Murray, Joseph, b. Belfast, e. Belfast, 3743, Pte., k. in a., F. & F., 14/4/18.
Murray, Robert Inglis, b. Holyhead, Anglesey, e. Clifton Street, E.C., Middx. (Clapham, S.W., Surrey), 18981, Pte., k. in a., F. & F., 12/10/16, formerly 21138, Hussars of the Line.
Murray, Thomas, b. Dublin, e. Dublin, 10491, L/Cpl., k. in a., F. & F., 25/4/15.
Murtagh, John, b. Dromiskin, Co. Louth, e. Dundalk, Co. Louth (Dromiskin), 18477, Pte., k. in a., F. & F., 12/10/16.
Murtagh, Thomas, b. Ballinagh, Co. Cavin, e. Cavan (Ballinagh), 3295, Pte., k. in a., F. & F., 25/4/15.
Myers, Edgar Charles, b. New Cross, S.E., Kent, e. Camberwell, S.E., Surrey (Gillingham, Kent), 50007, Pte., d. of w., F. & F., 3/10/18, formerly 555687, 16th Res. London Regt., M.M.
Mynes, Thomas, b. Dromiskin, Co. Louth, e. Dundalk (Dromiskin), 18473, Pte., k. in a., F. & F., 1/7/16.
MacPhillips, James, b. Smithborough, Co. Monaghan, e. Cavan (Smithborough), 19745, Pte., k. in a., F. & F., 21 3/18.
McAleavey, Patrick Bernard, b. Belfast, e. Glasgow (Lochwinnoch, Renfrews), 23551, Pte., k. in a., F. & F., 11/7/17. formerly 21110, R. Innis Fus., M.M.
McAlindon, James, b. Derrytrasna, Co. Armagh, e. Lurgan, Co. Armagh, 11168, Pte., d., F. & F., 28/2/17.
McAllister, James, b. Newry, Co. Down, e. Dundalk (Newry), 18600, Pte., k. in a., F. & F., 19/6/16.
McArdle, James, b. Inniskeen, Co. Monaghan, e. Dundalk, Co. Louth, 21420, Pte., k. in a., F. &. F., 16/2/17.
McArdle, James, b. Gilford, Co. Down, e. Newry, (Gilford), 27464, Pte., k. in a., F. & F., 27/9/17.
McArdle, Thomas, b. Dundalk, Co. Louth, e. Armagh (Dundalk), 11219, L/Cpl., k. in a., F. & F., 12/10/16.
McAteer, John, b. Newry, Co. Down, e. Coatbridge, Lanarks, 18124, Pte., k. in a., F. & F., 2/7/16.
McAvoy, Michael, b. Newry, Co. Down, e. Coatbridge, Lanarks (Newry), 17680, Pte., d., F. & F., 29/6/18.
McBrien, James, b. Dublin, e. Dublin, 20098, Pte., k. in a., F. & F., 1/7/16.
McCabe, Patrick, b. Drogheda, Co. Louth, e. Drogheda, 17481, Pte., k. in a., F. & F., 17/7/18.
McCaffrey, Bernard, b. Drumgoon, Co. Cavan, e. Armagh (Cootehill, Co. Cavan), 22740, Pte., k. in a., F. & F., 23/11/17.
McCaffrey, Hugh, b. Drumreilly, Co. Cavan, e. Cavan (Belturbet, Co. Cavan), 24362, Pte., k. in a., F. & F., 9/7/15.
McCaffrey, John, b. Ballybay, Co. Monaghan, e. Belfast (Tydavnet, Co. Monaghan), 24162, Pte., k. in a., F. & F., 11/4/17.
McCaldin, Robert, b. Armagh, e. Hamilton, Lanarks (Whitecross, Co. Armagh), 17814, Pte., d. of w., F. & F., 4/6/15.
McCann, Francis, b. Portadown, Co. Armagh, e. Armagh (Portadown), 6135, Pte., k. in a., F. & F., 1/7/16.
McCann, Michael, b. Shankill, Co. Armagh, e. Portadown, Co. Armagh (Lurgan, Co. Armagh), 6362, Pte., k. in a., F. & F., 11/4/17.
McCann, Thomas John, b. Portadown, Co. Armagh, e. Portadown, 11495, Pte., d. of w., F. & F., 21/10/14.
McCarron, William, b. Castlerock, Co. Londonderry, e. Londonderry (Castlerock), 49979, Pte., k. in a., F. & F., 1/10/18, formerly 3/30279, R. Innis. Fus.
McCartney, James, b. Donaghcloney, Co. Down, e. Lurgan (Donaghcloney), 11312, Pte., d. of w., Home, 5/5/15.
McCartney, John, b. Dublin, e. Hamilton, Lanarks (Laurencetown, Co. Down), 7856, Pte., k. in a., F. & F., 25/4/15.
McCartney, William John, b. Shankhill, Belfast, e. Belfast, 8101 Pte., k. in a., F. & F., 26/4/16, formerly 6972, S. Lancs Regt.
McClaren, Barclay Warren, b. Halifax, Nova Scotia, e. Liverpool, 27888, Pte., k. in a., F. & F., 23/11/17, formerly 28496, R. Innis. Fus.

McClarnan, William, b. Preston, Lancs, e. Preston, 11295, Pte., k. in a., F. & F., 25/4/15, formerly 7939, Dragoons of the Line.
McCleary, David, b. Dumfries, e. St. Paul's Churchyard, E.C., Middx. (Battersea Rise, S.W., Surrey), 45846, Pte., k. in a., F. & F., 11/4/18, formerly 6500, 3/21 County of London.
McCleery, Robert, b. Shankill, Belfast, e. Belfast, 8260, Cpl., k. in a., F. & F., 1/10/18.
McClelland, Thomas, b. Middleton, Co. Armagh, e. Armagh (Middletown), 18542, Pte., k. in a., F. & F., 11/5/17.
McClurg, Nathaniel, b. Shankhill, Belfast, e. Belfast, 23681, Pte., d. of w., F. & F., 5/11/17.
McConnell, Samuel, b. Waterford, e. Waterford, 42391, Pte., k. in a., F. & F., 1/10/18, formerly 22529, R. Irish Rif.
McConnell, William, b. Shankill, Belfast, e. Belfast, 3589, Pte., d. of w., F. & F., 4/5/17.
McConville, Charles Vincent, b. Shankill, Co. Armagh, e. Lurgan, Co. Armagh, 11215, Pte., k. in a., F. & F., 26/8/14.
McConville, Francis, b. Cavan, e. Cavan, 11499, A/Sgt., k. in a., F. & F., 12/10/16.
McConville, Matthew, b. Shankill, Co. Armagh, e. Lurgan (Belfast), 5726, Pte., k. in a., F. & F., 28/4/15.
McCormack, Edward, b. Cavan, e. Armagh (Cavan), 5788, Pte., k. in a., F. & F., 25/4/15.
McCormack, Nicholas, b. Chapelizod, Co. Dublin, e. Dublin (Chapelizod), 18959, Pte., d. of w., F. & F., 8/11/18, formerly 13461, Hussars of the Line.
McCormack, Patrick, b. Dublin, e. Dublin, 19962, Pte., d. of w., F. & F., 2/7/16.
McCormick, Thomas, b. Randalstown, Co. Antrim, e. Randalstown, 20909, Pte., k. in a., F. & F., 24/3/18.
McCourt, Michael, b. Coatbridge, Lanarks, e. Newry, Co. Down (Camlough, Co. Armagh), 5904, Pte., k. in a., F. & F., 25/4/15.
McCrea, Alexander, b. Belfast, e. Belfast, 8534, Pte., k. in a., F. & F., 24/6/15.
McCrory, Patrick James, b. Patrick, Glasgow, e. Randalstown, Co. Antrim, 20910, Pte., k. in a., F. & F., 9/5/17.
McCulloch, Peter, e. Cambuslang, Glasgow (Blantyre, Glasgow), 16374, Pte., d. of w., F. & F., 14/4/17.
McCullough, Henry, b. Shankill, Co. Armagh, e. Lurgan, Co. Armagh, 23231, Pte., k. in a., F. & F., 1/10/18.
McCurrie, John, b. Shankill, Belfast, e. Belfast, 8154, Pte., k. in a., F. & F., 26/8/16.
McDermott, James, e. Paisley, 49854, Pte., k. in a., F. & F., 1/10/18, formerly 26024, R. Innis. Fus.
McDermott, Richard, b. Carrickfergus, Co. Antrim, e. Carrickfergus, 12892, Pte., k. in a., F. & F., 16/2/17, formerly 11772, R. Irish Rif.
McDermott, Thomas, b. Belturbet, Co. Cavan, e. Cavan (Ballyconnell, Co. Cavan), 17529, Pte., d. of w., F. & F., 2/7/16.
McDermott, Thomas, b. Keighley, Yorks, e. Colne, Lancs, 17774, L/Cpl., k. in a., F. & F., 9/12/16.
McDonald, James, e. Cavan (Bailieborough, Co. Cavan), 21643, Pte., k. in a., F. & F., 21/3/18.
McDonald, John, b. Lisnaskea, Co. Fermanagh, e. Armagh (Gilford, Co. Down), 8467, Pte., k. in a., F. & F., 14/11/14.
McDonnell, Alexander, b. Belfast, e. Belfast, 21161, Pte., k. in a., F. & F., 11/4/17, formerly 2519, Connaught Rangers.
McDonnell, James, b. Shankill, Co. Armagh, e. Finner Camp, Co. Donegal (Lurgan, Co. Armagh), 3937, Pte., k. in a., F. & F., 11/4/17.
McDonough, Thomas, b. Paisley, Renfrewshire, e. Paisley, 29448, Pte., k. in a., F. & F., 18/4/18, formerly 6930, Connaught Rangers.
McDowell, Samuel, b. Shankill, Co. Armagh, e. Finner Camp, Co. Donegal (Lurgan, Co. Armagh), 4329, Pte., k. in a., F. & F., 25/4/15.
McElroy, Peter, b. Newry, Co. Down, e. Newry, 5430, Pte., d. of w., F. & F., 13/4/15.
McEneaney, Alexander, b. Lanark, e. Glasgow, 20082, Pte., k. in a., F. & F., 28/7/16.
McEvoy, Gordon, b. St. Giles, Middx., e. London (Clapham Rd., S.W., Surrey), 9354, Sgt., k. in a., F. & F., 21/10/14.
McEvoy, Peter, b. Shercock, Co. Cavan, e. Glasgow (Shercock), 17851, Pte., k. in a., F. & F., 3/5/17.
McFarlane, John, b. Keady, Co. Armagh, e. Armagh (Glasgow), 12000, Pte., d., Home, 12/12/16.
McFerran, Walter, b. Shankill, Belfast, e. Belfast,, 24614 L/Cpl., k. in a., F. & F., 23/11/17.
McGaley, Richard, b. Dublin, e. Dublin, 21513, Pte., k. in a., F. & F., 11/4/17.
McGaughey, Patrick James, b. Letterkenny, Co. Donegal, e. Hamilton, Lanarks (Mossend, Lanarks), 16331, Pte., k. in a., F. & F., 11/4/17.
McGeehan, Neil, b. Templemore, Co. Londonderry, e. Londonderry, 40134, Pte., k. in a., F. & F., 2/9/18, formerly 24817, Hussars of the Line.

McGeown, Francis, b. Shankill, Co. Armagh, e. Lurgan, Co. Armagh, 5971, Pte., k. in a., F. & F., 25/4/15.
McGeown, John, b. Belfast, e. Belfast, 49878, Pte., d. of w., F. & F., 22/10/18, formerly 19/424, R. Irish Rif.
McGill, James, b. Tandragee, Co. Armagh, e. Armagh (Tandragee), 20230, Pte., k. in a., F. & F., 11/4/17.
McGillin, George, b. Londonderry, e. Hamilton, Lanarks (Londonderry), 10825, Pte., k. in a., F. & F., 12/10/16.
McGinley, Bernard, b. St. Peter's, Co. Antrim, e. Belfast, 3844, Pte., k. in a., F. & F., 3/5/17.
McGlade, John, b. Shankill, Belfast, e. Belfast, 24067, Pte., k. in a., F. & F., 24/6/17.
McGlone, John, b. Glasgow, e. Glasgow, 6741, Pte., k. in a., F. & F., 10/11/14.
McGlynn, Edward, b. Armagh, e. Armagh, 19961, L/Cpl., d., Home, 10/10/18.
McGowan, James, b. Lisburn, Co. Antrim, e. Lurgan, Co. Armagh (Lisburn), 8546, Pte., k. in a., F. & F., 12/10/16.
McGrath, John, b. Seapatrick, Co. Down, e. Portadown (Seapatrick), 11237, Pte., d of w., F. & F., 15/10/14.
McGrath, John, b. Dublin, e. Stirling (Dublin), 24661, Pte., k. in a., F. & F., 15/4/17.
McGrath, Joseph, b. Enniskillen, e. Dublin, 9730, Pte., k. in a., F. & F., 26/8/14.
McGregor, John, b. Belfast, e. Newry, Co. Down, 6080, Pte., d., Home, 26/2/16.
McGruddy, John Michael, b. Shercock, Co. Cavan, e. Dundalk, Co. Louth (Shercock), 23922, Pte., k. in a., F. & F., 11/4/17.
McGucken, William, b. Belfast, e. Belfast, 12881, Pte., k. in a., F. & F., 9/6/15, formerly 11828, R. Irish Rif.
McGuigan, Henry, b. Moy, Co. Tyrone, e. Armagh (Dungannon, Co. Tyrone), 5695, L/Cpl., d., F. & F., 31/5/17.
McGuire, George, b. Ballinasloe, Co. Galway, e. Cork, 9334, A/Sgt., k. in a., F. & F., 21/3/18, M.M.
McGuire, James, b. Enniskillen, e. Glasgow (Arney, Co. Fermanagh), 10967, Pte., k. in a., F. & F., 11/4/17.
McGuirk, John Joseph, b. Cootehill, Co. Cavan, e. Armagh (Cootehill), 23924, Pte., k. in a., F. & F., 11/4/18.
McGurk, James Joseph, b. Shankill, Belfast, e. Belfast, 22695, Pte., k. in a., F. & F., 23/11/17.
McIlroy, Alfred, b. Belfast, e. Lurgan, Co. Armagh, 14512, Pte., k. in a., F. & F., 30/9/18.
McIlveen, William, b. Ballymena, Co. Antrim, e. Belfast, 6140, Pte., d., F. & F., 1/9/18.
McInally, James Stokes, b. Lanark, e. Glasgow (Partick, Glasgow), 27531, Pte., d., F. & F., 3/6/18, formerly 37076, R. Scot. Fus.
McIntyre, David, e. Glasgow (Whiteinch, Glasgow), 17744, Pte., k. in a., F. & F., 31/7/16.
McIntyre, Malcolm, b. Calton, Glasgow, e. Glasgow (Partick, Glasgow), 18110, Pte., k. in a., F. & F., 12/10/16.
McKenna, Edward, b. Omagh, Co. Tyrone, e. Carlow, 41762, Pte., k. in a., F. & F., 14/4/18, formerly S/4/094647, R.A.S.C.
McKenna, Francis, b. Dundalk, Co. Louth, e. Cavan (Dundalk), 11038, Pte., d. of w., F. & F., 21/10/14.
McKenna, Leo, b. Armagh, e. Glasgow (Milford, Co. Armagh), 23424, Pte., k. in a., F. & F., 11/4/17.
McKenna, Michael, b. Kingscourt, Co. Cavan, e. Dundalk (Kingscourt), 27781, Pte., k. in a., F. & F., 1/10/18.
McKeown, Charles, b. Portadown, Co. Armagh, e. Portadown (Gilford, Co. Down), 11142, Pte., k. in a., F. & F., 25/4/15.
McKeown, Daniel, b. Belfast, e. Dublin (Belfast), 25203, Pte., k. in a., F. & F., 11/4/17.
McKeown, Patrick, b. Blackrock, Co. Louth, e. Newry (Blackrock), 6023, Pte., k. in a., F. & F., 12/10/16.
McKevitt, James, b. Newry, Co. Down, e. Newry, 8279, Pte., d. of w., F. & F., 26/4/15.
McKnight, David, b. Ballymacarrett, Co. Down, e. Belfast, 42302, Pte., k. in a., F. & F., 24/10/18, formerly 22046, R. Irish Rif.
McLaughlin, Joseph, b. Londonderry, e. Londonderry, 24542, Pte., k. in a., F. & F., 23/11/17.
McLean, Albert, b. Belturbet, Co. Cavan, e. Cavan (Belturbet), 11472, Pte., k. in a., F. & F., 21/3/18, M.M.
McLean, George Henry, b. Croydon, Surrey, e. Croydon (Addiscombe, Surrey), 17822, Pte., k. in a., F. & F., 3/5/17, formerly 6549, 5th Lancers.
McLintock, Robert, b. Ballymena, Co. Antrim, e. Ballymena, 3622, Pte., k. in a., F. & F., 11/4/17, formerly 5706, R.G.A.
McLoughlin, James, b. Oristown, Co. Meath, e. Drogheda, Co. Louth (Navan, Co. Meath), 20413, L/Cpl., k. in a., F. & F., 24/6/17.
McLoughlin, Robert, b. Portadown, Co. Armagh, e. Finner Camp, Co. Donegal (Portadown), 3880, Sgt., k. in a., F. & F., 12/10/16.
McMahon, Featherston, b. Ballymacarrett, Co. Down, e. Belfast, 3528, Pte., k. in a., F. & F., 3/5/17.

McManus, James, b. Enniskillen, e. Enniskillen, 8962, Pte., k. in a., F. & F., 27/5/15.
McManus, Matthew, b. Clones, Co. Monaghan, e. Clones, 8951, L/Cpl., d., F. & F., 6/6/18.
McMullan, James, b. Portrush, Co. Antrim, e. Portrush, 22855, Pte., k. in a., F. & F., 15/7/16.
McMurray, William Thomas, b. Clones, Co. Monaghan, e. Clones, 10615, Pte., k. in a., F. & F., 25/4/15.
McNally, James, b. Lambeth, S.E., Surrey, e. Guildford, Surrey (Lambeth, S.E.), 8884, Pte., d., F. & F., 16/11/17.
McNally, John, b. Sandymount, Co. Dublin, e. Dublin, 3147, Pte., d. of w., F. & F., 30/3/18.
McNally, Peter, b. Cootehill, Co. Cavan, e. Cavan (Cootehill), 10462, Pte., k. in a., F. & F., 27/8/14.
McNally, Thomas, b. Castleraghan, Co. Cavan, e. Belturbet, Co. Cavan, 9295, Pte., d., F. & F., 22/6/18.
McNulty, William, b. Ballybofey, Co. Donegal, e. Belfast (Ballybofey), 21255, Pte., k. in a., F. & F., 26/8/16.
McParland, Bernard, b. Kilmore, Co. Armagh, e. Armagh (Richhill, Co. Armagh), 8444, Pte., k. in a., F. & F., 24/5/15.
McQuaid, John, e. Glasgow, 6237, Pte., d., Home, 10/7/17.
McQuilkin, Daniel, b. Carrickfergus, Co. Antrim, e. Lurgan, Co. Armagh (Carrickfergus), 7080, d. of w., Home, 24/6/15.
McShane, Bernard, b. Holywood, Co. Down, e. Belfast (Holywood), 21021, Pte., k. in a., F. & F., 11/4/17, formerly 2774, Connaught Rangers.
McShane, Robert, b. Dungannon, Co. Tyrone, e. Armagh, 8751, Pte., k. in a., F. & F., 27/8/14.
McStravick, John, b. Shankill, Co. Armagh, e. Lurgan, Co. Armagh, 11438, Pte., k. in a., F. & F., 25/4/15.
McSwiney, Denis, b. Ballincollig, Co. Cork, e. Cork (Middleton, Co. Cork), 21437, L/Cpl., k. in a., F. & F., 2/10/17.
McVarnick, James, b. Belfast, e. Belfast, 24014, Pte., k. in a., F. & F., 11/4/17.
McVeigh, John, b. Arboe, Co. Tyrone, e. Ballymena, Co. Antrim (Draperstown, Co. Londonderry), 26124, Pte., k. in a., F. & F., 23/3/18.
McVeigh, Patrick, b. Randalstown, Co. Antrim, e. Antrim (Randalstown), 3667, Pte., d. ,F. & F., 14/6/18.
McVicker, Patrick, e. Ballymena, 29728, Pte., k. in a., F. & F., 1/10/18.
McWhinnie, Samuel, b. Achavarrie, Co. Antrim, e. Hamilton, Lanarks (Rutherglen, Glasgow), 27418, Pte., k. in a., F. & F., 1/10/18.
Neill, George, b. Portadown, Co. Armagh, e. Portadown, 10772, Pte., k. in a., F. & F., 27/8/14.
Neill, William, b. Whitehaven, Cumberland, e. Belfast, 12475, L/Cpl., k. in a., F. & F., 24/3/18.
Nevin, Patrick, b. Limerick, e. Dublin (Limerick), 3141, Pte. k. in a., F. & F., 25/4/15.
Newell, Thomas, b. Belfast, e. Belfast, 23977, Pte., d. of w., F. & F., 18/10/16.
Newman, Harold Charles, b. Trimley, Suffolk, e. Ipswich, Suffolk (Trimley), 41764, Pte., d. of w., F. & F., 15/4/18, formerly S/4/094770, R.A.S.C.
Nicholas, Joseph, b. Hereford, e. Caerphilly, Glam. (Llanbradach, Glam.), 13611, Pte., k. in a., F. & F., 3/5/17.
Nicholls, James, b. Chiswick, W., Middx., e. Hammersmith, W., Middx. (Fulham, S.W., Middx.), 18796, Pte., k. in a., F. & F., 25/4/16, formerly 24162, Hussars of the Line.
Nichols, Horatio George, b. St. Margaret's, Norfolk, e. King's Lynn, Norfolk, 41691, Pte., k. in a., F. & F., 27/3/18, formerly 022680, R.A.O.C.
Noblett, Thomas, b. Dublin, e. Dublin, 3274, Sgt., k. in a., F. & F., 21/3/18.
Nolan, Michael, b. Dublin, e. Dublin, 11169, Pte., k. in a., F. & F., 18/10/14.
Nolan, Michael, b. Dublin, e. Dublin (Kingstown, Co. Dublin), 18696, Pte., d., F. & F., 19/10/18.
Nolan, William, b. Ballymore-Eustace, Co. Kildare, e. Dublin, (Ballymore-Eustace), 26302, Pte., d. of w., F. & F., 27/6/17.
Nordon, Cyril Montague, b. Haywards Heath, Sussex (Forest Gate, E., Essex), 41663, Pte., k. in a., F. & F., 1/10/18, formerly T/4/037603, R.A.S.C.
Norris, Francis, b. Killyleagh, Co. Down, e. Belfast, 11137, Pte., k. in a., F. & F., 11/4/17.
Norton, Thomas, e. Dublin, 24345, Pte., k. in a., F. & F., 21/3/18.
Notley, Henry, b. Ballymore Eustace, Co. Kildare, e. Maryborough, Queen's Co. (Dublin), 24837, Pte., k. in a., F. & F., 11/5/17.
Oates, George, b. Granard, Co. Longford, e. Cavan (Granard), 3251, Pte., k. in a., F. & F., 6/7/15.
O'Boyle, John, b. St. Matthew's, Co. Down, e. Belfast, 20480, Pte., d., F. & F., 15/7/18.

O'Brien, James, b. Millwall, E., Middx., e. Woolwich, Kent (Millwall), 18979, Pte., k. in a., F. & F., 12/10/16, formerly 15721, Hussars of the Line.
O'Brien, John, b. Liverpool, e. Seaforth, Lancs (Liverpool), 6291, Pte., d. of w., F. & F., 15/5/15.
O'Brien, John, b. Shercock, Co. Cavan, e. Dundalk, Co. Louth (Shercock), 23177, Pte., d. of w., F. & F., 11/4/18.
O'Brien, Joseph, b. Charleville, Co. Cork, e. Charleville, 8980, Pte., k. in a., F. & F., 26/8/14.
O'Brien, Patrick, b. Clonmel, Co. Tipperary, e. Clonmel, 16221, L/Cpl., k. in a., F. & F., 24/8/18.
O'Bryne, Felix MacHugh, b. Dundalk, Co. Louth, e. Drogheda, Co. Louth (Dundalk), 11360, Pte., k. in a., F. & F., 12/10/16.
O'Callaghan, Michael, b. Colchester, Essex, e. Belfast (Castlebar) Co. Mayo), 24167, L/Cpl., d. of w., F. & F., 16/4/18.
O'Connor, Henry, b. Newry, Co. Down, e. Hamilton, Lanarks (Coatbridge, Lanarks), 6964, Cpl., k. in a., F. & F., 2/9/18.
O'Hagan, James, b. Belfast, e. Sheffield, 12972, Pte., k. in a., F. & F., 11/4/17.
O'Hanlon, John, b. Shankill, Co. Armagh, e. Belfast (Lurgan, Co. Armagh), 23684, Pte., d. of w., F. & F., 27/4/18.
O'Hara, Michael, b. Shankill, Co. Armagh, e. Belfast, 24624, Pte., k. in a., F. & F., 9/4/17.
O'Hara, Robert James, b. Shankill, Co. Armagh, e. Belfast, 8161, Pte., d., F. & F., 28/3/15.
O'Hara, William, b. Dublin, e. Dublin, 7498, Pte., k. in a., F. & F., 6/7/15.
O'Hare, Patrick, b. Newry, Co. Down, e. Armagh (Newry), 10610, Pte., d., F. & F., 29/4/18.
O'Keefe, Alfred, b. Reading, Berks, e. Reading, 19992, Pte., k. in a., F. & F., 3/5/17.
O'Keefe, John, b. Limerick, e. Whitehall, S.W., Middx., 23461, Pte., d., Home, 24/11/16.
O'Keeffe, Daniel, b. Mountrath, Queen's Co., e. Maryborough, Queen's Co. (Mountrath), 11706, Pte., k. in a., F. & F., 6/9/15.
O'Keeffe, Patrick, b. Dublin, e. Dublin, 10987, Pte., k. in a., F. & F., 12/10/16.
O'Malley, Timothy, b. Cappamore, Co. Limerick, e. Cork (Coote-hill, Co. Cavan), 5367, C.S.M., k. in a., F. & F., 11/5/17.
O'Neill, Alfred, b. Whitehouse, Co. Antrim, e. Belfast, 8011, Pte., k. in a., F. & F., 21/10/14.
O'Neill, Francis, e. Hamilton, Lanarks (Coatbridge, Lanarks), 27497, Pte., k. in a., F. & F., 9/7/17.
O'Neill, John, b. Maygill, Co. Londonderry, e. Coatbridge, Lanarks (Knockcloghrim, Co. Londonderry), 20882, Pte., k. in a., F. & F., 11/4/17.
O'Neill, Luke, b. Portglenone, Co. Antrim, e. Coatbridge, Lanarks (Rasharkin, Co. Antrim), 22128, Pte., k. in a., F. & F., 12/10/16.
O'Neill, Thomas, b. Thomastown, Co. Kilkenny, e. Dublin (Thomastown), 10135, Pte., d. of w., F. & F., 22/4/18.
O'Rawe, Edward, b. Belfast, e. Portadown, Co. Armagh (Tandragee, Co. Armagh), 9807, Pte., d., F. & F., 2/3/16.
Orchard, Patrick, b. Dublin, e. Dublin (Cavan), 9137, Sgt., k. in a., F. & F., 23/11/17.
O'Reilly, James, b. Londonderry, e. Uddington, Lanarks, 18968, Pte., k. in a., F. & F., 6/7/15, formerly 11909, Hussars of the Line.
O'Reilly, William, b. Kingscourt, Co. Cavan, e. Edinburgh (Kingscourt), 9190, L/Sgt., d., Home, 6/1/17, formerly 191, R. High.
Orr, James, b. Newtownstewart, Co. Tyrone, e. Belfast (Newtownstewart), 3777, A/Sgt., k. in a., F. & F., 23/11/17.
Osborne, Bertie, b. Farnham, Essex, e. Bury St. Edmunds, Suffolk (Hockerhill, Herts), 45015, L/Cpl., d., F. & F., 27/11/18, formerly 20523, Norfolk Regt.
Owens, Hugh, b. Ballybay, Co. Monaghan, e. Armagh (Ballybay), 3498, L/Cpl., k. in a., F. & F., 22/10/18.
Parfitt, Frank Ernest, b. Stoke Newington, N., Middx., e. Lewisham, S.E., Kent (Catford, S.E., Kent), 50018, Pte., k. in a., F. & F., 2/9/18, formerly 557148, London Regt.
Parks, Robert, b. Shankill, Co. Armagh, e. Portadown, Co. Armagh (Lurgan, Co. Armagh), 9990, Pte., k. in a., F. & F., 26/8/14.
Partington, Miles Robert, b. Atherton, Lancs, e. Leigh, Lancs (Atherton), 49980, Pte., k. in a., F. & F., 2/9/18, formerly 141583, R.A.S.C.
Patrick, Alexander, b. Nottingham, e. Nottingham, 41810, Pte., d. of w., F. & F., 24/3/18, formerly S/4/044667, R.A.S.C.
Patterson, Peter, b. Ballyconnell, Co. Cavan, e. Cavan (Ballyconnell), 29565, Pte., d. of w., Home, 7/10/18.
Patterson, Samuel, b. Saintfield, Co. Down, e. Belfast (Boardmills, Co. Down), 8229, Pte., k. in a., F. & F., 25/4/15.
Pembroke, Harry Jack, b. Burghfield, Berks, e. Reading, Berks, 41771, Pte., k. in a., F. & F., 1/10/18, formerly 125256, R.A.S.C.
Peploe, Frederick William, b. Peckham, S.E., Surrey, e. Camberwell, S.E., Surrey (Peckham), 42047, Pte., k. in a., F. & F., 1/10/18.

APPENDICES

Perrin, Charles, Alfred, b. Barnstaple, Devon, e. Barnstaple, 49938, Pte., d. of w., F. & F., 22/8/18, formerly 40849, Som. L.I.
Perrins, Albert, b. St. Helens, Lancs, e. Chesterfield (Calow, Derbyshire), 40153, Pte., d., F. & F., 7/7/18, formerly 36367, Notts & Derby Regt.
Perry, Sidney, b. Penzance, Cornwall, e. Penzance, 41773, Pte., k. in a., F. & F., 21/10/18, formerly S/4/094600, R.A.S.C.
Peters, Frederick James, b. Paddington, W., e. Paddington, W., 42006, Pte., d. of w., F. & F., 21/7/18, formerly 67192, R.W. Surrey Regt.
Pettican, Robert, e. Whitehall, S.W., Middx. (Walworth, S.E., Surrey), 41997, Pte., k. in a., F. & F., 11/10/18, formerly 67213, R.W. Surrey Regt.
Petticrew, Patrick, b. Shankill, Belfast, e. Belfast (Holywood, Co. Down), 22628, Pte., k. in a., F. & F., 11/4/17.
Phillips, William John, b. Belfast, e. Belfast, 12586, Pte., k. in a., F. & F., 19/4/17.
Plunkett, Michael, b. Drogheda, Co. Louth, e. Drogheda, 10846, Pte., k. in a., F. & F., 10/6/15.
Pollard, Patrick, b. Randalstown, Co. Antrim, e. Belfast, 12195, Pte., k. in a., F. & F., 11/4/17.
Pollard, Thomas, b. Randalstown, Co. Antrim, e. Belfast, 6733, Pte., k. in a., F. & F., 18/10/14.
Pope, Charles George, b. Farningham, Kent, e. London (Brixton Hill, S.W., Surrey), 10832, A/Sgt., k. in a., F. & F., 16/8/17. M.M.
Portch, Charles, b. Peckham, S.E., Surrey, e. New Kent Road, S.E., Surrey (Nunhead, S.E., Surrey), 41919, k. in a., F. & F., 13/4/18, formerly 30856, R.A.S.C.
Porter, John, b. Shankill, Belfast, e. Belfast, 7181, Pte., k. in a., F. & F., 11/4/17.
Porter, William, b. Poyntzpass, Co. Armagh, e. Newry, Co. Down (Poyntzpass), 19849, Pte., k. in a., F. & F., 11/4/17.
Potter, George, b. Moira, Co. Down, e. Belfast, 5923, Pte., k. in a., F. & F., 8/9/15.
Pratt, Thomas, b. Clones, Co. Monaghan, e. Belfast, 7725, Pte., k. in a., F. & F., 26/8/14.
Pretlove, Charles Henry, b. Winchmore Hill, N., Middx., e. Enfield, Middx. (Winchmore Hill), 19024, L/Cpl., k. in a., F. & F., 7/5/17, formerly 146776, R.F.A.
Price, William, b. Newport, Mon., e. Newport, 18962, L/Cpl., k. in a., F. & F., 11/4/17, formerly 5633, Dragoons of the Line.
Prier, Oliver, e. Battersea, S.W., Surrey (Euston Square, N.W., Middx.), 43480, Pte., d. of w., F. & F., 17/7/18, formerly 2982, London Regt.
Pritchard, William, b. Cromhall, Glos., e. Mountain Ash, Glam. (Cromhall), 41665, Pte., k. in a., F. & F., 11/4/18, formerly 39183, R.A.S.C.
Quigley, Michael, b. West Calder, Midlothian, e. South Queensferry, West Lothian, 23121, Pte., k. in a., F. & F., 11/4/17, formerly 22256, R.D. Fus.
Quinn, Frank, b. Monaghan, e. Hamilton, Lanarks (Three Mile House, Co. Monaghan), 13310, Pte., d. of w., F. & F., 20/9/18.
Quinn, James, b. Dublin, e. Dublin, 11276, Pte., k. in a., F. & F., 11/7/16.
Quinn, James Andrew, b. Gilford, Co. Down, e. Armagh (Tandragee, Co. Armagh), 1141, Pte., k. in a., F. & F., 3/5/17.
Quinn, Thomas, b. Shankill, Belfast, e. Belfast, 49752, Pte., k. in a., F. & F., 24/8/18, formerly 21758, R. Innis. Fus.
Quinn, William, b. Shankill, Belfast, e. Lurgan, Co. Armagh, 7777, Pte., d. of w., F. & F., 27/4/15.
Radmilovic, Paul, b. Cardiff, Glam., e. Cardiff (Folkestone, Kent), 9293, Sgt., k. in a., F. & F., 6/5/15.
Rafferty, James, b. Armagh, e. Armagh, 3240, Pte., d. of w., F. & F., 6/5/15.
Rafferty, John, b. Maynooth, Co. Kildare, e. Dublin, 11308, Pte., d. of w., F. & F., 29/11/14.
Rafferty, William J., b. Shankill, Belfast, e. Belfast, 8330, Pte. k. in a., F. & F., 6/5/15.
Ramsay, William J., b. Govan, Lanarks, e. Govan (Glasgow), 17852, Cpl., k. in a., F. & F., 18/10/15.
Ranaghan, Patrick, b. Strathblane, Stirlings, e. Glasgow (Maryhill, Glasgow), 9058, Pte., k. in a., F. & F., 25/4/15.
Rayner, Sidney William, b. Ryburgh, Norfolk, e. Norwich, 18843, Pte., k. in a., F. & F., 12/10/16, formerly 19575, Hussars of the Line.
Reaney, Edward Thomas, b. Shankill, Belfast, e. Armagh, 9467, Pte., k. in a., F. & F., 25/4/15.
Redmond, Edward, b. Dublin, e. Dublin, 9147, Pte., k. in a., F. & F., 11/4/17.
Regan, Thomas, b. Charleville, Co. Cork, e. Dublin (Charleville), 12274, Pte., d. of w., F. & F., 13/10/16.
Regan, William, b. Charleville, Co. Cork, e. Charleville, 8981, Pte., k. in a., F. & F., 26/8/14.
Reilly, Francis, e. Cavan (Drung, Co. Cavan), 17607, Sgt., d. of w., F. & F., 24/9/18.

Reilly, George Bernard, b. Granard, Co. Longford, e. Cavan (Carrick-on-Shannon, Co. Leitrim), 8088, Pte., k. in a., F. & F. 15/10/14.
Reilly, James, b. Dublin, e. Dublin, 11424, Pte., k. in a., F. & F., 26/8/16.
Reilly, James, b. Phibsborough, Dublin, e. Ballinasloe, Co. Galway (Kells, Co. Meath), 16722, Pte., k. in a., F. & F., 24/3/18, formerly 681, Conn. Rangers.
Reilly, Peter, b. Shankill, Belfast, e. Belfast, 7046, Pte., k. in a., F. & F., 12/10/16.
Reynolds, Patrick, b. Dublin, e. Dublin, 20514, Pte., d., F. & F., 15/10/18.
Rice, Harry, b. Gilford, Co. Down, e. Armagh (Laurencetown, Co. Down), 11138, Pte., k. in a., F. & F., 4/9/18.
Rice, William, b. Seapatrick, Co. Down, e. Lurgan, Co. Armagh (Banbridge, Co. Down), 7257, Pte., d. of w., F. & F., 14/10/16.
Richmond, William, b. Portglemone, Co. Antrim, e. Glasgow, 49882, Pte., k. in a., F. & F., 21/10/18, formerly 21898, R. Innis. Fus.
Riddy, Walter Charles, b. North Crawley, Bucks, e. Bletchley, Bucks (Great Linford, Bucks), 41667, Pte., k. in a., F. & F., 11/4/18, formerly T/4/088236, R.A.S.C.
Riley, James, e. Liverpool (San Jose, California), 20145, Pte., k. in a., F. & F., 21/3/18.
Riley, Walter, b. Burton-on-Trent, Staffs, e. Holloway, N., Middx. (Tollington Park, N., Middx.), 41845, Pte., d., F. & F., 15/8/18, formerly T/4/124213, R.A.S.C.
Robbins, Percy, b. Castleford, Yorks, e. Castleford, 41847, Pte., d. of w., F. & F., 22/3/18, formerly T/4/088724, R.A.S.C.
Roberts, Edwin, b. Newport, Mon., e. Newport (Rogerstone, Mon.), 41666, Pte., k. in a., F. & F., 11/4/18, formerly T/3/029639, R.A.S.C.
Roberts, James, b. Manchester, e. Manchester, 41676, A/Cpl., k. in a., F. & F., 21/3/18, formerly 03663, R.A.O.C.
Roberts, Leonard Arthur, b. Willenhall, Staffs, e. Willenhall (Coventry, Warwick), 41846, Pte., d., F. & F., 7/5/18, formerly T/37296, R.A.S.C.
Roberts, Richard, b. Birkenhead, Ches., e. Birkenhead, 41900, Pte., k. in a., F. & F., 11/4/18, formerly S/4/125339, R.A.S.C.
Robinson, David, b. Broughshane, Co. Antrim, e. Ballymena, Co. Antrim (Broughshane), 40140, Pte., k. in a., F. & F., 11/4/17, formerly 24784, Hussars of the Line.
Robinson, John, b. Sandyford, Dublin, e. Dublin (Foxrock, Co. Dublin), 10368, Pte., k. in a., F. & F., 11/4/17.
Robson, Robert, b. Ballygraney, Co. Down, e. Clandeboye, Co. Down (Donaghadee, Co. Down), 41865, Pte., k. in a., F. & F., 21/3/18, formerly T/4/128737, R.A.S.C.
Roddy, Daniel, b. Londonderry, e. Clydebank, Glasgow (Londonderry), 17723, Pte., k. in a., F. & F., 2/1/16.
Rodgers, Samuel, b. Shankill, e. Belfast (Ballyhackamore, Co. Down), 7567, Pte., d. of w., F. & F., 31/5/15.
Roe, Hubert, b. Bradford, Yorks, e. London (Wealdstone, Middx.), 41147, Cpl., d. of w. F. & F., 8/4/18, formerly 4392, 2nd Dragoon Guards, D.C.M.
Rooney, John, b. Shankill, Co. Armagh, e. Lurgan, Co. Armagh, 16161, Pte., d. of w., F. & F., 15/5/15.
Rooney, Patrick James, b. Cabra, Co. Down, e. Newry, Co. Down, 6081, Pte., d. of w., Home, 3/11/16.
Rose, Harry, b. St. Peter Port, Guernsey, C.I., e. Guernsey (St. Peter Port), 21895, A/Cpl., k. in a., F. & F., 12/10/16.
Ross, William John, b. Armagh, e. Armagh (Portadown, Co. Armagh), 11217, Pte., k. in a., F. & F., 15/9/16.
Rowlandson, George, Philip, b. Newent, Glos., e. Chiswick, W., Middx. (Bedford Park, W., Middx.), 50056, Pte., k. in a., F. & F., 1/10/18, formerly 304551, 5th City of London.
Rufford, Augustus Frederick, e. Ipswich, 42376, Pte., d. of w., Home, 10/10/18, formerly 26850, Norfolk Regt.
Rutledge, David, b. Ballybay, Co. Monaghan, e. Enniskillen (Ballybay), 3384, Pte., k. in a., F. & F., 3/5/17.
Ryan, Richard, b. Bermondsey, S.E., Surrey, e. London (Streatham Hill, S.W., Surrey), 9330, Pte., k. in a., F. & F., 25/4/15.
Scott, Cedric Harold, e. Margate, Kent, e. Margate, 50030, Pte. k. in a., F. & F., 4/10/18, formerly 636148, 20th London Regt.
Scott, George, b. Glasgow (Partick, Glasgow), 17590, Pte., k. in a., F. & F., 12/10/16.
Scott, Robert, b. Skreen, Co. Sligo, e. Glasgow (Skreen), 9605, Sgt., d. of w., F. & F., 26/10/14.
Scott, William, b. Hammersmith, W., Middx., e. London (Hammersmith), 9642, Pte., k. in a., F. & F., 27/8/14.
Scullion, Peter, b. Motherwell, Lanarks, e. Hamilton, Lanarks (Wishaw, Lanarks), 17510, Pte., k. in a., F. & F., 7/5/17.
Scully, John Richard, b. Bradford, Yorks, e. Bradford, 42369, Pte., k. in a., F. & F., 1/10/18, formerly 11563, W. Riding Regt.
Seagrott, Albert Edward, b. Camberwell, S.E., Surrey, e. London, 6663, Sgt., k. in a., F. & F., 24/5/15.

Seymour, Robert, b. Benburb, Co. Tyrone, e. Partick, Glasgow, 24648, Pte., k. in a., F. & F., 11/4/17.
Sharp, John, b. Rutherglen, Lanarks, e. Glasgow, 6927, Pte., k. in a., F. & F., 25/4/15.
Shaughessy, Michael, b. Ballinasloe, Co. Galway, e. Ballinasloe, 10823, L/Cpl., k. in a., F. & F., 12/10/16.
Shea, John, b. Bantry, Co. Cork, e. Liverpool (Bantry), 12335, Pte., k. in a., F. & F., 25/8/16.
Sheehan, Henry, e. London (Portman Square, W., Middx.), 9802, Pte., k. in a., F. & F., 2/2/16.
Sheekey, William, b. Dublin, e. Dundalk, Co. Louth, 17887, L/Cpl., d., F. & F., 29/9/18.
Sheil, Andrew, b. Dublin, e. Dublin, 9180, L/Cpl., k. in a., F. & F., 18/10/14.
Sheilds, Edward, b. Monaghan, e. Cowdenbeath, Fife (Shantonagh, Co. Monaghan), 16311, Pte., k. in a., F. & F., 23/11/17.
Sheridan, James Francis, b. Carrigallen, Co. Leitrim, e. Cavan (Ballinagh, Co. Cavan), 9736, A/Cpl., d. of w., F. & F., 8/5/17.
Sheridan, Patrick, b. Cootehill, Co. Cavan, e. Armagh (Cootehill), 23754, Pte., k. in a., F. & F., 2/9/18.
Sherlock, Cassio, b. Brazil, S. America, e. Liverpool, 41675, Pte., k. in a., F. & F., 11/4/18, formerly T/4/128641, R.A.S.C.
Sherman, Ephraim, b. Portadown, Co. Armagh, e. Finner Camp, Co. Donegal (Portadown, Co. Armagh), 4777, Pte., k. in a., F. & F., 6/7/16.
Shields, Humphrey, b. Paisley, Renfrews, e. Glasgow (Coatbridge, Lanarks), 8562, Pte., k. in a., F. & F., 25/4/15.
Shields, John, b. Uddingston, Lanarks, e. Cambuslang, Lanarks, 27703, Pte., d. of w., Home, 6/9/18.
Shingfield, James Robert, b. Shropham, Norfolk, e. Norwich (Shropham), 41784, Pte., k. in a., F. & F., 18/4/18, formerly S/4/070884, R.A.S.C.
Shiveral, Samuel, b. Keady, Co. Armagh, e. Hamilton, Lanarks (Sittingbourne, Kent), 9115, Pte., k. in a., F. & F., 14/10/14.
Short, James, b. Shankill, Co. Armagh, e. Finner Camp, Co. Donegal (Lurgan, Co. Armagh), 4562, Pte., d. of w., Home, 18/6/15.
Short, Patrick, b. Armagh, e. Finner Camp, Co. Donegal (Armagh), 3832, Pte., k. in a., F. & F., 27/6/15.
Sidell, Samuel Frederick, b. Thetford, Norfolk, e. Norwich (Thetford), 41952, Pte., k. in a., F. & F., 24/8/18.
Simpson, Jas, b. Moneymore, Co. Londonderry, e. Finner Camp, Co. Donegal (Moneymore), 49824, Pte., k. in a., F. & F., 16/8/18, formerly 16006, R. Innis. Fus.
Simpson, Peter, b. Portadown, Co. Armagh, e. Portadown, 17299, Pte., k. in a., F. & F., 11/4/17.
Sinclair, Peter, b. Glasgow, e. Glasgow (Bridgeton, Glasgow), 18483, Pte., k. in a., F. & F., 26/8/16.
Skelton, Francis, b. Moy, Co. Tyrone, e. Armagh (Moy), 23583, Pte., k. in a., F. & F., 3/5/17.
Small, William Francis, b. Limerick, e. Mallow, Co. Cork (Buttevant, Co. Cork), 11387, Pte., k. in a., F. & F., 25/4/15.
Smith, Allen Reginald, b. Nottingham, e. Putney, S.W., Surrey (Balham, S.W., Surrey), 50014, Pte., d. of w., F. & F., 2/9/18, formerly 557144, 16th London Regt.
Smith, Charles Percy, b. Lichfield, Staffs, e. Birmingham, 18851, Pte., k. in a., F. & F., 12/10/16, formerly 24125, Hussars of the Line.
Smith, Frederick, b. Hailey, Oxon, e. Oxford (Witney), 41782, Pte., k. in a., F. & F., 11/4/18, formerly S/4/128426, R.A.S.C.
Smith, Frederick George, b. Woodville, Derbyshire, e. Derby (Woodville), 16301, Pte., d. of w., F. & F., 7/7/15.
Smith, Jesse, b. Northampton, e. Northampton, 7571, Pte., k. in a., F. & F., 25/10/14.
Smith, William, b. Lambeth, S.E., Surrey, e. Southwark, S.E., Surrey (Walworth, S.E., Surrey), 18646, Pte., k. in a., F. & F., 11/4/17.
Smith, William, b. Dublin, e. Whitehall, S.W., Middx. (St. Pancras, N.W., Middx.), 24778, Pte., d. of w., F. & F., 12/4/17.
Smyth, John b. Salford, Manchester, e. Newry, Co. Down, 22960, Pte., k. in a., F. & F., 11/4/17.
Sneddon, John, b. Craigneuk, Lanarks, e. Hamilton, Lanarks (Craigneuk), 17753, Pte., k. in a., F. & F., 18/4/18.
Soutar, Charles, b. Dundee, Forfars, e. Dundee, 41779, Pte., d., F. & F., 17/10/18, formerly SS/1790, R.A.S.C.
Southgate, Stanley Reginald, b. Ipswich, Suffolk, e. Ipswich, 41930, Pte., k. in a., F. & F., 1/10/18, formerly 685591, 22nd London Regt.
Spink, Harry, b. Sheffield, Yorks, e. Sheffield, 43068, Pte., k. in a., F. & F., 3/5/17, formerly 3096, Connaught Rangers.
Sproule, Joseph, b. Kesh, Co. Fermanagh, e. Monaghan (Clones, Co. Monaghan), 7917, Sgt., k. in a., F. & F., 8/12/14.
Stackpool, James, b. Liverpool, e. Liverpool, 41913, Pte., d. of w., F. & F., 2/9/18, formerly T/2/10033, R.A.S.C.
Stanbridge, Henry Arthur, b. Marylebone, Middx., e. London (Lower Edmonton, N., Middx.), 9264, Pte., k. in a., F. & F., 11/4/17, formerly 6303, Dragoons of the Line.

Stanley, Henry, James, b. Saltcoats, Lanarks, e. Poole, Dorset (Parkstone, Dorset), 18970, Pte., k. in a., F. & F., 15/7/15, formerly 10198, Dragoons of the Line.
Stapleton, James, b. Bagnalstown, Co. Carlow, e. Carlow (Bagnalstown), 8921, Pte., k. in a., F. & F., 1/7/16.
Stapleton, John, b. Thurles, Co. Tipperary, e. Dundrum, Co. Tipperary (Thurles), 20486, Pte., k. in a., F. & F., 6/7/16.
Steele, Thomas William, b. Cookstown, Co. Tyrone, e. Cookstown, 11376, Pte., k. in a., F. & F., 16/9/14, formerly 11376, R. Innis. Fus.
Steven, John, b. Blantyre, Lanarks, e. Hamilton, Lanarks (Blantyre), 12753, L/Cpl., k. in a., F. & F., 3/5/17.
Stevenson, Joseph, b. Shankill, Co. Armagh, e. Portadown, Co. Armagh (Lurgan. Co. Armagh), 5639, Pte., d. of w., F. & F., 27/3/18.
Stewart, John, b. Wemyss Bay, Renfrews, e. Belfast, 49876, Pte. k. in a., F. & F., 23/10/18, formerly 20993, R. Irish Rif.
Stewart, Joseph, b. Doe, Co. Donegal, e. Port Glasgow, Renfrews, 24930, Pte., k. in a., F. & F., 23/11/17.
Stewart, Waring, e. Belfast (Dunmurry, Co. Antrim), 22775, k. in a., F. & F., 23/11/17.
Stewart, William, b. Shankill, Belfast, e. Belfast, 24200, Pte., k. in a., F. & F., 3/5/17.
Stickler, George, b. King's Cross, N., Middx., e. Leyton, N.E., Essex, 42024, Pte., k. in a., F. & F., 1/10/18, formerly 67277, R.W. Surrey Regt.
Stimpson, Victor Joseph, b. Cardiff, Glam., e. Cardiff (Dublin), 25194, L/Cpl., k. in a., F. & F., 23/11/17.
Stone, Henry Joseph, b. Wandsworth, S.W., Surrey, e. Kingston-on-Thames, Surrey (Wandsworth, S.W.), 9557, Sgt., d. of w., F. & F., 25/6/17.
Stone, Herbert Edward, b. White Roding, Essex, e. Chelmsford, Essex (White Roding), 41783, Pte., d. of w., Home, 7/4/18, formerly S/35355, R.A.S.C.
Stone, Horace Sydney, b. London, e. Hammersmith, W., Middx., 49857, Pte., k. in a., F. & F., 1/10/18, formerly 5153, 13th London Regt.
Stritch, Joseph, b. Longford, e. Longford, 8610, L/Sgt., d. of w., Home, 5/3/17.
Strong, Thomas Henry, b. Clerkenwell, E.C., Middx., e. Whitehall, S.W., Middx. (Finsbury, E.C., Middx.), 41996, Pte., d. of w., F. & F., 30/9/18, formerly 67106, R.W. Surrey Regt.
Sullivan, John, b. Cavan, e. Glasgow (Cavan), 11172, Pte., d. of w., F. & F., 20/10/14.
Sullivan, John, b. Cardiff, Glam., e. Cardiff (Roath, Glam.), 12968, Pte., k. in a., F. & F., 12/10/16.
Sullivan, Joseph, b. Cavan, e. Cavan, 11204, Pte., k. in a., F. & F., 27/8/14.
Sullivan, Patrick, b. Ballyagran, Co. Cork, e. Cardiff, Glam. (Charleville, Co. Cork), 18937, Pte., k. in a., F. & F., 11/4/17, formerly 23683, Hussars of the Line.
Summerville, William, b. Portadown, Co. Armagh, e. Portadown, 11402, Pte., d. of w., F. & F., 17/9/14.
Sweeney, George, b. Dundalk, Co. Louth, e. Dundalk, 6160, Pte., d. of w., F. & F., 4/4/16.
Sweeney, Patrick, b. Shankhill, Belfast, e. Belfast (Ligoniel, Belfast), 3396, Pte., k. in a., F. & F., 1/10/18.
Sweeney, Thomas, b. Laghey, Co. Donegal, e. Glasgow (Laghey), 24818, Pte., k. in a., F. & F., 11/4/17.
Sycamore, Ernest, b. Hackney, N.E., Middx., e. Hackney, N.E., 40142, Pte., k. in a., F. & F., 5/5/17, formerly 24640, Hussars of the Line.
Taylor, Harry, b. Dagshai, India, e. Aldershot, Hants (Ash Vale, Hants), 10909, L/Sgt., k. in a., F. & F., 11/4/18.
Taylor, Percy, b. Accrington, Lancs, e. Blackburn, Lancs (Accrington), 18891, Cpl., k. in a., F. & F., 3/5/17, formerly 41678, Hussars of the Line.
Taylor, Stephen, b. Battersea, S.W., Surrey, e. London (Battersea, S.W.), 9361, Pte., k. in a., F. & F., 9/11/14.
Taylor, William, b. Portadown, Co. Armagh, e. Newry, Co. Down, 11072, L/Cpl., k. in a., F. & F., 6/7/16, M.M.
Taylor, William, e. Worcester (Oldbury, Birmingham), 49946, Pte., d. of w., F. & F., 15/10/18, formerly 50532, Worcs Regt.
Tedford, Charles, b. Portadown, Co. Armagh, e. Portadown (Coatbridge, Lanarks), 7354, Pte., k. in a., F. & F., 25/4/15.
Tedford, James, b. Portadown, Co. Armagh, e. Portadown, 25204, Pte., k. in a., F. & F., 21/3/18.
Teirney, Thomas, b. Baillieston, Lanarks, e. Clydebank, Glasgow, 24460, Pte., k. in a., F. & F., 7/5/17.
Thickens, Ralph Cook, b. Kings Norton, Worcs., e. Aylesbury, Bucks (Waddesdon, Bucks), 49925, Pte., d. of w., F. & F., 19/5/18, formerly 8/3629, Hamps. Regt.
Thomas, Elwin, b. Dublin, e. Dublin, 11082, Pte., k. in a., F. & F., 26/10/14.

Thomas, Frederick, b. Camberwell, S.E., Surrey, e. Warley, Essex (Colchester, Essex), 4880, Sgt., d. of w., F. & F., 25/6/15.
Thompson, John, b. Templepatrick, Co. Antrim, e. Lurgan, Co. Armagh (Belfast), 9928, Pte., k. in a., F. & F., 19/10/16.
Thompson, John, b. Govan, Lanarks, e. Glasgow (Partick, Glasgow), 17808, Pte., k. in a., F. & F., 26/6/15.
Thompson, Patrick John, b. Church Hill, Co. Fermanagh, e. Clones, Co. Monaghan, 22099, Pte., k. in a., F. & F., 11/4/17.
Thompson, Thomas, b. Liverpool, e. Leeds (Wakefield, Yorks), 10827, Pte., k. in a., F. & F., 15/2/17.
Threadgold, Charles James, b. Hackney, N.E., Middx., e. Southwark, S.E., Surrey (Walworth, S.E., Surrey), 42137, Cpl., k. in a., F. & F., 22/7/18, formerly S4/060061, R.A.S.C.
Tierney, James, b. Kildare, e. Dublin (Robertstown, Co. Kildare), 9075, Pte., k. in a., F. & F., 3/5/17.
Tinnany, Francis, b. Cavan, e. Dumbarton (Belturbet, Co. Cavan), 17591, Pte., k. in a., F. & F., 21/3/18.
Titterington, Robert, b. Tandragee, Co. Armagh, e. Armagh (Scarva, Co. Down), 9914, Sgt., d. of w., F. & F., 25/5/15.
Toal, Bernard, b. Old Monkland, Lanarks, e. Coatbridge, Lanarks, 29687, Pte., k. in a., F. & F., 1/10/18.
Todd, James Lowry, b. Lambeg, Co. Antrim, e. Glasgow (Partick, Glasgow), 29248, Pte., d. of w., F. & F., 7/11/18.
Todd, William Francis, b. Shankhill, Belfast, e. Portadown, Co. Armagh, 7365, Pte., k. in a., F. & F., 22/10/14.
Tollerfield, Charles Edwin, b. Portsmouth, Hants, e. Portsmouth (Southsea, Hants), 49927, Pte., k. in a., F. & F., 1/10/18, formerly 3493, Hamps Regt.
Toman, John, b. Lurgan, Co. Armagh, e. Lurgan (Portadown, Co. Armagh), 5180, Pte., k. in a., F. & F., 25/4/15.
Toole, Edward, b. Lisburn, Co. Antrim, e. Lurgan, Co. Armagh (Lisburn), 8475, Pte., k. in a., F. & F., 12/10/16.
Tracey, John, b. Drogheda, Co. Louth, e. Drogheda, 5903, Pte., k. in a., F. & F., 24/5/15.
Trainor, John, b. Belfast, e. Belfast, 3524, Cpl., k. in a., F. & F., 7/5/17.
Tuplin, William, b. Kermington, Lincs, e. Hull (Grimsby, Lincs), 41922, Pte., k. in a., F. & F., 16/8/18, formerly T/4/092104, R.A.S.C.
Turkington, Joseph, b. Lurgan, Co. Armagh, e. Portadown, Co. Armagh (Lurgan), 5435, Pte., d. of w., F. & F., 11/6/15.
Turkington, Samuel James, b. Shankhill, Co. Armagh, e. Armagh (Lurgan, Co. Armagh), 8402, L/Cpl., k. in a., F. & F., 21/3/18.
Turner, Sidney Herbert, b. Twickenham, Surrey, e. Marylebone, Middx. (St. John's Wood, N.W., Middx.), 41850, Pte., k. in a., F. & F., 21/3/18.
Varley, John, b. Pendleton, Lancs, e. Manchester (West Gorton, Manchester), 6373, Sgt., d. of w., F. & F., 12/10/16.
Vaughan, Henry, b. Eastleigh, Hants, e. Southampton (Armagh), 9332, Pte., d. of w., F. & F., 15/4/17.
Venables, Walter, b. Cheshunt, Herts, e. Stratford, E., Essex (Lr. Edmonton, N., Middx.), 9371, Cpl., k. in a., F. & F., 23/11/17.
Vinters, John, b. Belfast, e. Glasgow, 23867, A/Cpl., k. in a., F. & F., 16/2/17.
Vokins, Wesley, b. Ramsbury, Wilts, e. Marlborough, Wilts (Ramsbury), 41792, Pte., k. in a., F. & F., 21/3/18, formerly S4/060382, R.A.S.C.
Wakeham, William, e. Dudley, Worcs, 49947, Pte., k. in a., F. & F., 1/10/18, formerly 50548, Worcs Regt.
Walker, Alfred, b. Fulham, S.W., Middx., e. London (Fulham), 41993, Pte., k. in a., F. & F., 21/10/18.
Wall, Reginald Edmund, b. St. Mary's, London, e. London (Stamford Hill, N., Middx.), 41705, A/Sgt., k. in a., F. & F., 24/3/18, formerly 1295, R.A.S.C.
Wallace, Patrick, b. Newtownbutler, Co. Fermanagh, e. Clones, Co. Monaghan (Donagh, Co. Fermanagh), 10513, L/Cpl., k. in a., F. & F., 3/5/17.
Walmsley, William, b. Dundalk, Co. Louth, e. Armagh (Dundalk), 5787, Pte., k. in a., F. & F., 25/4/15.
Walsh, Charles, b. Castleblayney, Co. Monaghan, e. Armagh (Castleblayney), 15103, Pte., k. in a., F. & F., 1/10/18.
Walsh, John, b. Sligo, e. Sligo, 7106, Pte., d. of w., F. & F., 27/10/14.
Walsh, Patrick, b. Shankill, Belfast, e. Belfast, 3669, Pte., k. in a., F. & F., 3/5/17.
Ward, George Henry, b. Little Weighton, Yorks, e. Beverley, Yorks (Little Weighton), 49796, Pte., k. in a., F. & F., 24/8/18, formerly 41531, R. Innis. Fus.
Ward, Harry, b. Welwyn, Herts, e. Marylebone, Middx. (Welwyn), 22414, Pte., d. of w., F. & F., 18/4/17, formerly 13187, Beds Regt.
Ward, James, b. Dublin, e. Newcastle-on-Tyne (Dublin), 28313, Pte., k. in a., F. & F., 23/11/17, formerly 9866, Herts Regt.
Ward, William, b. Southwark, S.E., Surrey, e. Stratford, E., Essex (Borough, S.E., Surrey), 9373, Pte., d. of w., F. & F., 19/9/14.

Ward, William, b. Galway, e. Galway, 16495, Pte., d. of w., F. & F., 6/9/18, formerly 1859, R. Irish Regt.
Watson, James, b. Ballymacarrett, Co. Down, e. Belfast, 49874, Pte., k. in a., F. & F., 1/10/18, formerly 676, R. Irish Rif.
Watson, William, b. Shankill, Co. Armagh, e. Finner Camp, Co. Donegal (Lurgan, Co. Armagh), 4734, Pte., k. in a., F. & F., 27/11/14.
Watson, William, b. Holywood, Co. Down, e. Cavan (Saintfield, Co. Down), 11529, Pte., k. in a., F. & F., 12/4/15.
Watt, Richard, b. Tartaraghan, Co. Armagh, e. Portadown, Co. Armagh, 24853, Pte., k. in a., F. & F., 24/3/18.
Webb, Joseph Henry, b. Portadown, Co. Armagh, e. Armagh (Portadown), 6151, A/Cpl., k. in a., F. & F., 12/10/16.
Weir, James Henry, b. Portadown, Co. Armagh, e. Armagh (Portadown), 6128, Pte., k. in a., F. & F., 11/4/17.
Wheaton, Sydney, b. St. Peter Port, Guernsey, e. Guernsey, 23259, Pte., k. in a., F. & F., 27/9/17.
Wheeler, Charles Edward, b. Walworth, S.E., Surrey, e. London (Armagh), 9309, Sgt., k. in a., F. & F., 11/4/17.
Wheelwright, Charles Joseph, b. Stepney, E., Middx., e. Woolwich (Dunmurry, Co. Antrim), 8877, Sgt., k. in a., F. & F., 26/6/17.
Whelehan, Christopher, b. Mullingar, Co. Westmeath, e. Mullingar, 11496, Pte., k. in a., F. & F., 13/4/15, formerly 4565, 5th Leinster Regt.
Whelton, John, b. Dunmanway, Co. Cork, e. Cork (Dunmanway), 9652, Pte., k. in a., F. & F., 3/11/14.
Whetstone, Walter George, b. Hook, Surrey, e. Hounslow, Middx. (Claygate, Surrey), 50031, Pte., k. in a., F. & F., 21/10/18, formerly 636146, 20th London Regt.
White, David Joseph, b. Templemore, Co. Tipperary, e. Liverpool (Garston, Lancs), 12700, Pte., d. of w., F. & F., 26/5/15.
White, Edward Thomas, b. Shankill, Belfast, e. Belfast, 10650, Pte., k. in a., F. & F., 3/5/17.
White, Patrick, b. Dundalk, Co. Louth, e. Llanelly, Carmarthens (Dundalk), 24035, Pte., k. in a., F. & F., 18/2/17.
Whitfield, Arthur, b. Peckham, S.E., Surrey, e. Camberwell, S.E., Surrey (Peckham), 43486, Pte., k. in a., F. & F., 9/8/18, formerly 1715, 21st London Regt.
Whitley, George, b. Ballymacarrett, Co. Down, e. Belfast, 42394, Pte., d. of w., F. & F., 6/10/18, formerly 22479, R. Irish Rif.
Whitley, William John, b. Moy, Co. Tyrone, e. Armagh (Moy), 10921, Pte., k. in a., F. & F., 12/10/16.
Whyte, Charles, b. Dublin, e. Dublin, 8350, Pte., k. in a., F. & F., 26/10/14.
Wickham, Frederick, b. Pittsdeep, Hants, e. Exeter (Barnstaple, Devon), 49887, Pte., k. in a., F. & F., 1/10/18, formerly 3011, Hants Regt.
Wild, Frederick Bromley, b. Rickmansworth, Herts, e. Watford, Herts (Bushey, Herts), 50006, Pte., k. in a., F. & F., 2/10/18, formerly 556787, 16th London Regt.
Wilding, David, b. Preston, Lancs, e. Dunfermline, Fife (Wellwood, Dunfermline), 17653, Sgt., k. in a., F. & F., 3/5/17.
Williams, John, b. Portmadoc, Carnarvons, e. Merthyr, Glam. (Blaenau Festiniog, Merioneth), 3645, Pte., k. in a., F. & F., 16/1/16, formerly 50483, R.G.A.
Willis, Francis, b. Shankill, Co. Armagh, e. Portadown, Co. Armagh (Lurgan, Co. Armagh), 6363, Pte., d. of w., F. & F., 14/1/16.
Wilson, George, b. Glasgow, e. Glasgow, 10012, Pte., d. of w., Home, 18/6/15, D.C.M.
Wilson, John, b. Dundalk, Co. Louth, e. Dundalk, 2719, Pte. k. in a., F. & F., 10/10/16.
Wilson, Matthew, b. Ballymena, Co. Antrim, e. Belfast, 49873, Pte., k. in a., F. & F., 21/10/18, formerly 1003, R. Irish Rif.
Wisener, John, b. Garvagh, Co. Londonderry, e. Ballymena, Co. Antrim, 42380, Pte., k. in a., F. & F., 23/10/18, formerly 441, R. Irish Rif.
Woodhouse, Thomas, b. Portadown, Co. Armagh, e. Armagh (Portadown), 8355, Pte., k. in a., F. & F., 21/10/14.
Woods, Samuel James, b. Portadown, Co. Armagh, e. Portadown, 11355, Pte., k. in a., F. & F., 25/4/15.
Woods, William John, b. Portadown, Co. Armagh, e. Portadown (Cowcaddens, Glasgow), 7445, Pte., k. in a., F. & F., 14/11/14.
Wright, Alfred George, b. Clerkenwell, E.C., Middx., e. St. Pancras, N.W., Middx. (Kentish Town Rd., N.W., Middx.), 41828, Pte., k. in a., F. & F., 16/8/18, formerly S4/126085, R.A.S.C.
Wright, James, b. Stratford, E., Essex, e. New Kent Road, S.E., Surrey (Deptford, S.E., Kent), 9631, Cpl., k. in a., F. & F., 25/4/15.
Wright, John, b. Shankill, Belfast, e. Belfast (Enniskillen), 7064, Pte., k. in a., F. & F., 25/4/15.
Wright, Richard, b. Kirkdale, Lancs, e. Liverpool, 42367, Pte., k. in a., F. & F., 1/10/18, formerly 070916, R.A.S.C.
Yeates, John, b. Dublin, e. Dublin, 11455, Pte., k. in a., F. & F., 25/4/15.
Young, Thomas, b. Belfast, e. Belfast, 29156, Pte., d. of w., F. & F., 3/9/18.

APPENDIX III.

DECORATIONS AND HONOURS AWARDED TO COMMISSIONED OFFICERS OF THE 1ST BN. ROYAL IRISH FUSILIERS.

C.M.G.

Lieut.-Col. A. R. BURROWES, D.S.O., 18/2/15.
Lieut.-Col. A. B. INCLEDON-WEBBER, D.S.O.
Lieut.-Col. R. J. KENTISH, D.S.O.
Lieut.-Col. H. C. W. H. WORTHAM, D.S.O.

D.S.O. AND TWO BARS.

Captain Gerald Victor Wilmot HILL, Royal Irish Fusiliers.
(*London Gazette*, January 14th, 1916.)

For personal gallantry and good leading in the attack on St. Julien on April 5th, 1915. This officer has already been brought to notice on two previous occasions.

Captain and Brevet Major (T./Lieut.-Col.) Gerald Victor Wilmot HILL, D.S.O., Royal Irish Fusiliers, attached 8th Bn. Suffolk Regiment.
(*London Gazette*, April 17th, 1917.)

For conspicuous gallantry and good leadership when in command of his Battalion. He formed up his Battalion under very heavy fire and under the most difficult conditions. The successful start of his Battalion and the accomplishment of its task in the attack was in a great measure due to his personal example and fine leadership.
(S. Miraumont Trench, February 18th, 1917.)

Captain and Brevet Major (T./Lieut.-Col.) Gerald Victor Wilmot HILL, D.S.O., Royal Irish Fusiliers.
(*London Gazette*, September 26th, 1917.)

For conspicuous gallantry and devotion to duty when in command of his Battalion in support. Seeing that the troops in front were held up, he at once decided to attack the enemy, in co-operation with another battalion, in order to gain high ground that was of great tactical importance. It was mainly owing to his personal gallantry and leadership that the attack of his battalion, which had to be conducted without the help of artillery was successful, and the position gained.
(E. of Ypres-Menin Road, July 31st, 1917.)
(The above statement of services was announced in the *London Gazette* dated January 8th, 1918.)

APPENDICES

D.S.O. AND ONE BAR.

Captain (A./Lieut.-Col.) Heffernan William Denis MCCARTHY O'LEARY, M.C., Royal Irish Fusiliers.

For conspicuous gallantry and devotion to duty. During a heavy hostile counter-attack, which had driven in his advance post and recaptured part of the position, he went forward with one runner, rallied his men, and led them forward again, driving the enemy back and restoring the situation. He remained encouraging his men until he was himself severely wounded half an hour later, but he did not leave the field until he had reported the situation to his brigadier.

(Zonnebeke Redoubt, August 16th, 1917.)

(*London Gazette*, September 26th, 1917.)

(The above statement of services was announced in the *London Gazette* dated January 8th, 1918.)

Capt. (A./Lieut.-Col.) Heffernan William Denis MCCARTHY-O'LEARY, D.S.O., M.C., Royal Irish Fusiliers.

For conspicuous gallantry and devotion to duty. He was wounded, but refused to be evacuated, and during the severe fighting which ensued he remained in action in command of his battalion until again severely wounded. He displayed marked ability in encouraging and handling his troops, and showed great cheerfulness and total disregard for his own personal safety.

(Villiesclue, March 26th, 1918.)

(*London Gazette*, September 16th, 1918.)

D.S.O.

Captain and Brevet Major (T./Lieut.-Col.) George BULL, Royal Irish Fusiliers.

For good service as an Officer Commanding a Battalion since November 1st, 1915.

(*London Gazette*, June 3rd, 1916.)

Lieut.-Colonel Arnold Robinson BURROWES, C.M.G., Royal Irish Fusiliers.

An excellent officer who has done very good service during the past eight months. He is fully capable of occupying a higher rank and position than at present. For valuable services rendered in connection with military operations in the field.

(*London Gazette*, January 1st, 1918.)

Major (A./Lieut.-Col.) Stuckburgh Upton Lucas CLEMENTS, Royal Irish Fusiliers, Special Reserve, attached 1st Battalion.

Major Clements commanded the 1st Bn. Royal Irish Fusiliers during the offensive operations at Cambrai in November, 1917, when he was wounded. He showed great energy and zeal.

Although wounded, he refused to be evacuated, and remained in command of his battalion until ordered to go to hospital.

(*London Gazette*, June 3rd, 1918.

Captain (T./Major) Gilbert Eric Graham COCKBURN, M.C.

For conspicuous gallantry and devotion to duty. At a most critical and obscure period of an attack he was sent out with orders to clear up the situation, if possible, and to assume control of his battalion if he could reach the front line. This he eventually succeeded in doing, under heavy fire, during which he was shot through the right eye. Undeterred by this, he stuck most gallantly to his mission, and, although wounded again in the shoulder by a sniper, he displayed the most magnificent fearlessness and determination in reorganizing and leading his men against the enemy's position. Though under intense fire, he sent in invaluable and accurate reports on the situation, and remained directing operations until nightfall. His great gallantry and initiative and the example of devotion to duty which he set to all ranks were beyond all praise.

(*London Gazette*, September 17th, 1917).

Captain C. J. ELKAN, Royal Irish Fusiliers.

It has not been possible to trace in the *London Gazette* the particulars for which this honour was awarded.

It was awarded for personal gallantry near Houplines on October 17th, 1914, in the same circumstances as that awarded to Capt. R. J. Kentish, and also for personal gallantry at the attack on Frelinghien.

(*London Gazette*, February 18th, 1915.)

Major (T./Lieut.-Colonel) Adrian Beare INCLEDON-WEBBER, Royal Irish Fusiliers.

Carried out the duties of Brigade Major for two months until Major Elles came back. During this time he was invaluable and carried out his duties to my entire satisfaction, always ready for more than his share of risks, which came fairly often from April 25th to the middle of June, 1915. On April 25th, when the Brigade was forced to give ground, I sent both him and Major Elles, my Brigade Major, to assist in forming a line on which to rally. This was successfully done. This action on this day, apart from anything else, is worthy of record.

(*London Gazette*, January 14th, 1916.)

Captain Reginald John KENTISH, 1st Bn. Royal Irish Fusiliers.

Captain Kentish, on October 17th, 1914, near Houplines, set fire to a farm building occupied by some Germans, who had killed and wounded many of the attacking party. It was then found that some of the wounded lying close to the door were suffering from burning débris. He organized a rescue party, and himself, at the range of a few feet, endeavoured by firing down the passage, to keep down the fire of the occupants whilst the wounded were being removed.

(*London Gazette*, November 11th, 1914.)

Lieutenant (T./Captain and A./Lieut.-Colonel) Thomas Alfred LOWE, M.C., Royal Irish Regiment, attached 1st Bn. Royal Irish Fusiliers.

For conspicuous gallantry and devotion to duty on October 1st, 1918, near Dadizeele. He was visiting his forward posts when the enemy suddenly attacked under cover of shell and machine gun fire, inflicting numerous casualties. He went round encouraging his men, collecting ammunition from the dead, and inspiring such confidence that the attack was beaten off and the line properly reorganized.

(*London Gazette*, February 1st, 1919.)

Captain (A./Lieut.-Colonel) Redmond Barry NEILL, Reserve of Officers, Royal Irish Fusiliers.

This officer rejoined the battalion in February, 1917, on recovering from wounds received in action on July 1st, 1916, whilst in command of the 15th Bn. West Yorkshire Regiment. He has served with great distinction in this battalion in various capacities, including command. Has organized and superintended two successful raids on the enemy lines. Commanded the battalion, May, 1917, and on May 12th, in final taking of Chemical Works near Fampoux. His personal example, gallantry, and never-failing cheerfulness, on every occasion, set a fine example to all ranks. Before attack on May 12th these qualities were most marked and undoubtedly resulted in attack being a success.

This officer took over his present command in July, 1917, under very difficult circumstances, which included the heavy shelling of the battalion in camp near Coxyde on

APPENDICES

July 10th, 1917. On this occasion, and on all others, he has always shown most consistent devotion to duty, and the present efficiency of his battalion is largely due to his personal energy and example.

(*London Gazette*, January 1st, 1918.)

Captain William SCOTT, M.C., Royal Irish Fusiliers, Special Reserve.

For conspicuous gallantry and devotion to duty. When a strong point on the way to the assembly position was found to be still in the possession of the enemy he took command of the battalion, the commanding officer being wounded, and led them to the capture of the position with the greatest gallantry. His coolness, courage, and leadership, under heavy fire, at a critical moment were of the greatest value.

(Near Mœuvres, November 23rd, 1917.)

(*London Gazette*, February 18th, 1918.)

(The above statement of services appeared in the *London Gazette* dated July 18th, 1918.)

Captain Thomas John Chichester Conyngham THOMPSON, Royal Irish Fusiliers, Special Reserve, attached 2nd Bn. Royal Irish Rifles.

For conspicuous gallantry and devotion to duty. He led his company with great dash and success to their objective, afterwards by his initiative rendering valuable assistance to another unit by co-operating on their flank. The spirit and dash of his company were largely due to his personality and gallantry on this as on all other occasions.

(Messines-Wytschaete Ridge, June 7th, 1917.)

(*London Gazette*, August 16th, 1917.)

Captain Alexander James TROUSDELL, M.C., Reserve of Officers, Royal Irish Fusiliers, Special Reserve.)

This officer has carried out his duties as Brigade Major, whether in or out of the line, with exceptional ability and zeal.

During the recent fighting and the period covered by the Despatch his work was of a high order. His gallant example and energetic service were worthy of great praise.

(*London Gazette*, June 3rd, 1919.)

Captain Geoffrey Machel Hungerford WRIGHT, M.C., Royal Irish Fusiliers.

Since September, 1917, he has shown exceptional zeal in carrying out his staff duties, and apart from his ordinary duties has been untiring in his efforts to promote the welfare of the Brigade. He has rendered invaluable service in organizing the line in the battle areas, more particularly in December, 1917, in the Passchendaele Area, and owing to his assistance and organization many difficult situations have been overcome.

(*London Gazette*, June 3rd, 1918.)

Major and Brevet Lieut.-Colonel (T./Lieut.-Colonel) Harold Charles Webster Hale WORTHAM, Royal Irish Fusiliers.

A most zealous and capable staff officer who has spared no pains to ensure the efficiency of the administrative services of the Division.

He has carried out his duties in a highly satisfactory manner during the fourteen months he has been A.A. and Q.M.G. of the Division.

(*London Gazette*, June 3rd, 1918.)

MILITARY CROSS.

Lieut. G. W. N. Barefoot	22/9/16
2/Lieut. R. Brennan	14/1/16
T./Lieut. J. L. Chalmers	18/2/19
2/Lieut. G. Craiger Watson	18/2/18
Lieut. G. E. G. Cockburn	
T./2/Lieut. H. H. E. Q. Coles	21/1/20
Lieut. W. A. Colhoun	
T./Lieut. F. L. Crilly	3/6/18
2/Lieut. J. Cullen	26/7/18
Lieut. A. E. McM. Cuming	16/9/18
	Bar 16/9/18
2/Lieut. J. Darling	16/9/18
	Bar 15/2/19
Lieut. N. E. V. Dicks	1/1/18
Lieut. A. L. Dobbyn	
2/Lieut. R. O. Eaton	7/11/18
T./Capt. T. de C. Falle	2/12/18
Lieut. G. F. Gough	
Capt. G. M. P. Hornidge	17/9/17
Lieut. B. St J. Galvin	
Lieut. H. Haughey	7/11/18
2/Lieut. T. Houston	17/9/17
T./Capt. R. W. Kingham	16/9/18
Lieut. W. H. Liesching (Carden-Roe)	1/1/15
2/Lieut. J. Lennon	16/9/18
T./2/Lieut. S. Logan	1/2/19
	Bar 8/3/19
Capt. T. A. Lowe	
Lieut. A. Low	1/1/17
Lieut. V. J. Lynch	
Capt. H. W. D. McCarthy-O'Leary	
	Bar
Lieut. H. A. MacMullen	3/6/16
Capt. J. C. O'Brien	1/1/17
Capt. M. J. W. O'Donovan	1/1/17
T./Major L. C. C. Owen	1/1/19
2/Lieut. A. G. Porter	20/12/16
Lieut. N. Russell	16/5/16
2/Lieut. G. Reeve	18/7/17
Capt. W. Scott	16/8/17
Lieut. J. I. Smith	
Capt. A. J. Trousdell	1/1/18
2/Lieut. M. W. Taylor	18/2/18
Capt. G. M. H. Wright	18/10/17

O.B.E.

Capt. (T./Major) R. P. Power	1/1/19
Lieut.-Col. C. J. Elkan, D.S.O.	
Capt. D. A. Davison	
Capt. H. F. Stokes	

APPENDICES

M.B.E.

Capt. J. F. R. Massy-Westropp ... ...

FOREIGN DECORATIONS.

Capt. T. E. Bunting, D.C.M., Croix de Guerre avec étoile	19/6/19
Lieut.-Col. A. R. Burrowes, C.M.G., D.S.O., Croix de Guerre avec palme ...	
Bt. Lieut.-Col. C. J. Elkan, D.S.O., O.B.E., Legion of Honour, Croix de Chevalier	29/1/19
Bt. Lieut.-Col. R. J. Kentish, C.M.G., D.S.O., Legion of Honour, Croix d'Officier	14/2/17
2/Lieut. W. H. Liesching (Carden-Roe), M.C., Legion of Honour A.R.O.	8/11/14
A./Lieut.-Col. T. A. Lowe, D.S.O., M.C., Croix de Guerre, Belgian	
A./Lieut.-Col. H. W. D. McCarthy-O'Leary, D.S.O., M.C., Belgian Ordre de la Couronne	
Lieut. N. A. Rattray, Croix de Guerre, French	19/6/19
Bt. Lieut.-Col. H. C. W. H. Wortham, C.M.G., D.S.O., Croix de Guerre ...	15/12/19

APPENDIX IV.

DECORATIONS EARNED BY WARRANT OFFICERS, NON-COMMISSIONED OFFICERS, AND MEN OF THE 1ST BN. ROYAL IRISH FUSILIERS.

VICTORIA CROSS.

Regtl. No.	Rank.	Name.	Gazette
10531	Pte.	R. MORROW	22/5/15

"For most conspicuous bravery near Messines on April 12th, 1915, when he rescued and carried successively to places of comparative safety several men who had been buried in the débris of trenches wrecked by shell fire. Private Morrow carried out this gallant work on his own initiative, and under very heavy fire from the enemy."

MILITARY CROSS.

6982	C.S.M.	J. Butler	18/2/15

D.C.M. AND BAR.

McKENNA, No. 6333 Pte. J. (*London Gazette*, 10/11/14.)

For conspicuous gallantry on October 17th near Houplines in volunteering to rescue under heavy fire some wounded men who were lying close to the door of a burning house held by the enemy. They were successful in recovering one wounded man.

Bar. (*London Gazette*, 23/6/15.)

For conspicuous gallantry on January 2nd, 1915, when on the River Douve, near Messines, he carried wounded men to safety through water up to his waist. Pte. McKenna has since continually volunteered for dangerous enterprises, and has shown remarkable coolness under fire.

D.C.M.

ADAMS, No. 8084 Pte. H. (*London Gazette*, 11/12/16.)

For conspicuous gallantry in action. He tended many wounded men in "No Man's Land," and rescued a wounded man under intense fire. He has on many previous occasions done fine work.

BAGOT, No. 9828 Pte. W. (*London Gazette*, 5/8/15.)

For conspicuous bravery on May 24th, 1915, near Wieltje. Pte. Bagot carried messages throughout the day under a very heavy fire, displaying the greatest coolness and courage in the performance of his hazardous duties.

APPENDICES

BARTON, No. 10580 Pte. L. (*London Gazette*, 10/11/14.)

For conspicuous gallantry on October 17th near Houplines in volunteering to rescue under heavy fire some wounded men who were lying close to the door of a burning house held by the enemy. They were successful in recovering one wounded man.

BORLEY, No. 9400 Sergt. (A./C.Q.M.S.) F. W. (*London Gazette*, 23/6/15.)

For great gallantry and ability during the campaign, up till the time he was wounded in the Douve trenches. A very valuable non-commissioned officer.

BRADY, No. 10601 Pte. E. (*London Gazette*, 6/6/17.)

For conspicuous gallantry and devotion to duty. During operations he displayed the greatest courage and determination as a runner in getting messages through under heavy fire. Killed in action, 12/4/17.

BRANNIGAN, No. 7351 Sergt. A. (*London Gazette*, 14/1/16.)

For conspicuous gallantry, when he carried messages on many occasions under heavy fire. He has always volunteered for any hazardous work in front of the trenches.

CAHILL, No. 24423 L./Cpl. J. (*London Gazette*, 3/6/19.)

On September 30th, 1918 at Dadizeele, during an enemy counter-attack, he was in charge of a Lewis gun, and rushed forward under heavy fire to a flank with his gun and inflicted many casualties on the enemy. In a previous operation he handled his gun with such skill that he enabled his platoon, which had been held up by enemy fire, to advance and take their objective.

CATHCART, No. 8245 C.S.M. J. S. (*London Gazette*, 14/1/16.)

For conspicuous gallantry. Company Sergeant-Major Cathcart invariably exhibited the greatest bravery and devotion in the performance of his duties, and was at all times of great assistance to his company commander.

CORISH, No. 10777 Sergt. P. (*London Gazette*, 3/6/18.)

For conspicuous gallantry and devotion to duty. He has invariably shown fine courage in action, and only left the field on an occasion when carried away wounded in two places. Also he has done patrol work with skill and judgment. He has set a high example to his men.

FARRELL, No. 8001 Cpl. J. (*London Gazette*, 29/11/15).

For conspicuous gallantry and determination on the night of Octover 4th, 1915, near Beaumont village. Corporal Farrell led out a party of five men to capture Germans. He finally saw two, and disposed his patrol so as to capture them alive, but on charging up the party fell into wire close to the Germans, who, reinforced by eight or ten others, commenced bombing the British party, wounding Corporal Farrell and one other man, and forcing them to retire. When they got back it was discovered that one man was missing, and Corporal Farrell, though wounded in three places, insisted on going out again to find him. He met him crawling in badly wounded in eight places, and assisted him to reach safety under heavy fire.

HAMILTON, No. 5330 R.S.M. H. (*London Gazette*, 12/12/19.)

For gallantry and devotion to duty between February, 1917, and March, 1918. His fine example on many occasions was invaluable in the action in which the battalion took part, especially on March 24th, 1918, when he handled a portion of the rearguard with great skill, covering the retirement and evacuating all our wounded.

HUGHES, No. 4517 Sergt. J., M.M. (*London Gazette*, 3/9/18.)

For conspicuous gallantry and devotion to duty. He went forward with a Lewis gun and knocked out an enemy machine gun which was firing on our right flank. When his team were disabled, although wounded himself, he kept the gun in action until reinforcements came up.

JONES, No. 8740 Sergt. C. (*London Gazette*, 3/9/18.)

For conspicuous gallantry and devotion to duty. His conduct throughout the fighting has been magnificent. Twice, at most critical times, under severe enemy barrage of shell and machine-gun fire, he succeeded in obtaining ammunition for the battalion, and enabled them to carry on.

JONES, No. 9560 Sergt. D. C. (*London Gazette*, 10/11/14.)

For conspicuous gallantry on October 17th near Houplines in volunteering to rescue under heavy fire some wounded men who were lying close to the door of a burning house held by the enemy. They were successful in recovering one wounded man. Died of wounds, 20/10/14.

KEARNEY, No. 8977 Pte. W. (*London Gazette*, 1/5/18.)

For conspicuous gallantry and devotion to duty. During a raid by the enemy he advanced along a sap with his men until he came within range of the enemy's grenades. He then left the trench under heavy rifle and machine-gun fire, and led an attack on a party of the enemy who were covering the advance of the raiders. He captured an officer and three men and killed two others, while the rest of the enemy party retired. He showed magnificent courage and initiative.

KEENAN, No. 9766 L./Cpl. R. (*London Gazette*, 23/6/15.)

For conspicuous gallantry and devotion to duty in going out in broad daylight and bringing to safety four wounded men under heavy shell and rifle fire. This non-commissioned officer has previously been reported on for good service.

KIRKHAM, No. 8809 Pte. J. (*London Gazette*, 14/1/16.)

For conspicuous gallantry. When all the wires had been cut, Private Kirkham volunteered to carry an important message. He had to pass over about a thousand yards of ground swept by rifle fire, and, although wounded, he successfully accomplished the task. Died 9/4/18.

LEDDY, No. 6374 Pte. B. (*London Gazette*, 10/11/14.)

For conspicuous gallantry on October 17th near Houplines in volunteering to rescue under heavy fire some wounded men who were lying close to the door of a burning house held by the enemy. They were successful in recovering one wounded man. Died of wounds, 26/5/15.

LEDWIDGE, No. 3130 Pte. J. J. (*London Gazette*, 14/1/16.)

For conspicuous gallantry. After the enemy had exploded a mine in our trenches, by which he was partially buried, Private Ledwidge refused to leave the spot, but assisted in digging out his comrades. Later he volunteered for dangerous work within a few yards of the enemy's sap-head.

APPENDICES

LENNON, No. 9820 Sergt. J. (*London Gazette*, 18/7/17.)

For conspicuous gallantry and devotion to duty. Taking command, he led his platoon forward to an advanced position in the enemy lines. While doing so, he took forty men prisoners and captured two machine guns. There were with him at the time only ten men.

LIGGETT, No. 6114 Pte. J. (*London Gazette*, 15/3/16.)

For conspicuous gallantry when acting as orderly to two officers who were visiting posts. Both officers were hit by snipers, but Private Liggett dragged them both into a disused trench, bandaged them, went across the open to fetch stretchers, and returned with the stretcher party. All this time he was under heavy fire.

McCREEDY, No. 8625 L./Sergt. J. (*London Gazette*, 15/11/18.)

When his platoon commander had been killed he took command, and controlled his men with great ability during a difficult and trying time, when an intense bombardment was causing many casualties. He held on to his own position, and helped another platoon to reach their objective by pushing forward the remnants of his men and opening a heavy fire on the enemy. He displayed great gallantry throughout the operations, and very high qualities of leadership and determination.

McGALEY, No. 10853 Sergt. P. (*London Gazette*, 3/6/19.)

He behaved with marked gallantry in the operations near Neuve-Eglise on September 2nd to 4th, 1918. Again, at Dadizeele on October 1st, he collected and rallied men, and led them forward again under intense machine-gun fire. Later that day he took charge of three platoons whose officers had been killed, and placed them in a good position, which they consolidated under his direction.

NEVILLE, No. 8333 C.S.M. R. (*London Gazette*, 18/7/17.)

For conspicuous gallantry and devotion to duty. He took command of the company and held the ground won, beating off two bombing attacks. On being relieved, he withdrew his men in good order, with great skill, during an intense bombardment.

ROABUCK, No. 10703 Cpl. A. (*London Gazette*, 22/9/16.)

For most conspicuous gallantry when assisting stretcher-bearers. He went backwards and forwards under very heavy fire, bringing in wounded in broad daylight. He was wounded when bringing in the eighteenth man. His conduct has been brought to notice on many previous occasions.

SCRAFIELD, No. 5741 C.S.M. E. B. (*London Gazette*, 18/2/15.)

For gallant conduct and ability near Haucourt during a night charge by the Germans. Has set a fine example to the men of his company.

WILSON, No. 10012 Pte. G. (*London Gazette*, 5/8/15.)

For conspicuous gallantry on May 24th, 1915, near Wieltje. When all the men of a gun team were killed or wounded, and the gun blown out of the emplacement, Private Wilson carried it to a new position and brought it into action. Died of wounds, 18/6/15.

MERITORIOUS SERVICE MEDAL.

Regtl. No.	Rank.	Name.	Gazette.
9368	C.Q.M.S.	F. Callaway	3/6/19
8683	Q.M.S.	P. J. Clancy	18/1/19
10514	Sergt.	J. Donnelly	18/1/19
9810	Cpl.	C. Robinson	17/6/18
10357	Sergt.	W. Sullivan	18/1/19
10423	A./Sergt.	P. J. Toal	22/2/19
8499	C.S.M. (A /R.S.M.)	F. Tynan	18/1/19

MILITARY MEDAL.

Regtl. No.	Rank.	Name.	Gazette.
11153	Cpl.	T. Ashford	18/7/17
	Sergt.	T. Ashford	Bar 7/10/18
10033	Sergt.	C. Austin	9/11/16
13845	Sergt.	F. Baker	3/6/16
8085	Pte.	P. Bannon	14/6/17
10542	Sergt.	D. Barry	16/8/17
6175	Pte.	H. Barton	9/7/17
			Bar 11/2/19
10400	Cpl.	J. Boyd	9/7/17
10372	Sergt	J T Bridges	9/11/16
43495	Pte. (L./Cpl.)	A. Buck	7/10/18
29471	Pte.	J. Burke	11/2/19
6083	Pte.	W. D. Campbell	18/7/17
22539	Pte.	H. Cherry	17/6/19
49967	Pte.	J. C. Clarke	24/1/19
17151	Cpl.	F. Clements	21/9/16
10086	Sergt.	M. Conway	16/8/17
8973	Sergt.	G. Craig	9/11/16
6124	L./Cpl.	A. Crawford	9/11/16
11864	Pte.	D. Crichton	24/1/19
18385	Pte.	R. Crimmins	24/1/19
9444	Sergt.	J. Donaldson	25/4/18
11242	Pte.	J. Donohoe	14/5/19
7233	Pte.	J. Dougan	9/11/16
7038	Sergt. (A./C.S.M.)	R. Dunn	13/3/18
10678	Sergt.	P. Evans	9/11/16
17335	Sergt.	M. J. Fallon	11/2/19
18944	Pte.	W. E. Fearne	13/3/18
26908	Pte.	P. A. Fitt	24/1/19
10071	Pte.	J. Fraser	9/11/16
8784	Pte.	R. Gilbert	14/12/16
10387	Sgt.	H. Goode	9/11/16
18926	Pte.	W. Graham	9/7/17
10268	Pte.	J. Gray	13/3/18
41657	Pte.	J. B. Harrison	11/2/19
27664	Pte.	J. Heaney	11/2/19
43341	Pte.	W. Hoar	13/3/19
4517	Sergt.	J. Hughes	9/7/17

APPENDICES

Regtl. No.	Rank.	Name.	Gazette.
3383	Pte.	G. Irwin	18/7/17
			Bar 13/3/18
10279	Sergt.	J. Kearns	14/5/19
15995	Pte.	H. Kelly	24/1/19
6095	Pte.	P. Kelly	25/4/18
2741	Pte.	M. Lawless	9/7/17
3130	Cpl.	J. J. Ledwidge	9/7/17
9820	Sergt.	J. Lennon	9/11/16
3392	Pte.	R. Lindberg	13/3/18
			Bar 13/3/19
45826	Pte.	W. Littlebury	11/2/19
23551	Pte.	P. McAleavey	16/8/17
20165	L./Cpl.	W. M. M. McCall	2nd Bar* 29/8/18
10449	Pte.	P. McCann	14/12/16
22696	Pte.	H. McCluney	29/8/18
22156	Pte.	J. McDonald	17/6/19
17504	Pte.	M. McLaughlin	13/3/18
			Bar 7/10/18
18800	Pte.	J. McIntosh	11/2/19
11472	Pte.	A. McLean	13/3/18
11468	Pte. (L./Cpl.)	J. McLoughlin	13/3/18
6923	Sergt.	S. McMillan	9/11/16
			Bar 18/7/17
6957	Pte.	G. McNab	14/12/16
11132	Sergt.	J. Mahoney	3/6/16
9249	Pte. (L./Cpl.)	J. Martin	30/1/20
11243	Sergt.	R. Mason	19/2/17
6668	Pte.	W. Mitchell	9/11/16
47737	Pte.	T. E. Morton	18/12/19
11170	Pte.	M. Murtagh	29/8/18
50007	Pte.	E. C. Myers	13/3/19
50020	Pte.	E. Nash	17/6/19
10985	Sergt.	P. Nicholson	9/11/16
			Bar 6/1/17
20007	Pte.	H. O'Flanagan	24/1/19
23549	Pte.	W. L. Packer	29/8/18
			Bar 13/3/19
49783	Pte.	H. Parke	11/2/19
7239	Pte.	T. Parker	9/11/16
10832	Cpl. (A.Sergt.)	C. Pope	13/3/18
9610	Cpl.	G. H. Powell	9/7/17
11070	Pte.	J. Quinlan	13/3/18
9431	Pte.	W. Radcliffe	9/11/16
7574	Sergt.	G. Reeve	9/11/16
16971	Pte.	J. Reilly	14/6/17
10703	Cpl.	A. Roabuck	3/6/16
9810	Cpl.	C. Robinson	9/7/17
10652	L./Cpl.	F. Ryan	7/10/18

* L/Cpl. McCall earned the M.M. and the 1st Bar while serving with the 7th and 7/8th Battalions respectively.

Regtl. No.	Rank.	Name.	Gazette.
10996	L./Cpl.	R. Semple	9/11/16
	Sergt.	R. Semple	Bar 18/7/17
17181	Pte.	T. Smith	7/10/18
			Bar 13/3/19
11221	Pte.	J. Sweeney	18/7/17
	L./Cpl.	J. Sweeney	Bar 13/3/18
41825	Pte.	C. H. Tasker	11/12/18
11072	L./Cpl.	W. Taylor	19/2/17
11167	Pte.	J. Thompson	9/7/17
49848	Pte.	R. Vogan	14/5/19
9428	Sergt. (A./C.S.M.)	G. A. Williams	25/4/18
6239	Pte.	H. G. Williams	7/10/18
49785	Pte.	W. Wright	11/2/19
41066	Pte.	R. Wynne	11/12/18

FOREIGN DECORATIONS.

Regtl. No.	Rank	Name.	Gazette.	Decoration.
5732	Dr.	M. Corrigan	A.O. 1/12/14	Médaille Militaire.
10514	Sergt.	J. Donnelly	15/12/19	Medaille d'Honneur avec glaives en argent.
11284	Pte.	C. Hayden	25/8/15	Russian Medal of St. George, 4th Class.
42078	Cpl.	A. Jones	4/9/19	Croix de Guerre.
6374	Pte.	B. Leddy	25/8/15	Russian Medal of St. George, 4th Class.
5054	S./Dmr.	E. Leverett	4/9/19	Croix de Guerre, Belgian.
10531	Pte.	R. Morrow	25/8/15	Russian Medal of St. George, 3rd Class.
11168	Pte.	J. McAlindon	25/8/15	Russian Medal of St. George, 4th Class.
11038	Pte.	F. McKenna	25/8/15	Russian Medal of St. George, 4th Class.
9334	Cpl. (A./Sgt.)	G. McGuire	1/5/17	Médaille Militaire.
11316	A./C.S.M.	D. R. Magill	19/6/19	Croix de Guerre, French.
47737	Pte.	T. E. Morton	21/8/19	Decoration Militaire, Belgian.
8333	Sergt.	R. Neville	1/12/14	Médaille Militaire.
10183	L./Sergt.	C. Neville	26/11/19	Croix de Guerre, Belgian.
10610	Pte.	P. O'Hare	12/7/18	Croix de Guerre, Belgian.
10703	Cpl.	A. Roabuck	15/2/17	Russian Cross of St. George.
8375	Sergt.	S. Rosbotham	12/7/15	Croix de Guerre, Belgian.
5741	C.S.M.	E. B. Scrafield	A.O. 1/12/14	Médaille Militaire.
11221	A./Cpl.	J. Sweeney	10/10/18	Médaille Militaire.
8499	R.S.M.	F. Tynan	21/8/19	Médaille Militaire.
10012	Pte.	G. Wilson	25/8/15	Russian Medal of St. George, 3rd Class.
9676	Sergt.	H. A. Wilson	A.O. 466/14	Médaille Militaire.

APPENDIX V.

REINFORCEMENTS AND STRENGTH IN OTHER RANKS OF THE FIRST BATTALION ROYAL IRISH FUSILIERS FROM AUGUST, 1914, TO OCTOBER, 1918, BOTH MONTHS INCLUSIVE.

The actual number who joined the 1st Battalion Royal Irish Fusiliers in the field are shown in the statement below. The figures are only approximately accurate from January 1st, 1916, onwards :—

	1914.	1915.	1916.	1917.	1918.
January	—	142	232	166	299
February	—	67	42	37	327
March	—	67	38	208	104
April	—	64	15	181	792
May	—	363	115	257	63
June	—	236	68	118	42
July	—	284	141	72	20
August	Nil.	55	62	50	18
September	388	35	133	6	241
October	57	24	131	61	79
November	220	Nil.	104	Nil.	—
December	103	59	165	79	—
Total	768	1,396	1,246	1,235	1,985

Grand Total ... ... 6,630.

Add to this the number of other ranks who disembarked with the Battalion *vide* War Establishments, Part I, Expeditionary Force, 1914, p. 142, viz. :—971, making the total number of warrant officers, non-commissioned officers and men up to 7,601.

Of this number 1,051 lost their lives *vide* " Soldiers Died in the Great War, 1914-19," Part 68. But the percentage of deaths was greater than these figures imply, because the sick and wounded were struck off the strength and when they rejoined were counted as reinforcements. A large number of men rejoined many times, and it is probable that the percentage of deaths amongst the rank and file did not fall far short of that amongst the commissioned ranks.

Although the Battalion was, on several occasions, reduced to a mere handful of men in the field, it was strong on paper, and from January, 1916, to the end of the war was never below 1,000 of all ranks.

The average strength of the Battalion for thirty-two months from February, 1916, to October, 1918, omitting June, 1918, for which the figures are not available, taken from Part II Orders was 51 officers and 1,343 other ranks.

The lowest recorded strength was on January 1st, 1918, when the numbers were 59 officers and 963 other ranks.

The highest recorded strength was on May 1st, 1918, when the numbers were 57 officers and 1,776 other ranks.

The reinforcements were in the main Irish. It is true that in the early part of 1918, when a process of combing out was going on in the Departmental Corps, the Irish Fusiliers got a proportion of these drafts, as an instance, on January 14th, 1918, a draft of 65 was composed entirely of Army Service Corps bakers. But that the Battalion maintained its national character is shown by the official lists of those who lost their lives.

APPENDIX VI.

A List of Some of the Stores Brought into use for Trench Warfare.

" A " frames for revetting deep or waterlogged trenches.
Armour plate loopholes for snipers.
Air photographs.
Ammunition reserves of all sorts.
Alcohol solidified.
Armour-body for patrols and small raids.
Arm-racks.
Anti-frostbite grease.
Arm-bands of distinguishing colours.
Bass Brooms.
Barbed wire.
" Baby " elephants for making trench shelters.
Bangalore torpedoes.
Boxes for storing grenades.
" Blob " sticks for cleaning the chambers of rifles.
Boots, rubber, both short and thigh.
Body shields.
Bolt covers.
Camouflage—clothes, trees, screens, etc.
Corrugated iron.
Chloride of lime.
Concertina wire.
Creosol.
Catapults.
Cocoanut matting to conceal new trenches.
Chain-visors for steel helmets.
D.3 telephones.
Duck-boards.
Expanded metal for revetments.
Fan discs for signalling.
Fur waistcoats, goat-skin.
Grenades, hand and rifle, of many patterns.
Gas Stores:
    Respirators, helmets, masks, rattles, gongs, Klaxon horns, Strombos horns, saturated blankets for entrances to dug-outs, Vermoral sprayers, goggles, fans, " Ayrton " gas flappers, Salvus breathing sets, wind vanes.
Hurdles.
Hammers.
Hedging gloves.
Inventories of trench stores.
Knife rests, a form of wire obstacle when opposing trenches were very close.
Leather jerkins.

Listening sets, very secret and known as " I.T."
Metal discs for signalling to contact aeroplanes.
Mauls.
Mackintosh capes.
Nails, assorted.
Notice and direction boards.
Pigeons.
Pumps.
Periscopes.,
Pickets of iron and wood for entanglements.
Plain wire.
Rockets of all descriptions.
Rifle batteries.
Rocket stands.
Reserve rations.
Screens, coloured, put up in rear of trenches to help artillery observing officers.
Solidified petroleum.
Steel helmets.
Schemes of defence.
Sand trays for modelling.
Sandbags.
Saws.
Screw pickets.
Sanitary appliances of various kinds.
Smoke bombs.
Tarred felt.
Thermos food containers.
Trench scoups.
Telescopic sights.
Trench ladders.
Tommy cookers.
Trench mortars.
Trench maps.
Timber of all descriptions.
Very pistols, 1" and 1½".
Venetian discs for signalling.
Wire cutters.
Wire breakers for use with the rifle.
Whale oil for the feet.
Wire gooseberries made of barbed wire.
Water tins.
Water crates for pack transport of tins.
Yukon packs, a device for carrying loads.

APPENDIX VII.

The "Barrosa" song, supposed to have been written by a private soldier of the Regiment, is sung at the "Barrosa" Dinner whilst the "Barrosa" Cup passes round. Since 1890 the cup is accompanied by the original scroll of "Barrosa," taken from the old colours when new ones were presented at Port Louis, Mauritius, on March 5th, 1838, and in the possession of Major R. S. O'Brien, who was Adjutant at the time. Major General T. O'Brien, brother of Major R. S. O'Brien, was appointed to the 87th when about twelve years of age by Sir John Doyle, and when the 2nd Battalion was broken up the former received as his share of the officers' plate a silver spoon and fork.

Lieutenant-Colonel T. O'Brien, son of Major-General T. O'Brien, when Governor of Newfoundland in 1890, in a letter dated from Government House on April 1st of that year, presented the scroll and spoon and fork to the Regiment on condition that the two latter be used by the President at the Mess Dinner.

BARROSA.

(March 5th, 1811.)

On the 21st of February from Cadiz we set sail,
As many a gallant Frenchman had reason to bewail ;
Straightway for Gibraltar our gallant fleet did steer,
And on the 23rd my boys, we landed in Algeciras.

Chorus :

For we are lads of honour, boys, belonging to the Crown,
And death to those who dare oppose, the saucy " Prince's Own."

The next place we arrived at was called Tarifa Bay,
Where waiting for the Spaniards, in a Convent long we lay ;
But when the Spaniards joined us there, we marched both night and day,
Determined when we met the foe, to show them British play.

Our officers explained to us the hardships we should bear.
Well knowing British Courage would triumph everywhere ;
O'er plains and lofty mountains our army marched along,
And though our numbers were but few, our courage it was strong.

The Spaniards took the front my boys, their country for to free,
And bade our troops bring up the rear, that glorious day to see ;
But when Barrosa's Plains appeared we never saw them more,
Their columns drew behind the wood, upon St. Petri's shore.

Bold Graham, who was our General, not knowing their design,
Resolved that British Soldiers should never stay behind ;
But whilst advancing through a wood not dreading any snare,
The enemy in ambush lay and closed upon our rear.

Some watchful eye the foe espied and to the General flew,
Which news an oath of anger from the gallant Graham drew ;
" Oh ! Cursed is my lot," he cried, " this is a wretched day,
When Britons must deplore their fate, by Spaniards led astray."

" Turn to the right about, my boys, for Britons know no fear,
Extend your files, my Irish lads, and keep your outflanks clear ;
Look back to Cape Trafalgar, where Nelson bled before—
The blood that conquered on the sea shall triumph on the shore ! "

We jumped into their lines, my boys, their ranks were overthrown,
And in confusion forced to fly, charged by the " Prince's Own."
Two Generals left behind them, their Guns and Eagle, too,
Whilst the " Faugh-a-Ballaghs " cheered and charged, and boldly did pursue.

The 87th and 95th formed a hollow square,
All in the dead hour of the night, to keep their wounded clear
'Midst hollow sighs and dismal cries, 'twould grieve your heart full sore,
Like lions we protected them upon St. Petri's shore.

Here's a health to Gough and Graham and the soldiers on that field,
Who, though they fought them ten to one, soon taught their foes to yield ;
Who put them in confusion, and their Eagle took away—
Long live our Irish lads to cheer, on each Barrosa Day.

Then this cup to all the living, and in memory of the slain,
Who so bravely fought in freedom's cause upon Barrosa's Plain ;
Pass it round beside the Eagle which our Soldiers bore away,
Long live our Irish lads to cheer on each Barrosa Day.

APPENDIX VIII

BATTLE HONOURS IN THE GREAT WAR

LE CATEAU.
Retreat from Mons.
MARNE, 1914.
Aisne, 1914.
Armentières, 1914.
YPRES, 1915.
YPRES, 1917.
YPRES, 1918.
St. Julien.
Frezenberg.
Bellewaarde.
SOMME, 1916.
SOMME, 1918.
Albert, 1916.
Le Transloy.
ARRAS, 1917.
Scarpe, 1917.
MESSINES, 1918.
Cambrai, 1917.
St. Quentin.
Rosières.
LYS.
Bailleul.
Kemmel.
Courtrai.
France and Flanders, 1914-18.

Honours shown in CAPITAL LETTERS are borne on the Colours.